Cultural Integration and the Gospel in Vietnamese Mission Theology

A Paradigm Shift

KimSon Nguyen

© 2019 KimSon Nguyen

Published 2019 by Langham Academic (Previously Langham Monographs)
An imprint of Langham Publishing
www.langhampublishing.org

Langham Publishing and its imprints are a ministry of Langham Partnership

Langham Partnership
PO Box 296, Carlisle, Cumbria, CA3 9WZ, UK
www.langham.org

ISBNs:
978-1-78368-738-1 Print
978-1-78368-739-8 ePub
978-1-78368-741-1 PDF

KimSon Nguyen has asserted his right under the Copyright, Designs and Patents Act, 1988 to be identified as the Author of this work.

All rights reserved. No part of this publication may be reproduced, stored in a retrieval system or transmitted, in any form or by any means, electronic, mechanical, photocopying, recording or otherwise, without the prior written permission of the publisher or the Copyright Licensing Agency.

Requests to reuse content from Langham Publishing are processed through PLSclear. Please visit www.plsclear.com to complete your request.

Unless otherwise stated, Scripture quotations are from the New Revised Standard Version Bible, copyright © 1989 National Council of the Churches of Christ in the United States of America. Used by permission. All rights reserved.

Scripture quotations marked ESV are from The Holy Bible, English Standard Version® (ESV®), copyright © 2001 by Crossway, a publishing ministry of Good News Publishers. Used by permission. All rights reserved.

British Library Cataloguing-in-Publication Data
A catalogue record for this book is available from the British Library

ISBN: 978-1-78368-738-1

Cover & Book Design: projectluz.com

Langham Partnership actively supports theological dialogue and an author's right to publish but does not necessarily endorse the views and opinions set forth here or in works referenced within this publication, nor can we guarantee technical and grammatical correctness. Langham Partnership does not accept any responsibility or liability to persons or property as a consequence of the reading, use or interpretation of its published content.

To Ngọc-Ái,
my dear wife,
and
to Việt-Thái, Grace Quỳnh-Anh, and Hannah Phương-Anh,
our dear children,
who shared abundant love, faith, and countless sacrifices
until this endeavor came to fruition.

Contents

Acknowledgements xi

Abstract xv

List of Abbreviations xvii

Introduction 1
    Problem Statement 1
    Significance of the Study 5
    Context and Key Definitions 6
    Limitations of the Study 16
    Outline and Methodology 17

Chapter 1 21
East Asian Syncretistic Context
    Encountering Christianity 22
    Daoism 24
        Philosophical Daoism 25
        Religious Daoism 28
    Confucianism 31
        Heaven 33
        The "Way" of Man 37
        Encountering Buddhism 38

Chapter 2 43
Contextualization in Christian Mission Theology
    "Outsider" View 43
        Communication 44
        Interpretation 50
        Syncretism 55
    Alternative Evangelical View 65
        Within Cultural Context 65
        God's Intention 70
        Translatable Faith 79
    Chapters 1 and 2 Conclusion 83

Chapter 3 85
   Vietnamese Syncretistic Spirituality
      Popular Animist Beliefs 86
         Belief in the Twenty-Seven Spirits..88
         Ancestor Veneration 89
      Syncretistic Spirituality 90
         Encountering the Three Teachings...91
         Rationalizing the Essentials...95
         Belief in Heaven and Other Folk Beliefs 100
      Contextual Integrated Belief..106
         The Way of Heaven...107
         Unifying Spirituality..109
         Chapter Conclusion...117

Chapter 4 121
   Christian Missionary Movements in Vietnam
      Early Accounts of Christianity..122
      French Protestant Missions in Resurgence.......................................125
      Protestant Evangelization 131
         From the Pioneering Stage to the National Church.......................131
         French Protestant Mission Initiative..139
         Attitudes toward Vietnamese Socio-Cultural and Religious
           Contexts...146
         Chapter Conclusion...150

Chapter 5 153
   Christian Faith in Context
      A Catholic Attempt at Addressing the "Three Teachings" 153
      Protestant Missions in the Colonial Context 156
         Christian Mission and Colonization...157
         The Adjectives *American* and *français* 166
      "Foreign" Faith: An Issue of the Vietnamese Evangelicals 170
         "The Fourfold Gospel" 170
         Evangelism and Conversion: Tension with the Culture 177
         Fundamentalist Doctrines...179
         Chapter Conclusion...182

Chapter 6 187
   A Paradigm Shift Proposal for Vietnamese Mission Theology
      Mission Theological Principles 188
          Being Asian Evangelical 188
          Early Christian Assimilation Efforts 195
          Vietnamese Evangelical Mission Theology 198
      God in Our Midst: A Vietnamese Concept of God 206
          The Đạo 206
          The Supreme One 211
      God with Us: A Vietnamese Hermeneutic 215
          Jesus Christ: The Incarnate God 216
          The Church: The Center of God's Purpose 222
      Chapter Conclusion 232

Conclusion 235
   Theological Missiological Reflections

Appendix 241
   Inculturation vs Contextualization

Bibliography 243

Index of Names 269

Index of Subjects 273

Acknowledgements

With deep gratitude to God I acknowledge the contributions of many faithful people and institutions; without their significant roles, this study would not have been possible.

At Fuller Theological Seminary, I am grateful to Dr Scott W. Sunquist, Dean of the School of Intercultural Studies and Professor of World Christianity, for his patient and untiring efforts in mentoring me during the past five years of study. His academic guidance, insights for the writing, and encouragement through prayer, at each time of our meeting together, have been invaluable for my academic and spiritual development. I am grateful to my doctoral committee members: Dr Amos Yong, Professor of Theology and Mission and Director of the Center for Missiological Research, and Dr Diane B. Obenchain, Professor of Religion and Director of the China Initiative, and the dissertation outside reader, Dr Jonathan Y. Tan, the Archbishop Paul J. Hallinan Professor at Case Western Reserve University. I am indebted to their careful review, critical feedback, input and direction from the writing of the proposal until the present. Also, thanks to Wendy Walker of the office of the School of Intercultural Studies, and Johnny C. Ching of the Center for Missiological Research for their enormous assistance.

For academic resources that enriched my academic journey, thank you to these Professors: Dr David H. Scott, Dr Sherwood G. Lingenfelter, Dr Wilbert R. Shenk, Dr Daniel R. Shaw, and Dr Veli-Matti Kärkkäinen, among others at Fuller Theological Seminary, for their excellent teaching and guidance all along. Thank you to Dr George E. Dutton, Professor of Vietnamese History and Southeast Asia Studies at the University of California, Los Angeles (UCLA), for his valuable guidance in the Vietnamese study, and for introducing me to various important resources in the field. Thanks to my peers and colleagues Matthew Krabill, Dr Yukikazu Obata, Shi-Min Lu, Dr Tu

Thien Van Truong, Dr Vince Le, and other fellow doctoral students at Fuller Theological Seminary. Thanks also to my peers who responded with helpful feedback during my presentations at the 2014 Conference of the American Society of Missiology, and at the Yale-Edinburgh Group, particularly the 2015 Annual Meeting at Yale University, and the 2016 Annual Meeting at Edinburgh University. Lastly, thanks to the librarians and archivists who were incredibly helpful, making my visits successful: the staff of Fuller Theological Seminary's David Allan Hubbard Library, Madame Claire-Lise Lombard at Bibliothèque du Défap of the Société des Missions Évangéliques de Paris (SMEP), Mr David Fitzstevens for sharing his valuable collection on the CMA mission in Vietnam, and Mr Terrance Brown at Mid-America Baptist Theological Seminary's library.

I wish to acknowledge the award and grants received during the past five years of study: (1) the Robert and Dorothy King PhD Fellowship Award from Fuller Theological Seminary for three consecutive academic years, 2012–2015; (2) the Scholarship from the ScholarLeaders International. Thank you particularly to President Larry A. Smith, Dr Evan Hunter, and other members of the Board of Directors whom I was privileged to meet in person: Dr and Mrs Douglas C. McConnell, Mrs Linda Prinn, Dr David Fung, and Dr Paul Pierson. Thank you for your prayer, encouragement, and generous support; and (3) the grants received from the Foundation for Theological Education in Southeast Asia in 2012, the Presbyterian Church (USA) in 2012 and 2013, and the Research Grants from the Center for Missiological Research in 2015 and 2016.

I am grateful for the prayers and financial assistance from many faithful people and churches during the years of study in the United States. Thank you to the following people: Dr Duc Xuan Nguyen, Dr Gordon T. Smith, Dr Martinez T. Salvador, Rev Hồ Tấn Khoa, and Dr Steve Hyde for their recommendation to this doctoral studies program; Rev and Mrs Nguyễn Hữu Bình for their faithful prayer and encouragement for our family all along; Mr and Mrs Julian Khoo, Mrs Elizabeth Lee, Dr and Mrs Young Kim, Mr Yong Tok Chu, and Mr and Mrs Nguyễn Hiền Hoà for their generous financial support; Mr and Mrs Gerry Keener and the Eastern Mennonite Missions for their prayer and support; Dr and Mrs Isaiah E. Suhdir for their prayer and support; Dr Tan Kok Beng, Pastor Robert Yeo, and the Mennonite Church of Singapore for their prayer and support; Mr and Mrs Bill Fisher, Mr and Mrs Ken Farner, and the Gateway Presbyterian Church for their prayer and support; Mr and Mrs Anthony S. Yarbrough for their friendship in warmly welcoming our family to Tennessee during the writing of the dissertation; Dr Steve Marcum, Mrs Marilyn Hawkins at the mission office, and Bellevue Baptist Church for their hospitality to let our family stay at the mission house; and Pastor and Mrs Tieu Ly and the Grace Baptist Church, Highland Park, California, Dr and Mrs Doanh Van and the Ever-Living World Evangelical Church in Memphis, Tennessee (the CMA's Vietnamese District) for the fellowship and opportunity to minister the Word to the church.

I wish to express my appreciation to Dr Danielle Storia for providing critical reviews for the manuscript. Thank you for your inspiration and comments which have been invaluable. Thank you to the late Mrs Patricia Nachtrab-Smith and Miss Orpha E. Gehman for editing my tutorial papers in the years of study. Thank you especially to Miss Orpha E. Gehman for her enormous efforts in patiently proofreading this manuscript several times. Thank you very much for your love.

I am grateful to my extended family: the late Mr Nguyễn Thái Bưởi, the late Mr Nguyễn Văn Mạnh, my parents (the late Rev) and Mrs Nguyễn Kim Long, and my parents-in-law, Mr and Mrs Nguyễn Hữu Nghị. Thank you for your love and prayer and to all whom we owe what we are today.

Lastly, thanks be to God for his grace for physical and mental strength, and for spiritual refreshment during the years of study so that I could finally complete this work. To God be the glory.

Abstract

This study argues that it is necessary to present the Christian faith in such a way that it allows the Vietnamese to follow Christ and yet remain within their Vietnamese culture. To do so, the study resonates theologically with what has already been done, and offers some relevant contributions to the Vietnamese contextualization efforts by proposing a paradigm shift in the development of a Vietnamese mission theology that requires it to be both evangelical and Vietnamese. The proposed paradigm shift seeks to narrow the gap between the way evangelical mission theology has been practiced and the Vietnamese syncretistic spirituality. Within the larger context of East Asia, the study has navigated the religio-cultural dimensions of Vietnamese spirituality that have hindered the Christian faith being assimilated into the Vietnamese spirituality. The failure of the Christian missionaries to identify the simultaneous "resisting" and "assimilating" forces characteristic of Vietnamese spirituality became the reason why Christian contextualization efforts failed. At the same time, however, it seems promising that contextualization efforts could be possible once the dual force nature of Vietnamese spirituality is recognized, that is, identifying what needs to be resisted and what are the crucial religio-cultural elements or concepts that need to be assimilated. This nature would serve as the lens through which the contextualization processes would review the essential elements of Vietnamese spirituality which can be redeemed for evangelical Christian beliefs and practices, for instance, the concept of God the *Đạo* (the Way) and the Vietnamese extended family perspective for both the Trinitarian relationship and the Vietnamese Christian community of both the living people and the ancestors. A Vietnamese mission theology must begin with the Vietnamese concept of God the *Đạo*. Acknowledging that the *Đạo* is Christ, the Incarnate God, is the key to unlocking the problem of believing in a God who is alien and strange to the Vietnamese. Any attempt at Christian contextualization in Vietnam, therefore, cannot overlook the dual forces of "resisting and assimilating," and the nature of the *Đạo* of Vietnamese spirituality.

List of Abbreviations

BFBS	British and Foreign Bible Society
CMA	Christian and Missionary Alliance
CMV	Christian Mission of Vietnam
ĐVSKTT	*Đại Việt sử ký toàn thư* (Complete book of the historical records of Great Viet)
ECIC	Evangelical Church of (French) Indochina
ECVN	Evangelical Church of Vietnam
EMBMC	Eastern Mennonite Board of Missions and Charities
ESV	English Standard Version
ETR	The Errors of the Three Religions
IMC	International Missionary Council
LMS	London Mission Society
LNCQLT	*Lĩnh nam chích quái liệt truyện* (Arrayed tales of collected oddities from south of the passes)
LWR	Lutheran World Relief
MCC	Mennonite Central Committee
MEP	Société des missions etrangères de Paris
NRSV	New Revised Standard Version
SMEP	Société des missions évangéliques (or Mission de *Paris*)
TEF	Theological Education Fund
TKML	*Truyền kỳ mạn lục* (Collection of Strange Tales)
TSPM	Three-Self Patriotic Movement
VĐULT	*Việt điện u linh tập* (Departed spirits of the Việt realm)
WCC	World Council of Churches
WSCF	World Student Christian Fellowship
YMCA	The Young Men's Christian Association

Introduction

Problem Statement

The Evangelical Church of Vietnam (ECVN)[1] has long sought to develop an indigenous church in Vietnam modeled after the "three-self" concept: self-governing, self-supporting, and self-propagating.[2] The concept had reached Vietnam in the early twentieth century as reflected in the early missionary work of the Christian and Missionary Alliance (CMA) and ECVN. Rev Lê Hoàng Phu concluded in his findings that "a large number of local churches of the Evangelical Church of Vietnam were actually organized" on these "three principles of self-support, self-government, and self-propagation" in Vietnam.[3] He states that, "this indigenous movement [the ECVN] was well grounded and fully developed" from,

> its beginning through the efforts of the Christian and Missionary Alliance with the establishing [of] the first local churches (1911–1927); its official organization in 1927 and its subsequent development as an "indigenous church" through 1941; its struggles for survival during World War II (1941–1945) and

---

1. The Evangelical Church of Vietnam or *Hội Thánh Tin Lành Việt Nam* in Vietnamese (ECVN), the former Christian and Missionary Alliance (CMA) church in Vietnam is the evangelical church having the longest history and the largest membership of any evangelical church in Vietnam. *Vietnamese evangelicalism* (*Tin Lành*, in Vietnamese) is the term used in this study to discuss the Vietnamese evangelical Christianity and to differentiate it from the Vietnamese Catholicism (*Công Giáo*, in Vietnamese). Also, by the Vietnamese evangelicals, the writer means both the evangelical registered and the non-(and/or pre-)registered churches in Vietnam.

2. For background of this "three-self" concept, see in "Context and Key Definitions", 6–16.

3. Lê Hoàng Phu, "A Short History of the Evangelical Church of Viet Nam (1911–1965)," PhD diss. (New York University, 1972), iii.

the War of Independence (1945–1954); and its advances during the brief lull (1955–1960) and the first years of the Vietnam War (1960–1965).[4]

The "three-self" concept is a reflection of the manner in which national Christians can govern, give, and evangelize in a way that addresses the sociological aspects of the evangelization process, but yet, it does not relate to the cultural aspects. Rev Lê recommended that,

> in addition to the three basic principles of the indigenous church policy universally accepted in Protestant mission circles, the Evangelical Church of Vietnam should also concentrate its efforts on "self-nurture" and "self-expression," which are vital to any indigenous movement and constitute a basis for a significant contribution of a national church to the worldwide Christian Church and to the cultural heritage of its own country.[5]

There is a fourth self, "self-theologizing," but the Church has shown little evidence of having a specific Vietnamese contextual theology.[6] In other words, the Church has not "nurtured" or "expressed" itself theologically in the cultural context in which it has existed. Its architecture, liturgy, music, homiletical style and organizational structure have all reflected the foreign culture of the missionary, thus being completely discontinuous from Vietnamese cultural patterns.[7] The Church remains to this day, for the most part, a Western CMA church in Vietnam, rather than a contextualized and culturally appropriate ECVN as Violet James stated in her doctoral dissertation, "the ECVN was but another American denomination."[8]

---

4. Lê Hoàng Phu, "Short History," iii, 7.

5. Lê Hoàng Phu, iv.

6. Paul G. Hiebert, *Anthropological Insights for Missionaries* (Grand Rapids, MI: Baker, 1985), 193–224. This fourth self was proposed and articulated firstly by Hiebert.

7. For instance, Robert J. Priest discusses this similar situation elsewhere. See in Robert J. Priest, "Researching Contextualization in Churches Influenced by Missionaries," in *Communities of Faith in Africa and the African Diaspora: In Honor of Dr. Tite Tiénou with Additional Essays on World Christianity*, ed. Casely B. Essamuah and David K. Ngaruiya (Eugene, OR: Pickwick, 2013), 299–318.

8. Violet B. James, "American Protestant Missions and the Vietnam War," PhD diss. (University of Aberdeen, 1989), 354.

The vision of a fully contextualized evangelical mission theology in Vietnam – had past efforts not failed – was the initial thought and driving force behind the present study. The fully contextualized Evangelical Church of Vietnam would now, perhaps, have its own form or style of expression rooted in the culture where it exists. Contextualization (or inculturation) efforts – a continuing issue for Asian Christianity – remain an ongoing task for Vietnamese evangelicalism.[9] Christian faith, then, is expected to be both relevant and indigenous in Vietnamese form, style, language, and so forth. For instance, incorporating the Vietnamese way of venerating ancestors into Christian theology and liturgical practices is one of many forms that could be contextualized for the Vietnamese evangelicals. The church should present Christian faith in such a way that meets Vietnamese people's deepest needs and penetrates their worldview, allowing them to follow Christ while remaining rooted in their Vietnamese culture.[10] Efforts of contextualization have been made in Asia in the sixteenth and seventeenth centuries by the Jesuits Francis Xavier in Japan, Matteo Ricci in China, and Alexander de Rhodes in China and other kingdoms of the Orient, including today's Vietnam.[11] They put great effort into learning local languages and cultures to contextualize Christian faith in these Asian societies as a chance for Christianity to "re-encounter" Asia in the seventeenth century.[12] In fact, "what the Jesuits had done in contextualization, particularly in Vietnam, and generally in Asia in

---

9. See Appendix for the explanation of the terms "contextualization" and "inculturation."

10. A similar effort has been done among Thai Christians, for instance, Ubolwan Mejudhon, "The Way of Meekness: Being Christian and Thai in the Thai Way," DMiss. diss. (Asbury Theological Seminary, 1998). See also Darrell L. Whiteman, "Contextualization: The Theory, the Gap, the Challenge," *International Bulletin of Missionary Research* 21, no. 1 (1997): 2.

11. For instance, Ricci was quite successful in assimilating himself into the social, cultural, and religious life of China. He proved to be a good student of Confucianism, in which he found a philosophical connection between the Chinese concept of *heaven* and the Christian understanding of a personal God. From this connection, Ricci developed a theological defense in 1603, called *The True Meaning of the Lord of Heaven (T'ien-chu Shih-i)* which became the first attempt by a Catholic scholar to use a Chinese way of thinking to introduce Christianity to Chinese intellectuals. See in Dale T. Irvin and Scott W. Sunquist, *History of the World Christian Movement*, 2 vols., vol. 2: Modern Christianity from 1954–1800 (Maryknoll, NY: Orbis Books, 2012), 169–174.

12. Kenneth Scott Latourette, *A History of Christianity*, 1st ed. (New York: Harper, 1953), 853–854; Simon Ditchfield, "The Jesuits: In the Making of a World Religion," *History Today* 57, no. 7 (2007). Latourette revealed that in the sixteenth century the Society of Jesus, which was founded by Ignatius Loyola (c.1491–1556), was the largest and most powerful new religious order since the birth of the Franciscans and Dominicans, and as great mystics as

the previous centuries, became a foundational premise for a better picture of holistic contextualization for the Vietnamese Catholic Church (*Công Giáo*) in the twentieth century."[13]

In contrast, the French and American Protestant missionaries in early twentieth-century Vietnam seemed to be intent on making the native Vietnamese a more Western Christian, overlooking perhaps, that in the process, they were also making one less Vietnamese.[14] Should not a genuine Vietnamese evangelical Christian be expected to be a good Vietnamese as well? Nguyễn Ái Quốc in his letter to a French pastor in 1921 lamented,

> Whether students of illiterate peasants, they are Annamites, and Annamites they should remain. Being good Annamites does not stop them from being good Christians . . . and thus if you want to find a true Christian in Indochina [Vietnam], look for him in a good Indochinese [Vietnamese] man, but nowhere else.[15]

Mr Nguyễn Ái Quốc was living in Paris at the time this letter was written, arguing that French Christian mission and colonization should not go together, as he said, "every civilizing mission – whether it is in the Antilles, Madagascar, Indochina, or Tahiti – is always towed by a so-called evangelizing mission."[16] Rather, he believed there is "goodness" for Vietnamese people if

---

the Church has ever seen. According to Latourette, Loyola is considered as "a product of the Catholic Reformation."

13. For further discussion on how the Church has been able to contextualize its Christian faith relevantly to the culture in terms of theological approaches, art works, and rituals, see Nguyen KimSon, "The Catholic Church in Vietnam: An Example of Contextualization," *Asia Journal of Theology* 29, no. 1 (2015): 74.

14. "History will help us evaluate the critique of missions and empires, of missionaries creating 'rice Christians,' and of missionaries 'making one more Christian and thus one less Chinese.'" See Scott W. Sunquist, *Understanding Christian Mission: Participation in Suffering and Glory* (Grand Rapids, MI: Baker Academic, 2013), 14.

15. In Nguyễn Ái Quốc's (known as Hồ Chí Minh) original writing, "Etudiants ou paysans illettrés, annamites ils sont annamites ils doivent le rester. Etre bons annamites n'empêche pas d'être bon chrétiens . . . si vous voulez trouver un vrai chrétien en Indochine, cherchez le chez le bon Indochinois, mais pas ailleurs." See Hồ Chí Minh, "Unpublished Letter by Hồ Chí Minh to a French Pastor (September 8, 1921)," trans. by Kareem James Abu-Zeid, *Journal of Vietnamese Studies* 7, no. 2 (2012): 3; Pascal Bourdeaux, "Notes on an Unpublished Letter by Hồ Chí Minh to a French Pastor (September 8, 1921) or the Art of Dissenting Evangelization," *Journal of Vietnamese Studies* 7, no. 2 (2012): 14.

16. See Nguyen Ai Quoc, *Le procès de la colonisation francaise* [The process of French colonization], (Paris: Imprimerie et Librairie du Travail, Première Série, Mœurs Coloniales, 1926).

Buddhism, Confucianism (Vietnamese or "Orientals" value), and Christianity ("Occidentals" value) work in harmony, because only "one Truth" exists regardless "whatever side we find ourselves on."[17] His statement above reflects the struggle of the Protestant missionaries to communicate the gospel in a manner that was both relevant and indigenous to Vietnamese people. Because of the lack of cultural sensitivity, the Protestant mission and its mission fruit (the Evangelical Church of Vietnam) have not yet found the optimal solution for contextualizing the gospel relevantly to the diverse cultural and religious contexts of Vietnam.

The purpose of this study, therefore, is three-fold: (1) to situate the Vietnamese evangelical mission theology, and critically evaluate its cultural integration within the larger context of East Asia, and of the Vietnamese syncretistic spirituality context; (2) to show how the present paradigm of Vietnamese mission theology has developed through the missionary movement of Protestant Christian missions by raising the issue of indigenous acceptance and/or rejection of Protestant Christianity in the colonial and postcolonial Vietnamese context; and (3) to propose a paradigm shift towards a more integrative role of a Vietnamese evangelical mission theology. Here, the Vietnamese concept of God and the Vietnamese extended family perspective, for both the Trinitarian relationship and the Vietnamese Christian community of both the living people and the ancestors, must be redeemed.

Significance of the Study

This study shows that it is necessary to present the Christian faith in such a way that allows the Vietnamese to follow Christ and yet remain within their Vietnamese culture. To do so, the study offers some relevant contributions to Vietnamese contextualization efforts by proposing a paradigm shift in Vietnamese mission theology that honors being both "evangelical" and "Vietnamese." A robust Vietnamese mission theology has some outstanding characteristics that are considered necessary for Vietnamese evangelicals to make the Christian faith both evangelical and Vietnamese at the same time.

---

17. Hồ Chí Minh, "Unpublished Letter by Hồ Chí Minh," 2. More regarding Hồ Chí Minh's criticism of the French mission is discussed in "Protestant Missions in the Colonial Context" of chapter 4.

More specifically, this new paradigm promotes continuity with the Christian tradition at large. A Vietnamese mission theology must be faithful to continue the redemptive work of the Trinitarian God, and the saving work of God through Jesus Christ (the Đạo) by the Holy Spirit that has been passed down through the church of Christ since Pentecost. Such theology then enables the church to proclaim the good news of the gospel as reconciliation and restoration of the relationship between humankind and God through Christ, the Đạo. And in the power of the Holy Spirit, Christ the Đạo enlightens the minds and hearts of the Vietnamese so that the Bible continues to speak God's truth in fresh ways to them.

The missiological significance of this study lies in its contribution to the understanding of the Vietnamese evangelical mission history and the social, political, and cultural context of this one-century-old Vietnamese evangelicalism, so that, through the process of contextualization, the Vietnamese mission theology is engaged profoundly in the present-day context of Vietnam. The research also adds a Vietnamese perspective to the contemporary conversations on the notion of "God in our midst," and "God with us," as well as the consideration of ancestor veneration practices, by articulating theological missiological reflections on what it means to be an evangelical church in Vietnam.

This study is not suggesting things that have not been done, but those that have been resisted among the Vietnamese evangelicals, for instance, the Đạo application in Vietnamese Bible translations and in theological text books. The approach of this study, therefore, would resonate theologically more closely with what is already being done, making the Vietnamese concept of God (the Đạo) clearer, based on the cultural and theological practices of the Church. Moreover, the contribution of this study is to make a more global theological synthesis, a Vietnamese evangelical theological textbook for use in theological education, that would help the leadership of the Vietnamese evangelicals to move forward, consistently with the practices of the local churches.

Context and Key Definitions

The context of this study is twentieth-century Vietnam. In 1954, in Geneva, Switzerland, the 1954 Geneva Accords were signed to bring about the end to the war in Indochina. A ceasefire was signed and France agreed to withdraw its troops from the region of French Indochina. This region was then split into three independent countries, Vietnam, Laos and Cambodia.[18] In 1975, the northern Communist army of the Democratic Republic of Vietnam gained a final victory over the alliance between the United States and the Republic of Vietnam respectively under the United States President Richard M. Nixon and the South Vietnamese President Nguyễn Văn Thiệu.[19] Since then, the country has been united and renamed the Socialist Republic of Vietnam.

The study is carried out among the *Kinh* Vietnamese people and the *Kinh* Vietnamese culture.[20] For instance, the tales of *Lĩnh nam chích quái liệt truyện* [*Arrayed tales of collected oddities from south of the passes*] (*LNCQLT* hereafter) show that the *Việt* people had their own records of their origin, culture and regional land. To explain the nation's origin, the *LNCQLT* reveals who the Vietnamese were. In the *LNCQLT*, the name *Việt Nam*[21] is derived from the combination of two words, *Việt* (or *Yueh* 越 in Chinese) and *Nam* (or *Nan* 南 in Chinese), which together mean the Vietnamese (or *Việt*) people in the south.[22] The national identity is reflected in the legend of Lạc Long Quân

---

18. See Nicholas Tarling, *The Cambridge History of Southeast Asia, Vol. Two: The Nineteenth and Twentieth Centuries*, 2 vols. (New York, NY: Cambridge University Press, 1992), 365–374; Pierre Asselin, *Hanoi's Road to the Vietnam War, 1954–1965*, Series from Indochina to Vietnam 7 (Berkeley: University of California Press, 2013); Jessica M. Chapman, *Cauldron of Resistance:Ngo Dinh Diem, the United States, and 1950s Southern Vietnam* (Ithaca, NY: Cornell University Press, 2013).

19. See David L. Anderson, *The Columbia History of the Vietnam War* (New York: Columbia University Press, 2011), http://2001-2009.state.gov/r/pa/ho/time/dr/17411.htm, accessed 11 August 2014.

20. The *Việt* people, their origin, culture and land are beyond the scope of this study. Some notable contemporary resources include Trần Ngọc Thêm, *Cơ sở văn hóa Việt Nam* [Vietnamese culture]. (Nxb Giáo Dục, 1999); Nguyễn Ngọc Thơ, "Văn Hoá Bách Việt Vùng Lĩnh Nam Trong Quan Hệ Với Văn Hoá Truyền Thống Ở Việt Nam" [Bach Viet culture of the Linh Nam in the relation with traditional culture in Vietnam] (Luận Án Tiến Sĩ Văn Hoá Học (Doctoral diss.), HoChiMinh City University of Social Sciences and Humanities, 2011); Tạ Chí Đại Trường, *Thần, Người và Đất Việt* [Spirits, people and the lands of the Việt], (Hà Nội: Nxb Nhã Nam & Nxb Tri Thức, 2014).

21. See Alexander Woodside, *Vietnam and the Chinese Model: A Comparative Study of Nguyen and Ching Civil Government in the First Half of the Nineteenth Century* (Cambridge, MA: Harvard University Press, 1971). According to Woodside, when the new Nguyễn dynasty went to Peking to establish diplomatic relationships with China, the name Nam Viet (Nan Yueh) was used. But the Chinese changed the name to Viet Nam, and in the twentieth century, the name Vietnam has been generally accepted among the Vietnamese.

22. See Trần Thế Pháp, *Lĩnh nam chích quái liệt truyện* [Arrayed tales of collected oddities from south of the passes], trans. Lê Hữu Mục (Saigon: Khai Trí, 1960); Trương Bửu Lâm, *A Story of Viet Nam* (Honolulu, HI: Kindle Edition, 2012). According to Trương Bửu Lâm, as

in *Tale of the Hồng Bàng Clan*. The *Việt* people are proud, calling themselves "offspring of a dragon and a goddess/princess" (*con rồng cháu tiên* or *Long Phụ Tiên Mẫu*), a myth of Vietnamese origin.

The beginning of *Việt Nam* ("Vietnam" in contemporary English) as it is today, in terms of the people and culture, started with Nguyễn Ánh (or Nguyễn Phúc Ánh) who moved the capital to Thăng Long in the summer of 1802, beginning the Nguyễn dynasty under the Gia Long Emperor (1802–1945).[23] Nguyễn Ánh chose the name *Gia Long* for the Nguyễn imperial dynasty, a combination of two significant locations, *Gia Định* and *Thăng Long* in the northern and southern regions of *Đại Việt*. Politically, the Nguyễn emperor united *Đại Việt*[24] for the first time after similar efforts of the Nguyễn Lord (Nguyễn Hoàng) and the *Tây Sơn* regimes earlier, and ruled *Đại Việt* after a long, brutal, destructive century of civil war that "had drained the

---

some theories have proposed, the *Kinh* were one of the numerous Chinese tribes who originally resided in central China, south of the Yangtze River, and who eventually migrated to the southern region. Together, these tribes are identified as the "Hundred Yueh" (The Chinese ideograph for *Yueh* is pronounced Viet in Sino-Vietnamese). However, other scholars find that the Vietnamese share some of their basic religious beliefs and some of their social institutions with the Malayo-Polynesian speaking peoples. If so, they would then be related to other Malayo-Polynesian peoples such as the Chams, the Malays, and the Indonesians. This theory argues that the Vietnamese are simply a Malayo-Polynesian tribe that has been heavily influenced by the Chinese culture during thousands of years of Chinese domination and cohabitation.

23. Nguyễn Ánh chose the name *Gia Long* for the Nguyễn imperial dynasty, a combination of two significant locations, *Gia Định* and *Thăng Long* in the northern and southern regions of *Đại Việt*.

24. George E. Dutton, Jayne S. Werner, and John K. Whitmore, *Sources of Vietnamese Tradition* (New York: Columbia University Press, 2012), 258–259. At this point, the country called itself *Đại Việt* (Great Viet), but the Chinese court did not recognize it and persisted in calling the Vietnamese state *An Nam* (Pacified South). Ironically, the very name Viet Nam in the present-day, set forth by the Nguyễn emperor (*Gia Long* [1802–1945]) in his edict that is recorded in *Đại Nam thực lục*, was bestowed by the Chinese themselves (the Qing court) when the Nguyễn sent a diplomatic delegation to the Qing court, requesting permission to call their country *Nam Việt* (Southern Viet, or Nan Yueh in Chinese). The Qing court did not agree and insisted on reversing the order of the terms to *Việt Nam*. The Qing court was afraid that the term "Nam Việt" recalling a third-century BCE southern kingdom that had resisted Chinese authority, that might result in the possibility of the "Viets" claiming their territory on Chinese lands. Also, the Chinese were particularly sensitive to the possibility of a military campaign to "recapture" the two southern Chinese provinces of Guangdong and Guangxi, which had just been threatened by the Quang Trung emperor. Nevertheless, the term *Việt Nam* was largely ignored by both the Vietnamese and the Chinese until the twentieth century, with the Chinese continuing to use the name *An Nam*, and the Vietnamese reverting to *Đại Việt* in 1813 and later adopting *Đại Nam*, a name formalized under the Minh Mạng emperor.

country's resources and exhausted its people."25 The south, central, and north of *Đại Việt* now were united into one nation for the first time, beginning a new chapter in Vietnam's history, drawing from the rich political, social and cultural diversity of the Cham, the Khmer, several ethnic tribes, and a number of Chinese immigrants in the south. To accommodate this uniting ambition, the Gia Long Emperor sought to deal with a significant element of Vietnamese national identity, respectively naming the country *Việt Nam* through the 1804 edict.26 The unity was a long awaited moment after several regional conflicts, at least before the colonial period. Nevertheless, Vietnam in the Nguyễn dynasty experienced relative independence from the northern kingdom (China) and yet was harshly bombarded by European colonial threats just as other countries in Asia were, particularly the threat of French colonization.27

Culturally, Vietnamese beliefs and practices have been reflected through Vietnamese literature in various ways. Despite sharing the social, cultural, and religious contexts of Eastern and Southeastern Asia – particularly in the context of the Three Religions (Confucianism, Daoism, and Buddhism) – Vietnamese culture has its unique identity in both philosophical beliefs and practices. Understanding this context will provide various cultural approaches that bridge the gap between the Christian faith and the culture of Vietnam. As a result, the Evangelical Church of Vietnam, like its counterpart, the Catholic Church of Vietnam, could break out from the western cultural hegemony of the Western church in order to become a truly Vietnamese evangelical church.

This study is carried out with Vietnamese evangelicalism, or the *Tin Lành* in mind. Though Vietnamese people might have encountered Christianity

---

25. Dutton, Werner, and Whitmore, *Sources of Vietnamese Tradition*, 253.

26. See *Dai Nam thuc luc* [The veritable records of Đại Nam], 9 vols. (Tokyo: Keio Institute of Linguistic Studies, 1961); *Dai Nam thuc luc* [The veritable records of Dai Nam], trans. Nguyễn Ngọc Tỉnh, vol. 10 (Hà Nội: Nxb Khoa Học Xã Hội, 2004). For the Gia Long's edict (1804) and the Minh Mạng's edicts in English, see Dutton, Werner, and Whitmore, *Sources of Vietnamese Tradition*, 258–260.

27. See Jacob Ramsay, *Mandarins and Martyrs: The Church and the Nguyen Dynasty in Early Nineteenth-Century Vietnam* (Stanford, CA: Stanford University Press, 2008). There were several significant aspects to note during the Nguyễn dynasty in the nineteenth and early twentieth centuries, including the relationship between the Nguyễn dynasty and missionary Catholicism represented by the Paris-based Foreign Missions Society, and the Catholic communities of southern Vietnam from 1802 to 1867, the year of France's annexation of southern Vietnam's "six provinces."

from the East, for instance, the East Syrian Church, it was not until the arrival of the Jesuit priests in the seventeenth century, that the Christian church was able to be somewhat established in Vietnam. Despite the east Syrian Christians probably having visited ancient Vietnam on their way to China, there is no indication that they accomplished any significant evangelistic work in Vietnam during their visits.[28] Rather, Christianity in Vietnam can turn for its earliest accounts, in the seventeenth century to the Catholic Church in Vietnam (*Công Giáo*),[29] and two centuries later to the Vietnamese evangelicals (or the *Tin Lành*).[30] By the year 2009, both Vietnamese Catholicism and Vietnamese evangelicalism were two among the six largest religions of Vietnam according to the 2009 Vietnam Population and Housing Census.[31]

Both the registered and the non- (and/or pre-) registered evangelical churches hold similar beliefs, but they differentiate themselves in organizational practices. In terms of beliefs, most of the Vietnamese evangelicals hold a high view of the Scripture, evangelism, and devotion to a life of holiness. Moreover, they have inherited the Christian and Missionary Alliance (CMA) foundational characteristics, including *The Fourfold Gospel*, which is

---

28. See Phạm Văn Sơn's *Việt Sử Tân Biên* (1961) and J. Despon's *L'Eglise d'Indochine* (1964) cited by Lê Hoàng Phu, "Short History," 97.

29. See Latourette, *History of Christianity*, 853–854; Irvin and Sunquist, *History of the World*, 54. This 400-year-old Catholic Church in Vietnam is called *Giáo Hội Công Giáo*, or *Công Giáo*, in short, is a result of the spread of transnational Christianity, led by zealous Jesuits of the early Roman Catholic missions in previous centuries who gave Christianity a chance to "re-encounter" Asia, particularly Vietnam in the seventeenth century.

30. For an extensive and notable history of Vietnamese Catholicism written in English, see Phan Phát Huồn, *History of the Catholic Church in Việt Nam*, vol. 1: 1533–1960 (Long Beach, CA: Cứu Thế Tùng Thư, 2000); Charles Patrick Keith, "Catholic Vietnam: Church, Colonialism and Revolution, 1887–1945," PhD diss. (Yale University, 2008); Charles Patrick Keith, *Catholic Vietnam: A Church from Empire to Nation* (Berkeley, CA: University of California Press, 2012). For Vietnamese evangelicalism, there are a number of notable sources in English, for instance, Lê Hoàng Phu, "Short History"; James, "American Protestant Missions"; Reginald Eugene Reimer, "The Protestant Movement in Vietnam: Church Growth in Peace and War among the Ethnic Vietnamese," MA Thesis (Fuller Theological Seminary, 1972); Reginald Eugene Reimer, *Vietnam's Christians: A Century of Growth in Adversity* (Pasadena, CA: William Carey Library, 2011).

31. See Tổng Cục Thống Kê, "The 2009 Vietnam Population and Housing Census: Completed Results" (Hanoi, Vietnam, 2009); Nguyễn Cao Thanh, "Đạo Tin Lành ở Việt Nam từ 1975 đến nay, tư liệu và một số đánh giá ban đầu" [The Evangelicalism in Vietnam from 1975 to the present, sources and initial comments], Ban Tôn giáo Chính phủ, http://btgcp.gov.vn/Plus.aspx/vi/News/38/0/240/0/2737/Dao_Tin_lanh_o_Viet_Nam_tu_1975_den_nay_tu_lieu_va_mot_so_danh_gia_ban_dau, accessed 29 November 2014.

the preaching of Jesus Christ as Savior, sanctifier, healer, and coming King.[32] For the discussion on the Vietnamese evangelicals' perspective, the current research engages with a number of theologians and their work that influenced Vietnamese evangelicalism, including Albert B. Simpson's works and John Drange Olsen's two-volume *Thần đạo học* (Theology) which was strongly influenced by a famous Baptist theologian Augustus Hopkins Strong's *Systematic Theology* (1907).

From an organizational perspective, however, the Vietnamese evangelicals or the *Tin Lành*, distinguish themselves as two main groups: the registered churches and the non- (and/or pre-) registered churches. The evangelical registered churches are those which received their legal status in Vietnam after the year 2000 as they met certain criteria by law, for example, being present in Vietnam before 1975 and continually after 1975. These registered churches include Vietnam Christian Mission (2007), The United Christian Church (2007), the Seventh Day Adventist Church (2008), Vietnam General Baptist and Vietnam Southern Baptist Church (2008), Vietnam Presbyterian Church (2008), the Vietnam Assembly of God (2009), Jehovah's Witness Church (2009), and Vietnam Mennonite Church (2009).[33] For the Evangelical Church of Vietnam (ECVN), there are two different denominational entities called the ECVN (South) and the ECVN (North). An interesting note here is that the ECVN (South) received legal status in 2001 while the ECVN (North) was granted this status in 1958.

The Evangelical Church of Vietnam (ECVN), or *Hội Thánh Tin Lành Việt Nam* in Vietnamese is the largest evangelical registered church, the

---

32. See http://www.cmalliance.org/about/history/, accessed 29 August 2014. For more information of the CMA's history, see details of the four periods provided on the website: The Founding Years (1887–1919), Sacrifice and Expansion (1919–1946), The Evangelical Era (1947–1974), and the Missionary Church Era (1974–Present). For the Vietnamese Pentecostal-oriented churches, see Vince Le, "The Pentecostal Movement in Vietnam," in *Global Renewal Christianity: Spirit-Empowered Movement Past, Present, and Future*, ed. Vinson Synan and Amos Yong, vol. 1: *Asia and Oceania* (Lake Mary, FL: Charisma House, 2016), 181–195.

33. See Nguyễn Cao Thanh, "Đạo Tin Lành ở Việt Nam từ 1975 đến nay, tư liệu và một số đánh giá ban đầu." This figure also appeared in other articles by the Government Committee for Religious Affairs, for instance, in Đỗ Quang Hưng, "Đạo Tin Lành ở Việt Nam: Một cái nhìn tổng quát" [Protestantism in Vietnam: An overview], Ban Tôn giáo Chính phủ (Government Committee for Religious Affairs), http://btgcp.gov.vn/Plus.aspx/vi/News/38/0/240/0/1395, accessed 20 February 2014; Đoàn Triệu Long, "Đạo Tin Lành buổi đầu vào Việt Nam," [Beginning of Evangelicalism in Vietnam] *Nghiên Cứu Tôn Giáo [Journal of Religious Studies]*, no. 1 (2012).

national church having been established in 1927, first known under the name *Hội Tin Lành Đông Pháp* (Evangelical Church of [French] Indochina) (ECIC). The church again changed its name to *Hội Thánh Tin Lành Việt Nam* (Evangelical Church of Vietnam) in 1950. This Church was an offspring of the CMA missions started in the late nineteenth and early twentieth century in the Indochinese field, which included the countries of Vietnam, Laos, and Cambodia today. Historically, the ECVN should be reviewed through a few critical moments of its mission history in Vietnam: the early CMA mission in Vietnam in the 1900s; the efforts of indigenizing evangelical practices modeled after the "three-self" movement during the 1920s; the institutionalizing process, giving the church an indigenous face as the national evangelical church in Vietnam and writing its first constitution; and the departure of the Western mission in 1975 and the separation of the ECVN (North) and the ECVN (South) since 1955.[34]

Four Protestant mission theorists are generally given credit for the "three-self" concept – self-government, self-support, and self-propagation. These theorists include two administrators, one missionary, and one missionary-pastor theorist: Henry Venn (1796–1873), of the Anglican Church Missionary Society in Britain; Rufus Anderson (1796–1873), a Congregationalist of the American Board of Commissioners for Foreign Mission; Roland Allen (1868–1947), an Anglo-Catholic with Pentecostal sensitivities; and John L. Nevius (1829–1893), missionary to Shandong, China, from the American Presbyterian Church.[35] The purpose of the "three-self" principle was to help indigenous churches, planted in various colonies around the world, to become independent of "Western leadership and financing."[36] However,

---

34. In 1954, in Geneva, Switzerland, an agreement called "The 1954 Geneva Accords" was settled to bring about an end to the Indochina war. A ceasefire was signed and France agreed to withdraw its troops from the region of French Indochina.

35. Sunquist, *Understanding Christian Mission*, 104–106. "The concern for 'three-self' churches and the focus on the lower classes would be resisted by many missionaries, but it came a standard phrase in mission thinking." Thus, the "self-support" was not only financial issue but also the concern of education in terms of teaching English for the elite instead of local languages and dialects.

36. A. Scott Moreau, *Contextualization in World Missions: Mapping and Assessing Evangelical Models* (Grand Rapids, MI: Kregel Academic, 2012), 123–126. Moreau stated that, "in the height of the colonial era, when churches planted in various colonies around the world were largely dependent on Western leadership and financing, missionary leaders Rufus Anderson and Henry Venn utilized 'indigenization' to promote the idea of planting national

the implementation of this principle was problematic because the Western missionaries were not confident handing over "the control to local people who had less education and less experience as administrators and church leaders."[37] Rufus Anderson, however, encouraged missionaries to promote indigenous leadership. Based on his trip to visit mission fields in Syria, India, and Constantinople, Anderson convinced the missionaries of the logic of his "recommendations to break up the large stations, found village churches, ordain native pastors for them, and give up English language secondary schools in favor of vernacular-language schools."[38] His mission policy also clearly stated that, "missions are instituted for the spread of a scriptural, self-propagating Christianity. This is their aim only."[39] In 1949 and 1950, the "three-self" concept used by Anderson was used in the same way by the founders of the Three-Self Patriotic Movement (TSPM), a partner group of the China Christian Council: Wu Yaozong, Han Wenzao, and others in the People's Republic of China.[40] Nevertheless, John L. Nevius was radical when he applied the three-self principles from his early work in Shandong for indigenous localized education when he "established a church and leadership training program and moved away in less than three years, handing the ministry over

---

churches that were (1) self-propagating, (2) self-governing, and (3) self-financing." Although Moreau did not provide the source where he quoted Anderson and Venn's "indigenization" of the "three-self" concept, he provided an overview study of the term "indigenization," including the "Indigenization and Contextualization Compared" table by Simon S. M. Kwan, "From Indigenization to Contextualization: A Change in Discursive Pratice Rather Than a Shift in Paradigm," *Studies in World Christianity* 11, no. 2 (2005): 240. Moreau also believed that "'self-theologizing' and 'self-missiologizing' demonstrates the continuing validity of indigeneity as a guiding concept for evangelicals in contextualization."

37. Sunquist, *Understanding Christian Mission*, 104–106, 57. The "control of the church remained, for long periods of time, in missionary hands – with little understanding as to how the local people would ever be able to lead their own local churches." This was perhaps the tension between the missionary organization and the ECVN church after 1927 that Lê Hoàng Phu stated.

38. Pierce R. Beaver, "The Legacy of Rufus Anderson," *Occasional Bulletin of Missions Research* 3, no. 3 (1977): 94–97.

39. Beaver, "Legacy of Rufus Anderson," 94–97.

40. Sunquist, *Understanding Christian Mission*, 105. Also, there is background and detailed discussion about the implementation of "three-self" in Chinese Protestantism in chapter 10 "Y. T. Wu: A New Understanding of 'Three-Self' Development in Chinese Christianity," in Peter Tze Ming Ng, *Chinese Christianity: An Interplay between Global and Local Perspectives*, vol. 4, Religion in Chinese Societies, ed. Kenneth Dean, Richard Madsen, and David Palmer (Leiden, the Netherlands: Koninklijke Brill NV, 2012), 201–220.

to fresh converts."[41] Though Nevius was not successful implementing this concept in China overall, his idea was applied by the Presbyterians working in Korea, especially by the Underwoods and Moffets in northern Korea.[42]

The evangelical non-(and/or pre-) registered churches are usually called the Vietnamese House Churches (*Hội thánh Tư gia*).[43] These churches have not been studied or written about in academic literature, though the current study engages them in spite of the limited sources available which have been published by the state of Vietnam. Prior to their receiving legal status in 2000, many evangelical registered churches had been gathering and conducting their religious activities in private houses, sometimes in rented venues of the registered churches and of the Catholic Church in Vietnam. This "in house" phenomenon excludes those evangelical churches having their own church buildings which existed before 1975. These churches, which had their own buildings and which were allowed to operate their religious activities with unofficial, though limited, permission, included the Evangelical Church of Vietnam (both the North and the South), Vietnam Christian Mission (in Đà Nẵng and Quảng Ngãi province, in central Vietnam), the United Christian Church (in Hóc Môn district, Hồ Chí Minh City), Vietnam Southern Baptist Church / the Grace Baptist Church (in Hồ Chí Minh City), and the Seventh Day Adventist Church (in Hồ Chí Minh City).

---

41. Sunquist, *Understanding Christian Mission*, 105. From Nevius's *Chinese Recorder* in 1886 that later reprinted as a book entitled *Methods of Mission Work* (1895). Nevius criticized the old way of doing missions: paying foreign agents, paying for buildings, relying on foreign missionaries to do most of the evangelism, building big institutions, and so on. Moreover, he focused on training church leaders in their local villages rather than sending them away for three or four years of education in a big city.

42. Sunquist, *Understanding Christian Mission*, 106. For the Nevius Method in Korea, see Samuel H. Moffett, *A History of Christianity in Asia*, 1st ed., Series 2 (San Francisco, CA: HarperSanFrancisco, 1992); Allen D. Clark, *A History of the Church in Korea* (Seoul: Christian Literature Society of Korea, 1971), 112–116.

43. Luke S. Martin and Violet B. James believe the American Mennonites had the first North American Protestant relief organization in Vietnam in 1954 under two agencies: Mennonite Central Committee and Eastern Mennonite Board of Missions and Charities. See James, "American Protestant Missions," 171–191; Luke S. Martin, "An Evaluation of a Generation of Mennonite Mission, Service and Peacemaking in Vietnam 1954–1976: Vietnam Study Project," (Akron, PA: Mennonite Central Committee, 1977), 3–16. Reg Reimer states that the Southern Baptists arrived in 1959 and the Assemblies of God arrived in 1972. See Reimer, *Vietnam's Christians*, 41.

The fast-growing Vietnamese house church phenomenon was the new ecclesiastical movement in the 1980s,[44] characterized by and formed for various reasons. For instance, there were those who left or were forced to leave (excommunicated)[45] the ECVN due to conflicts regarding the understanding of various doctrines (e.g. spiritual baptism, speaking in tongues) and organizational policy. These ECVN pastors and members then joined other existing "in house" evangelical groups/churches such as the Assemblies of God or formed their own groups. In fact, many of them (e.g. "Inter-Evangelistic Movement" or "United Gospel Outreach Church") have chosen the latter, to have their own church names or to affiliate with other international churches institutionally (not necessarily in doctrine), such as with the Baptists, the Presbyterian Church (of the USA), the Methodists, or the Anglicans. Nevertheless, a very distinct characteristic of the Vietnamese house church movement is the association with the phenomena of Pentecostal speaking in tongues, revival prayers, and other spiritual gifts manifestation.

Adding to this house church phenomenon is the influx of the Vietnamese Christians returning from refugee camps in Asia, mainly Hong Kong in the 1990s, from former Communist countries in Eastern Europe, the former Soviet Union, the former East Germany, and from some Asian countries having Vietnamese immigrants such as South Korea, Taiwan, Malaysia, and Singapore. In addition, there are several missionary efforts recently from outside Vietnam that have made the house church landscape more diverse and complex, including Korean missionary agencies (denominations), the Methodists, the Anglicans, and the Free Churches (e.g. *Lời Sự Sống* [Living Word] church), just to name a few. Today, most of these churches associate with a few existing networks of churches, such as two Vietnamese Evangelical Fellowships in the South and Hanoi Christian Fellowship in the North of Vietnam.

---

44. See Nguyễn Cao Thanh, "Đạo Tin Lành ở Việt Nam từ 1975 đến nay, tư liệu và một số đánh giá ban đầu."

45. A number of the ECVN pastors were excommunicated due to their practices of tongues and healing prayers for the sick. See Hội Thánh Tin Lành Việt Nam (miền Nam), Church Memo 21/TLH/VP, June 24, 1989.

Limitations of the Study

This study is limited to research of the Christian missions among the *Kinh* Vietnamese people, of the French missions and the Christian and Missionary Alliance (CMA) in Indochina, the Evangelical Church of Indochina (ECIC) starting from 1927, and the Evangelical Church of Vietnam (ECVN) from 1950. Though the study contains some broader historical data, it is neither a comprehensive study of the history of the ECVN, nor a documentary of the church through the years. For scholars interested in the definitive history of the ECVN or its growth, there is extensive and notable literature on the history of the church by authors such as Edwin Franklin Irwin (1937), Violet B. James (1989), Reginald Eugene Reimer (1972 and 2011), Lê Hoàng Phu (1972), and Dale Sims Herendeen (1975).[46]

The study focuses only on those elements of Vietnamese culture and the worldview or outlook on life of Vietnamese people as documented in the Vietnamese literature, specifically relating to communal life and worship (ancestor veneration and views of the spiritual world). How does the literature reveal people's view of the world, beliefs and daily practices? What are some elements of Vietnamese culture that both shape and reflect their belief systems? How have Vietnamese people been affected by their cultural encounters with other ethnic populations, including the Chinese, the Cham, and the Khmer, and how have these impacted their belief structures? There are a number of cultural values in Vietnamese academic literature that are visible expressions of Vietnamese people and culture and their outlook on life. Also, the ritual practices of worshiping *Ông Trời* (Mr Heaven/God) and respecting *Đất* (Earth), and *Bàn thờ Ông Thiên* (Mr Heaven's altar) among the southern people in Mekong Delta, have reflected the cosmological worldview and outlook on life among the *Kinh* Vietnamese people. Based on the review of Vietnamese literature, the Vietnamese people believe in a spiritual world, in the existence of the spirits of their ancestors "living" all around them to bless and protect them. For instance, *Việt điện u linh tập* (Departed Spirits of the

---

46. See Edwin Franklin Irwin, *With Christ in Indo-China: The Story of Alliance Missions in French Indo-China and Eastern Siam* (Harrisburg, PA: Christian Publication, 1937); James, "American Protestant Missions"; Reimer, "Protestant Movement in Vietnam"; Reimer, *Vietnam's Christians*; Lê Hoàng Phu, "Short History"; Dale Sims Herendeen, *Conversion and Indigeneity in the Evangelical Church of Viet Nam* (Pasadena, CA: Fuller Theological Seminary, 1975).

Viet Realm) is a valuable source in Vietnamese literature that brings to light the Vietnamese religious values, especially venerating those "fully" human figures – seeing human life as a continual process from birth through life to death and after their death as they pray for their assistance. Some practices related to this belief can become visible examples for constructing Vietnamese contextual theology, for instance, ancestral veneration, which is manifested through placing the ancestor's pictures on the altar.

Outline and Methodology

The following chapter by chapter overview presents the study's objectives and outlines the methods used.

Within the very specific cultural and religious context of East Asia which is different from the Western world, chapters 1 and 2 seek to create a new set of information to understand the syncretistic spirituality, and to explain how and why appropriate contextualization of the gospel matters in this context. While chapter 1 is chiefly an introductory study of the East Asian context of Daoism, Confucianism, and Buddhism before encountering Christianity, chapter 2 is a literature review of Christian "contextualization," a concept that has been developed and practiced in Christian missionary activity and mission theology. In chapter 2, the study takes the alternative evangelical perspective on contextualization to argue that as God's intention through God's incarnation into the world of human flesh, God would have some specific, unique and translatable ways to reveal who he is for all human beings, regardless of their cultural contexts. Therefore, in the process of theologizing (not borrowing), without the fear of "syncretism," contextualization in Christian mission theology should come to the point of acknowledging (or "knowing") where and how God has been at work in the midst of the East Asian people.

From a Vietnamese cultural perspective, chapter 3 engages the Vietnamese syncretistic spirituality, with a special emphasis on the dual force of "resistance and assimilation" in the Vietnamese culture throughout the history of the Vietnamese people, and the essence of the East Asian-Vietnamese spirituality, that is the *Đạo*. First, we see how this dual force has shaped how the Vietnamese were able to both resist the religio-cultural influences from the outside and to assimilate moderately the essentials of the outside influences that were of specific interest to them. Second, the Vietnamese understanding of the divine nature of the *Đạo* indicates that the Vietnamese would be, by analogy, open to God's intent to be known, or simply to experience God in our midst. The failure of contextualization was indicative of a particularly Vietnamese cultural dimension that also gave birth to the special brand of Vietnamese syncretism (the Cao Dai or Caodaism).

Chapter 4 offers a historical perspective and overview of both the French and American Protestant missions in the nineteenth-century and the Evangelical Church of Vietnam (ECVN) in the twentieth-century in Vietnam. Several crucial historical moments, key missionaries, and national leaders are discussed in this early and exploratory stage of the evolution of evangelical Christianity in Vietnam. These include the evangelistic efforts, and attitudes of missionaries toward the religion, culture, and political context of Vietnam. The chapter seeks to show how the present paradigm of mission theology has been created through the historical evolution of Christian missions in Vietnam, particularly through and by the French and American Protestant missions. Thus, two questions can be answered in this chapter: How did Protestant Christian missions contribute to the formation of the present Vietnamese evangelicalism? And, to what extent have the French and American Protestant missions missed opportunities to contextualize the gospel to the Vietnamese culture relevantly and indigenously? Because of the nature of the Vietnamese culture to resist the complete assimilation of one single religious doctrine, it is possible to argue that this is also the reason why Christian contextualization efforts failed.

Chapter 5 situates evangelical theology in the particular framework of the Vietnamese context to evaluate the relationship between "mission" and "theology." Evangelical theology, done by Western missions in nineteenth-century Vietnam and carried out in present-day context, being focused on individual evangelism and conversion efforts, has critically missed considering contextualization (cultural integration) as being appropriate to the authentic message of the gospel. Thus, the chapter argues that Christian mission is to participate in the mission of the triune God.[47] It means that theology done in any missionary context – Vietnamese in this case – must be oriented

---

47. The Latin phrase *missio Dei* means the mission or sending of God. It was coined by Karl Hartenstein to summarize the teaching of Karl Barth. Further discussion of the phrase, see "God's Intention" in chapter 2.

and practiced biblically and theologically within the Trinitarian framework. Thus, to participate in *missio Dei*, the mission of the triune God, Vietnamese evangelical mission theology must integrate and express itself within its own cultural heritage.

Lastly, in chapter 6, the study proposes a cultural integration for a renewed evangelical mission theology in Vietnam. The chapter offers a Vietnamese perspective on how local and Christian concepts and their practice can merge, creating a paradigm shift required by a renewed evangelical mission theology. This redeems the Vietnamese concept of God, and the Vietnamese extended family perspective for both the Trinitarian relationship – the Father, the Son and the Holy Spirit – and the Vietnamese Christian community, both the living people and the ancestors. Such mission theology is an ongoing task for Vietnamese evangelicalism because it helps to point the evangelical Christian community in the right direction, which is fulfilling God's purposes as reflected in the ministry of Jesus Christ and in its response to the triune God's mission in which it has been called to participate. Thus, the study is a humble invitation and guide for others attempting to present the gospel that is relevant and connects with the Vietnamese people in their cultural context.

CHAPTER 1

East Asian Syncretistic Context

Contextualization and syncretism have been going on hand in hand in East Asia for millennia. Several doctrines (for instance, Christianity) have taken root and been blended in particular ways for different people for centuries.[1] Vietnam, however, has been singled out as a country resistant to Christian faith despite the early Jesuits' missionary work in the late sixteenth century. This chapter seeks to create a new set of information to understand why syncretism that happened generally throughout Asia presents with different degrees of manifestation.[2] When Western missionary movements arrived in Asia to convert the people (as seen with the Catholic missionaries), contextual syncretistic forms were established in most regions of the continent, meaning the majority of the continent was already contextualized. How is it possible that the entire continent of Asia was already subjected to syncretism by the time Christianity arrived? This is a very specific cultural religious context of Asia which is very different from the Western world. Therefore it is important to understand the syncretistic spirituality of East Asia, because Christian contextualization should be viewed from within the context of this continent that has already been syncretistically contextualized. In this first

---

1. For instance, some countries in Asia have high percentages of Christianity, including the Philippines and South Korea. A larger number of Christians does not mean better Christian contextualization or "over-contextualization," because an authentic contextualization is that it communicates the gospel clearly and accurately. But it could be indicative that Christians in these countries have synthesized their Christian faith with a number of aspects of their cultural traditions into some contextual syncretistic forms that are specific to them.

2. Historical migration, trade and imperialism work together to explain why some countries in Asia are more subjected to Islam (e.g. Indonesia, Malaysia, Pakistan), to Buddhism (e.g. Thailand, Myanmar, Cambodia), to Christianity (e.g. the Philippines), and to Daoism and Confucianism (e.g. Korea, Japan, Vietnam).

chapter, chiefly an introductory study of the East Asian context, the focus is given to Daoism and Confucianism with some references to how these two indigenous "religions" encountered Buddhism (coming from India). As we will see, other faiths had already been contextually syncretized before the arrival of Christianity.

Encountering Christianity

The religio-cultural context of East Asia is such that a named religion found in one country may not be similar to the religion of the same name found in another country. For instance, the Buddhism of China, Japan and Vietnam may have significant differences when compared with one another, and may have little resemblance to the original Buddhism which came out of Hinduism in India. Although Mahayana Buddhism of China and Zen Buddhism of Japan may resemble more closely the original Buddhism that came out of India, the Buddhism of Thailand and that of Vietnam differ greatly when compared with one another, bearing little resemblance to the original Buddhism. This has occurred because of patterns of contextualization and syncretism as the Buddhism moved from one cultural context to another. The Buddhism of China (originating in India) has been influenced much by Chinese folk religion, and has much common ground with the indigenous beliefs of Confucianism and Daoism, sharing certain beliefs, rituals, and values. Thus, one may consider Buddhism to be a Chinese religion, yet it may be more accurate to consider it "a religion of foreign origin."[3]

Before encountering Christianity, East Asia in particular had already been contextualized and syncretized in its spirituality by a plurality of traditions, especially the three religious traditions of Confucianism, Daoism, and Buddhism, assimilated with local beliefs in spirits (e.g. Animism in Vietnam and Shintoism in Japan). In fact, the coexistence of the three religious traditions, and the possibility for the same persons to be involved in all three of

---

3. See Julia Ching's chapter 4, "Buddhism: A Foreign Religion in China" in Hans Küng and Julia Ching, *Christianity and Chinese Religions* (New York: Doubleday, 1989), 195–230. Ching argued that "the meeting of the Buddhist religion and Chinese culture became the occasion for conflicts and controversies, which were resolved only when Buddhism adjusted itself to the Chinese environment-taking account of Confucian moral values such as filial piety while making use of Taoist ideas and terminology for its own survival and advancement."

them, testifies to a certain pluralism within the Chinese and the East Asian civilizations, a pluralism that was not known in the West.[4] The outward assimilation of Christianity was also expressed through the East Syrian Christian visitors and settlers in East Asia (e.g. the Persian monk A-lo-pen who arrived in Xian in 635 CE). These Christians spread Christianity into India, Vietnam (which comprised different kingdoms at that time), Java, Tibet, Central Asia, and China (in 578 CE) in the sixth or seventh century.[5] Principally, though the Vietnamese might have encountered the East Syrian Christians, there is no clear evidence that these Christians accomplished any significant work in Vietnam during their visits. It was not until the arrival of the Jesuit priests in the seventeenth century, that the church was able to be somewhat established in Vietnam.[6] Unlike in Vietnam, the spread of the East Syrian Christianity in China is preserved on the famous stele of Xian from the year 781 CE, written in Syrian and Chinese and excavated in 1623.[7]

Although there is no concrete evidence for the presence of the East Syrian Christianity in the lands of the *Việt* people in these early centuries, it is not necessary to make a geographical distinction between Vietnam and China since this boundary was not firm at that time. As invited Buddhist teachers of that time crossed the geographical boundary of the lands of the North (the northern Kingdom or China today) and of the South (the southern indigenous people which originated in the northern region of Vietnam today) to share their faith, the East Syrian Christians might have done the same. In fact, what early East Syrian Christianity had done in sharing their faith, perhaps, was quite different compared with the later Christian missionaries (the Catholic missionaries in the late sixteenth century and the Protestants in the nineteenth century) who focused on "converting" the natives. It appears that

---

4. Küng and Ching, *Christianity and Chinese Religions*, 225. This spiritual and religious context of East Asia, particularly China's Daoism and Confucianism, greatly influenced the development of Vietnamese syncretistic spirituality (discussed in ch. 2).

5. Jingyi Ji, *Encounters between Chinese Culture and Christianity: A Hermeneutical Perspective* (Münster: Lit Verlag, 2007), 23–37.

6. See Nguyen KimSon, "Mission History of Vietnamese Evangelicalism in the Pioneering Stage: A Vietnamese Perspective," *Journal of Asian Mission* 16, no. 2 (2015).

7. For Syrian Christians in China, see Li Tang, *East Syriac Christianity in Mongol-Yuan China* (Wiesbaden: Harrassowitz, 2011); Li Tang and Dietmar W. Winkler, *From the Oxus River to the Chinese Shores: Studies on East Syriac Christianity in China and Central Asia*, Orientalia-patristica–oecumenica, v. 5 (Zürich; Berlin: Lit Verlag, 2013).

the East Syrian Christians assimilated as migrants who sought to "survive" amid an alien culture.[8]

Christianity "re-encountered" Asia in the late sixteenth century.[9] As Christianity re-encountered the region it struggled to assimilate into the cultural context of East Asia, particularly Daoism, Confucianism, and Buddhism.[10]

Daoism

The study of Daoism is necessary for two reasons: first, the philosophical nature of Daoism, the *Đạo* (or *Tao*)[11] concept in particular (the Daoist philosophy) that manifested itself as the oldest indigenous philosophic-spiritual tradition in East Asia; and second, the religious nature of Daoism (the Daoist religion), specifically as "a salvation religion" in the East Asian spirituality.[12] The source is *Dao De Jing* (or *Tao Te Ching*) which is the most important canon of Daoist philosphy, as well as the most important scripture of Daoist religion.[13]

---

8. Küng and Ching, *Christianity and Chinese Religions*, 198.

9. Irvin and Sunquist, *History of the World*, 54.

10. For instance, at the end of the *Ming* dynasty (1368–1644) in China, Confucianism (Neo-Confucianism) became the religious-philosophical system of the state. The ruling system, then, considered any other religious system (including Buddhism and Daoism) as enemies of the state. See, for example, Wang, *Christianity and Imperial Culture*, 217–219. In Japan, although the country was open to making political alliances with the West, it was resistant to the spread of Christianity because Western culture and beliefs clashed with Japan's native culture and belief system. Over the previous centuries, Japan had adopted and had been shaped by the rich and diverse religious life of a mixture of Shintoism, Buddhism, and Confucianism that defined the national identity of its people.

11. 道 in Chinese is translated into two Romanization system of transliterations, the Wade-Giles (*Tao*) and Pinyin (*Đạo*). For the Wade-Giles to Pinyin conversion table, see in https://www.lib.uchicago.edu/about/directory/departments/eastasia/find/wade-giles-pinyin-conversion-table/. While the authors' quotations use the Wade-Giles transliteration of *Tao* remain, the preferred use of this term is the Pinyin one, *Đạo* in this chapter.

12. For a comprehensive study of Daoism, see Julia Ching's "Taoist Naturalism: Philosophy and Religion" in Küng and Ching, *Christianity and Chinese Religions*, 129–158.

13. See "On the Dao De Jing (Tao Te Ching)" in Yi Jie Tang, *Confucianism, Buddhism, Daoism, Christianity, and Chinese Culture*, vol. 3, Cultural Heritage and Contemporary Life 3, Asia (Peking; Washington, DC: University of Peking; Council for Research in Values and Philosophy, 1991), 61–65.

Philosophical Daoism

Daoism is the oldest philosophic-spiritual tradition of China and one of the most ancient of the world's spiritual structures.[14] It is difficult to know precisely what Daoism is because the term denotes not one school, but a whole conglomeration of doctrines.[15] The word *Đạo* which means the "Way," is used by every school of Chinese thought or religion.[16] In fact, the concept of *Đạo* (the Way) is what has given the school its name, "Daoism." This philosophical concept of *Đạo* (Daoist philosophy) is especially found in the texts of both Lao-tzu (*Lão tử*) and Chuang-tzu (*Trang tử*), Chinese philosophers whose writings were compiled over a period of fifteen centuries along with other writings of an electic nature.[17]

The famous line that begins the text of Lao-tzu says, "The Tao that can be trodden is not the enduring and unchanging Tao. The name that can be named is not the enduring and unchanging name."[18] Or "The Way (*Tao*) that can be spoken of, is not the constant [true] Way (*Tao*)" is the famous line that begins the text of Lao-tzu.[19] Julia Ching explains, "There is a double play on words here, since the term *tao* [*dao*] is also a verb, 'to speak.' It is really saying, 'The

---

14. Ronnie L. Littlejohn, *Daoism: An Introduction* (London: I. B. Tauris, 2009), 15. "The name 'Daoism' comes from the term *dao*, which is often used for a 'way' or a 'road' through the field or to one's village. It is also used as the 'way' to do something, such as the way a master craftsman carves a candlestick, make a bell or even butchers an ox."

15. See Julia Ching's "Taoist Naturalism" in Küng and Ching, *Christianity and Chinese Religions*, 131.

16. 道 in Chinese and *Đạo* in Vietnamese. The English word *Daoism* is used to refer to both Daoist philosophy (*Đạo lý*) and Daoist religion (*Đạo giáo*). See "Daoist Philosophy," particularly "The Daoist Religion of China" in Tang, *Confucianism, Buddhism, Daoism*, 81–85.

17. See "Origin and Characteristics of Daoism" in Tang, *Confucianism, Buddhism, Daoism, Christianity*; Küng and Ching, *Christianity and Chinese Religions*, 132. The text *Lao-tzu* is also called *Tao Te Ching* (Dao De Ching), or the Classic of the Way and Its power. This is a brief but cryptic text, containing a little more than 5,000 words presented in parallel verses and poetic stanzas.

18. Lao Tse, *Tao Te Ching, or, the Tao and Its Characteristics*, trans. James Legge. ([S.l.]: The Floating Press, 2008), 8. *Dao De Ching* (Tao Te Ching) is translated by other translators besides James Legge, for example, Lao Tse, *The Wisdom of Laotse*, trans. Lin Yutang (New York: Modern Library, 1948); Jonathan Star, *Tao Te Ching: The New Translation from Tao Te Ching* (New York: Jeremy P. Tarcher; Penguin, 2008).

19. Quoted in Küng and Ching, *Christianity and Chinese Religions*, 132. Ching argues that the Chinese word *Tao* is an equivalent of *both* the Greek word *logos*, the Word, and the Greek word *hodos*, the Way. It has been used in translations of St John's Prologue – "In the beginning was the Tao" – and its contents therefore echoes the line "I am the Way, the Truth and the Life."

Tao that can be *tao*-ed, is not the constant *Tao*.'"[20] Ching argues that this line shows "the dialectical method in Taoist thinking and the effort to point to the nameless *Tao* as the first principle – indeterminate, and yet that from which all things proceed to become determinate."[21]

Other lines in the text also reflect the nature of the *Đạo*:

"Deep, it is like the ancestor of the myriad creatures" (4:11).
"It images the forefather of the Lord (Ti)" (4:13).

And also:

There is a thing confusedly formed,
Born before Heaven and Earth.
Silent and void
It stands alone and does not change,
Goes round and does not weary (25:56).[22]

These verses appear to show that the *Đạo* existed "before the universe came to be, an unchanging first principle, even as the ancestor [creator] of all things, that by which all things come to be. It appears to be a philosophical attempt to conceptualize an earlier, religious belief."[23] Thus, Daoist philosophy sees "the nameless *Đạo* (or *Tao*)" as the unidentified Way in the text of Lao-tzu.[24] *Đạo* is not the supreme being of Daoism, even though there are certain numinal or holy entities and powers named.[25] But *Đạo* constitutes the origin of the universe within the natural law of the universe which is the beginning

---

20. The verse also appeared as "A *Tao* that can be told of is not the Permanent *Tao*," in Paul S. Chung, "The Mystery of God and Tao in Jewish-Christian-Taoist Context," in *Asian Contextual Theology for the Third Millenium: Theology of Minjung in Fourth-Eye Formation*, ed. Paul S. Chung, Kyoung-Jae Kim, and Veli-Matti Kärkkäinen (Eugene, OR: Wipf & Stock, 2007), 247; Paul S. Chung, *Constructing Irregular Theology: Bamboo and Minjung in East Asian Perspective*, Studies in Systematic Theology (Leiden, Netherlands), v. 1. (Leiden: Brill, 2009).

21. Küng and Ching, *Christianity and Chinese Religions*, 132.

22. Quoted in Küng and Ching, 132–133.

23. Küng and Ching, 133.

24. Will this be helpful to contrast with "Christian appropriation" of the Word (John 1:1) and the Way (John 14:6) as Ching explains?

25. Littlejohn, *Daoism: An Introduction*, 15. The highest numinal powers of Daoism are called the Celestial Worthy of Primordial Beginning (*Yuanshi tianzun*) or the Jade Emperor (*Yuhuang Shangdi*), or the Perfected Warrior (*Zhenwu*). But these are expressions of *dao* in specific *shen*, they are not identical with *dao*.

of all beings, including human beings.[26] In that sense, our lives are governed by the law of the universe.

In Lao-tzu, *Đạo* is the natural Way as well as the human way, and *Đạo* is the Way of all ways. And because the *Đạo* is not identified as a personal diety, *Đạo* remains as a model for human behavior.[27] In the Daoist philosophical writings of Chuang-tzu, the concept of *Đạo* is different from that of Lao-tzu. *Đạo* is more clearly identified in Chuang-tzu. "Đạo" did not completely disappear or take over "Heaven" as obviously as in Lao-tzu's text. Such understanding of the term can be viewed alongside the classic Confucianist terms "Lord-on-high" (a supreme diety) and "Heaven" which has been given a progenitor's or creator's role as that which gives birth to all things.[28]

Because Đạo is the Way of all ways, Daoism covers a wide variety of phenomena, from a bibliographic classification of philosophical texts to vaguely defined attitudes: the love of nature, the pursuit of personal freedom, and a concomitant antipathy toward the Confucian inspired social order, an antipathy shared by a number of recluses and disillusioned former officials throughout the course of Chinese history.[29]

Because *Đạo* is the Way of all ways, then the goal of human beings is not to control the way(s) but to let go of everything, and more importantly, to unite with the *Đạo*. Lao-tzu and the Daoists recognize the "power" (*te* in Chinese) by which the universal *Đạo* becomes specific.[30] So, the *Đạo* can be gained by human beings as they follow the example of the *Đạo* which means that they should have the power (*te*) or the way to reach the *Đạo*, and those who follow the *Đạo* are sages.[31] As the Sage said: "I take no action, and people of themselves become correct. I engage in no activity, and the people of themselves become prosperous. I have no desire, and the people of themselves become

---

26. Đào Duy Anh, *Việt Nam văn hóa sử cương* [An outline of Vietnamese culture]. (Hà Nội: Nxb Văn học, 2010), 252–257.

27. Küng and Ching, *Christianity and Chinese Religions*, 133.

28. Küng and Ching, 133.

29. See "The Worldview of the Daoist Religion: General Perspectives and Definitions" in Stephen R. Bokenkamp and Peter S. Nickerson, *Early Daoist Scriptures*, Taoist Classics (Berkeley: University of California Press, 1999).

30. Küng and Ching, *Christianity and Chinese Religions*, 133.

31. Tang, *Confucianism, Buddhism, Daoism*, 64.

simple" (line 57).³² Human beings need "nonaction" (the term *wu-wei*); rather, their whole life needs to contemplate the universe as it leads to the discovery of the nameless first principle (the Đạo) and of the disposition that should accompany such contemplation.³³ "By eliminating all things that bear names and forms, in other words, without any so-called knowledge, you can know the *dao* naturally."³⁴ And, this explains why "Taoism tends to be a tradition of the recluses, of persons who prefer to keep their distance from political involvement."³⁵ It contrasts with Confucianism, especially in the political dimension, which promotes the ability to live in harmony with the world.³⁶

The universal Đạo is the power of the natural, of simplicity, even of weakness. For instance, "There is nothing softer and weaker than water, and yet there is nothing better for attacking hard and strong things."³⁷ Thus, one needs to be concerned about finding absolute happiness through perfect union with the Đạo, which leads to the religious aspect of Daoism as a "salvation" religion. Chuang-tzu's central concern is the union with the Đạo which comes by mystical knowledge, or simply by "forgetting" the knowledge of all things – especially that of the self, as Chuang-tzu says, "fasting of the mind, which is different from fasting of the body. This requires the emptying of the senses and of the mind itself. Let your ears and your eyes communicate with what is inside . . . Then even gods and spirits will come to dwell . . ."³⁸

Religious Daoism

Unlike the philosophical Daoism of Lao-tzu and Chuang-tzu, the religious dimension of Daoism came down from the very early times, assimilating the animistic belief in spirits.³⁹ Tang Yi-Jie believed that "Daoism (Taoisim)

---

32. Cited by Tang, 64.
33. Küng and Ching, *Christianity and Chinese Religions*, 133.
34. Tang, *Confucianism, Buddhism, Daoism*, 64.
35. See Julia Ching's "Taoist Naturalism: Philosophy and Religion" in Küng and Ching, *Christianity and Chinese Religions*, 131.
36. Küng and Ching, *Christianity and Chinese Religions*, 192.
37. Cited by Tang, *Confucianism, Buddhism, Daoism*, 64.
38. *Chuang-tzu*, chapter 4, quoted in Küng and Ching, *Christianity and Chinese Religions*, 134–135.
39. Küng and Ching, 137–138. It came from the times of oracles, bones and divination, in a society where the diviners and shammans were venerated for their ability to communicate with the spiritual world – the world of the Lord-on-high, and of the other gods, including the ancestral spirits – to bring down rain to the dry earth and to heal the sick.

is a religion of the Han people and has certain concrete features that come from this association. It has a large influence on Chinese culture, psychology, customs, science and technology, medicine and hygiene, philosophy and even on Chinese politics and economics."[40] The religious doctrine of Daoism came mainly from the teachings of both Lao-tzu and Chuang-tzu which accumulated and interpreted a huge body of scripture called *Tao-tsang* (Taoist canon). This collection (over a thousand volumes compiled over fifteen centuries) has a very eclectic character, since it comprises as well certain Buddhist, Manichaean,[41] and even Christian works, which religious Daoism has simply appropriated and called its own.[42] The things which make up religious Daoism are from several strands, including the *yin-yang* school, the school of the Five Elements or Agents, and of course, the philosophical Daoism (the Đạo) as seen above.[43] These three schools exercised a formative influence in early attempts to understand the universe. They penetrated both Confucian and Daoist philosophy, and became even more prominent in the Daoist religion. In addition, the legendary Yellow Emperor and Lao-tzu were worshiped as the "Hoang-Lao" (Lao-tzu and Chuang-tzu) in a cult of alchemy that involved attempts to change base metal into gold and to find immortality. There was also a cult of hygiene which taught yoga exercises and gymnastics as well as the quest of elixirs, through alchemy or from the so-called "isles of the immortals."[44]

---

40. Tang, *Confucianism, Buddhism, Daoism*, 81.

41. A Christian sect that came to China from East Turkestan by way of the Silk Road in the 6th or 7th century. It was founded by Mani (the 3rd century CE) in the Judeo-Christian milieu of Mesopotamia, it spread to Spain in the West all the way to China in the East. See Küng and Ching, *Christianity and Chinese Religions*, 235–236.

42. Küng and Ching, 138. The principal books are alleged to be divine revelations made to Taoist adepts during a state of trance. None bears the name of the author or the date of composition; many are written in a coded, esoteric language which can only be understood by the initiated. Philosophical treatises such as Lao-tzu and Chuang-tzu have been incorporated into the Taoist canon and given their own interpretations; the *Book of Changes*, a Confucian classic and a divination manual, is also part of this canon.

43. Küng and Ching, 138. The *yin-yang* school understands the natural order under the two complementary yet antithetical aspects of the Đạo; the school of Five Elements (metal, wood, water, fire, earth), a group of physical substances which also represent cosmic forces.

44. Küng and Ching, 138–139. Daoist philosophy was actually reinterpreted in the light of such cults, which had as their goal the prolonging of life.

Daoism is a religion with longings for "salvation."[45] Ching argues, in the quest for immortality, that the Daoist intends to escape from deathlessness (from the fallen state that is followed by the present human condition, to a belief in an original state of bliss), and to seek a happy eternity beyond this transitory life.[46] To be saved from this fallen state, a reliance on supernatural powers for help and protection is definitely needed.[47] Thus, the authentically Chinese core of the Daoist religion is the survival of the whole person.[48] And to achieve such wholeness, they have developed the doctrine of the three life principles of breath (*ch'i*), vital essence or semen (*ching*), and spirit (*shen*), each of which has two dimensions, being present at the same time in the human being as microcosm and in the cosmos as macrocosm.[49] Ching says:

> Religious Taoism tends to associate human weakness and sickness with sin, that is, offense against both the conscience and the deity, and Taoists also associate the healing of such ills with the confession of sin, and the forgiveness and help of higher powers. On the other hand, their attention to physiology as well as to pharmacology has led to many contributions in the area of Chinese medicine.[50]

Religious ritual expressions, given special attention in Daoist religion, are performed mainly by Daoist priests. Several important rituals are performed by the priests on particular occasions, including the examination of the individual's ritual knowledge, and exorcism rituals for sickness believed to be caused by the evil spirits.[51] Many other well-known rituals are regularly performed around the Lunar New Year and its festivals, for instance, dragon

---

45. Küng and Ching, 149.

46. Küng and Ching, 149.

47. Some of these feaures represent greater Buddhist influence.

48. Küng and Ching, *Christianity and Chinese Religions*, 150. Ching explains, "Taoists do not conceive of eternal life in terms of spiritual immortality alone. Since there is no strict separation of spirit and matter in Chinese thought, they look forward to the survival of the whole person, including the body."

49. Küng and Ching, 150. For their proper cultivation, techniques are developed – of breath circulation, sexual hygiene (a blending of sex and yoga), and meditative exercises. Much of this teaching is esoteric and is transmitted in secret from master to disciple.

50. Küng and Ching, 150.

51. Since the Sung dynasty, the Daoist priests were *licensed* for this task and in return for a fee.

dances and firecrackers to chase away the demons, and prayers to Ông Táo, the kitchen god (a very important Daoist deity). Other more soteriological rituals include the rite of cosmic renewal and the general amnesty (*p'u-t'u*) ritual (freeing all the souls from hell). Food, wine and fruit, and incense and fire are elements used for these rituals. In fact, incense is central to Daoist rituals, together with the sacrificial offering of sacred writings, such as the burning of paper talismans. The Daoist priest plays several roles in the ritual, including that of shaman, soothsayer, or spirit-medium, assisting the faithful with their counsels and fortune-telling, explaining the baleful influence of the stars, and assisting communication with the spirits of the beloved dead. Within the religion itself, those priests who practice rituals as an expression of meditation or inner alchemy, usually earn more respect than do those who perform "external" exercises of exorcisms and healing for the sake of making a living.[52] These religious and practical aspects were apparent in late second-century CE Vietnamese spirituality, and more obviously in modern Vietnamese Caodaism (the Cao Dai).[53] Nevertheless, it is impossible to disentangle Daoism from many aspects of Chinese culture because Daoism is intertwined and integrated with China's calendar, traditional medicine, national artifacts and treasures, and even China's holidays and festivities, which have also influenced Vietnamese culture until today.[54]

Confucianism

Confucianism (or Ruism, known in Chinese as *ju chia* or School of the Literati) is also an influential tradition rooted in Chinese culture.[55] It has

---

52. Küng and Ching, *Christianity and Chinese Religions*, 153–154.

53. Both Vietnamese spirituality and the Cao Dai (or *Cao Đài* in Vietnamese) are discussed in the next chapter.

54. Littlejohn, *Daoism*, 18.

55. Peter C. Phan, *Christianity with an Asian Face: Asian American Theology in the Making*. (Maryknoll, NY: Orbis Books, 2003), 126–128. The literati are scholars and teachers of the ancient literature, especially of the Five Classics allegedly edited by Confucius: *Book of Poetry, Book of Rites, Book of History, Spring and Autumn Annals,* and *Book of Changes*). Confucianism is conventionally divided into (1) classical Confucianism, as embodied in the Four Books (*The Analects, The Great Learning, The Doctrine of the Mean,* and *Mencius*); (2) Han Confucianism, that is, Confucianism that was established as state orthodoxy during the Han dynasty (206 BCE–220 CE); it was during this time that the Confucian canon was established and the cult of Confucius emerged as part of the state religion; and (3) Neo-Confucianism, that is, Confucianism as it was revived from the Sung dynasty (960–1279) with the School of

deeply impacted the life of all East Asian people for centuries. This section describes two important aspects: first, the will of Heaven and how it is related to the way of man (*jen* or *nhân*), and second, the syncretistic and inclusive nature of Confucianism.

Confucius or K'ung Fu-tzu (552?–479 BCE) is believed to have developed Confucian tradition, rather than founding it. He strictly preserved religious ritual, yet he never saw himself as the leader or founder of a religious tradition.[56] What he did, was merely to transmit the ancient culture, which in his mind was the model for the present and the guarantee for the future.[57] In China, there was no religious equivalent for "Confucianism," the venerable, all-encompassing tradition of socio-ethical precepts and philosophical norms governing human conduct and social relations in Chinese antiquity that was presumed to be articulated by the historical "Confucius."[58] The term "Confucianism" was, in fact, coined as an interpretation of the ancient Confucian tradition by the Jesuit missionaries (Mateo Ricci) in the sixteenth and seventeenth centuries in China.[59] "The Jesuits' understanding of Confucianism had only a limited impact, mostly in the missionary realm

---

Principle (in particular with Cheng I and Chu Hsi) through the Ming dynasty (1368–1644) with the School of Mind, whose main representative is Wang Yang-Ming, until the present day. In 1905 the imperial examination system, whose source was the official Neo-Confucian orthodoxy, was abolished, and in 1928 the cult of Confucius in the Confucian temple was terminated, thus ending the status of Confucianism as a state religion. See details in Wing-tsit Chan, ed. *A Source Book in Chinese Philosophy* (Princeton, NJ: Princeton University Press, 1963); Julia Ching *To Acquire Wisdom: The Way of Wang Yang-ming*, Studies in Oriental Culture, no. 11; Oriental Monograph Series 16 (New York: Columbia University Press, 1976); Weiming Tu, *Neo-Confucian Thought in Action: Wang Yang-ming's Youth (1472–1509)* (Berkeley: University of California Press, 1976); Weiming Tu, *Centrality and Commonality: An Essay on Chung-yung*, Monograph no. 3 of the Society for Asian and Comparative Philosophy (Honolulu, HI: University Press of Hawaii, 1976).

56. Xinzhong Yao, *An Introduction to Confucianism* (New York, NY: Cambridge University Press, 2000), 26.

57. Yao, *Introduction to Confucianism*, 26.

58. Jonathan Y. Tan, "Encounter between Confucianism and Christianity," in *The Oxford Handbook of Christianity in Asia*, ed. Felix Wilfred (New York: Oxford University Press, 2014), 428–429.

59. Julia Ching, *Confucianism and Christianity: A Comparative Study* (Tokyo: Kodansha International, 1977), 12–19; Paul A. Rule, *K'ung-Tzu or Confucius?: The Jesuit Interpretation of Confucianism*, East Asia Series (Sydney; Boston: Allen & Unwin, 1986), 15, 26; Ken Gnanakan, "Some Insight into Indian Christian Theology," in *Global Theology in Evangelical Perspective: Exploring the Contextual Nature of Theology and Mission*, ed. Jeffrey P. Greenman and Gene L. Green (Downers Grove, IL: IVP Academic, 2012).

rather than in the larger social world."⁶⁰ "What is meant by 'Confucianism' is more a traditional neologism generally rooted in Chinese culture and nurtured by Confucius and Confucians rather than a new religion created, or a new value system initiated, by Confucius himself alone."⁶¹ In fact, "Confucius and the school named after him offered a moral or ethical answer to the questions regarding life's meaning and order in society, an answer that would dominate Chinese philosophical thinking for about two millennia."⁶²

Heaven

Confucius held a deep faith in Heaven and had a heart to follow the will of Heaven.⁶³ A profound sense of reverence for the will of Heaven is found in these lines of the *Analects*:

> At fifteen I set my heart on learning [to be a sage].
> At thirty I became firm.
> At forty I had no more doubts.
> At fifty I understood Heaven's Will.
> At sixty my ears were attuned [to this Will].
> At seventy I could follow my heart's desires,
> without overstepping the line.⁶⁴

The two most important terms in the Confucian Classics are *Shang-ti* (Lord-on-High) and *T'ien* (Heaven) which were used interchangeably as expression of the belief in one supreme diety.⁶⁵ In the language of prayer,

---

60. Anna Xiao Dong Sun, *Confucianism as a World Religion: Contested Histories and Contemporary Realities* (Princeton, NJ: Princeton University Press, 2013), 9.

61. Yao, *Introduction to Confucianism*, 17. In this sense, the word "Confucianism" is a misnomer for the tradition that is normally referred to as *ru jia* (literati family), *ru jiao* (literati teachings), *ru xue* (literati learning) or simply as *ru* (literati) in China and other East Asian countries (Korea, Japan, and Vietnam).

62. Küng and Ching, *Christianity and Chinese Religions*, 65–66.

63. In Chinese: *Shang-ti* (上帝) and *T'ien* (天). The term *T'ien* (天) in Chinese often translated as *Heaven*, has two apparent components: "one" (*yī* 一) and "great" (*dà* 大), namely, the "Great one." See Ching, *Confucianism and Christianity: A Comparative Study*, 117, 48 in fn. 9.

64. See *Analects* 2:4, quoted in Küng and Ching, *Christianity and Chinese Religions*, 67. See also Confucius, *The Analects of Confucius*, trans. Arthur Waley (London: Allen & Unwin, 1956); Confucius, *The Analects of Confucius: A Philosophical Translation*, trans. Roger T. Ames and Henry Rosemont, Classics of Ancient China (New York: Ballantine Books, 1999); Confucius, *Analects*, trans. David Hinton (Berkeley: Counterpoint, 2014).

65. Küng and Ching, *Christianity and Chinese Religions*, 116–117. In fact, there are many terms in the Confucian Classics which may refer to the notion of God. But the words *Ti* (Lord)

including the liturgical language of the "Sacrifice to Heaven," the Confucian Classics offer us adequate evidence in support of a belief in God as a personal diety.[66] "Heaven" carries the notion of a personal God, the Creator, and Lord of history that seems to affirm more than what is revealed as religious belief. Such profound understanding of God serves as concrete evidence of how Confucian Classics are deeply rooted in the worldview and lifeview of East Asian people, particularly the Chinese. Such understanding is clear from the importance assigned to the cult of Heaven itself. From the *Book of Changes* and other classical texts (including, *Book of Poetry, Book of Rites, Book of History, Spring and Autumn Annals*), Heaven was exalted above not only Earth (though Heaven and Earth refer sometimes to distinct hierophanies and to the power behind both), but also the gods of grain, of mountains and rivers, as well as of the ancestral spirits of kings and commoners.[67] In the *Book of Odes*, certain stanzas, coming also apparently from the time of the Chou dynasty, confirm this belief, referring to God sometimes as "Lord-on-High," and sometimes as "Heaven":

> How vast is the Lord-on-High,
> The ruler of men below:
> How arrayed in terrors is the Lord-on-High:
> His ordinances are full of irregularities.
> Heaven gave birth to the multitudes of the people, . . .[68]

And again:

> Heaven, in giving birth to the multitudes of the people,

---

and *T'ien* (Heaven) which appeared in the earliest writings called "oracle bones" have different meanings. *Ti* (Lord) was associated with sacrifices, and especially the God of the earliest Chinese dynasty in history: the Shang (begun around 1766 BCE). *Ti* belonged to a religion in which ancestral cults held a predominant place; according to some, it represented a divinization of the ancestral spirit of the ruling family. While *T'ien* does not refer to any God in the "oracle bones," only in the literature of the Chou period (1111–249 BCE) or the Confucian Classics, *T'ien* appears to have been the God of the Chou people, who were culturally and ethnically related to the Shang, but who came later to the central political stage.

66. Küng and Ching, *Christianity and Chinese Religions*, 126. There are a number of expressions of the notion of God in Confucian Classics, including the Books of Odes and Book of Documents (two of the Five Classics), the Analects of Confucius and the Book of Mencius.

67. Ching, *Confucianism and Christianity*, 117–118.

68. James Legge, tr., *The Chinese Classics* (Oxford: Clarendon Press, 1865), vol. 4, 541, quoted in Ching, *Confucianism and Christianity*, 118.

To every creature annexed its law.
The people possessing their constant nature,
They have a love of virtue.⁶⁹

Confucius believed in "Heaven," who represented for him a personal God, transcending all other spirits – as the "absolute Thou" of human prayer, as he alledgedly said, "He who offends against Heaven has none to whom he can pray" (17:19).⁷⁰ The religious horizon for Confucius was Heaven (*T'ien*, understood as effective power, order, law, or being). It had displaced the original lively gods of ancient China and is only named *Shang-ti* (Lord-on-high) once in the *Analects*.⁷¹ Heaven was supreme above all, and human beings (and epecially the ruler) were to hear and obey it (Heaven's Will): "He who sins against Heaven has no one to whom he may pray" (3:13).⁷² Thus, it appears that Heaven, as supreme diety, was regarded, at least during the Chou dynasty, as sole creator of the human race and the universe. Later on, Earth became associated with Heaven in the world of Creation, through the influence of the *yin-yang* school of thought.⁷³ Thus, Confucian Classics are much concerned with Heaven's will (the importance of knowing the will of Heaven) so that one might act in accordance with it. In the *Analects*, Confucius speaks of the will of heaven with reverence.⁷⁴ Unless one knows this will, he says, one cannot be a gentleman, that is, a person of high moral character (20:3). And yet, he also says of himself that he did not know the "Will of Heaven" until the age of fifty (2:4) as qouted above.⁷⁵

Heaven and the will of heaven change in their meaning when one studies Menicus (Confucius's successor) and later Neo-Confucianism. According to Mencius (the *Book of Mencius*), heaven is present within man's heart, so that he who knows his own heart and nature, knows heaven.⁷⁶ It represents,

---

69. Legge, *Chinese Classics*, 505, quoted in Ching, *Confucianism and Christianity*, 118.
70. See Analects 17:19, quoted in Ching, *Confucianism and Christianity*, 122.
71. Küng and Ching, *Christianity and Chinese Religions*, 109.
72. See *Analects* 3:13, quoted in Küng and Ching, *Christianity and Chinese Religions*, 109.
73. Ching, *Confucianism and Christianity*, 119. The Appendices to the *Book of Changes* show the intrusion of *yin-yang* concept into Confucianism itself.
74. *T'ien-ming*, 天命 in Chinese, *Thiên mệnh* in Vietnamese. The word *T'ien* (Heaven) is found 18 times in the *Analects* and always in connection with will, action, and emotion.
75. Quoted in Ching, *Confucianism and Christianity*, 122–123.
76. Ching, 123.

therefore, a greater immanence. It also refers more and more to the source and principle of ethical laws and values. Thus, when Mencius speaks of Heaven's will, it is usually with reference to the technical meaning of Heaven's mandate of rulership.

The mystical dimension of Confucianism is also attested to by the Doctrine of the Mean where the term "Way of Heaven" takes over. This way (*Đạo*) is eternal and unceasing, transcending time, space, substance and motion. It is characterized by the universal harmony found in nature as well as in Man.[77] It is a fuller expression of the "Unity of Heaven and Man," an integration of the cosmic-moral and human-social levels of thinking.[78] Nevertheless, heaven (*T'ien*) is always the central ruler over that relationship, and all human efforts.[79]

A side note on the "terms controversy" when the Jesuit missionaries (Matteo Ricci and his colleuages) translated the Latin term for God, *Deus* into Chinese[80] is important at this point: the word "God" points to at least four terms in the Chinese language which could be used to refer to a supreme being while frequently containing other meanings as well: *Shang-ti* (Lord-on-High), *T'ien* (Heaven), *Shen* (Spirit), *T'ai-chi* (the Ultimate).[81] After examining the Chinese classics, the Jesuits, who worked mainly with educated gentry, followed the example of Matteo Ricci in an effort of cultural accommodation. They argued between *Shang-ti* and *T'ien*, and settled for *T'ien-chu* (Lord of Heaven), Lord of whatever heaven may represent to the Chinese, while continuing occasionally to refer to the Lord of heaven as Lord-on-High or simply, Heaven.[82] Eventually, the Protestants (the new

---

77. For the classical Confucian concept of "man," see Donald J. Munro, *The Concept of Man in Early China*, Michigan Classics in Chinese Studies 6 (Ann Arbor: Center for Chinese Studies, University of Michigan, 2001).

78. This chapter 22 is quoted in Ching, *Confucianism and Christianity*, 123.

79. For Chuang-tzu's *Heaven*, see in Chuang-tzu, *Wandering on the Way: Early Taoist Tales and Parables of Chuang Tzu*, trans. Victor H. Mair (Honolulu: University of Hawaii Press, 1998), 102–143.

80. For an excellent discussion of the terms controversy, see ch. 4 in Paul Rule, *K'ung-Tzu or Confucius?: The Jesuit Interpretation of Confucianism*. Paul Rule has incorporated his work on the original sources and documents. Also, for an informative discussion on the seventeenth-century Chinese Rites Controversy between the Jesuits and the Franciscans, Dominican, and Missions Étrangères de Paris missionaries, see George Minamiki, *The Chinese Rites Controversy from Its Beginning to Modern Times* (Chicago, IL: Loyola University Press, 1985).

81. Ching, *Confucianism and Christianity*, 20. Shang-ti (上帝), T'ien (天), Shen (神), T'ai-chi (太極), in Chinese.

82. Ching, *Confucianism and Christianity*, 20. T'ien-chu (天主), in Chinese.

generation of China missionaries in the middle of the nineteenth century) adopted the term *Shang-ti* as God while the Catholics continued to adhere to *T'ien-chu* (Lord of Heaven).[83] This has signified in the minds of many Chinese Christians even today, the coexistence of two religions, that of the Lord of Heaven (Catholic) and that of Christ (*Chi-tu*) for the Protestants, each with its own God.[84]

The "Way" of Man

Central to the interests of Confucius was the "human person" ("man") with his or her natural, basic family and social relationships.[85] That means the "way" of man (*Jen-dao*) had to be in accordance with the "way" of heaven (*T'ien-dao*) or the "heavenly way."[86] Confucius's main concern was "with humans and with the fundamental principles of humanity."[87] He believed these principles were the root of social relationships, and the foundation for the stability, peace and prosperity of the state, the family and individuals. The relationships and the corresponding virtues are listed more fully:

> The duties of universal obligation are five, and the virtues wherewith they are practiced are three. The duties are those between sovereign and minister, between father and son, between husband and wife, between elder brother and younger, and those belonging to the intercourse of friends. Those five are the duties of universal obligation. Knowledge, magnanimity, and energy,

---

83. James Legge, a Protestant missionary and scholar in the 19th century, also examined the whole question of how to render the word God into Chinese, defending especially the thesis put forward by Jesuits earlier that *Shang-ti* (the Lord-on-High) is the true God. See James Legge, *The Notions of the Chinese Concerning God and Spirits: With an Examination of the Defense of an Essay, on the Proper Rendering of the Words Elohim and Theos into the Chinese Language*, ed. William J. Boone (Hong Kong, 1852). Further analysis of Legge's development of a universal Ruist (Confucian) theology based on his Sino-Christian perspective to these terms, see I-Hsin Chen, "Connecting Protestantism to Ruism: Religion, Dialogism and Intertextuality in James Legge's Translation of the Lunyu" (PhD diss., University of Manchester, 2014).

84. Ching, *Confucianism and Christianity*, 21–22. Christ (*Chi-tu*; 基督), in Chinese.

85. Küng and Ching, *Christianity and Chinese Religions*, 109.

86. Ching argues that the notion of a personal deity (Heaven) has survived up to the 20th century through an official cult offered to Heaven and through the popular belief in a Heavenly Ruler.

87. Yao, *Introduction to Confucianism*, 26.

these three, are the virtues universally binding. And the means by which they carry the duties into practice is singleness.[88]

He devoted himself wholeheartedly to solving human problems, propagating the value of education, virtue and self-cultivation (which is about this life rather than the life hereafter), and other religious matters such as serving "spirits and ghosts." And thus, "he developed his ethics around two central theses: that goodness can be taught and learned, and that society can only be in harmony and at peace under the guidance of wisdom."[89] He further developed a system of four concepts – the underlying ideas of the Confucian tradition – which later became the backbone of the ideological structure of a Confucian state, namely, the way (*đạo*), ritual/propriety (*lễ*), humaneness or benevolence (*nhân*) and virtue (*đức* or *nghĩa*). Later the great Neo-Confucian, Chu Hsi, achieved a philosophical synthesis of the speculative thought which blossomed forth during the tenth and eleventh centuries. He did not hesitate to borrow selectively from Buddhist ideas and vocabulary, in his reintepretation of Confucian teachings, bringing to light a transformed view of the world and of man.[90] This is why the Confucian tradition today can be seen as a syncretistic system in its understanding of the nature of man (the way of man) and the notion of heaven (the will or the way of heaven).

Encountering Buddhism

Confucianism in China has been syncretistic and inclusive in nature with "a flexible attitude towards different theories and practices," (even being open to religious values) as seen through five stages or dimensions, proposed by Yao Xinzhong as follows: "formation, adaptation, transformation, variation, and renovation."[91] In each stage, Confucian doctrines gained new characteristics so that the Confucian practices were enriched, and the range of Confucian teaching was broadened.[92]

---

88. The *Doctrine of the Mean*, chapter 20, verse 8, cited in Phan, *Christianity with an Asian Face*, 132.
89. Yao, *Introduction to Confucianism*, 26.
90. Ching, *Confucianismand Christianity*, 128–140.
91. See Yao, *Introduction to Confucianism*, 7–9, 224.
92. Yao, 7.

Such a syncretistic nature of Confucianism had already been developed during the time of the early Han emperor and ended with the declaration by Emperor Wu (140–87 BCE) that Confucian Classics were the state orthodoxy, and the worship of Confucius was the state cult. This was then the beginning of the "adaptation" stage, after the "formation" of Confucian tradition. Thus, the Confucians of the Han dynasty, on the one hand, were open and flexible, syncretistic and inclusive. On the other hand, they retained power to unify their ideology by controlling and yet accepting other doctrines, including the "Huang-Lao" doctrine. Thus,

> a new form of Confucianism took shape in the flow of eclecticism and inclusiveness. It accepted the cosmic view of the Yin–Yang School and partly adopted the Daoist view of life. It made some use of Legalist policies to strengthen the power of the rulers and took advantage of the Five Elements theory to explain the cyclical nature of history and the change of dynasties.[93]

The syncretistic nature in Confucianism, after adaptation, continued to "transform" itself to be relevant in the context where Daoism and Buddhism were more popular among the common people and the courts. Thus, the transformation dimension was apparent in a new form of Confucianism, called Neo-Confucianism.[94] Indeed, Neo-Confucianism did not only return to classical Confucianism, but fundamentally transformed its doctrines in a way that enabled this new form to "construct a comprehensive and complicated doctrinal system containing an evolutionary cosmology, a humanistic ethics and a rationalistic epistemology."[95] This was a result of encountering Buddhism, because "without the introduction of Buddhism into China [from India] there would have been no Neo-Confucianism."[96]

Although most of the Neo-Confucian masters spent their time studying Buddhism and Daoism, their system was by nature anti-Buddhist and its

---

93. Yao, 82–83.

94. See Ji, *Encounters between Chinese Culture and Christianity*, 116–121; Ching, *To Acquire Wisdom*.

95. Yao, *Introduction to Confucianism*, 97.

96. Carsun Chang, *The Development of Neo-Confucian Thought* (London: Vision Press, 1958), 43. quoted in Yao, *Introduction to Confucianism*, 97. See also Tu, *Neo-Confucian Thought in Action*; Tu, *Centrality and Commonality*.

underlying theme was to present a powerful argument against Buddhism.[97] For instance, Chu Hsi criticized Buddhist religious metaphysics, with its tendency toward cosmic pessimism and ethical indifference.[98] In fact, "Confucianism is portrayed as righteous and public-spirited, in contrast to the selfish and 'desiring profit' nature of Buddhism."[99] And yet, both Confucianism (from its "formation" stage) and Buddhism alike have not escaped being influenced by Daoism.[100] Observing this transformed Neo-Confucianism, Yao said,

> Neo-Confucianism vigorously supports the understanding of life in this world in opposition to the Buddhist doctrines of impermanence, *anataman* and other-worldliness; stressing the value of family and community and rebuking the life in Buddhist and Daoist monasteries as corrupt and disordered. Neo-Confucianism opts for the Confucian rites of passage in which tradition, human relations, social responsibilities and personal commitment replace "superstitious" (Pure Land) Buddhist worship of their "messiah" the Buddha, Bodhisattvas and gods. As a fully developed humanistic and rational doctrine, Neo-Confucianism greatly contributed to the absolute dominance of Confucianism in the politics, ethics, literature and culture of China for the next eight hundred years.[101]

This transformed new Confucianism later was what Vietnamese Confucians adopted in the sixteenth century. Thus, the "variation" stage began (by reshaping and redefining Confucian tradition), encouraging Neo-Confucianism to accommodate with the varied contexts of East Asia, specifically Vietnam.

---

97. See Yao, *Introduction to Confucianism*, 97, 227. Alongside the Neo-Confucian ascendancy, Daoists made a great effort in renovating their own doctrine in the light of the three-in-one theory.

98. Ching, *Confucianism and Christianity*, 129. However, from the Buddhist ideas and vocabulary, Chu Hsi also focused attention on the metaphysical First Principle, the Absolute that is given a place of central importance in the organismic philosophy of Neo-Confucianism.

99. Chan, *Source Book in Chinese Philosophy*, 576 (quoted in Yao, *Introduction to Confucianism*, 97.)

100. Wing-tsit Chan, "The Natural Way of Lao Tzu," in *A Source Book in Chinese Philosophy* (Princeton, NJ: Princeton University Press, 1963).

101. Yao, *Introduction to Confucianism*, 97–98.

To conclude this section one may ask the following question: Why in Asia, in the midst of both contextualization and syncretism, is Christianity readily accepted by some cultures (e.g. the Philippines) and resisted by others (e.g. Vietnam)? This study is not designed to explain why and how the contextualization of Christianity occurs differently across various East and Southeast Asian cultures. In addition, the study also does not intend to mean that a larger number of Christians in some countries in the region is because of better contextualization. Nevertheless, the next focus, that of chapter 2, explores two different directional perspectives on contextualization: (1) from the view of the "outsider," meaning the missionary entering a "new" culture, and (2) from the perspective of the "insider," the people of the local culture.

CHAPTER 2

Contextualization in Christian Mission Theology

Whenever different missionaries enter new cultures, it is inevitable that they bring with themselves diverse perspectives on Christian faith. The local people of the new cultures entered will also have their own perspectives of Christian faith that may be equally diverse. Given the probable differences in perspectives between the "insiders" and "outsiders," how does an "outsider" from a foreign culture achieve the goal of making the Christian faith and the Bible relevant (contextualized) to the "insiders" of the local culture? This chapter, first of all, discusses briefly a number of "outsider" perspectives on Christian contextualization (including communication and interpretation, as well as syncretism) that have been developed and practiced over the past several centuries of Christian missionary activity. It is important to understand the missionary nature of Christianity, but more importantly, how cultural context does matter, both to Christian faith in the past as well as in the present, and particularly in the diverse religio-cultural contexts of East Asia. Then, second, from the alternative evangelical perspective, the chapter discusses the cultural context and the divine act of incarnation as God's intention in terms of translatability, arguably the most effective process of making the gospel message relevant in terms of Christianity's origin and the ongoing process of Christianity's growth.

"Outsider" View

Before the term "contextualization" appeared and displaced "indigenization" in the late 1970s, the concept of communicating the gospel to the people of the world had been popularized, at least, in the practices of both Catholic and Protestant missionaries. For instance, Charles H. Kraft presents an excellent review of the historical evolution of contextualization through seven stages: (1) cultural encounter, (2) three selfs (formal indigeneity), (3) early impact of anthropology, (4) beyond "formal indigeneity," (5) transition to contextualization, (6) evangelical acceptance of the concept of contextualization, and (7) the period since 1980 (or the seventh stage).[1] The literature covering contextualization during the period from the 1970s to 1990s indicates that contextualization studies have increased greatly among both Protestants and Roman Catholics.[2] Rather than repeating the literature of contextualization, this section focuses on how contextualization has been defined. These definitions, from several wide-ranging perspectives in Christian mission, can fall under two categories: communication and interpretation.

Communication

Contextualization is commonly viewed as a communicative process. To communicate the gospel into a cultural context, missionaries use various approaches of communication to accommodate (or adapt) Christian terminology for the recipient culture. Perhaps one of the earliest conscious contextualization efforts done in this way was the Jesuits' accommodation in Asia in the sixteenth century. For instance, Alexander de Rhodes (1593–1660) focused on engagement with aspects of the Vietnamese culture in an attempt to accommodate the gospel to cultural forms familiar to the ordinary Vietnamese, specifically in his adaptation of his personal lifestyle to the local way of life.[3]

Contextualization means that the gospel is communicated relevantly in a meaningful way to a new culture. As David J. Hesselgrave and Edward Rommen define contextualization, it is,

---

1. See Charles H. Kraft, "The Development of Contextualization Theory in Euroamerican Missiology," in *Appropriate Christianity*, ed. Charles H. Kraft (Pasadena, CA: William Carey Library, 2005), 15–34.

2. This study highlights some critical aspects of contextualization for the argument of this particular theoretical chapter. For the historical evolution of *contextualization*, see Kraft, "Development of Contextualization Theory," 15–34.

3. For de Rhodes's *contextualized process*, see Nguyen KimSon, "Catholic Church in Vietnam."

the attempt to communicate the message of the person, works, Word, and will of God in a way that is faithful to God's revelation, especially as it is put forth in the teachings of Holy Scripture, and that is meaningful to respondents in their respective cultural and existential contexts.[4]

This definition shows that anyone doing contextualization must first of all have an authentic understanding of, and faithfulness to Scripture, because "the adequacy of an attempted contextualization must be measured by the degree to which it faithfully reflects the meaning of the biblical text."[5] Then, contextualization involves conceptions of God's revelation; of interpretation in how the reader or hearer perceives the intended meaning; of application, including how "the interpreter formulates the logical implications of his understanding of the biblical text" and how he "decides to accept the validity of the text's implications" by totally accepting it, accepting some parts and rejecting others, or superimposing his/her own meanings upon the text.[6] The last part of the definition assumes effectiveness in communicating the gospel which "grows out of an understanding of our respondents in their particular context and out of the active ministry of the Holy Spirit in us and in them."[7] In addition, Hesselgrave describes a seven-dimension grid (worldview, cognitive processes, linguistic forms, behavioral patterns, communication media, social structures, and motivational sources) as a tool for cultural analysis that equips the missionary to effectively communicate the gospel.[8]

Stephen B. Bevan's translation model (also called the accommodation or adaptation model) seems to be the model most popular among the evangelicals (e.g. David J. Hesselgrave), and among Catholics (e.g. Pope John Paul

---

4. David J. Hesselgrave and Edward Rommen, *Contextualization: Meanings, Methods, and Models* (Grand Rapids, MI: Baker, 1989), 200.

5. Hesselgrave and Rommen, *Contextualization*, 201. Quoted in Gailyn Van Rheenen, "Syncretism and Contextualization: The Church on a Journey Defining Itself," in *Contextualization and Syncretism: Navigating Cultural Currents*, ed. Gailyn Van Rheenen (Pasadena, CA: William Carey Library, 2006), 6.

6. Hesselgrave and Rommen, *Contextualization*, 201–102. More discussion on interpretative role in contextualization efforts in the next section.

7. Hesselgrave and Rommen, 199–200.

8. See Hesselgrave and Rommen, 202–203.

II).⁹ Western theologians often have the idea that "context is a vessel into which we insert faith, and proponents focus on the transmission of faith."¹⁰ This model encapsulates "translating the meaning of doctrines into another cultural context" because "there is 'something' that must be 'put into' other terms; there is always something from the outside that must be made to fit inside; there is always something 'given' that must be 'received.'"¹¹ In fact, the key idea of the model is "the supra-cultural nature of the Christian message;" that is, the "gospel core" or the "naked gospel" that can be unwrapped from its cultural husk, in order to communicate with other cultures.¹² Once the "receptor culture" finds the gospel kernel, that kernel can be rewrapped in the appropriate terms, action, or story so that the "never changing and supra-cultural message" is received well.¹³

Evangelicals most commonly hold to the translation model of contextualization as they believe "there is a core message of universal truth which must be translated into each new cultural setting in a way that remains faithful to the core. Because the content of that message is absolute and authoritative, the contextualizer's task is to change the form of the message."¹⁴ A. Scott Moreau defines contextualization as "the process whereby a Christian who is committed to world mission, adapts the forms, content, and praxis of the Christian faith as a whole so as to communicate it to minds and hearts of people with other cultural backgrounds."¹⁵ In that process of contextualizing theology, the gospel message must be presented in the context of a particular culture so that the gospel encounters minimal cultural barriers to its acceptance,

---

9. Bevans, *Models of Contextual Theology*, 37–46; Stephen B. Bevans, *Models of Contextual Theology* (Maryknoll, NY: Orbis Books, 2002), 44. Bevans categorized a contextual theology map into five models (1992): translation, anthropological, praxis, synthetic, transcendental. He added the sixth model, countercultural, in the revised edition in 2002.

10. Moreau, *Contextualization in World Missions*, 42. For Schreiter's contextual models, see in Schreiter, *Constructing Local Theologies*. See also in Robert Schreiter, "Contextual Theology," in *Christianity: The Complete Guide*, ed. John Bowden (London: Continuum, 2005), 281–282.

11. See Bevans, *Models of Contextual Theology*, 32–33.

12. Bevans, 33.

13. Bevans, 33, 37, 47. Supporters of this model have resource to a passage such as Acts 17 on which to base their authenticity.

14. See Scott A. Moreau, "Evangelical Models of Contextualization," in *Local Theology for the Global Church: Principles for an Evangelical Approach to Contextualization*, ed. Matthew Cook (Pasadena: World Evangelical Alliance Theological Commission, 2010), 169.

15. Moreau, *Contextualization in World Missions*, 36.

thereby calling forth faith and leading to the formation of a community that is culturally authentic and authentically Christian. In other words, contextualization is doing theology, based on the gospel of Christ, in which the contexts construct theology in different ways, making the gospel relevant to socio-cultural conditions in the contexts of "the totality of human experience arising from culture, nationality, history, geography, politics or economics."[16]

Roy Musasiwa believes that "a conservative evangelical view of contextualization limits it to communicate the gospel message in a way that is both faithful to the Bible and meaningful to respondents in their respective cultural and existential contexts."[17] T. D. Gener sees contextualization as local theologizing to mean "articulating biblical faith using vernacular terms and engaging local issues."[18]

At least two significant weak points seem to raise questions about the view of contextualization as "communication." The first question related to communication, is: What is it that needs to be known and understood about the gospel that the missionary wants to communicate? Charles E. Van Engen says, "Communication was deemed to be important, but the content of the message being communicated went unexamined because the missionary communicators assumed they knew and understood all there was to know and understand about the gospel they were communicating."[19] Once this perspective was mixed with an attitude of superiority on the part of Westerners, it became essentially a "non-contextual" approach as Paul G. Hiebert points out in the first level of his "four levels of contextualization."[20] The non-con-

---

16. See Roy Musasiwa, "Contextualization," in *Dictionary of Mission Theology: Evangelical Foundations*, eds. John Corrie, Samuel Escobar, and Wilbert R. Shenk (Downers Grove, IL: InterVarsity Press, 2007), 66.

17. Roy Musasiwa, "Contextualization," in *Dictionary of Mission Theology*, 66.

18. T. D. Gener, "Contextualization," in *Global Dictionary of Theology: A Resource for the Worldwide Church*, eds. William A. Dyrness and Veli-Matti Kärkkäinen (Downers Grove, IL: IVP Academic, 2008), 192.

19. See Charles Edward Van Engen, "Five Perspectives of Contextually Appropriate Missional Theology," in *Appropriate Christianity*, ed. Charles H. Kraft and Dean S. Gilliland (Pasadena, CA: William Carey Library, 2005a), 185. Earlier, Van Engen reviewed four "major models" of contextualization: communication, cultural relevance, liberation, interfaith dialogue, and suggested his fifth model called "knowing God in context," see in Charles Edward Van Engen, *Mission on the Way: Issues in Mission Theology* (Grand Rapids, MI: Baker Books, 1996), 72–89.

20. Four levels of contextualization are non-contextualization, minimal, uncritical, and critical. See Paul G. Hiebert, "The Gospel in Human Contexts: Changing Perceptions of

textualization level (Hiebert called it "the era of non-contextualization) sees the Christian faith as something that is not a part of human culture; it rejects the notion that culture shapes how one receives and practices Christianity. Considering the rejection by non-Western cultures, because of the "rise of colonialism" and the belief in the superiority of Western cultures, Hiebert says that in the "non-contextual level,"

> we see the gospel as acultural and ahistorical. It is unchanging and universal, can be codified in abstract rational terms, and communicated in all languages without loss of meaning. Neither the socio-cultural contexts of the listeners nor the messengers need be taken into account.[21]

The second question, related to communication, is: To what degree is a culture considered to be ready for the gospel when the beliefs and practices of the local people are rejected by the missionary as "pagan"? In this sort of situation, "the gospel was seen by the people as a foreign gospel. To become Christian one had to accept not only Christianity but also Western cultural ways."[22] As "the theory of cultural evolution" developed,

> Westerners could ignore other cultures by labeling them "primitive," "animistic," and "uncivilized." In fact, anthropologists until 1915 spoke of "culture," not of "cultures." They saw all cultures as different stages of development of the same thing; some were more advanced and others more primitive.[23]

Additionally, with the "triumph of science," Hiebert says:

> The same epistemological foundations were widespread among many conservative Christians, including most missionaries. Only here, theology replaced science, and revelation replaced experience. Carefully crafted, theology could be totally objective and absolutely true. In the light of this, other religions were seen

---

Contextualization," in *Missionshift: Global Mission Issues in the Third Millennium*, ed. David J. Hesselgrave and Ed Stetzer (Nashville, TN: B & H Academic, 2010), 84–99.

21. See Hiebert, "Gospel in Human Contexts," 84–99.

22. Paul G. Hiebert, "Critical Contextualization," *International Bulletin of Missionary Research* 11 (1987): 104.

23. Hiebert, "Critical Contextualization," 105.

as highly subjective and totally false. Consequently, Christians did not need to take other religions seriously, just as scientists refused to take other belief systems about nature seriously. The task of the missionary was to transmit his or her theology into new cultures unchanged.[24]

Earlier, Hiebert urged mission theologians to engage contextualization by translating and communicating "the gospel in the language and culture of real people in the particularities of their lives so that it may transform them, their societies, and their cultures into what God intends for them to be."[25] He then proposed "the third way of doing theology" or "missional theology" which is "a way of thinking biblically about God's universal mission in the context of the world here and now, with all its particularities, paradoxes, and confusions."[26] He argued that, "missional theology seeks to build the bridge between biblical revelation and human contexts." Thus, he asked Western theologians to overcome the "dualism" perspective dominant in the West when constructing "the third way of doing theology."[27] In other words, Western theologians should remove their dualistic glasses when communicating the gospel to a culture.[28] Nevertheless, at the end of the colonial era, Asian Christianity still encountered many challenges, such as the diversity

---

24. Hiebert, 105.

25. Paul G. Hiebert, *The Gospel in Human Contexts: Anthropological Explorations for Contemporary Missions* (Grand Rapids, MI: Baker Academic, 2009), 45.

26. Hiebert, *Gospel in Human Contexts*, 44.

27. "Western theology is deeply influenced by the Platonic dualism of supernatural/natural, spirit/matter, mind/body, evangelism/social ministry, religion/science, faith/fact, and miracle/natural. The biblical view is contingent dualism: Creator/creation, God/humans (in the incarnation), eternal/temporal. This is dualism, but it is contingent in that God is eternal and the source of all creation, and creation is constantly dependent on God's ongoing creation for its very existence every moment it exists. In biblical thought the incarnation of God is far more profound than in Greek thought, where an invisible god in the heavens involves himself in a material world." See Hiebert, *Gospel in Human Contexts* 45, fn. 12.

28. This is what Hwa Yung argued in his *Mangoes or Bananas?* Concurring with missiologists like Charles Kraft and Paul Hiebert, Yung argues that the Enlightenment rationality has bequeathed to the contemporary mind what Hiebert calls the "flaw of the excluded middle": the arbitrary reduction of reality to two tiers that erroneously dismisses or purposefully ignores the middle realm of spiritual and demonic beings. See in "The Roots of Divergences in Mission Theology: The Enlightenment and Western Dualism," in Hwa Yung, "Theology and Mission in the Asian Church" (DMiss diss., Asbury Theological Seminary, 1995), 71–92; Hwa Yung, *Mangoes or Bananas?: The Quest for an Authentic Asian Christian Theology* (Oxford: Regnum, 1997), 72–74.

of religions, differing worldviews, differing philosophies, cultures, and sociopolitical systems that obliged them to respond in a relevant manner.

Interpretation

Contextualization is also seen as the biblical-cultural process of interpretation. As Jackson Wu asserted "contextualization most basically is an act of interpretation. Only then can it be understood as communication or application. Contextualization is not primarily something we do to the gospel; rather, it is the minds' perception of and/or response to the gospel."[29] Wu categorizes contextualization into two kinds: "exegetical" contextualization, and "cultural" contextualization. The first means that Scripture is interpreted through a cultural lens, and the second refers to one's interpreting culture from a biblical perspective.[30] Hiebert is credited with this initiative for he discussed it as the highest level of contextualization, the "critical contextualization." This level seeks a balanced approach and requires critical interpretation of both gospel and culture. Hiebert says:

> The Bible is seen as divine revelation, not simply as humanly constructed beliefs. In contextualization, the heart of the gospel must be kept as it is encoded in forms that are understood by the people, without making the gospel captive to the contexts. This is an ongoing process of embodying the gospel in an ever-changing world. Here cultures are seen as both good and evil, not simply

---

29. Jackson Wu, "The Honor of God in the Shame of Christ for Salvation: A Theological Contextualization from Chinese Culture" (PhD diss., Southeastern Baptist Theological Seminary, 2012), 68. For details of this "two kinds of contextualization," see "Chapter 2: Theological Contextualization in Practice," particularly 33–68. This discussion also appeared on http://www.patheos.com/blogs/jacksonwu/2013/01/16/two-kinds-of-contextualization-and-why-they-matter-part-2/, accessed 10 August 2016.

30. The dual models of exegetical contextualization and cultural contextualization use Hiebert's "critical contextualization." This study agrees with Wu's dual models in arguing that the gospel message is critically interpreted through a cultural lens (e.g. "the Judaic roots and the Gentile culture" advocated by Andrew F. Walls and Lamin O. Sanneh), and any culture ought to be examined by the biblical perspective. The study, however, advances the importance of interpreting God's intention for human beings from a particular cultural lens in the light of biblical perspective (further discussion in the next section on "Alternative Evangelical View," and in chapter 6). For instance, I argue that to have a Vietnamese contextualized biblical theology – both true to God's intent and relevant within the Vietnamese context – is to have a way to acknowledge the insider's worldview, such as the concept of the Đạo, which might impact the way the Vietnamese understand the gospel and apply the gospel's truth into their daily lives.

as neutral vehicles for understanding the world. No culture is absolute or privileged. We are all relativized by the gospel.[31]

To achieve this "critical" contextualization, four steps need to be considered: exegesis of the culture, exegesis of the Scripture and the hermeneutical bridge, critical response, and new contextualized practices.[32]

The first step, exegesis of the culture, means that the local church leaders and the missionary lead the congregation in uncritically gathering and analyzing the traditional beliefs and customs associated with some question at hand. Hiebert believes that to "exegete" (interpret) the local culture is to understand the old ways, not to judge them. He warned that if at this point the missionary shows any criticism of the customary beliefs and practices, the people will not talk about them for fear of being condemned. We shall only drive the old ways underground. Unfortunately, this actually happens frequently because of a lack of awareness of the dynamics between the missionary and the local church leaders. For instance, who raises the questions, the missionary or the local leader? What are the criteria for examining the "old ways" of the local culture?[33]

The second step, exegesis of the Scripture and the hermeneutical bridge, means that the pastor or missionary leads the church in a study of the Scriptures related to the question at hand. Hiebert suggested that,

> the leader must also have a metacultural framework that enables him or her to translate the biblical message into the cognitive, affective, and evaluative dimensions of another culture. This step is crucial, for if the people do not clearly grasp the biblical message as originally intended, they will have a distorted view of the gospel . . . [He stressed,] without this [the metacultural

---

31. Hiebert, "Gospel in Human Contexts," 93.

32. Hiebert, "Critical Contextualization," 104–112. Similar discussion also appeared in Paul G. Hiebert, "Syncretism and Social Paradigm," in *Contextualization and Syncretism: Navigating Cultural Currents*, ed. Gailyn Van Rheenen (Pasadena, CA: William Carey Library, 2006), 41–43. Hereafter, the discussion of these four steps is taken from Hiebert's "Critical Contextualization."

33. In chapters 4, 5, and 6 of this dissertation, the study reveals that the missionary has set up the agenda most of the time when reviewing these "old ways" in Vietnam, for instance, ancestor veneration is idolatry, it is therefore necessary to prohibit its practices in any kinds/forms.

grids that enable him or her to move between cultures], biblical meanings will often be forced to fit the local cultural categories. The result is a distortion of the message.[34]

The third step, critical response, means that the people corporately need to evaluate critically their own past customs in the light of their new biblical understandings, and to make decisions regarding their response to their new-found truths. Eventually, the people may create new symbols and rituals to communicate Christian beliefs in forms that are indigenous to their own culture.[35] And of the last step, new contextualized practices, Hiebert believes that,

> having led the people to analyze their old customs in the light of biblical teaching, the pastor or missionary must help them to arrange the practices they have chosen into a new ritual that expresses the Christian meaning of the event. Such a ritual will be Christian, for it explicitly seeks to express biblical teaching. It will also be contextual, for the church has created it, using forms the people understand within their own culture.[36]

Seeking a balanced approach between the biblical text and cultural context as Hiebert advocated, Dean S. Gilliland and other evangelicals agreed (in 1989) on a statement of commitment to contextualization:

> The conviction behind this volume is that contextualization, biblically-based and Holy Spirit-led, is a requirement for evangelical missions today. Contextualization is incarnational. The Word which became flesh dwells among us. It clarifies for each nation or people the meaning of the confession, "Jesus is Lord." It liberates the church in every place to hear what the Spirit is saying. Contextual theology will open up the way for communication of the gospel in ways that allow the hearer to understand and accept. It gives both freedom and facility for believers to build up one another in the faith. Contextualization clarifies

---

34. Hiebert, "Critical Contextualization," 109–110.
35. Hiebert, 110.
36. Hiebert, 110.

what the Christian witness is in sinful society and shows what obedience to the gospel requires. These are the components of a theology for mission that meets the needs of today's world.[37]

Good communication requires good interpretation. That means, the person who communicates the gospel to a culture must interpret the gospel and engage the culture at the same time. As Charles H. Kraft suggests, contextualization must be "appropriate to the cultural context and also to the Bible."[38] He believes that, "There has been a lot of inappropriateness in the introduction of Christianity to peoples around the world. And because of this inappropriateness, the gospel has been interpreted in distorted ways (e.g. as Western religion rather than as a faith that can be at home in any culture)."[39]

The dynamic and comprehensive interpretation of the gospel text and cultural context is needed when mission theologians define contextualization. Dean E. Flemming argues, "I take contextualization, then, to refer to the dynamic and comprehensive process by which the gospel is incarnated within a concrete historical or cultural situation."[40] Louis J. Luzbertak, and later Susan S. Baker, affirm that "We understand contextualization as the various processes by which a local church integrates the gospel message (the 'text') with its local culture (the 'context')."[41] Bruce Riley Ashford calls this the process by which to "proclaim and embody the gospel in the midst of human cultures."[42]

Perhaps, the best example for this interpretive process is what Bevan calls the "Countercultural Model." This model, more than any other model, "recognizes that the gospel represents an all-encompassing, radically alternate,

---

37. Dean S. Gilliland, ed. *The Word among Us: Contextualizing Theology for Mission Today* (Dallas, TX: Word, 1989), 3.

38. Charles H. Kraft, "Why Appropriate?," in *Appropriate Christianity*, ed. Charles H. Kraft (Pasadena, CA: William Carey Library, 2005), 3–14.

39. Kraft, ed. *Appropriate Christianity*, xi.

40. Dean E. Flemming, *Contextualization in the New Testament: Patterns for Theology and Mission* (Downers Grove, IL: InterVarsity Press, 2005), 19.

41. Louis J. Luzbetak, *The Church and Cultures: New Perspectives in Missiological Anthropology*, American Society of Missiology Series 12 (Maryknoll, NY: Orbis Books, 1988), 69. Cited by Susan S. Baker, "The Social Sciences for Urban Ministry," in *The Urban Face of Mission: Ministering the Gospel in a Diverse and Changing World*, eds. Harvie M. Conn, Manuel Ortiz, and Susan S. Baker (Phillipsburg, NJ: P&R, 2002), 75.

42. See Bruce Riley Ashford, "The Gospel and Culture" in *Theology and Practice of Mission: God, the Church, and the Nations*, ed. B. R. Ashford (Nashville, TN: B&H Academic, 2011).

worldview that differs profoundly from human experiences of the world and culture that humans create."[43] The goal of this model is to "truly encounter and engage the context through respectful, yet critical analysis and authentic gospel proclamation in word and deed."[44] The method to theologize in this model is "commitment to the Christian story as clue to history; use the story as the lens to interpret, critique, and challenge context."[45] This model is similar to Charles Van Engen's epistemological approach that emphasizes "the sense that in each new context, in each new cultural setting, followers of Jesus Christ have an opportunity to learn something about God they had not previously known. Christian knowledge about God is seen as cumulative, enhanced, deepened, broadened and expanded as the Gospel takes new shape in each new culture."[46]

Contextualization as interpretation appears to be problematic if local people are not integrally involved in the process of interpreting the Scripture and constructing a theology from their own perspective and with their own resources. At the present time, based on the above discussion, outsiders (missionaries, Western theologians, or even non-Western theologians trained in the West) are mostly dominant in the process, whether in theory or practice. Contextualization is too often a one-way direction. But, what would happen if local people played the main role (or at least initiated the process) in the interpretative process? Clearly, the gospel would be read (and interpreted) by East Asians' own eyes. Thus, the perspective of the insider would be very important in critical interpretation.

The Jerusalem Council's decision in Acts 15 shows that the reaction of "Gentile" cultures (the non-Jewish believers who were some of the early disciples) mattered, not only to the shaping of Christianity, but also to the way these "Gentiles" understood and responded to the gospel from their own cultural perspective. This biblical example allowed local people to be involved in the process of contextualization to form an authentic Christian faith relevant to the Gentile culture, not an imported or alien one (the Judaic

---

43. Bevans, *Models of Contextual Theology*, 118.
44. Bevans, 119.
45. Bevans, 126.
46. Van Engen, "Five Perspectives," 196–201.

religion).⁴⁷ Within the process of constructing local theologies, Tite Tiénou rightly points out that,

> contextualization is the inner dynamic of the theologizing process. It is not a matter of borrowing already existing forms or an established theology in order to fit them into various contexts. Rather contextualization is capturing the meaning of the gospel in such a way that a given society communicates with God. Therein theology is born.⁴⁸

However, there is the fear that bringing in some cultural elements may dilute or compromise authentic Christianity, just as the early Jewish Christians at the Jerusalem Council worried about their Gentile counterparts. Even worse, for some people is the fear that the newly emerging local theology may be labeled as "syncretism."

Syncretism

Syncretism has been viewed as negative, but it is time to see it as a natural term, at least from the context of East Asia and Vietnam. For instance, "History of Religions" used "syncretism" to designate "any interpretation between religions and between cultures," and to make a distinction "between a wrong and right kind of syncretism" rather than rejecting it as a whole.⁴⁹ Merriam-Webster defines "syncretism" as (1) the combination of different forms of belief or practice, and (2) the fusion of two or more originally different inflectional forms.⁵⁰

The evangelical understanding of "syncretism" is generally about the fear of losing the essentials of the gospel, especially while over-emphasizing the culture, in the processes of contextualization. Robert J. Schreiter says:

---

47. Further discussion on how Christianity was assimilated to other cultures (e.g. "translatability" that Lamin Sanneh advocated) will be given in the next sub-chapter.

48. Tite Tiénou, "Contextualization of Theology for Theological Education," in *Evangelical Theological Education Today: 2 Agenda for Renewal*, ed. Paul Bowers (Nairobi, Kenya: Evangel Publishing House, 1982), 51.

49. Cited by Ken Christoph Miyamoto, *God's Mission in Asia: A Comparative and Contextual Study of This-Worldly Holiness and the Theology of Missio Dei in M. M. Thomas and C. S. Song*, American Society of Missiology Monograph Series 1 (Eugene, OR: Pickwick, 2007), 131–132.

50. https://www.merriam-webster.com/dictionary/syncretism, accessed 28 February 2017.

> Starting with Adolf von Harnack and continuing on with Karl Barth, Henrick Kreamer, and others, syncretism has been viewed as a distorted form of Christian faith, skewed by cultural and religious forces in the environment into which Christianity has come. The root of this negative attitude goes deep into Christian history and its early encounter with the variform map of religiosity in the Mediterranean basin. Theological assertions have served to sustain a negative view of syncretism.[51]

In the discussion of contemporary Christian mission theology, the debate of syncretism comes up every time mission theologians talk about contextualization. For instance, Hiebert's third level of contextualization, uncritical contextualization takes place when culture tends to be prioritized over the gospel. This means that it minimizes the eternal truths found in Scripture in order to emphasize cultural convictions and practices.[52] Both uncritical and minimal contextualization are not "appropriate" as seen in Kraft's discussion.[53] However, these two levels actually appear in Christian mission discussions whenever the processes of contextualization are addressed: (1) the minimal level that results in a foreign form of religion and/ or suppression of old ways and traditions which then go underground, or (2) the uncritical level that leads to the risk of syncretism.[54]

How is "syncretism" defined or understood by Christians? Christopher J. H. Wright when discussing syncretism has distinguished syncretism from the "modes" of God's "self-revelation using existing concepts and religious forms." He says:

> Syncretism is a conscious or unconscious attempt to combine divergent religious elements (beliefs, rites, vocabulary) in such a way that a new religious mixture evolves which goes beyond the contributing elements. It presupposes that none of the

---

51. Robert J. Schreiter, "Defining Syncretism: An Interim Report," *International Bulletin of Missionary Research* 17, no. 2 (1993): 50.

52. For four levels of contextualization are non-contextualization, minimal, uncritical, and critical, see detail in Hiebert, "The Gospel in Human Contexts: Changing Perceptions of Contextualization," in *Missionshift*, 84–99.

53. Kraft, "Why Appropriate?" 3–14.

54. See "Appendix: Contextualization Models" in Gilliland, *Word among Us*, 317.

contributing elements can be regarded as final or sufficient in itself. It must be distinguished from the modes by which God has communicated his self-revelation using existing concepts and religious forms, but then transcending and transforming them with a new theology. The latter process is usually called accommodation or assimilation. It is quite different from syncretism inasmuch as it recognizes the reality of unique divine revelation in history, whereas syncretism excludes such a category a priori.[55]

Van Rheenen believes that "syncretism cannot be defined without an understanding of contextualization since the two processes are inter-related . . . what is considered authentic contextualization by some may be interpreted as syncretism by others."[56] He then defines it:

> Syncretism occurs when Christian leaders accommodate, either consciously or unconsciously, the prevailing plausibility, structures or worldviews of their culture. Syncretism, then, is the conscious or unconscious reshaping of Christian plausibility structures, beliefs, and practices through cultural accommodation so that they reflect those of the dominant culture. Or, stated in other terms, syncretism is the blending of Christian beliefs and practices with those of the dominant culture so that Christianity loses it distinctiveness and speaks with a voice reflective of its culture.[57]

Van Rheenen believes that "syncretism occurs when Christianity opts into the major cultural assumptions of a society."[58] For Van Rheenen, "frequently," syncretism in Christianity is a result of making the gospel relevant,

---

55. Christopher J. H. Wright, "The Christian and Other Religions: The Biblical Evidence," *Themelios* 9, no. 2 (January 1984): 4–15.

56. Van Rheenen, "Syncretism and Contextualization," 3.

57. Gailyn Van Rheenen, "Modern and Postmodern Syncretism in Theology and Mission," in *The Holy Spirit and Mission Dynamics*, ed. C. Douglas McConnell (Pasadena, CA: William Carey Library, 1997), 173. Cited in Van Rheenen, "Syncretism and Contextualization," 7–8.

58. Van Rheenen, "Modern and Postmodern Syncretism," 173. Cited in Van Rheenen, "Syncretism and Contextualization," 7–8.

for example, accommodations that appeal to "those outside the fellowship."[59] When these accommodations become routinized, integrated into the narrative of the Christian community and inseparable from its life, meaning major worldview changes occur within the culture, then, the church struggles to separate the eternals from the temporals. In other words, "the church, swept along by the ebb and flow of cultural currents over a long period of time, loses her moorings."[60]

If syncretism is understood as this, it is problematic in at least three things: (1) most missionaries (the Jesuits among the Catholics, William Carey and Hudson Taylor among the Protestants) indeed consciously and even unconsciously accommodated or adapted the gospel to the local culture in their contextualization efforts. With "a desire to make the Gospel relevant" to their recipient cultures, they were on the verge of making Christianity syncretistic; (2) there is no clear and distinct line between gospel and culture in this understanding so that by just one step one may cross over to become syncretistic; (3) the meaning of "Christianity" is narrowed here. If argued that this Christianity is from the "translatable" and the "local" (Andrew F. Walls) perspective, then this "Christianity" is already a syncretistic one.[61] As Walls once said:

> No one ever meets universal Christianity in itself: we only ever meet Christianity in a local form and that means a historically, culturally conditioned form. We need not fear this; when God became man he became [a] historically, cultural[ly] conditioned man in a particular time and place. What he became, we need not fear to be. There is nothing wrong in having local forms of Christianity provided that we remember that they are local.[62]

A. Scott Moreau believes that syncretism "has generally referred to the replacement or dilution of the essential truths of the gospel through

---

59. Van Rheenen, "Modern and Postmodern Syncretism," 173. Cited in Van Rheenen, "Syncretism and Contextualization," 7–8.

60. Van Rheenen, "Modern and Postmodern Syncretism," 173. Cited in Van Rheenen, "Syncretism and Contextualization," 7–8.

61. Details of Sanneh's *translatability* will be discussed in the next sub-chapter.

62. Andrew F. Walls, *The Missionary Movement in Christian History: Studies in the Transmission of Faith* (Maryknoll, NY: Orbis Books, 1996), 235.

the incorporation of non-Christian elements"[63] Earlier, Dean Gilliland also explained:

> Contextualization [is] a delicate enterprise if ever there was one ... the evangelist and mission strategist stand on a razor's edge, aware that to fall off on either side has terrible consequences ... Fall to the right and you end in obscurantism, so attached to your conventional ways of practicing and teaching the faith that you veil its truth and power from those who are trying to see it through very different eyes. Slip to the left and you tumble into syncretism, so vulnerable to the impact of paganism in its multiplicity of forms that you compromise the uniqueness of Christ and concoct 'another gospel which is not a gospel.'[64]

Thus, to keep the gospel from being replaced or diluted, the contextualization process needs to be kept from becoming syncretistic. Ed Stetzer says, "Contextualization matters to those concerned about clear gospel proclamation. Yes, contextualization can be a dangerous thing. It is also a necessary thing. Without contextual considerations, we do not transmit the gospel, but we transmit more of our cultural adaptation of that gospel."[65]

Certainly, evangelicals have been struggling to rationalize "gospel and culture," and "faith and religion," together as they believe there are different emphases placed upon *either* Scripture *or* the cultural context in the processes of contextualization.[66] When Scripture is emphasized, contextualization and its models tend to be defined as the translation of biblical meanings into contemporary cultural contexts from outside the culture.[67] However, when context is prioritized, God's meaning is sought experientially within the

---

63. A. Scott Moreau, "Syncretism," in *Evangelical Dictionary of World Missions*, ed. A. Scott Moreau et al. (Grand Rapids, MI: Baker Books, 2000).

64. Dean S. Gilliland, "Contextual Theology as Incarnational Mission," in *Word among Us*, 10–11.

65. See Hesselgrave and Stetzer, eds., *Missionshift*. See also http://www.christianitytoday.com/edstetzer/channel/utilities/print.html?type=article&id=106692, accessed 10 August 2016.

66. A. Scott Moreau, "Contextualization: From an Adapted Message to an Adapted Life," in Michael Pocock, Gailyn Van Rheenen, and Douglas Mcconnell, *The Changing Face of World Missions: Engaging Contemporary Issues and Trends* (Grand Rapids, MI: Baker Academic, 2005), 321–348.

67. See Van Rheenen, "Syncretism and Contextualization," 2–3.

culture using the Bible as a guide, trying to find what God is already doing in the culture.[68] Van Rheenen agrees with Moreau's argument that this way of understanding contextualization describes anthropological inquiry as a "treasure hunt that uses Scripture as a map or guide to discover the treasures to be found in the culture."[69] Van Rheenen stresses that "an over-emphasis upon cultural context can lead to syncretism," and that evangelicals, who believe that God's revelation in Scripture is authoritative in life and ministry, see this option as syncretistic, because the "Scripture is marginalized in the contextualization process."[70]

In addition to struggling for a balance between "gospel and culture," the evangelical missiologists are also struggling with "faith and religion." As Robert Schreiter observed, "Missiology has not yet recovered from Barth's distinction between faith and religion, a distinction that can make some sense in a mono-religious situation but is less useful elsewhere."[71] Thus, to guard against "syncretism," several safeguards are suggested by Hiebert: for example, a high view of the authority of Scripture, and the ongoing work of the Holy Spirit in the lives of Christians.[72] Moreau also insists on some guidelines to help guard against syncretism:

> Because of the convoluted nature of culture, the declaration of syncretism in a particular setting cannot be simply left in the hands of expatriate missionaries. The local community must be empowered to biblically evaluate their own practices and teachings. Missionaries must learn to trust that indigenous peoples are able to discern God's leading and trust God and maintain biblically founded and culturally relevant faith and praxis in each local context. Finally, Christians of every culture must engage in genuine partnership with Christians of other cultures, since often the outsider's help is needed to enable the

---

68. Van Rheenen, 4.
69. Van Rheenen, 4. See also Moreau, "Contextualization," 336.
70. Van Rheenen, 4, 7.
71. Schreiter, "Defining Syncretism," 50.
72. Paul G. Hiebert, *Anthoropological Insights for Missionaries* (Grand Rapids, MI: Baker Book House, 1994), 91.

local believer, blinded by culture and familiarity, to see which contravenes scriptural adherence to the first commandment.[73]

Christians should not fear syncretism and abandon it as a negative force in Christian mission theology, at least from the context of Asia where the entire continent is already contextualized and has accepted syncretistic processes. Syncretism is followed by contextualization generally. Thus, evangelicals need to continue to grapple with it by redefining the term for the sake of theology, culture, and missiology, as Schreiter suggests. But why the need to keep "syncretism"? Schreiter gives three reasons why this term needs to be kept: (1) abandoning "syncretism" (called for by some missiologists) does not guarantee its passing out of our vocabulary; rather, it helps missiologists in conservative traditions to understand cultural processes in the proclaiming of the gospel; (2) to substitute "inculturation" or some other term for "syncretism" can obscure the very crucial point that syncretism raises – namely, the relationship between theological development and cultural processes; and (3) we are clearly in a time of considerable change within Christianity. Truly we seem to be coming into the age of the world church (to borrow Karl Rahner's much-quoted phrase). If so, we will see interactions of faith and culture that will be more varied and more acute at the same time.[74] Nevertheless, in the argument of what Christian faith looks like in a context of multiple religious encounters such as that of East Asia and Vietnam, a new definition of syncretism in missiology makes sense.

> Missiology's longtime concern about crossing boundaries is now becoming a central concern in theology as a whole. In this regard theology is becoming missiology. Missiology needs to take the lead, and a key area is the formation of religious identity in new circumstances. That is why, it seems to me, we must continue to speak of syncretism. We cannot ban its troubled history; we must, rather, come to terms with that past so as to understand the present.[75]

---

73. Moreau, "Syncretism," 924. See also Moreau's chapter 12, "Contextualization: From an Adapted Message to an Adapted Life," in Pocock, Van Rheenen, and Mcconnell, *The Changing Face of World Missions: Engaging Contemporary Issues and Trends*, 331–332.

74. See Schreiter, "Defining Syncretism," 50–51.

75. Schreiter, 53.

This section argues that a more comprehensive way to carry on the "syncretism" discussion and its meaning in mission theology is needed. First of all, one must be grounded biblically, particularly in the New Testament. As Dean Flemming suggested, "Scripture itself can offer us a more adequate approach to the challenge of re-appropriating the gospel," because "each book of the New Testament represents an attempt by the author to present the Christian message in a way that is targeted for a particular audience within a socio-cultural environment."[76] John Howard Yoder, an Anabaptist theologian, suggested that a sound biblical foundation for contextuality in mission can be learned from the New Testament where it shows how the apostolic writers resorted to a common pattern of response to an alien worldview, that of Christ's incarnation as Lord of the universe (five texts – John 1:1–14; Phlm 2:5–11; Col 1:15–23; Heb 1–2; and Rev 4:1–5:5).[77] These writers were completely familiar with the language and thought of the host culture. However, they did not fit Jesus and his message into the ready-made categories of the host culture but presented Jesus as transcendent Lord.[78] For instance, in Paul's message (to the Athenians in Acts 17:16–34), "there is an affirmation of God the Father, but this is precisely the God whom Jesus taught us to call Father, the one whom Jesus in a peculiar way claimed as the Father from whom he had his mission."[79]

Second, one must recognize the context of "multiple religious encounters" such as those of East Asian and Vietnamese insiders, not just looking left and right, but looking deep into why things are as they are. As an outsider observing these "multiple religious encounters," Schreiter says:

> There are instances of communities absorbing and embracing successive religious encounters. An example would be Vietnam, where local traditions had to deal with two thousand years of Chinese hegemony with its attendant Confucian ethic,

---

76. Flemming, *Contextualization in the New Testament*, 15–16.

77. John Howard Yoder, *The Priestly Kingdom: Social Ethics as Gospel* (Notre Dame, IN: University of Notre Dame Press, 1984), 49–53.

78. See Wilbert R. Shenk, "John Howard Yoder's Mission Theology: Context and Contribution," in *Theology of Mission: A Believers Church Perspective*, ed. Gayle Gerber Koontz and Andy Alexis-Baker (Downers Grove, IL: InterVarsity Press, 2014), 21.

79. Gayle Gerber Koontz and Andy Alexis-Baker, eds., *Theology of Mission: A Believers Church Perspective* (Downers Grove, IL: InterVarsity Press, 2014), 139–142.

the introduction of Theravada Buddhism, and, most recently, Christianity. All four traditions are often present together in contemporary Vietnamese people. How is such a mix negotiated into a religious identity?[80]

Seeing syncretism from within such a cultural context needs a thoroughly East Asian and Vietnamese perspective on the one hand. Such a process of accommodation or assimilation taking place, within East Asian and Vietnamese cultural concepts and religious forms would require a paradigm shift for mission theology. On the other hand, "the reality of unique divine revelation in history" (God communicating his self-revelation using existing concepts and religious forms during the patriarchal history of Israel in the Old Testament) needs to be recognized in the process of "thoroughly" seeing the Christian faith from a biblical perspective (Christopher J. H. Wright's "missional hermeneutic").[81]

Lastly and more importantly, syncretism needs to be seen as a natural expression of Christianity. Taking from this position together with observing Western Christianity which itself is a product of syncretism with Christ at its center, M. M. Thomas developed his distinctive "Christ-centred syncretism" with an emphasis on conversion, not of individuals but of whole religious systems to Christ-ultimately all religions and ideologies which will be found in Christ.[82] From the post-colonial context and his experience in

---

80. Schreiter, "Defining Syncretism," 52.

81. Wright, "Christian and Other Religions," 4–15; Andrew F. Walls, "In Quest of the Father of Mission Studies," *International Bulletin of Missionary Research* 23, no. 3 (1999): 98–104. Walls believes that Origen was able to contextualize theology cross-culturally because of being "thoroughly Greek, thoroughly Christian." Vinoth Ramachandra also argues that, "God accommodates his self-disclosure to fit the religious framework of the patriarchs, including the religious rituals, customs and divine titles of their culture. This is in preparation for an experience of his liberating act, a deeper and fuller revelation of his character and purposes, one that will in the course of time take them beyond their ancestral religious framework and shatter its central assumptions. Once they have walked with Yahweh in the wilderness, there is no going back." See Vinoth Ramachandra, *Faiths in Conflict?: Christian Integrity in a Multicultural World* (Downers Grove, IL: InterVarsity Press, 1999), 139–140.

82. M. M. Thomas, *Man and the Universe of Faiths* (Madras: Published for the Christian Institute for the Study of Religion and Society, Bangalore, by the Christian Literature Society, 1975), 157; M. M. Thomas, "Christ-Centred Syncretism," *Religion and Society* 26 (March 1979): 26–35; Miyamoto, *God's Mission in Asia: A Comparative and Contextual Study of This-Worldly Holiness and the Theology of Missio Dei in M. M. Thomas and C. S. Song*, 131–132; Gnanakan, "Some Insight," Kindle Locations 1187–1199.

the ecumenical movement, Thomas believed that the work of Jesus Christ is one that transforms all religions and ideologies from within. That means he traces some significant secular and religious movements and the individuals behind them to demonstrate the transforming effects of Christ.[83] Thomas sees Christian influence on these movements as a result of encountering Christ, regardless of their religions and ideologies.[84] What Thomas stresses here is the cosmic and universal lordship, the centrality of Jesus Christ to all of creation and history (an integral part of human history). He does not talk about the centrality of Christ only in terms of a commitment to the historic Jesus Christ, nor even any open acknowledgment of Christ in these movements. It is a cosmic Christ who remains a nebulous entity-an anonymous Christ. Such "cosmic" impact is to be accepted as religions are reforming, and there is definitely a noticeable influence of Christianity on society. Showing how Raja Ram Mohan Roy (1772–1833) brought a reformation to Hinduism in his time as he encountered the message of Jesus Christ is an example of how Thomas's cosmic Christ worked. Ken Gnanakan affirms that, "God is at work in the world even apart from saving men and women. He is also shaping history and all that is in it."[85]

What M. M. Thomas and other Asian theologians (as insiders) advocate is to see the work of God, particularly the cosmic Christ, not just in soul saving or individual conversion, but also in all that is in human history. Within the context of Asia where most of the countries struggled for independence and established a national post-colonial identity (post-colonialism), the merger of secular and Christian faiths into a specific form of syncretism is noteworthy to be considered as contextualization in Asia, specifically in Vietnam. This attempt was what the Cao Dai did in the early twentieth-century Vietnam (ch. 3) where a Christ figure was placed in the Vietnamese syncretistic spirituality. Nonetheless, syncretism as viewed as a natural approach by insiders is also part of making contextualization work in that context of Asia: Christian faith is authenticated as the evangelical faith and yet relevant to its cultural context.

---

83. See Gnanakan, "Some Insight," Kindle Locations 1187–1199.
84. See Thomas, "Christ-Centred Syncretism."
85. Gnanakan, "Some Insight," Kindle Locations 1198–1199.

Alternative Evangelical View

In this second section, the study presents an alternative evangelical view. How can East Asian Christians live and present their Christian faith in such a way that meets the deepest needs and penetrates the worldview of the people, and more importantly, allows them to follow Christ while remaining within their culture? For instance, if Vietnamese are not being transformed in their worldview, in their hearts, minds, and beings by the gospel, and if the church cannot bridge the gap between the gospel and the culture, conversion, then, may take place only at the outward level with Christian forms, but no real change will occur in their lives. Can the Vietnamese become Christians without first becoming Chinese, French, American, or whatever the cultural origin of the missionaries with whom they identify? The foremost issue for contextualization in East Asia is not about communicating the gospel relevantly into these cultures, but how to ensure that the gospel is understood biblically and culturally by the local people. In other words, to have an authentic gospel, the local people should be able to interpret the gospel from within their cultural perspective. More importantly, if God's intent is to be known by all human beings, then through God's incarnation into the world of human flesh, God would have some specific, unique and translatable ways to reveal who he is for all human beings, regardless of their cultural contexts. Thus, understanding cultural assimilation in the process of the translatability of Christianity is critical, and seeing God's incarnation as purposely making known who God is to all human beings is equally important. These perspectives need to be thoroughly examined before having Christian dialogue with the existing syncretistic religious traditions in East Asia and Vietnam. In short, this study explains three specific areas of contextualization that should be viewed as alternatives for evangelicals, namely cultural context, God's intention, and translatable faith.

Within Cultural Context

The process of contextualization must allow the people from *within* a cultural context to be involved and to form an authentic Christian faith relevant to their culture, not an imported or alien one. In fact, the term "contextualization" was coined at the close of the modern colonial era. It was first introduced and applied to Christian theological education in the *Ministry in Context Programme* of the 1970s by the Theological Education Fund Ministry Program of the World Council of Churches (WCC/TEF).[86] The emphasis on "contextualization," instead of "indigenization" (through the "three-self" concept promoted earlier for indigenous churches in Asia) has changed because indigenization tends to be used in the sense of responding to the gospel in terms of a traditional culture; therefore, it is in danger of being past-oriented.[87] Contextualization, while not ignoring this, takes into account the process of secularism, technology and the struggle for human justice, which characterized the historical movement of nations in the Third World.[88] This was the breakthrough in the interaction between the gospel and culture in Asia. According to Shoki Coe, younger churches in Asia (and in Third World countries) have shifted from indigenization to contextualization in the process of developing local theologies. Using the word "contextualization" seeks to "convey all that is implied in the familiar term 'indigenization,' yet to press beyond for a more dynamic concept which is open to change and which is also future-oriented."[89] Moreover, this timely development emerged in the context of "new nations struggling for their own life, and the mission enterprise needed new symbols to mark a needed separation from the colonialistic, Western-dominated past."[90]

Ironically, "whether one talked about the necessity of indigenization or inculturation, the initiative was thought to remain in the hands of foreign evangelists, who alone were considered qualified to determine how orthodox beliefs and settled practices ought to be expressed in new situations."[91] This

---

86. See William P. Russell, *Contextualization: Origins, Meaning and Implications* (Rome: Pontifica, 1995); Klas Lundström, "Gospel and Culture in the World Council of Churches and the Lausanne Movement with Particular Focus on the Period 1973–1996" (Svenska institutet för missionsforskning, 2006). See also WCC/TEF, "Ministry in Context: The Third Mandate Programme of the Theological Education Fund (1970–1977)," ed. the TEF-staff (Bromley, Kent: Theological Education Fund, 1972).

87. Shoki Coe, "Contextualizing Theology," in *Third World Theologies*, ed. Gerald H. Anderson and Thomas F. Stransky (New York: Paulist Press, 1976), 19; Kraft, "Why Appropriate?," 3.

88. WCC/TEF, "Ministry in Context," 20; Ruy O. Costa, *One Faith, Many Cultures: Inculturation, Indigenization, and Contextualization* (Maryknoll, NY: Orbis Books, 1988), xii.

89. Coe, "Contextualizing Theology," 19–24.

90. See Dean S. Gilliland, "Contextualization," in *Evangelical Dictionary of World Missions*, ed. A. Scott Moreau et al. (Grand Rapids, MI: Baker Books, 2000), 225–228.

91. Skreslet, *Comprehending Mission*, 88.

is the reality situation with many younger churches in Asia. Hiebert rightly calls this "contextualization" at the "minimal" level, meaning that there is acknowledgement that differences exist between cultures, but cultural adaptation is limited as much as possible. Under this level, a missionary might translate the Bible into a foreign language, but will likely arrange new church plants in a fashion similar to the churches in the missionary's home country (this was the situation in Vietnam which will be discussed further in chs. 3 and 4). Hiebert says:

> The more we live with and study the people we serve, the more we become aware of the depth and power of the people's culture, and the need to contextualize both the messenger and the message for them to understand and live the gospel; but we are afraid that this can distort the gospel, so it must be done minimally. We realize that we must speak and translate the Bible into their language and that we must organize their services and churches in ways the people understand, but we equate Christianity with our beliefs and practices.[92]

Contextualization is "part of the very nature of theology itself," because it is "the attempt to understand Christian faith in terms of a particular context."[93] That means all theologies are not done alone but within a certain context. Mission theologians recognize the need to facilitate the gospel's accessibility to all cultures by local theologizing. Thus, theology is constructed differently within each cultural context so that the gospel will be relevant to that culture. As Kosuke Koyama once reminded us, there is "no handle on the cross."[94] We do not have a privileged position when it comes to understanding and practicing Christianity, because "it cannot be the exclusive property of any one culture, for it refuses to be culture bound; it continually bursts free from the chains of bondage to cultural tradition."[95]

Contextualization was once understood in a narrow way and its practices in mission and evangelism heavily emphasized humanization, the impact

---

92. Hiebert, "Gospel in Human Contexts," 84–99.
93. Bevans, *Models of Contextual Theology*, 1.
94. Kosuke Koyama, *No Handle on the Cross: An Asian Meditation on the Crucified Mind* (Maryknoll, NY: Orbis Books, 1977).
95. Whiteman, "Contextualization," 4.

of socio-political, economic, cultural, and other forces on the task of doing theology in that context.⁹⁶ The so-called "contextual theologies" (Dalit theology from India, Minjung theology in Korea, Black theology in Africa and among African Americans) believe that context does matter, that in the act of reading and interpreting the Bible, the questions of who you are, where you are, and whom you live among as a reader make a difference.⁹⁷ However, to avoid slipping into syncretism, Christopher J. H. Wright warns against an over emphasis of "contexts and interests" that "contextual theologies" use in their approach to the Bible "to be read precisely in and for the context in which its message must be heard and appropriated."⁹⁸ There are also "justice and social development" issues among conciliar Protestantism that are part of "the theology-in-context discussion that ensued through the volatile 1960s and which polarized American Christianity on issues such as Vietnam and race."⁹⁹ In addition, the extreme tendency of liberation theology coming from the church in Latin America, being inspired by the socio-political conditions there as the source for theologizing, had "alarmed most evangelicals."¹⁰⁰

Johannes Christian Hoekendijk argued that "church based" mission thinking of the previous century by Rufus Anderson and other promoters of the three-self mission theology was an "illegitimate center."¹⁰¹ By "church based," Hoekendijk meant the church was only an instrument for bringing God's *shalom* (peace) to the world. Therefore, "If God is the primary missionary, and if God works in the whole world, then it is the world that sets the agenda for the church, not the church that is the sign and instrument of God's

---

96. See particularly "Appropriate Contextualization as Local Theologizing," in Van Engen, "Five Perspectives," 192–196.

97. Christopher J. H. Wright, *The Mission of God: Unlocking the Bible's Grand Narrative.* (Downers Grove, IL: IVP Academic, 2006), 41–43. Wright offers "a missional hermeneutic" as an alternative to see God's mission biblically.

98. Wright, *Mission of God*, 41–43.

99. Gilliland, *Word among Us*, 2. Also, the tension in relationship between the concept of the triune God's mission (*missio Dei*) and the missionary activities of the church to the point that the latter has become unnecessary or excluding the first, just right after 1952 (Willingen's IMC) to 1968 (Uppsala's WCC).

100. Gilliland, *Word among Us*, 2.

101. Johannes C. Hoekendijk, "The Church in Missionary Thinking," *International Review of Missions*, no. 41 (1952): 324–336, cited by Sunquist, *Understanding Christian Mission*, 135.

presence in the world."¹⁰² In other words, the world is the primary context for contextualization efforts in constructing mission theology for Christian missions. At the 1960 Strasbourg Conference of the World Student Christian Fellowship (WSCF), the idea surfaced that if the world provides the agenda for the church, the church has to identify completely with this agenda. The notion of *missio Dei* was secularized in a way that *missio Dei* meant that God needs no help in "articulating himself;" the church's missionary efforts only get in the way. If anything, the church "simply points to what God is doing in the world; that is all."¹⁰³

The conflict about the church and the world ended with a separation between evangelical and conciliar Protestants within the World Council of Churches (WCC). The evangelicals first shared their concern about Donald McGavran's "Church Growth" concept at both the 1968 WCC Assembly in Upsalat, and again at the 1974 International Congress on World Evangelization at Lausanne; the latter echoed much of Hoekendijk's emphasis on the horizontal aspect of mission with its primary goal being humanization rather than salvation.¹⁰⁴ And because of this narrow sense of contextualization, it was concluded that a balanced approach is needed to engage both gospel and culture critically from biblical, theological, and cultural perspectives.

John Howard Yoder also suggested that Ephesians 3 and 2 Corinthians 5 are the biblical "basic reorientation of our thinking about missions," whereas the classical definition of the church in which the church is present where the sacraments are administered and the word of God is preached to the faithful has sundered the essential relationship between church and mission.¹⁰⁵ Further, to assert that church and mission are inseparable "is not simply an affirmative statement about the church; it is also a radical questioning of her missionary methods."¹⁰⁶ Commenting on Yoder's position, missiologist

---

102. Bosch, *Transforming Mission*, 392. Cited by Stephen B. Bevans and Roger Schroeder, *Constants in Context: A Theology of Mission for Today* (Maryknoll, NY: Orbis Books, 2004), 291.

103. Bevans and Schroeder, *Constants in Context*, 290–291.

104. See "Evangelical and Conciliar Protestants in Mission" in Bevans and Schroeder, *Constants in Context: A Theology of Mission for Today*, 260–64.

105. See Shenk, "John Howard Yoder's Mission Theology," 20.

106. John Howard Yoder, "Anabaptist Vision and Mennonite Reality," in *Consultation on Anabaptist Mennonite Theology*, ed. A. J. Klassen (Fresno, CA: Council of Mennonite Seminaries, 1970), 32.

Wilbert R. Shenk said that the evangelical and ecumenical Protestant views of church and mission are problematic when both operate from the same Christendom model, that is, that mission initiatives were taken independently of ecclesial responsibility.[107] Shenk argues that lacking a robust ecclesiology, evangelicals were characterized by their preoccupation with personal piety, and they viewed mission as the work of a special society outside the church's purview.[108] Then, to have a robust biblical and theological foundation for contextualization, we need to explore what God's intention is which is the next discussion.

God's Intention

God's intention and purpose in incarnation is to be, and to be known by all human beings. The Lord Jesus certainly incarnated (or translated) himself into the world. The Word made flesh in John 1:1 is "a massive act of translation."[109] The central event on which the Christian movement rests is an astonishing act of divine translation, "divinity translated into humanity."[110] This divine act of incarnation in terms of "translation" which Andrew F. Walls advocated, is prefigured in many acts of divine "accommodation" in the Old Testament.[111] David Bosch calls for a "paradigm shift" with an accompanying shift in epistemological approach as being critical to theologizing, because, ". . . the Word became flesh and lived among us" (John 1:14 NRSV) is a powerful statement in the entire chapter of describing God's incarnation. God's intention is that the Word is for all human beings "from every nation, from all tribes and peoples and languages" (Rev 7:9 NRSV). For Bosch, the old paradigm is a monolithic approach to theology. Such a paradigm has to shift to a "critical hermeneutic" in which the biblical text is recognized as contextual in its very nature. Thus, God has interacted with human beings through time and space and in multiple contexts so as to communicate God's intent and God's

---

107. See Shenk, "John Howard Yoder's Mission Theology, 20.

108. Shenk, 20. Shenk believes that mainstream Protestantism was associated with state churches, which had large nominal memberships; since mission was not integral to its ecclesiology, the mission-minded among its membership formed independent mission societies.

109. Andrew F. Walls, *The Cross-Cultural Process in Christian History: Studies in the Transmission and Appropriation of Faith* (Maryknoll, NY: Orbis Books, 2002), 29.

110. See Walls, *Missionary Movement in Christian History*, ch. 3.

111. Ramachandra, *Faiths in Conflict?*, 39–40; Wright, "Christian and Other Religions," 4–15; Wright, *Mission of God*, 75–83.

desire to be in relationship with human beings, wherever they are found.[112] This affirms that the pre-incarnate Son/Word of God has been addressing all human beings, even those of cultures and histories other than Israel, working with them under forms and names that Christians may find strange and even repellent (John 1:1–3, 9; Heb 1:1). That is the self-humbling accommodation of God to a "fallen" human world.[113]

In a similar argument, Paul Hiebert also called for "critical" contextualization as discussed above. Hiebert indeed recognized that contextualization is "critical" when its processes are judged from the biblical standard for their relevance, not strictly from a local perspective.[114] That means that "Contextualization forces interactive reflection, and it is from the interplay between people's understanding of God's intention for all human beings, as well as for their particular environment, that transformation takes place, that is, transformation that is both true to God's intent and also relevant within the context."[115] Charles Van Engen, in the same fashion, examines the biblical theology of covenant as a model for "knowing God" in multiple cultural contexts.[116] He indeed calls "re-contextualization" as believing that human beings know God in their midst.[117] And thus for him, the mission of the

---

112. Bosch, *Transforming Mission*, 421–425.

113. Ramachandra argues that, "after all, what can be more repellent than a cross? This fact, however, far from obviating the need to proclaim the gospel of Christ to all cultures, actually *compels* it. For if it is Christ who has been speaking to human beings in their sin, then it is in order that Christians lead them out of what Paul calls (when addressing the learned citizens of Athens) 'the times of human ignorance' (Acts 17:30) that they may understand and experience the freedom that he wrought for them through the cross. The church is the bearer of the good news of freedom, and the Holy Spirit enables the church to discern those 'pointers' to Christ in every human situation, so that the word of Christ may be articulated powerfully and relevantly in every age." See Ramachandra, *Faiths in Conflict?*, 139–140.

114. Hiebert, "Critical Contextualization," 109–110.

115. Daniel R. Shaw, "Beyond Contextualization: Toward a Twenty-First-Century Model for Enabling Mission," *International Bulletin of Missionary Research* 34, no. 4 (2010): 212.

116. Van Engen, *Mission on the Way*, 75–89; Daniel R. Shaw and Charles E. Van Engen, *Communicating God's Word in a Complex World: God's Truth or Hocus Pocus?* (Lanham, MD: Rowman & Littlefield, 2003), 214.

117. See Charles Edward Van Engen, "Critical Theologizing: Knowing God in Multiple Global/Local Contexts," in *Evangelical, Ecumenical, and Anabaptist Missiologies in Conversation: Essays in Honor of Wilbert R. Shenk*, ed. Wilbert R. Shenk et al. (Maryknoll, NY: Orbis Books, 2006), 88–97.

church as God's called and sent people is to enable God's people to represent God's intention in the world.[118]

God wants to be known by all human beings, whether the Jews, the Greeks, or the Gentiles. The earliest Christian community understood this profound missionary nature of Christianity when stating their Christian beliefs, "For there is no distinction between Jew and Greek; the same Lord is Lord of all and is generous to all who call on him" (Rom 10:12). But, can the Jew and the Greek (and all human beings) hear and understand the authentic gospel according to their perception of time and space? Do the Greeks need to become Jews to enable their hearing capacity or vice versa? Here, the processes of contextualization determine not only that the gospel is communicated, either by a missionary or the local people, but also that it is interpreted, received and understood by the people of the culture. But what is the theological ground for the argument of God's intention?

Missio Dei

God wants to demonstrate himself to the world through missionary activity as God the Father sending Jesus the Son through the empowering of the Spirit (*missio Dei*). This is the major theological ground for the argument of God's intention initiated by God and implemented within the triune God. Mission theologians have recently called for a re-examination of "contextualization," going beyond it to understand the purpose of God's mission in this world. That is, we need to recognize that God is in our midst and that we participate in God's mission.[119] The modern understanding of mission has been undergirded by missiological instincts and a missiological consensus that is based on the concept of *missio Dei*.[120] Furthermore, *missio Dei* theology drew on

---

118. See Charles Edward Van Engen, "Mission Described and Defined," in *Missionshift: Global Mission Issues in the Third Millennium*, ed. David J. Hesselgrave and Ed Stetzer (Nashville, TN: B & H Academic, 2010), 7–29.

119. In the decades following World War I, a number of theological ideas fostered by theologians, such as Karl Barth, Emil Brunner, and Karl Hartenstein, were brought to the table to determine what perceptions were held about God's mission (*missio Dei*). For an excellent review, see John G. Flett, *The Witness of God: The Trinity, Missio Dei, Karl Barth, and the Nature of Christian Community* (Grand Rapids, MI: Eerdmans, 2010).

120. Rodman W. MacIlvaine, "What Is the Missional Church Movement?," *Bibliotheca Sacra* 167, no. 665 (2010): 99.

Barth's doctrine of the Trinity[121] in the 1930s in which David Bosch believed that Barth was the first to articulate mission as an activity within the triune God and thus, "the ground for mission was found in the triune God and his mission."[122] Such understanding of *missio Dei* is a crucial breakthrough in respect to the preceding centuries.[123] Mission, indeed, is "primarily and ultimately, the work of the triune God, Creator, Redeemer, and Sanctifier, for the sake of the world, a ministry in which the church is privileged to participate."[124] Twenty years later, at the fifth International Missionary Council (IMC) conference held in 1952 at Willingen, although the term *missio Dei* was not used once, it did appear in Karl Hartenstein's report from his essay in 1934.[125] Thus, Barth's approach was acknowledged, and the ground for mission was found in very nature of the triune God.[126]

Willingen is important in mission theology for what might be called "a recovery of fully Trinitarian engagement," instead of a radical christological orientations of neo-orthodoxy that had dominated most mission discussions until this point.[127] As Bosch summarizes the Willingen message:

> The classical doctrine on the *missio Dei* as God the Father sending the Son, and God the Father and the Son sending the Spirit was expanded to include yet another "movement": Father, Son, and Holy Spirit sending the church into the world . . . Willingen's

---

121. The intellectual origins of this shift are attributed to a lecture Karl Barth delivered in 1932, entitled, "Die Theologie and die Mission in der Gegenwart" (theology and mission in the present situation). See Bosch, *Transforming Mission*, 389–393.

122. Johannes Aagaard, "Some Main Trends in Modern Protestant Missiology," *Studia Theologica* 19, no. 1–2 (1965): 252.

123. Bosch, *Transforming Mission*, 393.

124. Lutheran World Federation, "Together in God's Mission: An Lutheran World Federation Contribution to the Understanding of Mission" (Geneva: Lutheran World Federation (LWF, 1988), 6–10. Cited by Bosch, *Transforming Mission*, 392.

125. Georg F. Vicedom, *The Mission of God: An Introduction to a Theology of Mission* (Saint Louis, MO: Concordia, 1965), 4–6. It was at the International Missionary Conference at Willingen, Germany, in 1952 that the concept of *missio Dei* began to reshape missiological thinking, even though the term *missio Dei* itself was not used at the conference. Rather, it appeared in Hartenstein's conference report. See Craig Ott, Stephen J. Strauss, and Timothy C. Tennent, *Encountering Theology of Mission: Biblical Foundations, Historical Developments, and Contemporary Issues*, Encountering mission (Grand Rapids, MI: Baker Academic, 2010), Loc. 1873–1875.

126. Aagaard, "Some Main Trends," 252.

127. Sunquist, *Understanding Christian Mission*, 136.

image of mission was mission as participating in the sending of God. Our mission has no life of its own: only in the hands of the sending God can it truly be called mission, not least since the missionary initiative comes from God alone.[128]

Since the concept of *missio Dei* was developed, a further study on mission, namely "missiology" has developed in academia as a theological discipline, in which missiologists (e.g. Johannes Verkuyl) may argue that the mission of the church, *missio ecclesiarum*, is subsumed within the *missio Dei*.[129] Because of that, *missio Dei* is understood as "the study of the salvation activities of the Father, Son, and Holy Spirit throughout the world geared toward bringing the kingdom of God into existence."[130] Nevertheless, the modern understanding of mission may be traced back to several historical developments of the missional church, such as the explosion of missionary activity after the 1792 publication of William Carey's *An Enquiry into the Obligation of Christians to Use Means for the Conversion of the Heathen*. Even earlier, in the sixteenth century, the Society of Jesus, a missionary order, founded by Ignatius Loyola (c. 1491–1556), was the largest and most powerful new religious order since the birth of the Franciscans and Dominicans, as the greatest mystics the church has ever known.[131] Subsequently, the church as mission to the world was taken seriously by various foreign mission associations focused on taking the gospel to other parts of the world, for instance, the World Missionary Conference in Edinburgh in 1910 with the goal to "evangelize the world in our generation." Other mission associations included the International Missionary Council (IMC) in 1921, Life and Work in 1925, and Faith and Order in 1927. The relationship between the older and younger church was thoroughly discussed which led to the formation of the World Council of Churches (WCC) in Amsterdam in 1948. The focus of the 1983 Tambaram

---

128. Bosch, *Transforming Mission*, 390. Cited from Van't Hof, I. P. C. 1972. *Op zoek naar het geheim van de zending: In dialoog met de wereldzendingsconferenties 1910–1963* (Wageningen: Veenman, 1972), 158–159.

129. See Johannes Verkuyl, *Contemporary Missiology: An Introduction* (Grand Rapids, MI: Eerdmans, 1978), 5.

130. Verkuyl, *Contemporary Missiology*, 5.

131. Latourette, *History of Christianity*, 853–854.

(Madras) International Missionary Council (IMC) was "what it means for the church – for any and every local church – to participate in God's mission."[132]

Biblically, the act of mission is and starts with God right from the beginning in Genesis 1:1 where the triune God – Father, Son, and Holy Spirit, first initiated this sending activity throughout the Bible. In short, God is a missionary God.[133] Christian mission is rooted in divine initiative and character of the missionary God because, "we confront a God in whom his very essence is the basis for mission today. Mission begins with God himself, not merely because he is the God of mission but because his very character is mission."[134]

The sending activity of the triune God is revealed in Jesus's statement to his disciples, "as the Father has sent me, I am sending you" (John 20:21b). The followers of Christ today are sent by Jesus to carry on God's mission into the world. The sending of the Holy Spirit empowers the church to fulfill God's mission in this world: "But the Advocate, the Holy Spirit, whom the Father will send in my name, will teach you everything, and remind you of all that I have said to you" (John 14:26).

The recognition that mission is the triune God's mission, *missio Dei* provides a new understanding of mission in which the church again reverts to a narrow, ecclesiocentric (church-centric) view of mission.[135] In other words, a theocentric focus on mission as the *missio Dei* replaced the former ecclesiocentric focus (*missio ecclesia*) or christological view of mission (*missio Christi*). This means that *mission* (singular) remains primarily the mission of the triune God, while *missions* (plural) means the missionary activities of the church or simply Christian missions, as Stephen Neill claimed in the post-Willingen period, "The age of missions is at an end; the age of mission has begun."[136] Thus, David Bosch believes that, "we cannot without ado claim that what we do is identical to the *missio Dei*; our missionary activities are

---

132. Sunquist, *Understanding Christian Mission*, 8–9.

133. Johannes Aagaard, "Trends in Missiological Thinking during the Sixties," *International Review of Mission* 62, no. 245 (1973): 11–15.

134. Ken Gnanakan, *Kingdom Concerns: A Biblical Exploration towards a Theology of Mission* (Bangalore, India: Theological Book Trust, 1989), 67.

135. See Bosch, *Transforming Mission*, 389, 393.

136. Stephen C. Neill, *A History of Christian Missions*, vol. 6, Pelican History of the Church (Harmondsworth, UK: Penguin Books, 1966), 572.

only authentic insofar as they reflect participation in the mission of God."[137] This helps to eliminate the danger of what Stephen Neill once noted, "if everything is mission, nothing is mission."[138] That means the primary purpose of the missionary activities of the church or Christian missions is not simply the planting of churches or the saving of souls, but "it has service to the *missio Dei*, representing God in and over against the world, pointing to God, holding up the God-child before the eyes of the world in a ceaseless celebration of the Feast of the Epiphany."[139] And that means, "in its mission, the church witnesses to the fullness of the promise of God's reign and participates in the ongoing struggle between that reign and the power of darkness and evil."[140]

Christian mission then participates in the mission of the triune God (*missio Dei*). More specifically, it is Christ's mission (*missio Christi*), and not ours.[141] By God's grace, we (the church) can participate in the mission of God. As David Bosch said, "the *missio Dei* is God's activity, which embraces both the church and the world, and in which the church may be privileged to participate."[142] In other words, God gives us (the church) the privilege to see the world from his perspective so that we can humble ourselves in preaching, serving and witnessing to the work of God in the world today. A better way of understanding the missionary God is that,

> Christian mission is the church's participation in the triune God through the suffering of Christ, who was sent by the Father for the redemption and liberation of the world, by means of the conversion of individuals and cultures, in the power of the Holy Spirit, to the end that God be glorified in the nations and in all of his creation.[143]

---

137. Bosch, *Transforming Mission*, 391.

138. Stephen C. Neill, *Creative Tension* (London: Edinburgh House Press, 1959), 81.

139. Bosch, *Transforming Mission*, 391.

140. James A. Scherer, *Gospel, Church, and Kingdom: Comparative Studies in World Mission Theology* (Minneapolis, MN: Augsburg, 1987), 84.

141. Lesslie Newbigin, *Trinitarian Faith and Today's Mission* (Richmond: John Knox Press, 1964), 78. "The Christian world mission is Christ's not ours" was the final statement of the International Missionary Council (IMC)'s Ghana assembly in 1957/1958, see Thomas, *Classic Texts in Mission and World Christianity*, 113–114.

142. Bosch, *Transforming Mission*, 391.

143. Sunquist, *Understanding Christian Mission*, 173.

Thus, mission is from the triune God, not the church nor any human agent. But the triune God's mission "must be understood as a foundational concept that launches the church from the place of worship and fellowship into frontiers of God's reign."[144] And since "mission begins with God himself, not merely because he is the God of mission, but because His very character is mission," then, the task of mission that the Christian church contextually participates in, is the mission of the triune God which will be fulfilled by his grace, not by its own efforts and strength.[145] In other words, Christian missions thus are involved in trinitarian dimensions: (1) proclamation of the reign of God or the kingdom of God's presence in the world; (2) proclamation that Jesus Christ is Lord of every culture. Christian mission is supposed to model Christ's way of humility and self-emptying and bold proclamation of God's "already" and "not yet" reign;[146] and (3) mission as participation in the work of the Holy Spirit in the world today.

To fully participate in the mission of the triune God, the local Christian church (as insiders) must respond to these "three trinitarian dimensions" above to be "the place of worship and fellowship into frontiers of God's reign."[147] As Daniel R. Shaw stresses, "Instead of outsiders reconfiguring local cultural forms to fit the shape of Christianity with which they are familiar, we need – following the theological implications of the incarnation – to allow local people to contemplate the implications of God-in-their-midst."[148] This position has been explicated by David Bosch in that "people must be allowed to find their own way to God. Using their own understanding, they can connect with the message that clearly impacts them and do so in ways that outsiders, in large measure, cannot fathom."[149] Based on the "relevance theory of communication" (or the inferential model), Shaw argues that the emphasis should be on the process, not the product, and asks, "How does God's intent

---

144. Sunquist, xiii.

145. Gnanakan, *Kingdom Concerns*, 67.

146. Bosch, *Transforming Mission*, 489; Bevans and Schroeder, *Constants in Context*, 284–285.

147. Sunquist, *Understanding Christian Mission*, xiii, 284. The church throughout its history has carried out the mission of proclamation and praise in the world. Such proclamation is temporary (until the *eschaton*), but worship is eternal.

148. Shaw, "Beyond Contextualization," 211.

149. Shaw, 209. Cited from Bosch, *Transforming Mission*, 307–308, 62.

become cognitively relevant to, and understood by human beings?" instead of "How is an understanding of God translated or transmitted from one set of cultural forms and meanings to another?"[150] Shaw intends to go "beyond contextualization" by shifting the focus from the "missionary product or result orientation" to the "both-and process orientation," the process that at the end both "outsiders and insiders" come to know God, and are transformed more fully into the image of God.[151] This study concurs with Shaw's call to go "beyond contextualization" to recognize that God is in our midst, that is Jesus, who came to connect with real people who express human need. "To do so, he entered their world, took up their language with its implicit categories, learning the shapes and contents of their mental and conceptual 'boxes.'"[152] Therefore, "We who call ourselves by his name must, as he did, go beyond our context, learn from those with whom we interact, and become God's intention to them – the Word in their midst."[153] To show that God's intention is to be known by all humans through God's incarnation (through Jesus Christ, John 1, the massive translation of the gospel into human history), the nature of translatability in Christian faith is the third dimension for an alternative evangelical view on contextualization.

---

150. For details of the comparison between the S-M-R code (Source-Message-Receptor, developed by Eugene Nida) and the relevance theory of communication (the inferential model or the process-oriented model), see Shaw, "Beyond Contextualization," 210. Shaw argues that, "the heart of mission hears the call to discern God's intent for human beings and to consider how we go in Christ's name can enable people everywhere to understand what that intent might mean for their spiritual well-being," see Shaw, "Beyond Contextualization," 208; Shaw and Engen, *Communicating God's Word*, 11–21.

151. See particularly two figures "Serial Processing of Codes" (focus on product or result), and "Parallel Distributive Processing of Ideas" (least effort for maximum understanding), in Shaw, "Beyond Contextualization," 209–210.

152. Shaw, "Beyond Contextualization," 214.

153. Shaw, "Beyond Contextualization," 214. Although Shaw's "beyond contextualization" is critical for mission theory, shifting the missionary "product or result" (or old model) to a "process" orientation, this theory focuses on some new approaches for communicating the gospel where "outsiders" (or message bearers) need to shift or transition *from* preaching the gospel *to* living the gospel within the context where the people live. This study, moreover, develops a Vietnamese contextualized biblical theology from an "insider" perspective to argue that the Vietnamese themselves perhaps have acknowledged "God in our midst" (*Đạo*) as God's intent to be known by the Vietnamese a long time ago. See further in chapter 6.

Translatable Faith

Translation of the gospel message is a process that involves the fundamental knowledge of the shaping of Christianity in terms of its origin and the ongoing process of Christianity's growth within a culture. The nature of translatability shows that "Christianity identified itself with the need to translate out of Aramaic and Hebrew, and from that position came to exert a dual force in its historical development"[154] Lamin O. Sanneh identified as "translatability" that which is formed by a "dual force of the Judaic roots and the Gentile culture."[155] Christianity would not have started or gone anywhere if Jewish followers of Jesus had not radically translated their Jewish traditions into the brand new Judaic sect by both "internal conditions" and "external circumstances."[156]

Christianity drew its origin from relativizing the "Judaic roots" because the early followers of Christ inherited Judaic traditions, such as keeping the Torah and gathering at the synagogue, which were considered to be "the defining standards of religion."[157] In fact, the early Christians purposely kept the law and socialized with others at the synagogue (traditions unfamiliar to the Gentiles). They carefully obeyed the teachings of Jesus and taught others the same, according to what Jesus had commanded them (Matt 28:19–20). This led to a theological shift in their concept of YHWH, the One True God of Israel. The early believers, after "the Easter experience," realized that their "Rabbi" and "Messiah" Jesus, who died and rose again, was their Lord and Savior. This Jesus is now Jesus Christ, the Lord who "begins the reign of God."[158] Sanneh believes that two other critical accounts, showing that Christianity in its early stage did not just end up as a new Judaic sect, are the Pentecostal moment and the believers' obedience to make disciples of all nations. At Pentecost, the disciples experienced the power of the Holy Spirit upon them as manifested in the tongues of fire (Acts 1–2). This experience gave them a fresh view about God's impartial action in all cultures. Furthermore, as they obeyed the commandment of Jesus to go out from Jerusalem to the ends of

---

154. Lamin O. Sanneh, *Translating The Message: The Missionary Impact on Culture*, 2nd ed., American Society of Missiology Series 42. (Maryknoll, NY: Orbis Books, 2009), 1.

155. Translatability is an "unusual" approach instead of "new." See Sanneh, *Translating the Message*, 1, 7.

156. Sanneh, 15–27.

157. Walls, *Cross-Cultural Process*, 67–68; Sanneh, *Translating the Message*, 53.

158. Sanneh, *Translating the Message*, 53.

the earth (Matt 28:19–20; Acts 1:8), they encountered a different world, that of polytheism, no longer monotheism.[159] This encounter is considered to be "the Gentile breakthrough," which became "the paradigm of the church's missionary call."[160]

In the process of translatability that contributed to the continuity and the growth of early Christianity, "cultural assimilation" (of Greek culture) played a major role as argued by Sanneh.[161] For instance, initially Christians were faced with a tendency to adjust to Roman cultural and religious terms and figures. Then during the Roman and Greek periods, Christians were also forced to translate their message into the Greek culture. Justin Martyr, Origen, and Clement of Alexandria were the pioneers who steered the church into alignment with Greek learning and culture, though at the same time, they had to deal with Greek ideals like Gnosticism without compromising their Christian faith. Origen, in particular, was the first to put theology into cross-cultural perspectives in such a way that Andrew F. Walls suggests that Origen be recognized as the "father of mission studies" because of his being "thoroughly Greek, thoroughly Christian."[162] The process continued with the challenge that the hellenized church faced with vernacular forces in its Slavic mission. Later the Slavic translation of the Bible deeply impacted Moravia and beyond. Eventually, the Reformation and the Western church continued the process of translatability, which extraordinarily marked Christianity as the most diverse religion in the world.[163]

In the New Testament, Jesus also commanded his disciples to carry the gospel throughout the world so that every human being should hear it, regardless of ethnic or religious background (Matt 28:19–20). He empowered his followers at Pentecost through his Holy Spirit to fulfill this mission, for this gospel is for the entire human race in every time and place (Acts 1:8). Thus, the gospel is equally reserved for everyone. To the Galatians, the apostle

---

159. Sanneh, *Translating the Message*, 42.

160. See Sanneh, *Translating the Message*, 38–53. This account is given in detail in "The Acts of the Apostles": Peter and others (Acts 1–13), Paul and Barnabas (Acts 14–17), and Paul then with the church in Galatia.

161. See particularly in chapter 2 "Mission and the Cultural Assimilation of Christianity" in Sanneh, *Translating the Message*, 56–96.

162. Walls, "In Quest of the Father," 98–104.

163. See Sanneh, *Translating the Message*, 56–96.

Paul wrote, "There is no longer Jew or Greek, there is no longer slave or free, there is no longer male and female; for all of you are one in Christ Jesus" (Gal 3:28). To the Colossians, he said, "In that renewal [being renewed in knowledge according to the image of its creator] there is no longer Greek and Jew, circumcised and uncircumcised, barbarian, Scythian, slave and free; but Christ is all and in all!" (Col 3:10–11). Perhaps, Darrell L. Whiteman is right when he argued, "missiological anthropology as a discipline and contextualization as a method are important in Christian mission to combat ethnocentrism in missionaries and cultural imperialism in the missionary enterprise."[164] Because of ethnocentrism and cultural imperialism, the gospel has often become distorted. As hearers are "in the most varied socio-cultural situations," they must be able to defend the gospel meaningfully, even within the framework of religious pluralism.[165]

Several other accounts given in the Bible show that the gospel of Christ is intended to be for all people in all cultures. For instance, one account is the vision that the apostle Peter received from God to preach the gospel to Gentile Cornelius in Acts 10. Another is the decision of the first church council at Jerusalem in Acts 15, when the Gentile believers were granted the freedom to worship God and "turn towards Christ," without the requirement of keeping Jewish religious traditions.[166] Furthermore, the apostle Paul's writings take a clear and consistent multicultural church perspective, when Hellenistic Christians used their indigenous methods as the agent to translate the Messiah of Jewish tradition into their *Kyrios,* providing key marks in Christian history that the gospel is meant to be for all, "without first becoming culturally a Jew," because "no cultural enclave may be said to stand outside of God's salvific intentions."[167]

---

164. See Darrell L. Whiteman, "Models of Contextualization," in *Encyclopedia of Mission and Missionaries*, ed. Jonathan J. Bonk (New York, NY: Routledge, 2007), 90.

165. See Hans Waldenfels, "Contextual Theology," in *Dictionary of Mission: Theology, History, Perspectives*, ed. Karl Müller et al. (Maryknoll, NY: Orbis Books, 1997), 86. See also Lesslie Newbigin, *The Gospel in a Pluralist Society* (Grand Rapids, MI: Eerdmans, 1989); Scott W. Sunquist and Amos Yong, *The Gospel and Pluralism Today: Reassessing Lesslie Newbigin in the 21st Century* (Downers Grove, IL: IVP Academic, 2015).

166. Walls, *Cross-Cultural Process*, 273–277.

167. Skreslet, *Comprehending Mission*, 86.

Since Christianity is a "translated religion," the gospel message continues to be translated into many local cultures and languages. This is the ongoing process of Christianity's growth. Through history, Christianity became a force for translation, not just for the church, but for culture.[168] All cultures have the right to receive the message in their own tongues. Thus, the encounter with Asian cultures in the process of translatability makes Christianity an even more diverse, translated, and assimilated faith. In a discussion of contextualization in Asia, Hwa Yung argues that,

> true contextualization must hold together in proper tension the indigenous and the pilgrim principles [of Andrew Walls]. That means the gospel must be incarnated into Asian soil without losing its distinctiveness. A contextualization that ends up in unfaithfulness to "the faith that was once for all delivered to the saints," cannot claim to be a genuine incarnation of the gospel.[169]

As Christianity itself has been culturally assimilated, then according to Hwa Yung, we must ask which "distinctiveness" of the gospel and which "faith" will "be a genuine incarnation of the Gospel"? Kraft and other evangelicals rightly used "appropriate" as a better way of understanding both gospel and culture. At least, Western scholars and theologians were urged to step into a different, pluralistic, and spirits belief-worldview.[170] That means, "appropriate Christianity will, therefore, be a Christianity that is appropriate to the Scriptures, on the one hand, and appropriate to the people in a given cultural context, on the other."[171] But, the "appropriate" processes must see that Christianity is a faith and not a religion in which the gospel has been interpreted in distorted ways.[172] And when this faith finds a home in any culture, the people then embrace that faith authentically and genuinely, as their own; it is no longer a stranger or alien in their cultural context.

---

168. Jonathan J. Bonk, "The Defender of the Good News: Questioning Lamin Sanneh," *Christianity Today* (October 2003): 7–8.

169. Hwa Yung, "Banana Or Mango?," 194. This dissertation is published later as, *Mangoes or Bananas?*

170. See six "remaining issues" in Kraft, "Development of Contextualization Theory, 31–34.

171. Kraft, "Why Appropriate?," 4–5.

172. See Kraft, "Is Christianity a Religion or a Faith?," 83–98.

Chapters 1 and 2 Conclusion

From chapters 1 and 2, we see that contextualization of the gospel in the context of East Asia matters when it: (1) is understood as the process of theologizing (not borrowing) the meaning of the gospel in such a way that the people are able to communicate with God without the fear of "syncretism"; and (2) goes beyond the current "contextualization" discussion of mission theology to the point of knowing where and how God has been at work in the midst of the East Asians.

First, the gospel reveals that God came down in human flesh to make himself known among human beings (John 1:1). This evidence of God's incarnation through Jesus the Christ is the "massive" translation of the gospel into human history. Such "translatability" of the gospel is fundamental in shaping Christianity's origin and the ongoing process of Christianity's growth. The encounters with other cultures (Greek and other Gentiles) in the early period of Christianity reveal that these cultures were assimilated into Christianity. Such processes required early Christians (e.g. Origen,) to thoroughly examine both their own culture and their Christian faith.[173]

Second and more importantly, is the ability to see God in the midst of the East Asian people from the inside perspective. This means that as insiders, the people have acknowledged the notion of God whether in the *Đạo* (Way) as in Daoism, and in the *T'ien* (Heaven) and *Shang-ti* (Lord-on-High) as in Confucianism, long before the arrival of the Christian missionary (to be discussed in chapter 6). Such forms of the way and obeying the will of the way of the East Asian do not diminish the visibility of seeing the truth, or knowing God. Certainly, such divine forms are not to equate "pagan" unknown gods with the Christian God. But, these divine phenomena and understandings of "God" indicate that the people in East Asia are open to God's intent to be known. Perhaps, it also indicates that the people are ready to come into the full knowledge of God's incarnation, Jesus the Christ, at least in the case of Vietnam's spirituality, which is the subject of the next chapter.

---

173. For a study on how Origen "not only lived out his Christian faith within the context of his church and culture, but that his spirituality was also very much a product of his church and cultural context," see Adonis Abelard O. Gorospe, "Spirituality and Christianity," in *The Gospel in Culture: Contextualization Issues through Asian Eyes*, ed. Melba Padilla Maggay (Manila: OMF Literature Inc., and Institute for Studies in Asian Church and Culture, 2013), 107–125.

CHAPTER 3

Vietnamese Syncretistic Spirituality

The spiritual and religious landscape of Vietnam and East Asia before the arrival of European Christianity is complex, blending the cultural and religious aspects of local animistic beliefs, together with the Confucianist-Daoist-Buddhist teachings. This chapter focuses on how the Vietnamese syncretistic system of beliefs became the Vietnamese spirituality of today within the context of Asia, and particularly China. This complex system is an integrated matrix of local beliefs in God(s), spirits, the Confucianist-Daoist-Buddhist faith, and a syncretistic hybrid assimilation of both Oriental and Western philosophical and socio-religious aspects. This integrated form of Vietnamese spirituality is unique because it is adapted by what is called a "dual force" – resistance and assimilation – in its historical development.

There is resistance in the nature of the Vietnamese culture to adoption or assimilation (moderate accommodation) of one single complete religious doctrine. On the one hand, Vietnamese spirituality was able to resist some of the religio-cultural influences from the outside. On the other hand, this unique form of spirituality has synthesized (moderately assimilated) the essentials of the outside influences that appeal specifically to the Vietnamese. To investigate whether there is a such "dual force," two hypotheses are stated in the process to understand an integrated unique form of spirituality specific to the Vietnamese. First, is it possible that the failure to completely adopt a religion or tradition was indicative of a particularly Vietnamese cultural dimension that also gave birth to the special brand of Vietnamese syncretism? Second, if there is such a nature in Vietnamese culture, then, is it possible that this is also the reason why Christian contextualization efforts failed?

This chapter, therefore, first navigates the origin of Vietnamese popular beliefs before the thousand-year Northern Kingdom (China today) occupation. Then the chapter identifies the essential aspects of the Confucianist-Daoist-Buddhist faith, brought in by the outside, which were "Vietnamized" to create an integrated unique form of spirituality specific to the Vietnamese. This unique form can best be observed in the way Vietnamese understood the core values of the Confucianist-Daoist-Buddhist (*Nho-Lão-Phật*) faith in their written and oral folklore traditions, as well as in the new indigenous religious movements of colonial Vietnam, the Cao Dai (or Caodaism) in particular.

The sources investigated for this chapter include Vietnamese folklore, literary works, and other documents. Vietnamese literature has existed in both oral and written traditions (in classical Chinese, *chữ nôm*, and the Romanized *quốc ngữ*) providing concrete resources from which to look at common and daily expressions of the people.[1]

Popular Animist Beliefs

The belief in spirits of the early *Việt* people is the oldest and most popular form of Vietnamese spirituality which has survived to this day.[2] It is the basis for the tradition of ancestor veneration. The belief in spirits from the Premodern Vietnam period emerged in the midst of blending several internal and external influences.[3] This was a "highly dynamic and transformative

---

1. Classical (or original) Chinese (*chữ Hán* or *chữ nho* in Vietnamese); *chữ nôm* is the demotic script used to represent the Vietnamese vernacular; and *quốc ngữ* is the Romanized alphabet, which was developed by early European Catholic missionaries as a means to facilitate the transmission of their religious message, and it was soon taken up by their literate converts. In the oral tradition (*truyền thuyết*), the Vietnamese view of their world has been preserved, to some extent, in a rich tradition of Vietnamese folklore (*văn học dân gian*), including folk narratives (*truyện cổ tích* or *truyện đời xưa*), Buddhist tales (*tích Phật*), aphorisms (*cách ngôn*), folk ballads and folk songs (*ca dao và dân ca*).

2. For an excellent study on cults venerating particular material objects – trees, rocks, landmarks, boundary, limits, hillocks, and other topographical features, see Léopold Cadière, *Croyances et pratiques religieuses des Viêtnamiens*, vol. 2 (Saigon; Paris: Ecole Française d'Extrême-Orient, 1955). Here, Cadière carefully employs philology to capture the Vietnamese concept of supernatural beings (on popular beliefs and practices found in Nguon Son valley of central Vietnam) – *ma, quỉ, thần, thiên*, and *con* – that make up their complex animist pantheon (cultural notions about animals and plants).

3. Some regional cultures are thought to have begun in the Southern region (the north of Vietnam today) before the third century BCE, (including the Sơn Vĩ culture in 18,000 BCE, the Hoà Bình culture in 10,000 BCE, and the Bắc Sơn culture in 8,000 BCE). Continuing

period" for northern Vietnam in which its southern indigenous society was stimulated externally by political, social, economic, religious, and cultural forces, and responded internally by "absorbing many of these elements into its own culture."[4] During these centuries of the first millennium CE, a number of Vietnamese patterns for later periods were set, including "the use of Chinese characters in writing, chopsticks for eating, money in the form of Chinese copper cash, and the Tang dynasty's poetry and laws."[5] Nevertheless, what we know about the *Việt* culture in these centuries consists of myths, legends, and traditions related to the history of Daoist, Confucianist, and Buddhist influences in Southern (Vietnamese) regional history.[6]

The early folk narratives, including *Việt điện u linh tập* (Departed spirits of the Viet realm), and *Lĩnh nam chích quái liệt truyện* (Arrayed tales of collected oddities from south of the passes) in particular are the sources to investigate the Vietnamese belief in spirits. These folk narratives were officially

---

with the Phùng Nguyên culture in 3,000 BCE, the Văn Lang or Lạc Việt (Hùng kings) in 1000 BCE, the Đông Sơn culture the Proto-Chàm culture in 500 BCE, and the iron-melting and forging techniques in upper Red River valley in 400 BCE, up to 1000 CE), it is obvious that a long period of "premodern" Vietnam existed, which paralleled the Northern Chinese Empire period. The *Premodern* Vietnam period is that during which the Viet people struggled against Northern domination (up to the tenth century, 939 CE), and finally established an independent nation under five different dynasties: Ngô, Đinh, Lê, Lý and Trần from the tenth to fourteenth centuries. The second period or *Early Modern* Vietnam, includes the fifteenth to nineteenth centuries, during which there was the expansion of the southward influence, encroaching upon existing populations of the Cham and Khmer ethnic groups under the Nguyễn dynasty. The last period or *Modern* Vietnam is that time in which Vietnamese literature found fresh, new ways to express itself in the vernacular Vietnamese, the *quốc ngữ*. For scholars and readers who want to know more about Vietnamese traditions, they can see the literature in Vietnam in three periods: Premodern, Early Modern, and Modern. I am indebted to Profs. Dutton, Werner, and Whitmore for their designations *"Premodern Vietnam," "Early Modern Vietnam,"* and *"Modern Vietnam"* to view Vietnamese literature in this way. For the full chronology, see Dutton, Werner, and Whitmore, *Sources of Vietnamese Tradition*, xxi–xxxiv.

4. Dutton, Werner, and Whitmore, *Sources of Vietnamese Tradition*, 4, 11. According to these scholars, Vietnam's own political style, at least from the Lý epoch, only formed after blending those internal and external influences to be a replica of the Northern state. However, the general geographical referents North and South are used to designate the peoples and polities of the Chinese and Vietnamese realms. The terms "China" and "Vietnam," whose modern territorial and political implications are readily apparent, are much less useful when discussing pre-twentieth-century geography.

5. Dutton, Werner, and Whitmore, *Sources of Vietnamese Tradition*, xxi–xxxiv.

6. See *The Birth of Vietnam*, Appendix O, "Sources for Early Vietnamese History," 349–359. See the Chinese sources, for instance, in Taylor (*Birth of Vietnam*, and *History of the Vietnamese*).

recognized by the royal court during the Lý and Trần dynasties.[7] They are not only the best sources – through many myths, legends and traditions – to present a real picture of the *Việt* people and culture of the premodern period, but are also the best sources on the origin and development of the Vietnamese people. These folk narratives frequently express various aspects of Vietnamese culture such as belief in spirits, religious practices, philosophical perceptions, social relationships, behaviors, and ways of self-expression.[8]

Belief in the Twenty-Seven Spirits

The Vietnamese have had the tradition of expressing gratitude and honor to good people who demonstrated excellent moral conduct as seen in putting communal and national interests above their own. This tradition of belief in spirits has been used to explain the reasons for certain phenomena which are recorded in *Việt điện u linh tập* (Departed spirits of the Viet realm," *VĐULT* hereafter).[9] The twenty-seven spirits, described in this collection of stories, are arranged under three headings: *Sovereigns, Ministers* and *the Spirits from Nature*.[10] They were venerated by the Vietnamese as the earliest form of spirit belief. Because of the existence of temples and shrines for the worship of deities in the land of *Việt* at the time, Lý Tế Xuyên questioned: "Have there ever been many to manifest signs of greatness and to secretly

---

[7]. Keith Weller Taylor, *The Birth of Vietnam* (Berkeley, CA: University of California Press, 1983), 354.

[8]. Công Huyền Tôn Nữ Nha Trang, *Vietnamese Folklore: An Introductory and Annotated Bibliography* (Berkeley, CA: Center for South and Southeast Asia Studies, University of California, 1970), x.

[9]. This 27-story collection compiled by Lý Tế Xuyên is divided into three parts: Lịch Đại Đế Vương (Sovereigns) (6 stories), Lịch Đại Phụ Thần (Ministers) (11 stories), and Hạo Khí Anh Linh (the Spirits from Nature) (10 stories). This collection is based on manuscript number A.751 and translated by Lê Hữu Mục and published in 1960 in Saigon. English translated version by Brian E. Ostrowski and Brian A. Zottoli under Cornell University's Southeast Asia Program in 1999.

[10]. The *Records Declaring the Ultimate* of the *VĐULT* (1329) was the major text of the early Lý dynasty in which the royal tradition was expressed as "the indigenous spirit beliefs with the continuity of localized Sinic power." See Dutton, Werner, and Whitmore, *Sources of Vietnamese Tradition*, 33–46. From the 10th and the 14th centuries, Buddhist poems were written by religious figures, including Khương Việt (993–1011), Vạn Hạnh (d.1025), Lý Thái Tông, Cửu Chi (1050s) of the *Eminent Monks of the Thiền Community* (1337) in such ways that express Đại Việt's Buddhist belief system.

assist the living?"[11] he believed, nevertheless, that the supernatural powers of these spirits may have manifested themselves: "Some have been the spiritual essences of mountains and streams, or other powerful and divine figures."[12] Thus, these spirits represent the reflection of the Vietnamese perception of reality or the world as it is.

The spirits of the *Sovereigns* and the *Ministers*, such as Sĩ Nhiếp, Phùng Hưng, Triệu Quang Phục, the Trưng Sisters, Lý Thường Kiệt, and so forth, were venerated as "fully" human figures, even after their death. These were real people in Vietnamese history. The living people were praying for assistance from these spirits, a popular practice in this belief system. Other spirits were from *Nature,* including the Goddess of the Earth, the Spirit of *Phù Đổng* (*Thánh Gióng*), the Mountain Spirit and the Water Spirit (*Sơn Tinh* and *Thuỷ Tinh*), and so forth. These are considered myths because of a lack of historical facts, but they help to explain certain realities of the supernatural forces in which the Vietnamese believed. Their daily encounter with nature in the early agricultural culture of wet rice, was reflected in the way they honored "the God of Agriculture, who taught the people to plant rice during the Chu times (1066–255 BCE)"[13] Therefore, the respect and honor shown to the spirits of their saints and heroes, as well as to supernatural forces in nature as recorded in *VĐULT*, demonstrates the rich and varied expressions of the Vietnamese spiritual life. Such animist beliefs have been popular up to this day, especially in the belief and practice of venerating ancestral spirits.

Ancestor Veneration

The Vietnamese have kept the tradition of venerating their ancestors through different tales which are told in *LNCQLT*.[14] For instance, in the legend of *Lạc Long Quân* in the "Tale of the Hồng Bàng Clan," the Vietnamese are proud, calling themselves *con rồng cháu tiên* (or *Long Phụ Tiên Mẫu*) – offspring of

---

11. See Lý Tế Xuyên, *Departed Spirits of the Viet Realm* [Việt Điện U Linh Tập], trans. Brian E. Ostrowski and Brian A. Zottoli, Southeast Asia Program (Ithaca, NY: Cornell University, 1999).

12. Lý Tế Xuyên, *Departed Spirits of the Viet Realm*, iii, 2.

13. Lý Tế Xuyên, *Departed Spirits of the Viet Realm*, 21.

14. See Trần Thế Pháp, *Lĩnh nam chích quái liệt truyện (Arrayed tales of collected oddities from south of the passes)*. Both Chinese and English translations of *LNCQLT* are available at "Translations of Vietnamese Historical Texts," History Department, University of Hawaii at Manoa, https://sites.google.com/a/hawaii.edu/viet-texts/home, accessed 14 April 2014.

a dragon and a goddess/princess, a myth of Vietnamese origin. According to the earliest oral traditions of the Vietnamese revealed in the *LNCQLT*, in the *Tale of the Hồng Bàng Clan*, Lạc Long Quân (literally Dragon Lord of the Lạc), was a hero who came to the Hồng river and became the second king of the Hồng Bàng dynasty. He seized Âu Cơ from a mountain of the Northern Kingdom to be his wife.[15] Eventually Âu Cơ gave birth to a pouch containing one hundred eggs, which became one hundred children. The Vietnamese are said to be the *Lạc*, the descendants of the Dragon Lord.[16] Subsequently, fifty children went with their mother back to the mountain and fifty followed their father to the sea. Their eldest son was made king of *Văn Lang*, which was located in the northwest Red River Delta region near the Chinese border and was claimed by the Vietnamese as their first kingdom. This son ruled in Mê Linh, taking the name of *Kinh Dương*, and inaugurated the first Vietnamese dynasty, the *Hùng*, which was comprised of eighteen generations of kings.[17] Today, the Vietnamese honor their ancestors and pay their respects through regional and national rituals, and annual festivals. The ancestor venerating tradition runs deeply in the life of the people, both in literature and in their spiritual practices even today. More importantly, these tales of ancestors give identity and guidance to the understanding of Vietnamese culture.

Syncretistic Spirituality

There has been an ongoing process of assimilation of sociopolitical and religio-cultural dimensions (a form of contextualization?) between the early Vietnamese folk beliefs and the three teachings of Confucianism (*Nho*), Daoism (*Đạo* or *Lão*), and Buddhism (*Phật*), all of which came from the outside. This process of assimilation has influenced the philosophical thoughts, religious beliefs, and socio-political ideas of the Vietnamese at all levels of Vietnamese society. Such a syncretistic contextualizing process appears visibly

---

15. Trần Thế Pháp, *Lĩnh nam chích quái liệt truyện* [Arrayed tales of collected oddities from south of the passes], (n.d.), 12–15.

16. See Trần Thế Pháp, *Lĩnh nam chích quái liệt truyện*.

17. See Trần Quốc Vượng, ed. *Việt sử lược* [Short history of Dai Viet] (1960. Reprint, Huế: Nxb Thuận Hoá, 2005). Trần Quốc Vượng, "Về danh hiệu 'Hùng Vương,'" in *Hùng Vương dựng nước* [King Hung established the nation], ed. Uỷ ban Khoa học Xã hội (Hà Nội: Khoa học Xã hội, 1973), 353–355; Taylor, *Birth of Vietnam*, 3.

in the three teachings' examinations in the sociopolitical realm and in the stele inscriptions in village temples in the religio-cultural realm.[18] The syncretistic (accommodating) nature had a critical impact that went far beyond the borders of China, shaping the worldviews of diverse East Asian societies.

Encountering the Three Teachings

In the late second century CE, the Southern region (or *Giao Chỉ*, which is northern Vietnam today) encountered the Northern (Chinese) patterns of thought and belief, including Confucianism, Daoism and Buddhism.[19] Because Vietnam was a small country, bordering this Northern Kingdom (or China today), the South (the Vietnamese) struggled in their relationship with the Northern dynasties. Thus, the Northern sociopolitical and religio-cultural patterns directly or indirectly influenced the South (the Vietnamese). Nevertheless, while both the Northern (Chinese) and local thought included ideas from the Five Classics of Confucianism and the classical thought that dominated the Han dynasty, Daoist influence was apparent in ideas about abstinence and the search for immortality.[20] There is no record of when Daoism arrived in Vietnam, but it seems to have already existed when Mou Bo (*Mâu Tử*) from the North arrived in the South. In his *Li hou lun*, Mou Bo based his objections toward the Daoist and spiritualists of that time on Confucianism. Mou Bo's *Li hou lun* may be the earliest example of Confucianist-Daoist (and later, Buddhist) syncretism in *Giao Chỉ* in the early days of the thousand-year period of Northern dominance (up to the tenth century, 939 CE):

> At that time, after the death of [the Han] Emperor Ling [189], the empire was in disorder; only Jiao Province (or *Giao Chỉ*) was relatively calm, and unusual men from the North came to live there. Many occupied themselves with the worship of gods and spirits, abstinence from cereals, and immortality. Many people of that time devoted themselves to these studies. Mou

---

18. For instance, the existence of a temple dedicated to the Three Teachings remained even at the end of the sixteenth century. See Nguyen Nam, "Writing as Response and as Translation: 'Jiandeng Xinhua' and the Evolution of the Chuanqi Genre in East Asia, Particularly in Vietnam" PhD diss., (Harvard University, 2005), 300. Since the Lý dynasty in 1195 it could be considered the first official notice of the combination of the Three Teachings in Vietnam.
19. Dutton, Werner, and Whitmore, *Sources of Vietnamese Tradition*, 16.
20. Dutton, Werner, and Whitmore, 16.

Bo unceasingly proposed objections based on the Five Classics; none of the Daoist and spiritualists dared argue with him.[21]

The encounter brought new challenges to the philosophical thought and the religions of the North which were brought into the South by some unusual men including Mou Bo (*Mâu Tử*), a Confucianist who came to the South to learn about Vietnamese Buddhism which came from India. Thus, Confucianism was introduced to Vietnam during the later Han dynasty (25–220 CE).[22]

Although Confucianism was brought into the South by the Northern people like Mou Bo, "the worship of gods and spirits," and especially Buddhism, had already made a major contribution into the life of the Southern people in terms of philosophy and religion. Buddhism in Vietnam (*Giao Chỉ*/ Jiaozhou/ Jiaozhi) had come through international trade with Central Asia, and was recognized as being ahead of that found in the Northern Kingdom.[23] Although there was no record when this version of Buddhism arrived in the Southern region, it seems that it had come before Confucianism and Daoism. By 480 CE, Tan Qian (542–607), a Buddhist master from Central Asia, reported to the Qi court that,

> the area of Jiaozhou has long been in communication with Tianzhu [India]. Early on, when the Buddha-Dharma reached Jiangdong (which was the capital of the state of Qi) and still had not been established [there], in Luy Lau (the main port area of Giao Chỉ, in the central Red River Delta) more than twenty

---

21. Mou Bo, *Li hou lun*, 1; trans. Taylor, *Birth of Vietnam*, 81 (quoted in Dutton, Werner, and Whitmore, *Sources of Vietnamese Tradition*, 16.)

22. Yao, *Introduction to Confucianism*, xv.

23. Jiaozhou/ Jiaozhi (or Giao Chỉ) which is northern Vietnam today was a far region in the South during the Han dynasty in the North (206 BCE – 220 CE). This imperial proclamation came to Shi Xie (Sĩ Nhiếp) a local strongman of Northern decent in Jiaozhou/Jiaozhi, saying, "Jiaozhou is a very distant region, so far beyond the rivers and seas to the south, a place where our beneficence can barely reach and whence the gratitude of the people can hardly flow back. It has come to our attention that the rebellious Liu Biao, viceroy of Zhang province directly to the north, has had the effrontery to have appointed Lai Gong to office and that he has his ambitious eye on our southern lands. Thus we now charge you to become our General of the gentlemen of the Household Who Comforts the South, in charge of all seven commandries, maintaining as before your authority as Grand Administrator of Jiaozhi," (Wu zhi 4, in Chen Shu, *San guo zhi*, trans. O'Harrow, "Men of Hu," 262), cited by Dutton, Werner, and Whitmore, *Sources of Vietnamese Tradition*, 11–12.

previous temples had [already] been built, more than five hundred monks had [already] been ordained and fifteen volumes of scriptures had [already] been translated [from Sanskrit into Chinese].[24]

The Southern region was already so rich in local spirit cults and folk beliefs. Many tales of the rivalry between the mountain and the stream, and the land and the water were recorded in *VĐULT*. Buddhism, then Confucianism and Daoism, by the ninth century, had enriched the process of constructing Vietnam's early philosophical and religious life. The early stage of the *Đại Việt* monarchy[25] closely embraced the Buddhist ethos and religious practices.[26] Confucianism played a major role in the socio-political realm throughout the Vietnamese imperial courts of early modern Vietnam, however, the Buddhist community had grown strong, as was evident in their building of temples and occupying of lands for its growing population in the eleventh and twelfth centuries.[27]

In the new Trần dynasty and later the Hồ dynasty from the thirteenth century, Buddhism together with other local spirit cults, offered a blended picture of the *Việt* people and its belief system. The three traditions of Confucianism, Daoism, and Buddhism were interrelated in complex philosophical ways in political and religio-cultural aspects of the Vietnamese culture.[28] For instance, during the Lý and the Trần dynasties, in order to pass the civil service examinations, a candidate had to know Buddhist and Daoist doctrines besides the

---

24. No direct evidence when Buddhism arrived in Vietnam, but this quotation is indirect evidence. This was later recorded in *Eminent Monk of the Thien Community* (1337), which appeared in *Thien uyen tap anh*, 20b; trans. adapted from Nguyen Tu Cuong, *Zen in Medieval Vietnam: A Study and Translation of the Thien Uyen Tap Anh* (Honolulu: University of Hawai'i Press, 1997), 129. Quoted in Dutton, Werner, and Whitmore, *Sources of Vietnamese Tradition*, 18.

25. *Đại Việt* (Great Viet): the establishment of Đại Việt's monarchy from the mid-tenth century to the mid-eleventh century was gradually being shaped as a result of the Tang dynasty in the north losing its control over various parts of the South, including northern Vietnam. Before the monarchy took shape, the "pattern of regionalism" emerged in the land of Viet among local chiefs who vied with one another for dominance. See Dutton, Werner, and Whitmore, *Sources of Vietnamese Tradition*, 28–31.

26. Works of literature in these epochs reflect the establishment of the Đại Việt monarchy from the mid-tenth century to the mid-eleventh century. See Dutton, Werner, and Whitmore, *Sources of Vietnamese Tradition*, 28–31.

27. Dutton, Werner, and Whitmore, 77.

28. Nguyen Nam, "Writing as Response," 293–294.

Confucian doctrine – no differentiation was made between the politically correct doctrine and the superstitious doctrine – one could not pass the exam without a broad education.[29]

A significant marker of Vietnamese imperial interest in Confucian orthodoxy was the Temple of Literature (*Văn Miếu*) built in Thăng Long (Hà Nội today) to honor the men who had achieved academic success in the civil service examinations.[30] The Temple was the central site for Confucian learning and ritual in *Đại Việt* in the fifteenth century, and remained the focus for the public recognition of scholarly achievement until the early twentieth century, when the examinations were finally abandoned.[31] Below is a mid-seventeenth century example of the wording on a commemorative stele erected in honor of those scholars who were successful on the examination held in 1623, showing the court's adherence to Confucian principles in its selecting of officials:

> These steles are chiefly the pillars of the names of the enlightened and the foundations of the Way of constant obligations or morality, and those who contemplate them will have some standards and also know what they must guard against. Truly, this has benefits for the [Vietnamese] emperor's system of governance for a hundred million years, and it will mean that our country will be eternally stable and secure like the great stones of Mount Tai.[32]

The relationship between Confucianism and Buddhism fluctuated, but they coexisted relatively peacefully from the fifteenth century, during the

---

29. See Phan Huy Chú's remark qouted in Vu Van Vinh, "Development of Confucianism in the Tran Dynasty and the Struggle of Confucian Scholars against Buddhism at the End of the XIV Century," *Vietnam Social Science* 2 (1999): 56.

30. Dutton, Werner, and Whitmore, *Sources of Vietnamese Tradition*, 200. These examinations were designed to serve as the basis for appointment to high positions in the bureaucracy, although more generally they provided an avenue for social advancement and prestige. The regular holding of examinations as a means of finding qualified officials began in the fifteenth century, and the triennial examination system itself was initiated in 1463.

31. Dutton, Werner, and Whitmore, *Sources of Vietnamese Tradition*, 108–109.

32. See "Temple of Literature Stele for the Examination of 1623" in *Le trieu lich khoa tien si de danh bi ky*, 136–137; Do Van Ninh, *Van bia Quoc Tu Giam Ha Noi*, 251–255, trans. George Dutton with Mathew Cochran (quoted in Dutton, Werner, and Whitmore, *Sources of Vietnamese Tradition*, 200–203.) Mount Tai is one of the sacred mountains of China.

Lê and Mạc epochs.³³ When Lê Thánh Tông (r.1460-1497) came to power, a new model of political control for Đại Việt was introduced. The new emperor established

> the triennial Confucian examination system, a centralized administration based on the Northern six ministries model, a provincial system reaching down into the countryside, and a regime of paperwork that made "legible" the realm's human and material resources through the creation of written records.³⁴

The Three Teachings indeed integrated and formed a syncretistic belief system in the Vietnamese spiritual life during the Lê dynasty (1428-1788).³⁵ Although Buddhism was not the central religion of the court of the Lê dynasty, the Buddhist temples and rituals remained spiritually significant across the realm.³⁶

Rationalizing the Essentials

The syncretistic belief system with its resisting and assimilating natures, is best revealed through a number of stele inscriptions (*văn bia*), particularly the stele inscription of the Three Teachings Temple (*Tam Giáo Tự*).³⁷ There were about 148 extant inscriptions from the Mạc dynasty (1528-1592), showing how Vietnamese Confucians viewed their predecessors' attitudes towards the other religions, and rationalized their involvements in their local communities' religious activities.³⁸ Though their aim was to preserve their Confucian

---

33. In 1428, Lê Lợi (Lê Thái Tổ [r.1428-1433], a local cheiftain based in the village of Mount Lâm, drove out the Ming's occupation (1407-1427) and became the king of a restored Đại Việt, whose capital was Thăng Long, forming the new aristocracy.

34. Dutton, Werner, and Whitmore, *Sources of Vietnamese Tradition*, 90.

35. One may need to look at the major law code of the transitional period in the history, the *Quốc Triều Hình Luật* (National Penal Code) to understand Vietnamese society during the Lê dynasty

36. Dutton, Werner, and Whitmore, *Sources of Vietnamese Tradition*, 106-109.

37. This inscription was very special because it was "built for and named as the Three Teachings [which] has never existed before." See Vũ Tuấn Sán and Đinh Khắc Thuân, "Bài văn bia tạo tượng Tam Giáo, chùa Cao Dương của Trình Quốc Công" [The stele inscription on the statues of the Three Teachings at Cao Duong Pagoda by Trinh Quoc Cong], *Tạp Chí Hán Nôm (Journal of Han-Nom Studies)* 1, no. 8 (1990): 85; Đinh Khắc Thuân, *Văn Bia Thời Mạc* [Stele Inscriptions of the Mac Period], (Hà Nội: Nxb Khoa học Xã hội, 1996), 335, quoted in Nguyen Nam, "Writing as Response," 300.

38. Nguyen Nam, "Writing as Response," 295.

primacy, the Confucians were willing to integrate elements of Daoist and Buddhist essential teachings into their Confucian ideology, thus the "common threads" woven through the Three Teachings.[39] Similarly to the Confucians of the early Han emperors (in China), Vietnamese Confucians from the Mạc dynasty were more or less forced to accommodate the Daoist and Buddhist spiritual practices, especially in village communal life. At the same time they had to maintain their Confucian orthodoxy in order to keep up their tradition as literati (*nhà Nho*) and their eligibility to serve at the court of the Mạc dynasty (social-political correctness). Eventually, in 1592, the Nguyễn and another Trịnh clan swept across the Red River Delta and drove out the Mạc, restoring the Lê (1592–1789) to the throne. Nevertheless, Vietnamese Confucians and Daoist/ Buddhist communities coexisted peacefully.

When Confucianism arrived in Vietnam, the dimensions of adaptation and transformation had developed into variation, creating a Vietnamese contextual Confucian tradition.[40] Vietnamese literati were playing a major role in integrating Confucianism with Daoism and Buddhism. Moreover, whenever invited to produce inscriptions for special occasions (the inauguration of a new temple, or the renovation of a pagoda), these Vietnamese Confucians, were able on behalf of Buddhist or Daoist communities, to speak in the voice of the other beliefs. This honorable task was given to Vietnamese Confucians because, as village intellectuals they played the central role in uniting and leading people in various public affairs; and as villagers, they shared in the community's multi-dimensional spiritual life.[41] In fact, by the early sixteenth century, the Neo-Confucian ideals were adopted by Vietnamese Confucian literati. "These orthodox Neo-Confucian ideals had strongly affected the intellectual and cultural patterns of the Vietnamese elite and, through them, began to change the way of life of the population at large."[42] Nevertheless,

---

39. Nguyen Nam, 292–295. During the Mạc dynasty, particularly in the reign of Mạc Đăng Dung begun 1527, many Vietnamese literati were put in a difficult position as they found themselves resisting more fundamental questions about "duty, religion, morality and social order."

40. The Confucian evolution has gone through five stages or dimensions: formation, adaptation, transformation, variation, and renovation, see in Yao, *Introduction to Confucianism*, 7–9.

41. Nguyen Nam, "Writing as Response," 296–297.

42. John K. Whitmore, "Social Organization and Confucian Thought in Vietnam," *Journal of Southeast Asian Studies* 2, no. 15 (1984): 296–306. Further understanding of Vietnamese

there was a common understanding between Confucians and Buddhists of "the goodness of human beings" so that as a result, there were a number of Confucian literati composing texts for inscriptions at the local Buddhist temples.[43]

The stele inscription of the Three Teachings Temple (*Tam Giáo Tự*) quoted below was composed by the most prominent Confucian of the sixteenth century, Nguyễn Bỉnh Khiêm (1491–1585), showing how a Confucian could integrate core teachings (common threads) of the three teachings.

> The ancient temple Thụy Anh at Cao Dương (Thái Bình) has long shown spiritual efficacy ... Now, the village literati Bùi Tử Trang, Nguyễn Lễ, Tống Mộc, Nguyễn Lãm, together with monks and nuns contributed money, and directed craftsmen to cast the precious statues of the Three Teaching and Miao Shan (Diệu Thiện).[44]
>
> After finishing the work, they asked me to compose the inscriptions to record the event. I also have a mind and heart fond of doing good, and dare not refuse. However, I am a Confucian. Although I am not well versed in Buddhism and Daoism, I have read broadly and dispelled my doubts and learned something of their theories. Generally speaking, the Buddhist teaching is rooted in illuminating physical forms and the mind, and analyzing cause and effect. Daoism is based on concentrating on the vital energy (*khí*) to make it supple, preserving oneness and keeping to genuineness. The sage of Confucius rooted his teachings in morality, benevolence and righteousness, literature, life's realities, loyalty, and good faith.

---

society at this time, one may need to look at the major law code of the transitional period in the history, the *Quốc Triều Hình Luật* (National Penal Code) of the Lê dynasty (1428–1788).

43. Dutton, Werner, and Whitmore, *Sources of Vietnamese Tradition*, 113–114.

44. Miao Shan (Guan Yin, or Quan Âm Nam Hải [Avalokitesvara of the South Sea] in Vietnamese) was worshipped popularly in the sixteenth century in Vietnam. Her statues could be found in both Buddhist pagodas and Daoist temples, for instance, in the Daoist temple Hoài Linh (Hà Tây province). See Đinh Khắc Thuân, "Contribution à l'histoire de la Mac (1527-1592) du Viet Nam" [Contribution to the History of the Mac (1527–1592) of Vietnam], (Ecole des hautes études en sciences sociales, 2000), 277.

Aren't all of them the teachings that follow human nature in order to cultivate the Way (đạo)?

Miao Shan got her reputation because of her goodness, which is nothing but the dwelling place of the mind and heart and human nature . . .

Accordingly, I have inscribed this on a solid piece of stone so that the transmission of their teaching shall endure through the ages. The inscription reads as follow,

> What Heaven imparts to man is called human nature
> To follow our nature is called the Way.
> It is rooted in the Mind and lodged in the Teachings.
> The forms through which it has been bequeathed to us are full of dignity,
> Eternal and ageless as Heaven.[45]

The statement "However, I am a Confucian" as stated above, reveals that Nguyễn Bỉnh Khiêm and other Vietnamese Confucians were not only affirming their Confucian identity, but they were also expected to comprehend common threads in the Three Teachings and the belief in Miao Shan (goodness).[46] More importantly, Nguyễn Bỉnh Khiêm revealed an attitude of religious accommodation toward the essential teachings of Buddhism and Daoism, and of Miao Shan which led him to a syncretistic conclusion "Aren't all of them the teachings that follow human nature in order to cultivate the Way (Đạo)." In fact, Trần Trọng Kim who regarded Confucianism as the "national essence" of Vietnam, believed that the essence of Confucianism started from the Way (Đạo).

> If humans adopt the middle course, behave according to the Way of Heaven (Đạo), and nurture their feelings, they will acquire

---

45. Nguyen Nam, "Writing as Response," 298–300. Han Nom Institute Library, nos. 2669–2697; trans. Nguyen Nam, "Being Confucian in Sixteenth Century Vietnam," 143. This quote is also appeared in Dutton, Werner, and Whitmore, *Sources of Vietnamese Tradition*, 115.

46. Nguyễn Bỉnh Khiêm was invited to compose the inscription on the occasion of making images of Buddha, Laozi, and Confucius, and Miao Shan at this Three Teaching Temple (*Tam Giáo Tự*).

benevolence (*nhân*). If, by means of self-cultivation, a person acquires benevolence, he will have a lively spirit, be able to distinguish right from wrong, and will always act in accordance with the law of Heaven and Earth. If *benevolence* is combined with *honesty* (*tín*), this person will become a sage. Honesty is in keeping with the natural path (way) of Heaven and Earth. An honest person is someone who has become pure, akin to the initial nature given to him by Heaven. Such a person comprehends the nature of all creatures and is capable of contributing to the creation and raising of humans by Heaven and Earth. He is on an equal footing with Heaven and Earth and is therefore considered to be a sage. This is the essence of Confucianism. All other notions, such as filial piety, righteousness, rites, wisdom, loyalty to the emperor, and trust, derive from this.[47]

One of the core teachings of Confucianism, benevolence (*nhân*), and the Buddhist virtue of goodness (*thiện*)[48] were addressed in the "Inscription of the Statues of the Three Teachings" above. Like Nguyễn Bỉnh Khiêm, other Vietnamese Confucians in the sixteenth century were also able to draw out the essentials of Buddhism and integrate them harmoniously, as seen in the following two stele inscriptions:

> As a Confucian, I do not adore Buddhism. However, I am fond of joining people in doing good things, thus, I dare not reject their demands [for an inscription].[49]

> I often hear the words "advocating goodness as the master." So I taught the *Shujing* [Book of Documents]. How can those who want to do good things not seek the truth from these words?[50]

---

47. Trần Trọng Kim, *Nho giáo* [Confucianism] (Sàigòn: Nxb Tân Việt, n.d.), i, ix–x, xii–xiii, xv–xvii, xix–xx, xxii–xxvi, 389–372, trans. Luu Doan Huynh, Jayne Werner, and John Whitemore, quoted in Dutton, Werner, and Whitmore, *Sources of Vietnamese Tradition*, 414–424.

48. In his stele inscription, Nguyễn Bỉnh Khiêm already recognized "goodness" (*thiện*) in Miao Shan (*Diệu Thiện*).

49. See Trần Quý Túc, *Stele Inscription of the Pagoda Thiên Hựu, 1571*, in Đinh Khắc Thuân, *Văn Bia Thời Mạc*, 148–150 (quoted in Nguyen Nam, "Writing as Response," 305).

50. See Tô Quý Khê, *Stele Inscription of the Pagoda Sùng Ân, 1578*, 182–183 (quoted in Nguyen Nam, "Writing as Response," 305).

Most importantly, the poem at the end of Nguyễn Bỉnh Khiêm's inscription reveals the syncretistic nature of the Vietnamese religious belief system, though Vietnamese Confucians had seen benevolence among other Confucian moral values as the logic for syncretism.[51] That means the essence of the Three Teachings (humaneness, benevolence, or goodness) is the way (following the path, or "the Way of Heaven" according to Trần Trọng Kim) to concede Heaven, as the Eternal and ageless One who imparts the forms of full dignity in our human nature.[52] Thus, heaven (*Thiên*), that is mentioned in this poem, is identified by Nguyễn Bỉnh Khiêm indeed as the Supreme Lord (*Thượng đế*), a concept which became very popular in sixteenth-century Vietnam.[53] The transcendent *Thiên* (heaven) is the one who "has given human goodness; [all people] must hold fast to their natural disposition."[54] Goodness, therefore, can be rewarded and evil will be judged by heaven, according to the Buddhist principle of karmic retribution and cause-and-effect,[55] and so worshiping *heaven* became a common ritual in Vietnamese religious belief system.

Belief in Heaven and Other Folk Beliefs

The teachings of Confucianism, Daoism and Buddhism have influenced the life of the Vietnamese, as seen in the belief in heaven and the traditional folk beliefs.

The belief in Heaven (*Thiên/Thượng đế*, or *Ông Trời* in common language) was one of the most prominent Daoist-Confucian influences on the life of the Vietnamese people, both in the practices of the royal courts and of the common people. As in China, the Confucian Vietnamese traditional government was, by nature, a theo-political entity, and functioned with the religious belief that political power was endowed by heaven and that heaven

---

51. Nguyen Nam, "Writing as Response," 306. Nguyen Nam believed that based on the thought of the *Zhongyong* (*Doctrine of the mean*), the poem at the end of the inscription considers "the syncretism in the spirit of Confucianism."

52. For the transcendental features of the *Zhongyong* (*Doctrine of the mean*), see Chan, "Spiritual Dimensions: The Doctrine of the Mean," in *A Source Book in Chinese Philosophy*. Tu, *Centrality and Commonality*.

53. *Tian/Thiên* was accorded with the cult of *Ngọc Hoàng Thượng Đế* (Great Lord – Jade Emperor) was popular in Vietnam in the sixteenth century, as well as in the Cao Dai in the 20th century. For the cult of *Ngọc Hoàng Thượng Đế*, see Đinh Khắc Thuân, "Contribution à l'histoire de la Mac (1527–1592) du Viet Nam," 275–284.

54. Tu, *Centrality and Commonality*, quoted in Nguyen Nam, "Writing as Response," 308.

55. Nguyen Nam, "Writing as Response," 308.

sanctioned political decisions legitimately.⁵⁶ This was called *the Mandate of Heaven*.⁵⁷ Thus, "in this respect all state affairs were religious and all religious practices had a political significance."⁵⁸

Though influenced heavily by Buddhism, Buddhist religious activities were greatly limited by King Lê Thánh Tông, as well the *Gia Long* emperor in 1804.⁵⁹ The belief in heaven's favor made an impact on Lê Thánh Tông as he changed the title of his reign from *Quảng Thuận* (Conforming [to Heaven's Will]) to *Hồng Đức* (Overflowing Virtue) in 1469. King Lê Thánh Tông then began to establish the ritual for Venerating heaven as the Sacrifice to Heaven (*Giao Lễ* or *Nam Giao*),⁶⁰ in which the king, as the representative of the entire population, offered a solemn sacrifice, a royal ritual that continued until the twentieth century.⁶¹

---

56. Yao, *Introduction to Confucianism*, 196; Küng and Ching, *Christianity and Chinese Religions*, 133. Ching believes that in the Confucian classics, Lord-on-high has referred to a supreme deity, while Heaven has sometimes been given a progenitor's or creator's role, as that which gives birth to all things. The term Heaven did not completely disappear from Taoist philosophical writings, appearing especially in Chuang-tzu alongside the term Tao, but "Tao" has obviously taken over "Heaven" in Lao-tzu, as the natural Way as well as the human way, even the political way. If the Tao is no longer a personal deity, it remains as a model for human behavior.

57. If people behaved in morally upright ways and the ruler did well, Heaven responded by creating harmony through appropriate weather patterns, fertility, and general wellness. It thereby showed its approval and granted the dynasty the right to rule, known as the "Mandate of Heaven." See "the Yijing or *Book of Changes*" in Livia Kohn, *Introducing Daoism* (State College, PA: Journal of Buddhist Ethics Online Books, 2008), 4–7.

58. Yao, *Introduction to Confucianism*, 196.

59. Dutton, Werner, and Whitmore, *Sources of Vietnamese Tradition*, 109, 320–324.

60. Phạm Đình Hổ, *Vũ trung tuỳ bút* [Following the brush amid the rains], trans. Đông Châu Nguyễn Hữu Tiến (Hồ Chí Minh City: Nxb Văn Nghệ, 1998), 351–353; Phạm Đình Hổ, *Vũ trung tuỳ bút* [Following the brush amid the rains], trans. Tran Thi Kim Anh (Hà Nội: Nxb Khoa học Xã hội, 2003). Also, see "Rituals for Venerating Heaven" in Dutton, Werner, and Whitmore, *Sources of Vietnamese Tradition*, 186–188.

61. Dutton, Werner, and Whitmore, *Sources of Vietnamese Tradition*, 109–110; Ngô Sĩ Liên, *Đại Việt sử ký toàn thư* [Complete book of the historical records of Great Viet], (Hà Nội: Viện Khoa học Xã hội Việt Nam, 1993). The Sacrifice to Heaven (Nam Giao) perhaps was the Ming pattern of ritual since Lê Lợi (King Lê Thái Tổ [r.1428–1433], a local chieftain based in the village of Mount Lâm, who drove out the Ming occupation (1407–1427) in 1428 and became the king of a restored Đại Việt, whose capital was Thăng Long, forming the new aristocracy. For further procedure for carrying out this ritual, see in Phạm Đình Hổ, *Vũ trung tuỳ bút*, 351–353. English translation is in "Rituals for Venerating Heaven" in Dutton, Werner, and Whitmore, *Sources of Vietnamese Tradition*, 186–188. See also in Léopold Cadière, *Croyances et pratiques religieuses des Viêtnamiens*, vol. 1 (Hanoi: Impremerie d'Etrême Orient, 1944), 85–129.

A similar description of this ritual is also found in the twelve-page *History of the Country of Annam*, written by Bento Thien in 1659.⁶² The *quốc ngữ* historical text is a rare very early account of Vietnamese ritual practices which were carried out throughout the year, starting with the *Tết* (Lunar New Year) ceremonies. These rituals offer insights into Vietnamese social structures, the expectations of rulers, and the origins of these rituals.⁶³ The ritual and ceremony are described thus:

> In Annamese (Vietnamese) tradition, the first date of New Year (Lunar) is called *Tết* (literally means season). People show their respect (by bowing down) to the King (emperor), the lords (superior king), then ancestors, grandparents, parents, and other respected persons respectively. Officials bow to the King, the lords, and the common people bow to Buddha (*Bụt*). During the three days of the New Year festival, an auspicious day is selected on which the King pays a visit to Heaven's altar (*giao*), to perform a ritual called the Sacrifice to Heaven and Earth ceremony. The supreme emperor (King) and the lords pray to Heaven for good harvests, and peace and prosperity for the people in the kingdom. The ceremony lasts until the seventh or the eighth day of the New Year, and ends with the King's provision of a feast for the people to celebrate for ten days . . . The Sacrifice to Heaven and Earth (*giao*) ceremony has been performed since the time of Emperor Lê Thái Tổ.⁶⁴

---

62. Bento Thien or *Thầy giảng Thiện* (indigenous priest) was a Vietnamese Catholic priest and yet wrote a brief history of Vietnam as a piece of secular writing rather than a Christian one. He was one of many intellectual Catholics who contributed significantly to the process of developing the early *quốc ngữ* literature. Bento Thien did not name this document as *History of the Country of Annam*, but it was named by Đỗ Quang Chính and his colleagues, see Đỗ Quang Chính, *Lịch sử chữ Quốc Ngữ 1620–1659* [History of Quoc Ngu writing, 1620–1659], (1972. Reprint, Hà Nội: Nxb Tôn giáo, 2008), 147–178.

63. Dutton, Werner, and Whitmore, *Sources of Vietnamese Tradition*, 223.

64. Đỗ Quang Chính, *Lịch sử chữ Quốc Ngữ 1620-1659*, 164–165, quoted in Bento Thien, *Letter to Gio: Filippo de Marini*, Jap.-Sin, 81, n. 148–259v (Rome: Archivum Romanum Societatis Iesu, 1659). "Thói nước Annam, đầu năm mùng một tháng giêng, gọi là ngày Tết. Thiên hạ thì đi lạy Vua, đoạn lạy Chúa, mới lạy ông bà ông vải, cha mẹ cùng kẻ cả bề trên. Quan quyền thì lạy Vua Chúa, thứ dân thì lạy Bụt trước. Ăn tết ba ngày, mà một ngày trước mà xem ngày mùng hai, mùng ba, ngày nào tốt thì vua đi đến giao, gọi là nhà thờ Trời, hiệu Thiên Thượng Đế Hoàng Địa Kì. Vua Chúa đi lạy mà xin cho thiên hạ được mùa cùng dân an. Đến mùng bảy mùng tám mới hết, cùng làm cỗ cho thiên hạ ăn mười ngày . . . Trước thì thờ Thiên Chúa

The ritual was performed once a year at *Tết* (the Lunar New Year's festival), and required the emperor's direct participation in an elaborate ceremony. Though the performance sought to ensure the favor of Heaven, as well as serving to legitimate imperial rule, it also revealed the religious beliefs about Heaven; if the ritual was observed properly, then suitable rainfall, good harvests, and peace and prosperity will be ensured for the entire kingdom. At this point, we see the king, in the name of his people, come to the altar to bow down (*lạy*) and pray (*cầu*) to Heaven – the personal, transcendent, benevolent, and just God, creator of the universe, source of life, and supreme judge, as *Ông Trời* who is placed above all deities, immortals, spirits, and genies.[65]

The religio-cultural values influenced by the Three Teachings, along with traditional folk beliefs are seen in *Truyền kỳ mạn lục* (Collection of Strange Tales) by Nguyễn Dữ,[66] and *Truyện Kiều* (The Tale of Kiều) by Nguyễn Du.[67] The twenty folk tales of *Truyền kỳ mạn lục* (*TKML* hereafter) reveal that spiritual practices were deeply rooted in the culture and were popular among the people and were not only royal rituals or festivals at the national level.[68] As the seventeenth-century *nôm* literature was characterized by efforts to de-emphasize Confucian orthodoxy and official views, in favor of more "popular" (*bình dân*) themes, Nguyễn Dữ took oral folk narratives from among the common

Thượng Đế một đàn, là một đàn từ Vua Lê Thái Tổ cho đến nay." (This is the original written quotation, but the English translation above is my own.)

65. Further discussion on the Vietnamese people's understanding of heaven and their native religion, see Peter C. Phan, *Mission and Catechesis: Alexandre de Rhodes and Inculturation in Seventeenth-Century Vietnam*, Faith and Cultures Series (Maryknoll, NY: Orbis Books, 1998), 24–28.

66. The volume is a series of twenty stories composed in Chinese by Nguyễn Dữ in the sixteenth century. The collection was first printed in 1768 and translated into *nôm* by Nguyễn Thế Nghi. Nguyễn Thế Nghi, *Tân biên truyền kỳ mạn lục: Tác phẩm Nôm thế kỷ XVI* [New version of Truyen Ky Man Luc: A Nôm work of the sixteenth century], trans. Hoàng thị Hồng Cẩm (Hà Nội: Nxb Văn hoá Dân tộc, 2000).

67. With 3,254 verses in the *lục-bát* (six-eight) poetry genre, taken from a novel named *Truyện Kim Vân Kiều* by Thanh Tâm Tài Nhân (Từ Văn Trường) in Zhejiang, China today, it was the first *Nôm* literature to appear as a transition from the early modern Vietnamese literature (using *Hán* Chinese) to *Nôm*. This is the most important classic masterpiece in the history of Vietnamese literature in which the poetic novel was written in a couplet form, popular with the native oral folk tradition (*ca dao*). There are at least five interlinear versions of *Truyện Kiều* in Nôm and *Quốc ngữ* that can be found online through the *Vietnamese Nôm Preservation Foundation (VNPF)*, http://nomfoundation.org/nom-project/tale-of-kieu/kieu-introduction, accessed 3 June 2014.

68. The collection was first printed in 1768 and translated into *nôm*. See Nguyễn Thế Nghi, *Tân biên truyền kỳ mạn lục: Tác phẩm Nôm thế kỷ XVI*.

people, rearranged them with structures and characters, and put them in writing in a collection of new stories.[69] Despite the mythical elements of the oral folk literature, these tales also reveal several social, cultural and religious aspects of the people. With a philosophy of life governed by Confucianism, moral values were considered as guidelines for the behavior of the people in society. Thus, *TKML* showed that these values were no longer important to the state when these dynasties and feudal lords became corrupt in many ways. At the same time, with a belief in cause and effect, particularly the nemesis belief of Buddhism, Nguyễn Dữ revealed the hope of these suffering people who now can only trust in a better reincarnation to a future life where good people receive rewards and bad people earned punishment. While Nguyễn Dữ criticized various superstitious practices among the people, he also encouraged people to take spirituality seriously with a belief that good people should never be afraid of bad spiritual forces, or in another way, good people would be protected by good spirits who may appear in forms of *bụt* (Buddha) or *tiên* (a fairy). Thus, in *TKML*, certain influences of Confucianism, Daoism, and Buddhism became the three philosophical and religious value systems that governed all aspects of life for the Vietnamese.

Truyện Kiều (The Tale of Kiều) reflects the philosophical and religious traditions of Confucianism and Buddhism that were deeply rooted in the worldview or outlook on life of the Vietnamese, as shown in the first few poetic lines:

> A hundred years – in this life span on earth
> Talent and destiny are apt to feud.[70]

These two lines show the integration between Confucianism and Buddhism in the Vietnamese traditional philosophical belief which was popular in the late eighteenth and early nineteenth centuries. This belief was that nothing can happen coincidentally in life, but that it occurs according to destiny (*mệnh*). No matter how great one's talent (*tài*), everything is destined. Kiều was a talented person, but her life was a succession of pain and sorrow as a result of her

---

69. Nguyễn Dữ, *Truyền kỳ mạn lục* [Collection of strange tales], trans. Trúc Khê and Ngô Văn Triện (Hồ Chí Minh City: Nxb Trẻ & Nxb Hồng Bàng, 1768), 288.

70. Nguyễn Du, *The Tale of Kieu: A Bilingual Edition of Truyen Kieu*, trans. Huỳnh Sanh Thông (New Haven, CT: Yale University Press, 1983), 3. (Trăm năm trong cõi người ta. Chữ tài chữ mệnh khéo là ghét nhau.)

destiny. Instead of living together happily with Kim Trọng, another talented person, she experienced many ups and downs in life. In Kiều, the tension between her impulsive tendencies and filial piety is evident. She tries to make right decisions, but ultimately follows her passions. More importantly, in Kiều we can see how the Vietnamese at that time constantly struggled between Confucian virtues, filial piety (*hiếu thảo*) to parents, and the Buddhist belief of *karma* from the evils of a previous life. Kiều indeed believes that she is fated to suffer due to the law of *karma*. Ultimately, Confucianism prevails, as, Kiều returns home to serve her parents and fulfill her role as a daughter and wife, "an affirmation of family solidarity despite the random violence of a world twisted with corruption and war."[71] Thus, the more things one encounters in life, the more disappointment and pain are possible, which was the sociopolitical situation of the people in the eighteenth and nineteenth centuries:

> You must go through a play of ebb and flow
> and watch such things as make you sick at heart.[72]

Thus, one may hypothesize that a *resisting* and *assimilating* nature exists in Vietnamese culture where the integration of the Three Teachings with each other and the encounter with the local religio-cultural traditions resulted in a syncretistic belief system specific to the Vietnamese. The integration took place because of the philosophical thought of the Vietnamese at that time (when the people accommodated the three teachings), a spiritual need, and the limited doctrinal content of each of the three teachings.[73] This means that although the people were governed by Confucian principles, which provided the understanding of political-social responsibility and morality, the people needed spiritual values, found in Daoism and Buddhism, to understand

---

71. Keith Weller Taylor, *A History of the Vietnamese* (New York, NY: Cambridge University Press, 2013), 405.

72. Nguyễn Du, *The Tale of Kieu*, 3 (Trải qua những cuộc bể dâu, Những điều trông thấy mà đau đớn lòng.)

73. Nguyễn Tài Thư, "'Tam Giáo Đồng Nguyên': Hiện Tượng Tư Tưởng Chung của Các Nước Đông Á" [Unified source of the Three Teachings: A common ideological phenomenon of East Asian countries]. *Tạp Chí Hán Nôm (Journal of Han-Nom Studies)* 3, no. 40 (1999): 17. The article argues, "Tam giáo đồng nguyên" (unified source of the Three Teachings) takes place in China, Korea, and Japan, besides Vietnam. But, unlike Vietnam, the ideological unity of the three traditions maybe promoted by the political unity in China, for instance, during the Sui and Tang Dynasties, or during the Song and Ming Dynasties that resulted a new type of Confucianism, or Neo-Confucianism.

their origin, life and death. When the outside religions and ideologies of Confucianism, Daoism, and Buddhism arrived in Vietnam, the dual forces of resistance and assimilation allowed them to become unified with each other in a unique harmonious and balanced way that was specific to the political, social, and religio-cultural needs in the context of Vietnam. This is the nature of Vietnamese religious belief.

Contextual Integrated Belief

Vietnam in the late nineteenth and early twentieth centuries was challenged by losing its traditional and cultural systems, those being replaced by French modernization. France systematically replaced traditional Vietnamese education and its language of *nôm* with its western models of schools and universities,[74] and *quốc ngữ* (which later became the national Romanized writing system) as the means of disseminating its policies of society, culture, and religion to make traditional Vietnam into another France in Asia.[75] One of the first results of the French colonial conquest was to deprive the Vietnamese of the right to call their country by its proper name and of the right to think of themselves as Vietnamese. Instead, they had to use the names of Tonkin, Annam, and later on Cochinchina for their country.[76] Vietnam was then under a new name, French Indochina (1884–1945) with the territory expanded to include Laos and Cambodia.

The imprint of French colonialism, however, did not manifest itself significantly until the beginning of the twentieth century, when it became evident that in the last three decades of the nineteenth century, Vietnam had changed

---

74. The new system took over from the Confucian scholar elite class beginning in 1884, just a year before the Nguyễn dynasty independent rule ended. See Pierre Brocheux and Daniel Hémery, *Indochina: An Ambiguous Colonization, 1858–1954*, trans. Ly Lan Dill-Klein et al. (Berkeley, CA: University of California Press, 2009), 227–229.

75. Although *quốc ngữ* was not popular in Vietnam until the early twentieth century, the early *quốc ngữ* developed by the Jesuits, that is, Alexandre de Rhodes (1591–1660) and other local Vietnamese Christians who were with them, was a historical beginning of the modern writing script of the Vietnamese. Further discussion on the role of *quốc ngữ*, see Nguyen KimSon, "Catholic Church in Vietnam"; Đỗ Quang Chính, *Lịch sử chữ Quốc Ngữ 1620–1659*.

76. Hue-Tam Ho Tai, *Radicalism and the Origins of the Vietnamese Revolution* (Cambridge, MA: Harvard University Press, 1992), 7.

tremendously in every aspect of life.⁷⁷ In this period, *quốc ngữ* played the most important role in popularizing Vietnamese cultural traditions and the continual process of decolonization of the French imperialism. Seeing how *quốc ngữ* had become popular in the life of the early twentieth century Vietnam, Đào Duy Anh commented, "from now on, the Europeanization of our society will deepen."⁷⁸ Moreover, numerous internal changes in Vietnamese society also occurred during the first half of the twentieth century, including the development of new religious movements such as Cao Dai and Hoà Hảo.⁷⁹

The Way of Heaven

The Cao Dai is *Đạo Trời* (the Way of Heaven) and is said to be the only true religious pathway for all human beings and yet, it is specific to the Vietnamese.⁸⁰

---

77. Hue-Tam Ho Tai, *Radicalism and the Origins*. Vietnam was then under a new name, *French Indochina* (1884–1945). They had to use the names of Tonkin, Annam, and later on Cochinchina for their country. "Loss of linguistic autonomy was so internalized that even revolutionaries referred to themselves by the name given them by their French masters – *Annamites* – a label that resonated with echoes of an earlier period of colonial rule under the Tang dynasty."

78. See Đào Duy Anh, *Việt Nam văn hóa sử cương*; Dutton, Werner, and Whitmore, *Sources of Vietnamese Tradition*, 424–429. In contrast to Trần Trọng Kim, Đào Duy Anh believed that Confucianism would also be influenced by economic, geographical, and social factors instead of only the development of Vietnamese civilization and culture. Thus, for him, Westernization (under the French) would inevitably have a large impact on Vietnamese society and culture.

79. Along with the Cao Đài, Hoà Hảo (Peace and Harmony) founded by Huỳnh Phú Sổ (who placed strong emphasis on national affairs), *Bửu Sơn Kỳ Hương* (a Buddhist sect founded by Đoàn Minh Huyên), and a Vietnamese Buddhist revival movement initiated by Trí Hải were other unique religions characteristic of the southern Vietnamese people. These religious practices in the South of colonial Vietnam are believed to be synthetic, rather than syncretistic, as a result of integrating traditional cultures of the Việt, Khmer, migrant Chinese, Cham and Indian with those religious philosophies and practices of Confucianism, Buddhism, and Daoism. This integrated system of beliefs is sometimes called the traditional beliefs of the Vietnamese people. See Dutton, Werner, and Whitmore, *Sources of Vietnamese Tradition*, 434–444; Phạm Bích Hợp, *Người Nam Bộ và Tôn Giáo Bản Địa: Bửu Sơn Kỳ Hương, Cao Đài, Hòa Hảo* [The southern people and local religions], (Hà Nội: Nxb Tôn Giáo, 2007); Đặng Thế Đại, "Tính đặc sắc Nam bộ và truyền thống văn hóa Việt Nam qua một dòng tôn giáo" [Southern characteristics and Vietnamese traditional cultures through a religious practice], *Tạp Chí Nghiên Cứu Tôn Giáo (Religious Studies Journal)* 58, no. 4 (April 2008): 43-52.

80. "For as long as we have seen, the southern country has not had it own religion. Its foundation must now be laid. . . . I, as the higest Master (Đức Cao Đài), have founded the Đạo in this southern region to compensate a country that since the beginning of its history has regularly suffered my vicissitudes. This time, I have decided to forgive you for your sins and redeem you in returning glory to your country. . . . I will give the greatest rewards to those disciples who show that they are most worthy of my favor. . . . From this day on, there is only one true religious pathway, the Đạo, and that is my pathway, which I have founded for my

The first paragraph of the preface of the Cao Dai's *New Code* (1926) reveals that the Mandate from the Supreme God (Đức Cao Đài, who called himself Master) was passed on to his disciples to guide humankind to this Đạo Trời.

During the autumn of 1926 and the spring of 1927, the early period when the movement was beginning to take shape, several spirit messages were believed to be transmitted directly from the Jade Emperor. The syncretistic dimension of Confucianism, Daoism, and Buddhism is revealed in the "Spirit messages" (*Thánh Ngôn Hiệp Tuyển*) which underlie the Cao Dai's rituals for worship and practices for its believers. These messages are included in the New Code (1926) and two collections of spirit writings.[81] The New Code contains the canonical laws regulating all aspects of the Cao Dai religious practice. The preface (below) outlines the religion's goals:

> All human beings must recognize what is over their heads. The infinite space over our heads is Heaven. The Supreme Being [God] who rules in this space is the Creator, the Celestial Jade Emperor and the Supreme Chief of all the Universe and the Cosmos. This Creator has come today under the name of Cao Dai Tien Ong Dai Bo Tat Ma Hat Tat to found in our Vietnam, through a supernatural and a mysterious communication with the Immortals, a pure religion of high moral and philosophical value to save humanity from the rigors of karmic law.
>
> This religion calls itself the Great Path/ Way [Đạo] or the Great Religion of the Third Salvation [Amnesty]. In his great love and mercy, the Celestial Jade Emperor calls himself Master and calls us his Disciples. Consequently, we must bring all our respectful adoration to the Creator and all our faith to the religion of his mysterious and miraculous Way.[82]

---

disciples and named as the national religion of this region," The first *spirit message* (in Noel 1925) by "the Jade Emepror written as Cao Dai – Teaching Religion to the Southern Country." Quoted in Janet Alison Hoskins, "An Unjealous God? Christian Elements in a Vietnamese Syncretistic Religion," *Current Anthropology (The University of Chicago Press Journals)* 55, no. S10 (2014): 304.

    81. Spirit messages were transmitted in séances conducted by a medium who wrote down the messages in trays of sand or on paper. Hence the author of a divine message identified himself or herself by means of a written symbol.

    82. Toà Thánh Tây Ninh (Tay Ninh Holy See), *Tân Luật (The New Code)*, The Cao-Dai Temple of New South Wales, E-book v.2011 ed. (Thủ Đức, Việt Nam: Nhà in Trung Tâm Giáo

Unifying Spirituality

The Cao Dai represents a massive contextualization effort done in Vietnam.[83] This religious organization articulated spiritual ambitions in response to the anti-colonialist and nationalist struggles by Vietnamese intellectuals, and made its own alternative form of conversion in a profound way.[84] With political overtones and colorful liturgy, Ngô Văn Chiêu (1878–1932) and eleven other founders (first disciples) sought to combine and unify the Vietnamese world's religious tenets of the Confucianist-Daoist-Buddhist belief, elements of Christianity and Islam, European Spiritualism (or Kardecism), and ideologies of Communist founders.[85] Major beliefs have been united in one single organization of religion, not in order to create another brand new religion, but to unify the existing religions through the emphasis of their inter-relatedness. In fact, assimilating other faiths has already been the second nature of the Vietnamese. The Cao Dai realized they needed to fill in the gap between the popular spirits belief of the Vietnamese and the faiths coming from the outside, including the three teachings, the European Christian faith, and other world religious precepts. More specifically, the Cao Dai incorporates "organizational elements from the Catholic Church and Chinese redemptive

---

Hoá Thiếu Nhi Thủ Đức, 1972), 3. Eng. trans. Jayne Werner (quoted in Dutton, Werner, and Whitmore, *Sources of Vietnamese Tradition*, 430–431.)

83. The Cao Dai is also known as *Đại Đạo Tam Kỳ Phổ Độ* (The Great Way of the Third Period of Salvation).

84. For instance, the growth of the Cao Dai in its beginning was partially a result of the Vietnamese and the southern Vietnamese traditional basis, and the political influence of the French. See "Đạo Cao Đài, con đường cách tân cải biên, hướng ngoại" [Cao Dai, the way to renovation and outreach] in Tạ Chí Đại Trường, *Thần, Người và Đất Việt*, 305–372.

85. The first *spirit message* (in Noel 1925) by "the Jade Emepror written as Cao Dai – Teaching Religion to the Southern Country" mentioned the first names of the first twelve disciples (founders) who were directly called by the Jade Emperor (Ngọc Hoàng Thượng Đế): "Chiêu Kỳ Trung độ dẫn Hoài sanh, Bản đạo khai Sang Quí Giảng thành. Hậu Đức Tắc Cư Thiên Địa cảnh, Huờn Minh Mân đáo thủ đài danh." See Toà Thánh Tây Ninh (Tay Ninh Holy See), *Thánh Ngôn Hiệp Tuyển (Official spirit messages)*, The Cao-Dai Temple of New South Wales' E-book v.2011 ed. (Thủ Đức, Việt Nam: Nhà in Trung Tâm Giáo Hoá Thiếu Nhi Thủ Đức, 1972), 3; Ralph B. Smith, "An Introduction to Caodaism 1: Origins and Early History," *Bulletin of the School of Oriental and African Studies, University of London* 33, no. 2 (1970): 335–349; Huệ Khải, *Lược Sử Đạo Cao Đài: Khai Minh Đại Đạo 1926* [A concise Cao Dai history: The 1926 inauguration], (Hà Nội: Nxb Tôn giáo, 2015).

societies, as well as Spiritist texts from French writers like Victor Hugo and Allan Kardec."[86]

By incorporating other religious elements and practices, together with local Vietnamese traditions (local spirits, ancestral veneration), the Cao Dai offers a unifying form of spirituality uniquely specific to the context of colonial Vietnam as well as the global context.[87] Perhaps, this is a first attempt at "globalization" in the twentieth century. Such contextualization effort could be best viewed in the five integrated levels of worship of the Cao Dai. The first level is acknowledging the Supreme Being, the Creator (*Đức Cao Đài, Đấng Cao Cả*),[88] then Buddhist enlightenment is at the top which is Immortal

---

86. Janet Alison Hoskins, *The Divine Eye and the Diaspora: Vietnamese Syncretism Becomes Transpacific Caodaism* (Honolulu, HI: University of Hawai`i Press, 2015), Kindle Locations 488–489. The Cao Dai's founders (e.g. Ngô Văn Chiêu) moved in between the world of French Spiritism (Allan Kardec, Victor Hugo) and ancient Chinese spirit writing. Allan Kardec (or Allan Jardec) (1804-1896) coined the word "Spiritism" for his experiments with *séances* and table tipping, eventually transitioning to the use of a "beaked basket" similar to the Chinese phoenix basket later used by Caodaists. Kardec's best-known writings include *Le Livre des Espirits* [The book of the spirits] (1857), *Le Livre des Mediums* [The spirit medium] (1861), and *L'Evangile selon Le Spiritisme* (1880). These "manuals for spirit mediums" became best sellers in French Indochina at that time. Victor Hugo (1802–1885) was also a great French writer and one of the Cao Dai's "saints" or spiritual teachers. Many years after his death, *Chez Victor Hugo: Les Tables Tournantes de Jersey* (1923) was published, a series of conversations that Hugo and his Spiritist circle had with Rousseau, Voltaire, Shakespeare, and even the spirit of Death. In this work, Jesus Christ appeared several times and "revised his thinking" about Christianity, predicting that a new world religion would emerge to unite Eastern and Western doctrines, and Victor Hugo would be a prophet for this new vision. For the English translation, see Victor Hugo, *Conversations with Eternity: The Forgotten Masterpiece of Victor Hugo*, trans. John Chambers, 1st New Paradigm Books ed. (Boca Raton, FL: New Paradigm Books, 1998); Victor Hugo, *Victor Hugo's Conversations with the Spirit World: A Literary Genius's Hidden Life*, trans. John Chambers, Rev. and expanded 2nd ed. ed. (Rochester, VT: Destiny Books, 2008).

87. This was part of the global spiritualism which emerged in the mid-nineteenth century, not only in Vietnam, but also can be seen in other spiritist movements around the world. For the Theosophists, Cargo Cults in the South Pacific, see Olav Hammer and Mikael Rothstein, *Handbook of the Theosophical Current*, Brill handbooks on contemporary religion (Leiden, Boston: Brill, 2013); G. W. Trompf, *Cargo Cults and Millenarian Movements: Transoceanic Comparisons of New Religious Movements*, Religion and Society 29. (Berlin: Mouton de Gruyter, 1990); Holger Jebens, *Cargo, Cult, and Culture Critique* (Honolulu, HI: University of Hawaii Press, 2004). Also, the Umbandist spiritist tradition, an Afro-Brazilian adaptation of Kardecism (Allan Kardec) in Brazil, see particularly chapter 8 "Pentecostalism and Umbanda: A Test Case," in Amos Yong, "Discerning the Spirit(s): A Pentecostal-Charismatic Contribution to Christian Theology of Religions" PhD diss., (Boston University, 1999), 319–389.

88. The influence of Confucianism is clearly shown by how the Cao Dai portrayed *Heaven*, the Jade Emperor, the Supreme Being, or the Creator (*Ngọc Hoàng Thượng Đế* or *Đấng Cao Cả* or *Đức Cao Đài*). Huệ Khải (the Vietnamese Caodai historian Lê Anh Dũng) notes that the term Cao Đài was already in use in Cochinchina, since it appeared in a text published in 1912 in Shanghai, where it was used to refer to the Supreme Being, see Huệ Khải, *The Emergence*

Bodhisattva-Mahasatva (*Tiên Ông Đại Bồ Tát Ma Ha Tát*), followed by the way of the Daoist Immortals, then the "way of the saints" which includes Jesus, Moses, and Mohammed,[89] the "way of local spirits," and ancestral veneration.[90]

The Vietnamese are God's chosen people. The Creator had chosen Vietnam ("the southern country") as the site for the third and final attempt to save human beings from its transgressions.[91] This was because the Vietnamese suffered the most oppressive colonial regime in Asia, but had still maintained their virtue, so they would be rewarded by receiving teachings directly from the Supreme God.[92] Moreover, the Vietnamese had already been able to unite the essences of Confucianism (the early Vietnamese Confucian syncretistic understanding of Heaven or the Supreme God), of Buddhism (three obligations and the five prohibitions), of Daoism (the three jewels and the five elements), of the *đạo* (way) of the world's "saints," of the popular Vietnamese spirits belief, and of the tradition of venerating ancestors. While the Three Teachings tradition had become widespread in Vietnamese society at large, the Supreme Being or Jehovah God (*Đức Cao Đài*) chose to reveal the "mysterious method" (the Cao Dai) to the Vietnamese:

> I wanted to tell you only once, [about] the sage Saint Moses on the Sinai mountain, but you hadn't been able to understand MY intention. MY promise for your Ancestors about atoning for guilt for you and the Birthday of the Savior is a matter existing in the prophetic saying already but you did not care. Nowadays, I must find the more mysterious method [the Cao Dai] to conquer you. You will be not able to deny any more when facing on the

---

of Caodaism in Cochinchina (Hồ Chí Minh City: Cơ quan Phổ thông Giáo lý Đại Đạo; Nxb Tôn giáo, 2008), 82.

89. Other "saints" were also incorporated as Cao Dai's spiritual teachers, including Victor Hugo, Jeanne d'Arc, Vladimir Lenin, and Joseph Smith.

90. Toà Thánh Tây Ninh (Tay Ninh Holy See), *Tân Luật (The New Code)*, 3. Eng. trans. Jayne Werner (qouted in Dutton, Werner, and Whitmore, *Sources of Vietnamese Tradition*, 430–431).

91. According to the Cao Dai, the First Period of Salvation was chronologically associated with Moses, Buddha Dipankara, and Chinese dieties Fu Hsi and T'ai Shan Dao Guan. The Second Period of Salvation was represented by Buddha Shakyamuni, Confucius, Lao Tzu, Jesus Christ, and Mohamed. See http://caodai.com.vn/en/news-detail/brief-outline-of-history-and-philosophy-of-caodaism.html, accessed 10 June 2016.

92. Hoskins, "An Unjealous God?," 305.

general judgment court that I would not save humankind by effective methods.⁹³

The Third Period of Salvation, however, is for all human beings who should follow this Way/Great Path (Đạo). They will reach the level of the Genie-Spirits, the Saints, the Immortals, and the Buddhas, which is the call to fulfill the Three Teachings of Confucianism, Daoism, and Buddhism:

> The aim of the Great Religion consists of embracing and synchronizing the doctrines of the three major religious teachings [of the East]: Confucianism, Buddhism, and Daoism, and harmonizing them into one. This is why in Caodaism, we must observe the basic principles of the Three Religions to improve and purify ourselves by strictly following the three duties and the five cardinal virtues [of Confucianism],⁹⁴ the three obligations and the five prohibitions [of Buddhism],⁹⁵ as well as the union of the three jewels and the five elements [of Daoism].⁹⁶ Whoever is able to fulfill these three religious teachings will reach the level of the Genie-Spirits, the Saints, the Immortals, and the Buddhas.⁹⁷

And to reach salvation is by a moral life and by following the religion:

> I, out of great love and mercy, have founded the Third Amnesty (Salvation) of the Great Way based on love of life, with the purpose of elevating the predestined spirits to higher levels, thereby

---

93. "Ngọc Hoàng Thượng Đế Viết Cao Đài (Jade Emperor written as Cao Dai), on October 27, 1926, Toà Thánh Tây Ninh (Tay Ninh Holy See), *Thánh Ngôn Hiệp Tuyển (Official spirit messages)*, 107–109, trans. Quách Minh Chương in http://www.daotam.info/booksv/pdf/pdf2/thanhngon-qI-hc.pdf, accessed 13 June 2016.

94. The three duties: between the king and subject, father and children, and husband and wife. The five cardinal virtues: love or brotherhood, justice or faithfulness, good behavior or politeness, wisdom, and loyalty.

95. The three obligations (or treasures): to the Buddha, to Buddhist law, and to Buddhist community (*sangha*). The five prohibitions: do not kill, do not steal, do not commit lewd acts, do not abuse the use of alcohol or live a high life, and do not tell lies.

96. The three jewels: matter, spirit, and soul. The five elements: metal, air, water, fire, and earth.

97. Toà Thánh Tây Ninh (Tay Ninh Holy See), *Tân Luật (The New Code)*, 3. Eng. trans. Jayne Werner, qouted in Dutton, Werner, and Whitmore, *Sources of Vietnamese Tradition*, 430–431.

avoiding reincarnation and bringing the virtuous to a more precious and peaceful domain free of struggle compared with this poor, vile earthly world.[98]

Nevertheless, humans cannot escape from the circle of reincarnation:

> For many thousands of years, all beings have been transformed through the cycle of reincarnation from minerals to plants to animals, finally reaching the stage of human beings. Human beings are themselves divided into different classes on this earth ... Then, they will reach the pinnacle, the Bach Ngoc Kinh. In Buddhism, this place is called nirvana.[99]

And yet, enlightenment comes from Cao Dai's missionaries' propagation of the faith:

> Children, many of you may think that in order to practice a religion, you have to be completely detached from secular activities, yearning day and night for a secluded place for religious self-improvement. I am telling you now that if you have not paid all your karmic debt and have not accrued enough merit, you cannot become enlightened. In order to be enlightened, you must first accrue merit by bringing salvation to all wandering souls. If you cannot do it in this way, then you may then find other ways, such as self-cultivation, that also can lead to the elevated position of enlightenment.[100]

---

98. See "Ngọc Hoàng Thượng Đế Viết Cao Đài – Giáo Đạo Nam Phương" (The Jade Emperor written as Cao Dai - teaching religion to the Southern Country), 6 December 1926, in Toà Thánh Tây Ninh (Tay Ninh Holy See), *Thánh Ngôn Hiệp Tuyển (Official spirit messages)*, 132–133. trans. Jayne Werner and Jeremy Jammes, quoted in Dutton, Werner, and Whitmore, *Sources of Vietnamese Tradition*, 431.

99. See "Ngọc Hoàng Thượng Đế Viết Cao Đài" (Jade Emperor), 19 December 1926, in Toà Thánh Tây Ninh (Tay Ninh Holy See), *Thánh Ngôn Hiệp Tuyển (Official spirit messages)*, 143–145, quoted in Dutton, Werner, and Whitmore, *Sources of Vietnamese Tradition*, 432-33.

100. See "Ngọc Hoàng Thượng Đế Viết Cao Đài" (Jade Emperor), 5 March 1927, in Toà Thánh Tây Ninh (Tay Ninh Holy See), *Thánh Ngôn Hiệp Tuyển (Official spirit messages)*, 186–187, quoted in Dutton, Werner, and Whitmore, *Sources of Vietnamese Tradition*, 433–434. This spirit message at *Great Altar* at Cầu Kho (in Saigon) is also an example of one of the main characteristics of the Cao Dai.

The Cao Dai has successfully assimilated (or inculturated) the Christian faith in such a way that they were able to resist European religious and political influences in colonial Vietnam (the Roman Catholics, and the French imperialists in Indochina), besides accommodating Confucianism, Daoism, Buddhism, and other world spiritual or political figures successfully. Janet Alison Hoskins argued that "Caodaism created a new religious field in French Indochina, and in doing so invested a number of very traditional elements with new significance and new dynamism."[101] Socio-politically, the Cao Dai oriented itself towards the belief that "the Vietnamese combination of Buddhism, Daoism, and Confucianism now needed to be defined explicitly against the pressures of European culture."[102] Religiously, "by integrating Christianity under the wider umbrella of East Asian cosmology, they have made themselves 'more catholic than the Catholics,' applying the Catholic theory of 'inculturation' to European religion and tolerating Christian rituals as 'sincere but unsophisticated practices' that approach the Jade Emperor as the supreme transcendent deity."[103] Thus, the Cao Dai gives a different picture of Christianity in Vietnam where its intellectuals during the colonial period often resisted actual conversion (to European Christianity) by incorporating Christian elements into new, more universal forms of spirituality.[104]

Several Christian elements are understood or re-interpreted from the Vietnamese-East Asian perspective. The Cao Dai applied the Vatican's hierarchy in building their own "*Toà Thánh Tây Ninh*" (Tay Ninh Holy See), a "Vatican in Vietnam." The biblical concept of "God's chosen people" is given new interpretation when applied to the Vietnamese.[105] Jesus was treated as Jehovah God's obedient child where the filial obligations are understood by the Confucian model (*Đức Chúa Jésus Christ làm con hiếu hạnh*). Jesus speaks to the Cao Dai disciples to follow the Đạo, and thus the new way was opened up by his father, which has superseded all earlier religions.[106] Jesus was also treated as a junior "brother" in this Vietnamese-East Asian pantheon on

---

101. Hoskins, "An Unjealous God?," 305.
102. Hoskins, 304.
103. Hoskins, 310–311.
104. Hoskins, 302.
105. Hoskins, 305.
106. Hoskins, 306.

the teaching of elderly sages, and was placed three levels below Confucius, Lao Tzu, and Buddha. In this position, Jesus does not offer a great number of teachings in the Cao Dai. The Jehovah God is incarnated and identified himself as *Đức Cao Đài* (the highest tower), or the Jade Emperor:

> Nothing in this world exists without my will. There are many poor spirits who pretend that they have the secrets of God. But I have not given my revelations to any human being. To make contact with me, you need to pray to me directly. I will not hesitate to respond to sincere prayers. I am the Jehovah of the Hebrews, the God of the Israeli armies, the unknown God of the Jews, and the true father of Jesus Christ, and you can call me with the name *Cao Đài* so that your wishes will be heard. You come to me with the sincere feelings of the oppressed people whom you represent. I ask you to spread this doctrine to all your protégés. It is the only one that will sustain humanity in the love of all creatures and bring you a lasting peace.[107]

The Vietnamese, as Jehovah God's chosen people, are called to carry on the mission of Jesus who was proclaimed by the gospel, but has not been heard of, or has been distorted by the French colonial presence and Vietnamese Catholics:

> Christ came among you. He spilled his blood for your redemption. How have you benefited during the roughly 2000 years that he has been gone? You preach his Gospel without understanding it. You distort the significance of his holy doctrine. Humanity suffers the vicissitudes of all his apostles. They have not known how to follow the same pathway as their Master.[108]

The urgency of proclaiming the good news (of Jehovah God or *Đức Cao Đài*) was prophesied by the prophets in the Bible, especially by Jesus.[109] While

---

107. See "Ngọc Hoàng Thượng Đế Viết Cao Đài" (Jade Emperor), 17 December 1926, in Toà Thánh Tây Ninh (Tay Ninh Holy See), *Thánh Ngôn Hiệp Tuyển (Official spirit messages)*, 140–142, trans. Hoskins, "An Unjealous God?," 305–306.

108. See "Ngọc Hoàng Thượng Đế Viết Cao Đài" (Jade Emperor), on 8 June 1926, in Toà Thánh Tây Ninh (Tay Ninh Holy See), 57–59, quoted in Hoskins, "An Unjealous God?," 306–307.

109. Ralph B. Smith believes that the Chinese term *Cao Đài* was used to refer to *Jehovah* in translations of the Bible by the British Bible Society, see Ralph B. Smith, "An Introduction

a few Christian New Testament verses and biblical figures (e.g. Moses, John the Baptist) were used as the prophecy of the forerunners of the coming of the Cao Dai ("For you yourselves know very well that the day of the Lord will come like a thief in the night," 1 Thess 5:2; also Matt 24:32–44), Jesus was treated as one of the prophets and religious teachers that were combined with the nineteenth century French spiritists, as seen in this Spirit message:

> Humanity suffers all sorts of vicissitudes. I sent Allan Jardec, I sent Flammarion as I had sent the prophet Elijah and John the Baptist, who came to announce the coming of Jesus Christ. One was persecuted, the other killed. And by whom? By humanity. My son [Jesus] was also killed by you. You have only venerated him in spirit, not in his full holiness.[110]

In conclusion, the Vietnamese spirituality has witnessed several crucial historical moments that have demonstrated this resistance and assimilation nature in every aspect of Vietnamese life. It was the socio-political context of colonial Vietnam (sovereignty was lost to the French) that fostered the 1925 formation of the Cao Dai as a response of Vietnamese intellectuals to meet a need for national unity. Then the refugee crisis in the post-colonial-communist Vietnam (after 1975), when thousands of the Cao Dai believers were scattered around the world, brought this religion into another process of resistance and assimilation with the challenge to appropriate its doctrines and practices in a new context.[111] Although the Cao Dai in Vietnam, much as other religions had faced new challenges of restriction for religious practice after 1975, the Cao Dai's diaspora has become a "transpacific" Cao Dai phenomenon, particularly in the United States and Australia.[112] Nevertheless, the Cao Dai, as a syncretistic religion emerging in Vietnam in the twentieth

---

to Caodaism 2: Beliefs and Organization," *Bulletin of the School of Oriental and African Studies, University of London* 33, no. 3 (1970): 573–589.

110. See "Ngọc Hoàng Thượng Đế Viết Cao Đài" (The Jade Emperor written as Cao Dai), quoted in Hoskins, "An Unjealous God?," 306.

111. For these two periods of crises, Hoskins argued, "the 1925 'conversion to modernity' was an effort to seek equivalence with French notions of what a religion could and should do in the public sphere. The 1975 conversion to a 'global faith of unity' was an effort to reformulate this religion so that it could be both practiced in other countries and normalized within the Socialist Republic of Vietnam." See Hoskins, "An Unjealous God?," 307.

112. For the Cao Dai diaspora, see Hoskins, "An Unjealous God?," 307–308. Also in Hoskins, *Divine Eye and the Diaspora*.

century, is not explicitly a new or surprising thing, if argued that the nature of resistance and assimilation is indeed rooted in Vietnamese spirituality. Through the development of the Cao Dai religion, such a nature is revealed quite clearly in the manner in which the Vietnamese (the Vietnamese intellectuals in the twentieth century) were successful in accommodating (contextual assimilation) their national interest (the loss of their country's sovereignty to the French) and having their faith "Vietnamized."[113]

Chapter Conclusion

This chapter has revealed that the syncretistic system of beliefs which has become the Vietnamese spirituality of today is a complex, and integrated matrix of local beliefs in God(s), spirits, the Confucianist-Daoist-Buddhist faith, and a syncretistic hybrid assimilation, the Cao Dai. Two crucial points can be deducted from this study.

First, the core or actual Vietnamese spirituality is the *Đạo* (the Way, not as the *Đạo* in Daoism) in which the process of syncretism has created an integrated unique form of spirituality specific to the Vietnamese. Centuries before encountering the Western Christian God, this *Đạo* had been important to the Vietnamese because the understanding had changed even before they assimilated the Three Teachings. The Vietnamese believed that there is the one and the only true God (*Thiên*, *Thượng Đế*, or *Ông Trời* in common language). However, the early Christian missionaries, upon their arrival in Vietnam, were faced with several practices including the belief in spirits, the common ritual ceremony (venerating Heaven, venerating ancestors), and the oral folklore traditions (e.g. *The Tale of Kieu*), all of which have been transmitted from generation to generation over many centuries. These things seemed strange, colorful, and boisterous to the missionaries, and yet, each story or ritual carried something of the essence of Vietnamese spirituality. But

---

113. Hoskins believed that "Caodaists are most 'Christian' in their acceptance of a Roman Catholic insitutional model (fused with the Confucian bureaucracy and its Ministry of Rites) and a 'theologizing of history' that identifies chosen people, a master and his 12 apostles (associated with the twelve animals of East Asian zodiac), a lost homeland, and a divine mission to reconquer it. Caodaists view themselves as followers of a modern, congregational religion that fuses the great philosophical ideas of the East with the great historical achievements of the West and that prophecies a fusion of Eastern ethics and Western statecraft in a new divinely mandated nationa state." See Hoskins, "An Unjealous God?," 310.

the missionaries overlooked these religio-cultural aspects, not knowing the essence underlying these manifestations. Thus, the early missionaries failed to find ways to contextualize the gospel to the Vietnamese. They didn't have the intuitive insight to see that these people also believed in the same God. The opportunity of contextualization existed all the time, but was completely ignored. For instance, it seems that Alexander de Rhodes did not know the full meaning underlying the concept called *đạo* or *đàng* (translated "way") nor the doctrinal spirituality behind the traditions, practices and beliefs shaping the *đạo* when he encountered it.[114] Honoring certain realities from daily encounters with nature, respecting the living saints or heroes when they were alive, or venerating them as spirits or deities after death, and venerating heaven (*Thiên, Ông Trời*) (the Sacrifice to Heaven) are just some of the manifestations of Vietnamese spirituality. The main concept of Vietnamese spirituality, thus, is the *Đạo*. All other things (venerating heaven, ancestral veneration, and honoring saints/ heroes) are just satellites around this concept. Thus, to follow the *Đạo* is to harmonize and observe fully all these realities regarded as truths.

Second, the Vietnamese integrated form of spirituality is unique because it has been adapted by what is called a dual force in the Vietnamese culture – resistance and assimilation – throughout the history of the Vietnamese people. Such a "dual force" demonstrates how Vietnamese spirituality was both able to resist the religio-cultural influences from the outside and assimilate moderately (not absorbing completely all of one single religious doctrine) the essentials of the outside influences that are of specific interest to the Vietnamese. The failure of contextualization was indicative of a particularly Vietnamese cultural dimension that also gave birth to the special brand of Vietnamese syncretism, the Cao Dai. Thus, because of the nature of the Vietnamese culture to resist the complete assimilation of one single

---

114. "Having heard of the Law which they call *đạo* in scholarly language and *đàng* in popular tongue, which means *way* . . . I decided to announce it to them under the name of the Lord of heaven and earth, finding no proper word in their language to refer to God . . . I decided to employ the name used by the apostle Saint Paul when he preached to the Athenians who had set up an altar to an unknown God." See *Histoire du Royaume*, 129–130, cited by Peter C. Phan, *In Our Own Tongues: Perspectives from Asia on Mission and Inculturation* (Maryknoll, NY: Orbis Books, 2003), 163.

religious doctrine, it is possible to argue that this is also the reason why Christian contextualization efforts generally failed.

This chapter has identified the unique Vietnamese cultural and spiritual premises that indicate the reason why Christian contextualization efforts failed – a lack of understanding Vietnamese spirituality which lay behind those visible religio-cultural forms and rituals. In other words, any attempt at Christian contextualization in Vietnam cannot overlook the *Đạo* and the resistance-assimilation characteristics of the Vietnamese cultural and spiritual dimensions. Thus, the insight learned from this chapter provides a hermeneutical interpretation for chapters 4 and 5, and the guiding principles for a constructive approach in chapter 6.

CHAPTER 4

Christian Missionary Movements in Vietnam

Although Vietnamese people might first have encountered Christianity from Asia, for instance, the East Syrians, it was not until the arrival of the European Catholic priests in the late sixteenth century that a Christian mission was able to enter Vietnam. Although East Syrians probably had visited ancient Vietnam on their way to China, there is no indication that the East Syrians accomplished any significant missionary work in Vietnam during their visits.[1] Aside from the Roman Catholic missions, there is also no clear evidence of other Protestant missionary activity done in Vietnam until the French and American Protestant missions arrived in the late nineteenth century. These two missions, especially the latter, anchored their missionary work in the land and enjoyed their mission "fruit" of hundreds of national converts and churches in the early twentieth century. But, how did these Protestant Christian missions contribute to the formation of the present Vietnamese evangelicalism (or *Tin Lành*)?[2] This chapter, therefore, seeks to answer that question. At the same time, it will show how the present paradigm of mission theology has been created through the historical evolution of Christian missions in Vietnam (particularly the French and American Protestant missions) as it answers another question: To what extent have the French and American Protestant missions and the Evangelical Church of Vietnam missed

---

1. Lê Hoàng Phu, "Short History," 97. Rev Lê quoted from Phạm Văn Sơn's *Việt Sử Tân Biên* (1961) and J. Despon's *L'Eglise d'Indochine* (1964).

2. The *Tin Lành* Church referred here is the Evangelical Church of Vietnam (ECVN). The word "Tin Lành" is also used for the Vietnamese evangelicals or Vietnamese evangelicalism in general in this study.

opportunities to relevantly and indigenously contextualize the gospel to the Vietnamese people?

This chapter gives a historical perspective and overview of both the French and American Protestant missions in the late nineteenth century and the Evangelical Church of Vietnam in the early twentieth century through archival and library research.³ Several crucial historical moments, key missionaries, and national leaders are discussed in this early and exploratory stage of the evolution of evangelical Christianity in Vietnam, including evangelism efforts, as well as missionary attitudes toward the religious, cultural, and political contexts of Vietnam. The chapter also covers the British and French missions' endeavors which have been missing or poorly covered in the current Vietnamese evangelical historiography.⁴ This section focuses on the missiology of the early missionaries in Vietnam in light of the socio-political contexts existing at the time.

Early Accounts of Christianity

The earliest accounts of Christianity in Vietnam date from the sixteenth century (for instance, Alexander de Rhodes arrived at *Đàng trong* or Annam in 1624) and relate to the Catholic Church in Vietnam (*Công Giáo*),⁵ and two centuries later, the Vietnamese evangelicals (*Tin Lành*).⁶ By the year 2009,

---

3. The archival data for the French Protestant missions is held at Bibliothèque du Défap (service Protestant de mission) at 102 Boulevard Arago, Paris 75015, France. There are two archival boxes of letters, pamphlets, published and unpublished articles/ reports which related to the French mission before and at the same time as the American mission (the CMA) in Vietnam. These two boxes are dated "Indochina 1860–1924" and "Indochina 1925–1952." Thank you especially to Madame Claire-Lise Lombard, the Défap's libarian for her wonderful assistance during the research done in March 2015.

4. Irwin, *With Christ in Indo-China*; James, "American Protestant Missions"; Reimer, "Protestant Movement in Vietnam"; Reimer, *Vietnam's Christians*; Lê Hoàng Phu, "Short History"; Herendeen, "Conversion and Indigeneity." Although the year 1911 is considered to be the beginning of Vietnamese evangelicalism, there is a serious question about its historical accuracy.

5. This 400-year-old Catholic Church in Vietnam called *Giáo Hội Công Giáo*, or *Công Giáo*, in short, is a result of the spread of transnational Christianity, led by zealous Jesuits of the early Roman Catholic missions in previous centuries who gave Christianity a chance to "re-encounter" Asia, particularly Vietnam in the sixteenth century. Latourette, *History of Christianity*, 853–854; Irvin and Sunquist, *History of the World Christian Movement*, 54.

6. For an extensive history of the Catholic Church in Vietnam, see Phan Phát Huồn, *History of the Catholic Church in Việt Nam*; Keith, "Catholic Vietnam"; Keith, *Catholic Vietnam*.

both Vietnamese Catholicism and Evangelicalism had become two of the six largest religions of Vietnam.[7] The Catholic Church, started by the Jesuits, who pioneered missions in Vietnam in the sixteenth century, opened the door for the gospel to reach the Vietnamese people. Although one may learn how colonialism had created new transnational links that were to the church's advantage, it must be noted that such transition during the Vietnam colonial period from a foreign-administered mission to an independent national church was not an overnight development.[8] From the sixteenth century to the first half of the nineteenth century, Vietnam witnessed a new era of social, political and cultural transformation in which Đại Việt (Great Viet, former Vietnam),[9] under the Trịnh-Nguyễn Lords, the Tây Sơn regime (1788–1802) and the Nguyễn dynasty (1802–1885), settled in the northern region and expanded to the farthest southern region establishing the national territorial boundaries Vietnam enjoys today, encroaching however upon, and attaching the existing southern territories of the Cham and Khmer people.

It is in this complex context that the Vietnamese people encountered Christianity from the West for the first time. This early East-West contact came about through commercial trade, followed by the international exchanges of socio-religio-cultural influences with Đại Việt during the sixteenth and seventeenth centuries. When Đại Việt (during the Mạc dynasty) opened trade with the Europeans and other Asian people at the trading post at Faifo (Hội An) in 1535, and also with the Dutch merchants trading in Phố Hiến in 1637, it was also opened to Western socio-cultural and religious influences. Amid these dynamic encounters, the most interesting event, perhaps, was the arrival of the Jesuit priests in the seventeenth century. They played

---

For Vietnamese evangelicalism, see Lê Hoàng Phu, "Short History"; James, "American Protestant Missions"; Reimer, "Protestant Movement in Vietnam"; Reimer, *Vietnam's Christians*.

7. See Tổng Cục Thống Kê, "2009 Vietnam Population"; Nguyễn Cao Thanh, "Đạo Tin Lành ở Việt Nam từ 1975 đến nay, tư liệu và một số đánh giá ban đầu."

8. Keith, *Catholic Vietnam*, xiii–ix.

9. Đại Việt (Great Viet): the establishment of Đại Việt's monarchy from the mid-tenth century to the mid-eleventh century was gradually being shaped as a result of the Tang dynasty in the north losing its control over various parts of the South, including northern Vietnam. Before the monarchy took shape, the "pattern of regionalism" emerged in the land of Viet among local chiefs who vied with one another for dominance. See Dutton, Werner, and Whitmore, *Sources of Vietnamese Tradition*, 28–31.

an important role in the conception of *quốc ngữ*, the modern Vietnamese national script.[10]

There were also several other significant Western influences during the Nguyễn dynasty in the nineteenth and early twentieth centuries, including the relationship between the Nguyễn dynasty and the Catholic missionaries. Catholicism was represented in Vietnam by the Paris-based Foreign Missions Society, and the Catholic communities of southern Vietnam (*Đàng trong*) from 1802 to 1867, the year of France's annexation of southern Vietnam's "six provinces."[11] Although Vietnam experienced relative independence from the northern kingdom (*Đàng ngoài*) during the Nguyễn dynasty, like other countries in Asia, it encountered European colonial threats.

The Catholic Church in the late nineteenth century was enmeshed in Western imperialism in Vietnam and was not in a position to avoid or prevent European expansionist incursions. The tension between the Church and Vietnamese nationalism and anti-colonialism (or self-realization)[12] continued into the early twentieth century when France annexed Laos and unified the areas of Tonkin, Annam, and Cochinchina, together with Cambodia, as Indochina under a French governor general. At the end of the twentieth century, the church has been challenged to make its Vietnamese mark on the social-cultural-political-religious dimensions of the "struggle for independence"[13] in post-colonial-communist Vietnam. Despite these struggles, the church has shown its role as the agent of social, cultural, religious, and even political transformation by adapting itself to a national mindset, belonging in and to the new Vietnam and opening a new chapter in the history of the Catholic Church of Vietnam. Leaving aside this early story of Christianity in Vietnam, that is Roman Catholicism, Protestant/ Evangelical Christianity in post-colonial-communist Vietnam has its own history. We

---

10. For further discussion on how *Quốc ngữ* has become a means of contributing to the Vietnamese Catholic Church's theology and practices, see Nguyen KimSon, "Catholic Church in Vietnam."

11. See Ramsay, *Mandarins and Martyrs*.

12. Landon Kenneth Perry, "Nationalism in Southeastern Asia," *The Far Eastern Quarterly (pre-1986)* 2, no. 2 (1943): 8.

13. Conrad Schirokauer and Donald N. Clark, *Modern East Asia: A Brief History* (Belmont, CA: Thomson/Wadsworth, 2004), 316.

turn now to the Protestant missions in Vietnam, including the French, the British, and the North American missions respectively.

French Protestant Missions in Resurgence

The historiography of the Evangelical Church of Vietnam (ECVN) has generally accepted 1911 as its founding date. The earlier Protestant missionary efforts are unknown to most historians.[14] It is important that this lost history be retrieved because this early history established patterns and trends that became part of the earliest Vietnamese evangelicalism.

The Vietnamese mission historiography has not emphasized strongly enough the contribution of the French Protestant mission in Vietnam, Protestant work that pre-dated English speaking work. Aside from the American mission, the French Protestant mission was a primary influence on Vietnamese evangelical Christianity.[15] Although there is evidence that the French mission was actively sending missionaries, pastors, and establishing churches throughout the country, that evidence has largely been ignored in most of the Vietnamese evangelical mission historiography. Thus, to present Vietnamese evangelical Christianity, the *Tin Lành*, from a more accurate perspective, one needs to reconstruct and rewrite the historiography in a more holistic way, to include the mission work of those forgotten Dutch, British, and especially the French missionaries in Vietnam prior to 1911.

The sociopolitical situation in that period was another significant element that contributed to both the growth and the decline of the French Protestant mission. By the mid-nineteenth century, the French community was the largest foreign community, after the Chinese, to have existed for hundreds of years in Vietnam. Unlike the Dutch and the British,[16] the

---

14. For further discussion of the early European Protestant missional efforts, see Nguyen KimSon, "Mission History of Vietnamese Evangelicalism."

15. For a brief history of the French Catholic mission in Vietnam, see Nguyen KimSon, "Catholic Church in Vietnam"; Keith, *Catholic Vietnam*.

16. Aside from the French, there were a number of Protestant missions actively involved in Vietnam, including the Dutch East Indies Company, the London Mission Society (LMS), the British and Foreign Bible Society (BFBS), and the Christian and Missionary Alliance (CMA) just to name a few. The Dutch attempted to evangelize the Indochinese while trading with the nationals. But besides the CMA, the missions of both the Reformed Church of France and the British Foreign Bible Society (BFBS) were considered the most active in the early missions to Vietnam. Also, a number of British missionary efforts besides the BFBS in Indochina greatly

French had a long and complex relationship with the Vietnamese in all three kingdoms of Tonkin, Annam, and Cochinchina in terms of social, political, and religious involvement. Moreover, a number of French Protestant agencies were present in Vietnam, including the Église Réformée de France (the Reformed Church of France), Société des Missions Évangéliques de Paris (SMEP or Défap), and Société d'Évangélisation des Colonies Françaises (Society for the Evangelization of French Colonies).[17] Among them, the Société d'Evangelisation des Colonies, one of the earliest missionary societies, sent pastor Théophile Boisset to Hải Phòng in 1884 to minister to the French and European Protestants. Pastor Boisset was the one who realized the need to evangelize non-Christians in this region and so he appealed to his Society to send missionaries to what he called "a field more vast than all of France" which "is open to us."[18] Though Boisset urged in his appeal letter that, "the time is short. Don't wait until it's too late," his call and other subsequent appeals went unheeded by the French Protestant Church.[19]

Under the *Église Réformée de France*, the first Protestant church was started in Hải Phòng in 1894. Subsequently, three other Protestant churches were founded: one in Hà Nội in 1902 which is now the Evangelical Church of Vietnam (ECVN) in the North, another in Sài Gòn (Hồ Chí Minh City, after 30 April, 1975), and one in Đà Lạt.[20] Though their missions focused on French colonies, they also attempted to evangelize among the nationals. Article no. 1 of *The Imperial Decree of December 4, 1929* (With regard to the Treaty of 6 June, 1884) states "French Protestant pastors are *unrestricted* in

---

facilitated the evangelical effort. Particularly commendable was the work of Charles Gutzlaff who was directly involved in translating many English works into Cochin-Chinese (Sino-Chinese or the *Nôm*).

17. Georges Bois, *Histoire des Missions en Indochine et les Protestants Francais* (Villeneuve-les-Avignon: Manuscrits, 1952), 40–42; E. Schloesing, *Les Missions Protestantes en Indochine*; A. Richemond, *L'évengile en Indo-Chine* (n.d.); Jacques Pannier, "Les Protestantes Francais in Extrême-Orient au XVII Siècle"; Jacques Pannier, *Trois Ans en Indochine*.

18. John S. Sawin, *The Christian and Missionary Alliance in Indo-China (1882–1924)* (unpublished manuscript), 1, quoting from Schloesing, *Les Missions Protestantes en Indochine*, 1.

19. Sawin, *Christian and Missionary Alliance*, 1, quoting from Schloesing, *Les Missions Protestantes en Indochine*, 1.

20. See Bois, *Histoire des Missions*; Georges Bois, "Les Resultats de L'Enquete Missionnaire en Indochine (The Results of Missionary Inquiry in Indochina)," (Archives of Société des Missions Evangéliques des Paris (SMEP/ Défap), 1924); Georges Bois, "Eglises et Missions Protestantes d'Indocine (de 1949 à 1951)," *Journal des Missions Évangéliques* 5, no. 23 (1952).

the exercise of worship and *evangelistic work*" (emphasis added).²¹ During the late French colonial period, the French Protestant mission in Vietnam grew tremendously.²²

Rev Lê Hoàng Phu's doctoral dissertation in 1972 entitled, "A Short History of The Evangelical Church of Viet Nam (1911–1965)," written from a Vietnamese perspective, is the most helpful source to understand the co-existence of two Evangelical missions, the French Protestant Mission, and the British and Foreign Bible Society (BFBS).²³ Though Rev Phu's work mainly focuses on the ECVN in the period 1911–1965, it also includes some crucial facts about the Protestant missions in addition to the American Christian and Missionary Alliance (CMA). In chapter 3 of his dissertation in particular, entitled "The Entrance of the Protestant Faith: The Work of the Christian and Missionary Alliance from 1911 to 1927," Rev Phu gives a brief history of the early "Evangelical Faith"²⁴ before shifting his main focus to the arrival of the North American CMA.²⁵

Remembering the American Protestant mission in Vietnam, Rev Lê Văn Thái,²⁶ one of the most prominent Vietnamese evangelicals in the ECVN's history, describes this period as "The Primary Stage from 1880–1915." Within a six-page section of *Bốn mươi sáu năm chức vụ: hồi ký của mục sư Lê Văn Thái* (Forty-six years in ministry: The memoir of Rev Le Van

---

21. See the *Decree* in Lê Hoàng Phu, "Short History," 520.

22. A. Encrevé, *Les Protestants en France de 1800 À Nos Jours (Protestants in France from 1800 to Today)*; Brocheux and Hémery, *Indochina*.

23. Besides, there is also James, "American Protestant Missions." This work mainly focuses on how American Protestant missions, especially those of the Christian and Missionary Alliance (CMA) and the Mennonites, were involved with the Vietnamese, particularly with the Evangelical Church of Vietnam (ECVN) during the Vietnam War and during the period of the 1950s to 1980s. Though a number of pieces in this research are peripheral and preliminary due to the researcher's limitations (e.g. chapter 1 on Vietnam is heavily reliant on foreign sources and the section on the ECVN mainly depended on Lê Hoàng Phu's 1972 work), Prof. James's thesis is fascinating and valuable in the way it reveals the nature of missions of the CMA and the Mennonite organizations MCC and EMBMC that shaped Vietnam, in particular the ECVN as a younger institution and a fruit of American mission agencies in several ways, including its theology and practices.

24. These include the British and Foreign Bible Society (BFBS), the Societe d'Evangelisation des Colonies of France, the Protestant Church of France in Indochina.

25. Lê Hoàng Phu, "Short History," 97.

26. Rev Lê Văn Thái was converted in 1919 in Tourane (Đà Nẵng) and was one of the first few Vietnamese Evangelicals at that time. Later, he was the president of the ECVN for 18 years (1942–1960).

Thai), pinpointing 1880 as a starting date, makes clear that the evangelical mission history in Vietnam began before 1911.[27] Furthermore, quoting from *With Christ in Indochina* by E. F. Irwin, one of the first few American missionaries in Vietnam at that time, Rev Thái notes that the Christian and Missionary Alliance based in southern China always directed their efforts toward Vietnam in the 1880s.[28]

Although Rev Phu states the fact that the French Protestant missions in Indochina carried out some mission work, he discounts their activity as having "had little if any bearing on the history of the propagation of the Protestant faith to the Vietnamese people."[29] He quotes Georges Bois' *Histoire des Missions Protestantes en Indochine*, confirming that the French Protestants indeed had arrived in Indochina in the seventeenth century. There is also the account dated 1794 of Jean Baptiste Chaigneaux, a French Protestant naval officer, who helped King Gia Long for twenty-nine years, both in the bitter Vietnamese Civil War and later during the reign of the Nguyễn dynasty. In 1884, under the *Société d'Évangélisation des Colonies Françaises*, a church was planted in Hải Phòng for European Protestants, both civilian and military personnel. There were two other French Protestant churches also established in Hà Nội and Sài Gòn in 1902.[30]

One important fact that Rev Phu recounts from Georges Bois is the conversion of only one Vietnamese national named Duong before 1911,[31] who might have heard of the gospel in Vietnam or in France.[32] Rev Phu argues that since these churches were overwhelmed by the great demands from the European constituency, "they had no time to undertake a missionary enterprise among the Vietnamese," therefore, "no French-speaking Vietnamese were drawn into their churches." Moreover, he states that the French could

---

27. Lê Văn Thái, *Bốn mươi sáu năm chức vụ (Hồi ký)* [Forty-six years in ministry: Memoir] (Sài Gòn: Nhà In Tin-Lành, 1970), 82–87.

28. See Lê Văn Thái, 82–87; Irwin, *With Christ in Indo-China*.

29. Lê Hoàng Phu, "Short History," 99.

30. Lê Hoàng Phu, 99. These churches prospered until 9 March 1945, when the Japanese army overthrew the General Government of Indochina and eliminated the French administration.

31. Perhaps he is Louis Đường who will be discussed later in "the French Protestant Mission" section.

32. Lê Hoàng Phu, "Short History," 100. This could have been a result of one of these early Protestant churches in Hải Phòng, Hà Nội, or Sài Gòn.

not even "master the Vietnamese language and were unable to communicate meaningfully with the native people."[33] In fact, there does not seem to be any concrete evidence that the French missions took root among the Vietnamese in this period. However, Adolphe de Richemond, one of the French leaders of the Hải Phòng, Hà Nội and Sài Gòn churches, wrote an article published in "*Foi et Vie*" (Belief and Life) by the Protestant Church of France in November 1906. The focus of the article was on the "three missionary principles" that the author advocated that the French Protestants follow for missionary work in Indochina: (1) sending to the mission field "persons of high culture" since the Vietnamese have been "civilized for fifteen centuries," (2) carefully selecting the mission location to "avoid the conflict with the Roman Catholic work," and (3) French missionaries to Indochina should refrain from "making Protestants" out of their inquirers but rather endeavor to "transform their spirit" and not to change only their "religious labels."[34] The articulation of these "three missionary principles" is the first account of an attempt at framing contextualization by any Protestant mission in Vietnam. These guiding principles are crucially significant for evangelical Christians in Vietnam because Christian faith should be introduced by Protestant missionaries who have an understanding within and between "civilized" cultural contexts (first principle). This means that they should have an attitude of learning about the long and rich culture of Vietnam, and be able to adapt into the culture. Moreover, Protestant missionaries should respect the Roman Catholics' work by avoiding the conflict with or stepping over their areas of missionary activity (second principle). And most importantly the job of the missionary is not to convert the local people to become "Protestants" by changing their "religious labels" but to "transform their spirit," meaning to allow the gospel to change their worldview (third principle).

Đỗ Hữu Nghiêm,[35] who in 1965 researched evangelicalism in Vietnam, says he was personally given, without hesitation, the manuscript of *Histoire*

---

33. Lê Hoàng Phu, "Short History," 100.

34. Lê Hoàng Phu, 100–101, quoted in Schloesing, *Les Missions Protestantes en Indochine*, 8.

35. He is one of the Vietnamese Catholic scholars who understands Vietnamese evangelicalism. Two of his works would help us to understand the evangelical missions in Vietnam. One is his Master's thesis in history submitted to the University of Saigon in 1968, "Phương pháp truyền giáo Tin Lành giáo tại Việt Nam" (Evangelistic Methods of Evangelicalism

des Missions Protestantes en Indochine (History of Protestant missions in Indochina) and other significant materials, by Georges Bois, who knew that Mr Đỗ was a Roman Catholic.³⁶ In a section entitled "The beginning (from the start to 1915)," he places the establishment of early evangelical missions during the 1600s, at the time of the Dutch East Indies Company, the Charles Harsingh Company in the Red River area, and numerous French pastors, and evangelists. Later, from 1790–1825, the French Protestant Jean Baptiste Chaigneau, who is mentioned above, was a French naval officer and became King Gia Long's advisor to unite Vietnam at that time.³⁷ Besides these, there were numerous other French pastors and evangelists who had worked in Vietnam.³⁸

Contrary to Rev Lê Hoàng Phu's assumption about the lack of success of the French missions in Vietnam, because of political agendas and language barriers as mentioned above, other significant sources have been identified that would reveal the impact of the French Protestant mission in the pioneering stage. These sources include Georges Bois's *Histoire des Missions Protestantes en Indochine* (History of Protestant Missions in Indochina), E. Schloesing's *Les Missions Protestantes en Indochine* (The Protestant Missions in Indochina), Hoàng Cơ Thụy's *Việt sử khảo luận* (Treatise of Vietnamese History), Adolphe de Richemond's *L'Évengile en Indo-Chine* (Evangelization in Indochina), and Jacques Pannier's *Les Protestantes Francais en Extrêême-Orient au XVII Siècle* (The Protestant French in the Far East in the Seventeenth

---

in Vietnam). Another is his unpublished article, "Lịch sử giáo hội Tin Lành Việt cận đại" (Contemporary History of the Evangelical Church of Vietnam) (2010).

36. See Đỗ Hữu Nghiêm, *Lịch sử giáo hội Tin Lành Việt cận đại* [History of the contemporary Evangelical Church of Vietnam] (unpublished manuscript, 2010). He said he was given this manuscript directly from George Bois. His work is an immensely useful resource for reclamation of the evangelical mission historiography in Vietnam.

37. Đỗ Hữu Nghiêm, "Phương pháp truyền giáo của Tin Lành giáo tại Việt Nam" [Mission methodology of protestant religion in Vietnam], (MA Thesis, s.n., 1968), 50–51.

38. See Đỗ Hữu Nghiêm, "Phương pháp truyền giáo của Tin Lành giáo tại Việt Nam"; Đỗ Hữu Nghiêm, *Lịch sử giáo hội Tin Lành Việt cận đại*. Mr. Đỗ named a number of French pastors: Théophile Boisset in Hải Phòng (from 1884), Jacques Pannier in Hà Nội (1902–1905), Métayer in Sài Gòn (1902), Louis de Saint-André in Hà Nội (1904–1911), Adolphe de Richemond in Hà Nội (1906–), and evangelists Mercadier and Bonnet in Hải Phòng (1902–1911), "mailing and literature distribution" evangelist Bonnet in Đà Nẵng (1902–), evangelist André de Richemond in Hà Nội, Ulysse Soulier in Hà Nội (1922–1923), Paul Monet in Hà Nội (1922–1925), Georges Bois in Hà Nội (1923–1925), Thomas Calas in Hà Nội (1930–), Bertrand de Luze in Sài Gòn and Đà Lạt (1949–), and Pierre Médard (1960–1975).

Century) (1904), and *Trois Ans en Indochine* (Three Years in Indochina) (1906). Besides these sources, there were a number of French believers who lived and worked in Vietnam as early as the seventeenth century and as late as the twentieth century, according to Jacques Pannier, a pastor in the French Protestant church in Hà Nội between 1902–1905.[39]

In light of the above mentioned findings, it becomes evident that the Vietnamese evangelical Christian mission needs to reconstruct its mission historiography in a more accurate and complete way that includes the work of those forgotten missions, particularly the French Protestant mission in Vietnam prior to 1911. If the French mission was important in the late nineteenth century colonial context of Vietnam, its investigation of activities and influences would be significant and shed a new light on the Vietnamese evangelical church's contextualization efforts. However, before attempting to have these forgotten missions included in Vietnamese evangelical mission historiography, there is a need to discuss and understand the concerns of these missions.

Protestant Evangelization

With French colonial power established in Vietnam in 1885, there were stirrings in the hearts and minds of the French, British and American Protestants about the need for evangelization in Vietnam. These Protestant missions included the British and Foreign Bible Society (BFBS), the Evangelization of French Colonies, and the Christian and Missionary Alliance (CMA).

From the Pioneering Stage to the National Church

The Christian and Missionary Alliance, or simply the Alliance, is a missionary society founded by Albert B. Simpson in Nyack, New York, as an alliance of churches for global outreach in 1887, just two years after the French

---

39. See Đặng Ngọc Phúc, *Những người Tin Lành tại Việt Nam trong giai đoạn thăm dò* [Protestant Christians in Vietnam in the exploratory period], (San Diego, CA: unpublished, 2011), 307–331. There were Francois Caron (1600–1673), Maximiliaan le Maire (1606–1654), Johannes Lamotius, Jean Baptist Chaigneaux, and Dr Alexandre Yersin (1863–1943). Of these French Protestants, Dr Alexandre Yersin became one of the most important figures in the history of Vietnam. Mr Phúc believes that Yersin was a Protestant Christian, "a quiet person and a hidden missionary," and that Yersin was the eighth Protestant descendant of a Huguenot Protestant in Switzerland.

established Vietnam as their colony. It was formally incorporated as a denomination in 1974 in the United States.[40] But, "Simpson never intended that the Alliance he had formed in 1887 would become a separate denomination; thus, he did not provide a catechism or confession for his followers."[41] Instead, "he affirmed all of the accepted creeds and doctrines of the Protestant traditions."[42] In addition, he stressed the uniqueness of the movement he led as follows:

> First, it stands for an absolute faith in supernatural things and a supernatural God. It represents a Christianity which is out-and-out for God, and it gathers to it those and only those who believe something, and believe it with all their heart and soul and strength. In a word, it represents intense spiritual earnestness. And secondly, along with this as the outgo and overflow of this deeper life of faith and consecration, it represents intense aggressiveness in its work for God, and overflow and outgo that is ever-reaching on to the regions beyond, and seeking to pass on to others the blessings we have ourselves received.[43]

Today, there are more than 2,000 CMA churches in the United States.[44] More than 800 missionaries and workers minister in fifty-plus countries, planting churches and training national church leaders, providing relief and development assistance, medical and dental care, and microenterprise projects.[45]

---

40. See http://indochina1911.com; http://www.cmalliance.org/about/history, accessed 29 August 2014.

41. T. V. Thomas and Ken Draper, "A. B. Simpson and World Evangelization," in *The Birth of a Vision: Essays on the Ministry and Thought of Albert B. Simpson*, ed. F. David Hartzfeld and Charles Nienkirchen (Beaverlodge, Alberta: Buena Book Services, 1986), 200.

42. Thomas and Draper, "A. B. Simpson and World Evangelization," cited from Albert B. Simpson, "Distinctive Teaching," *The Word, the Work and the World* 9 (July 1887): 1–5.

43. Albert B. Simpson, "Aggressive Christianity," *The Christian and Missionary Alliance Weekly* 23 (September 23, 1899): 260–262, cited by Thomas and Draper, "A. B. Simpson and World Evangelization," 200.

44. See http://www.cmalliance.org/about/history/, accessed 29 August 2014. See also "Minutes of the General Council" in *The Christian and Missionary Alliance* (1970); *The Alliance Witness* (1971).

45. See *The Alliance*, http://www.cmalliance.org/about/history/ (accessed 29 August 2014). For more information of the CMA's history, see details of the four periods provided on the website: The Founding Years (1887–1919), Sacrifice and Expansion (1919–1946), The Evangelical Era (1947–1974), and the Missionary Church Era (1974–present).

Dr Simpson[46] was the first American Protestant who wrote of his interest in Vietnam in *The Word, the Work, and the World* published in the August 1882 issue as he was focused on this region before it became a colony.

> Cochin China (Saigon) and Tonkin (Hanoi) so near to China on the South, have passed under the control of the French. Taking advantage of commercial difficulties and misunderstandings, a French expedition has recently occupied Hanoi, the capital of Tonkin and now the whole peninsula of Annam is virtually under their power. This region is rich in natural wealth, and closely connected by trade with the Chinese province of Yunnan.[47]

With this special interest in Vietnam (the three kingdoms of Tonkin, Annam, and Cochinchina), and Tibet, Simpson devoted three columns to an analysis of the people of Vietnam – their origin, the geography, religion and economy of the country and the Roman Catholic Church's efforts in the country. He notes that "there are several primitive people living in the center of the empire. These are very savage and seem to have no idea of God." He concludes:

> This land is one of those neglected regions that have long been crying out for Christian enterprise and faith and love to bring into it the sweet story of Jesus. May the time be not far distant when the whole land from Saigon (capital of Cochinchina) to the China frontier shall be claimed and won for Him . . . The southeast peninsula of Asia has been much neglected. The great kingdom of Annam (the center of Vietnam today) should be occupied for Christ. Why should it not, along with Tibet, be looked forward to as one of the earliest fields of new aggression by the people of God?[48]

Dr Simpson was not only writing in periodicals about his interest in Vietnam, but also preaching it. In 1892, he challenged American Christians:

---

46. See http://indochina1911.com; http://www.cmalliance.org/about/history/, accessed 29 August 2014.

47. This first recorded interest of Albert B. Simpson towards Vietnam cited by Sawin, *Christian and Missionary Alliance*, 2.

48. The Christian and Missionary Alliance, *The Word, the Work and the World* (February 1887): 112, 128. Cited by Sawin, 3.

> Shall we hold up to God the great unoccupied fields of the world this year, for His mighty power to open to the Gospel? They are Tibet, Annam, Arabia, et al . . . All nations must have the Gospel ere the Lord come.[49]

He continued in the same magazine:

> Paul's great ambition was to preach the Gospel where Christ was not named. Today there is still a great unknown world for the missionary – 900 cities of China, 300–400 tribes in Africa, Tibet, China, Annam, Cambodia, et al. Who will go?[50]

In his report to a missionary convention in October 1892, he wrote:

> It is also upon our hearts, as soon as suitable workers can be found, to endeavor to open a mission in the provinces of Annam, Cambodia, Cochin China and Tonkin, where among twenty millions of people there is not a single Protestant missionary. It is an unhealthy country and entirely occupied by the Roman Catholic religion whose opposition will undoubtedly be found most persistent. But we are asking the Lord for some wise and brave volunteers who can speak the French language and who shall be gifted with the wisdom of the Master to cope with these tremendous difficulties, and found a successful mission in this unoccupied field.[51]

Dr Simpson's heart was passionate for both South China and Vietnam. He urged the Missionary Alliance (the International Missionary Alliance at that time), every time he had a chance, to reach these "unreached" people for Christ. In 1893, Simpson sent David Lelacheur to Singapore and then to Sài Gòn on his behalf. He believed that Singapore was the base camp to enter Vietnam, and Sài Gòn (Cochinchina, in the south) the city to enter

---

49. The Christian and Missionary Alliance, *Christian Alliance* (15 January 1892): 33, 131. Cited by Sawin, 4.

50. The Christian and Missionary Alliance, *Christian Alliance* (15 January 1892): 33, 131. Cited by Sawin, 4.

51. See Sawin, 4.

Vietnam.[52] For the north of Indo-China (Tonkin) and the south China region, he urged readers in another article entitled, "A Cry from Quang-si," describing the destitution of the area and lamenting the absence of missionaries inside the province.[53] Simpson believed that as the French have built a railroad from Tonkin to Lung-Chow, Quang-si could be reached via Tonkin.[54] Simpson had a passion to reach the neglected field of Vietnam. Thus, in June 1894, he devoted a long descriptive editorial to Annam in which he gave a strong conclusion:

> When we were abroad a year ago, 1893, we were informed that an agent of the Bible Society had travelled over the whole Empire and found it open to the Bible. We believe that it is one of the loudest calls of the Spirit of God to the Church to plant a chain of Protestant missions in the cities of Hue, Hanoi, Haiphong and Saigon . . .
>
> We have long been praying the Holy Spirit to raise up some such company of pioneers, and to call some brave, true heart to lead us in this great movement. May God lay it upon the hearts of some chosen vessels, and give the high honor to someone who reads these lines, of planting the Standard of the Cross in the great centres of this neglected Asiatic Empire.[55]

Again, in his missionary sermon entitled "The Macedonian Cry," Simpson describes Vietnam as one of the world's areas of tremendous neglect and need.[56] The following year, 1895, he pleads for Vietnam "with its twenty millions of people and not a single Protestant voice to tell them of Jesus."[57] Then, a year later, in 1896, he reminded his readers again that only four

---

52. The Christian and Missionary Alliance, *Christian Alliance* (June 1893): 372. Cited by Sawin, 4–5.

53. The Christian and Missionary Alliance, *Christian Alliance* (January 1894): 98–100. Cited by Sawin, 7.

54. The Christian and Missionary Alliance, *Christian Alliance* (August 1895): 280. Cited by Sawin, 7.

55. The Christian and Missionary Alliance, *Christian Alliance* (June 1894): 690f. Cited by Sawin, 7–8.

56. The Christian and Missionary Alliance, *Christian Alliance* (August 1894): 199. Cited by Sawin, 8.

57. Albert B. Simpson, *Annual Report* (October 1895): 84. Cited by Sawin, 8.

years remained in the nineteenth century, "Shall it see Annam, Tonkin, Cochinchina and Cambodia all represented in the twentieth century convention of the Christian Alliance?"[58]

After all these writings and preaching on these "neglected" people of the world, several new missionaries from the Gospel Tabernacle, New York City, responded and were ready to be sent to Southern China. Among them was Robert A. Jaffray, twenty-three years of age, going to join the pioneers in Quang-si, South China. But Vietnam was upon Jaffray's heart so that Simpson commented about Jaffray in his address, "In going to Southern China, God had laid upon his heart more than twenty millions of unevangelized people just South of them, and he hoped God would use him in some way to reach them."[59] True enough, Jaffray later became one of the key persons of the CMA's South China Headquarters in Wuchow, Quang-si.[60] In this initial stage, the early CMA missionaries, whose mission work was based in South China, always directed their efforts toward Vietnam.

The Alliance missionaries attempted to reach various provinces in the northern part of Vietnam in 1889, 1897, and 1902 to "occupy Vietnam with the gospel as soon as possible."[61] Eventually, Clarence H. Reeves and his wife, Lillian H. Lamont, who were based in Southern China with Robert A. Jaffray, undertook an extensive exploratory trip within the province of Quang-si. They reached the city of Lang-son (a northern province of Vietnam today) to "extend their work into this neglected land (Vietnam)."[62] However, Vietnam was still the "neglected land" as evidenced by silence in the annual reports, as well as the in the 1904 and 1905 minutes of the South China Executive Committee.[63] Instead, Lung-chow became an object of missionary occupa-

---

58. Simpson, *Annual Report* (1896). Cited by Sawin, 8.

59. The Christian and Missionary Alliance, *Christian Alliance* (January 1896): 72. Cited by Sawin, 8.

60. Robert A. Jaffray, "Report of the Indo-China Mission, 1916," *The Alliance Witness* (23 June 1917): 184–185. See also in Sawin, 150–155.

61. See Phạm Xuân Tín, *The Gospel First Came to Vietnam* (Mennonite Biblical Seminary and Mennonite World Conference, 1970).

62. Albert B. Simpson, "The Evangelization of Annam," *The Christian Alliance* (15 January 1897): 49. Cited by Sawin, 10.

63. Lloyd G. Hughes, "Anam the Neglected," *The Alliance Witness* (January & February 1904): 2.

tion for the South China missionaries, and thus "Annam and Cochinchina are almost outside the influence of evangelical Christianity."[64]

However, Jaffray was highly motivated and made all efforts to carry on the work in Vietnam. In the Annual Report for 1905 which was given in 1906, Jaffray said, "The Lord still holds this neglected field before us. Oh, why are we so slow to go up?"[65] Again, Jaffray continued to impress North American Christians with the "lostness" of the people of Indochina, the unevangelized Vietnamese, in his article published in the *Alliance Magazine* in 1908.[66] In the CMA Council gathering of May 1908, the call for Vietnam as "a whole country absolutely neglected" was continued: "Shall we see a band of missionaries come out this year (1908) for Annam? If so, we firmly believe that the way is open for the conquest of this land for Jesus."[67]

The year 1910 was considered the final year before the time when the CMA missionaries would reach their goal and finally set foot on Vietnam soil to claim its people for Jesus and the Church. The three men to spearhead the advance were already located in Southern China: Paul Hosler, Lloyd Hughes and Robert Jaffray; two others who would join them a little later, William C. Cadman and Frank A. Soderberg, had arrived in Vietnam in 1910. Cadman, one of the key missionaries in Vietnam in 1911, had come as a printing press specialist for Southern China at the request of Jaffray. Hughes and Hosler were studying French and Vietnamese so that these earnest preparations were being undertaken with a view to soon enter Vietnam.[68] Even though there were still uncertainties and differences, the event of establishing a mission in

---

64. The Christian and Missionary Alliance, "The Missionary Review of the World," *Alliance Magazine* (1905): 602. Cited by Sawin, 28–29.

65. Robert A. Jaffray, "The Annual Report for 1905," *Alliance Magazine* (1906): 106. Cited by Sawin, 29.

66. Robert A. Jaffray, "The 'Lostness' of the People of Indo-China," *Alliance Magazine* (10 April 1908): 22f. Cited by Sawin, 30–34.

67. A. E. Funk, "The Need of Annam: Annual Report May 1908," (1908): 151. Cited by Sawin, 34; Robert A. Jaffray, "A Plea for the Perishing of South China and Annam," *The Christian and Missionary Alliance* 33, no. 4 (23 October 1909): 49–51.

68. The Christian and Missionary Alliance, "Annual Report for 1910," (1911): 16, 139. Cited by Sawin, 38–39; Lloyd G. Hughes, "A Personal Letter," *The Christian and Missionary Alliance* (7 July 1906): 418. In August 1910, Mr C. H. Colby of Brooklyn donated funds to build a mission home at Lung-chow. See "The South China Executive Committee minutes," (1910): 374, cited by Sawin, 39.

Vietnam was promising. A year later, in 1911, the work opened in Vietnam.[69] In Jaffray's 1916 report, the CMA had met its long-awaited goal since 1891 to enter French Indochina (also known as Annam). He wrote:

> But real work was permitted by the French authorities only five years ago (1911), and even yet, with perhaps the sole exception of one station in Laos, opened by the Plymouth Brethren, the Alliance Mission is the only Protestant Missionary Society at work in Indo-China. The British and Foreign Bible Society has, through it colporteurs, for some years scattered the Scriptures, principally the Chinese version, among the people, and the Paris Evangelical Association has also had French pastors working among the French population, including the soldiers and sailors, at the chief centers for many years. They have only one man on the field now.[70]

The Alliance missionaries, such as C. H. Reeves, arrived in Lạng Sơn province, the area of North Vietnam in 1897. Mr and Mrs Sylvan Dayan arrived in Hải Phòng in 1902; Robert A. Jaffray had already been in Hà Nội since 1889. However, these missions were not successful in planting churches. It was only on the second visit to Tourane in 1911, the landmark year in the mission history of Vietnamese evangelicalism, that Jaffray was successful in planting a church.[71]

By 1927, the year of forming the national church, the Evangelical Church of Indochina (ECIC), which later became the Evangelical Church of Vietnam (ECVN), the CMA was considered as a denomination in Indochina. From

---

69. The minutes of the Board meeting in New York on 17 June 1911 stated that because of financial conditions the Board should "seriously considered if it is advisable to open Annam." At 29 July meeting of the Board, Mr Simpson read a letter from South China urging the Board to open Annam. The South China Committee minutes, however, indicated the feeling that existed in New York. A letter had come from Mr Funk in which he stated four reasons why the Board cannot open Vietnam. They were: (1) Financial conditions at Home have first consideration; (2) The number of missionaries necessary to maintain the South China ranks; (3) The Board's attitude of discouraging the opening of new missions in other lands; and (4) Missionaries on furlough have a united sentiment against opening Vietnam as well as any other new areas. See "The South China Executive Committee Minutes" (16 Sep 1911): 404, cited by Sawin, 48.

70. Jaffray, "Report of the Indo-China Mission for 1916," 184f. Cited by Sawin, 150–155.

71. See Lê Văn Thái, *Bốn mươi sáu năm chức vụ (Hồi ký)*, 82.

1928 to 1975, the CMA remained in Indochina as the "Mother Mission" which functioned only in "an advisory capacity."[72]

French Protestant Mission Initiative

The French Protestant mission was recognized as one of the earliest Protestant missions in Vietnam. There are several accounts to consider as initial evangelical ventures by the French Protestants in the land where French Roman Catholicism had dominated for the previous three centuries. As early as 1884, the French Protestants had shown interest in mission work in Indochina (Vietnam). That year, the Society for the Evangelization of French Colonies sent pastor Théophile Boisset to Hải Phòng as mentioned. In 1886, though Boisset appealed to his Society to send missionaries to this field, the French Protestant church seemed not ready. Nevertheless, the French church – as they had two French pastors in Hải Phòng and Hà Nội who had come at the end of 1898 – restricted their ministry mainly with the French, but offered assistance to the CMA mission to enter the field. A. B. Simpson thought they could be the opening wedge to Vietnam. Though the plan didn't work out as expected, the relationship between the French Protestant missionaries and CMA's R. A. Jaffray was relatively smooth. On 10 February 1899, in his letter to Simpson, which was published in the *Christian Alliance,* Jaffray said:

> You [Simpson] will be much pleased to know that the Protestant church of France has pastors here now. I was pleased to meet Pastor G. M. Mereadier at Haiphong and Pastor Adolphe de Richemond[73] who is my kind host at this place (Hanoi). These two gentlemen with their families arrived here only three months ago and have begun their work, which is, of course, not of a missionary character, but simply among the Protestant French population of Tonkin and especially the soldiers. The number of Protestants is rather larger than I had expected. Mr.

---

72. See Lê Hoàng Phu, "Short History," 188–189. In 1975 (also called Vietnam War, or Second Indochina War), the northern Communist army of the Democratic Republic of Vietnam gained a final victory over the alliance of the United States and the Republic of Vietnam under the United States President Richard M. Nixon and the South Vietnamese President Nguyễn Văn Thiệu. Since then, the country has been renamed as the Socialist Republic of Vietnam. All missionaries were forced to leave the country.

73. He was the General Secretary of the *Société d'Évangélisation des Colonies Françaises* in which Pastor B. Couve was the President.

> Richemond's parish here in Hanoi consists of over 100. Their work is already very encouraging and will do much to prepare the way for the opening of the mission work in Tonkin. Mr. Richemond informs me that it is the desire of their society to establish mission work among the Annamese also in the future but this is as yet altogether indefinite.
>
> Mr. Richemond is much pleased that our Alliance anticipates opening work here and has encouraged me very much. He has over and over again, expressed himself most heartily, as willing to do all in his power to assist and cooperate. He says he does not believe the French government would offer any resistance whatever, but on the other hand would afford satisfactory protection.[74]

In 1901, Jaffray held some meetings among the French Protestants in Quebec, Canada, and presented to them the needs of Vietnam. The result was that Rev Sylvan Dayan and his wife offered themselves for missionary work in Vietnam. Later, they arrived in Hong Kong, and then Wuchow, where they were welcomed by Jaffray in May 1902. Dayan was authorized by the South China Executive Committee to take a trip to Tonkin in August 1902. Apparently Dayan disagreed with the idea of such an investigation, but nevertheless carried it out, as Dayan thought that "attempts to study Annamese (Vietnamese) on French territory would not only be fruitless, but fatal to our prospects for that field."[75] Thus, on this trip his purpose was to find and bring to Wuchow a Vietnamese language teacher, which he did.[76] Unfortunately, in 1904, the Dayans had to end their relationship with the Alliance because of some disagreements on principles between them and the South China Executive Committee, because of his ambition toward the fields ("Annam or Home") and the attitude toward the Board.[77] The conflict was actually about mission strategies that closed an effort with otherwise bright prospects for

---

74. Robert A. Jaffray, "To Dr. Simpson (10 February)," *Christian Alliance* (May 1899): 162f. Cited by Sawin, 12–14.

75. The Christian and Missionary Alliance, *Christian Alliance* (January 1903): 55. Cited by Sawin, 19–20.

76. The Christian and Missionary Alliance, *Alliance Magazine* (31 January 1903): 55f. Cited by Sawin, 20–24.

77. See Sawin, 25–29.

the potential field of Vietnam. The disagreement was between Mr Dayan and the Committee (in Wuchow) and the Board (in New York) about how to start effective activity in Vietnam ("the Committee felt that contacts with Chinese merchants would accomplish the task better and cheaper"). There was also disagreement about where and when was the best place and time to enter the country ("In October 1903, Mr Dayan had requested a copy of the Committee's letter to the Board. They sent him a synopsis of it. On December 2, a letter from the Board insisted that Tonkin be entered via Lung-Chow").[78]

Also in 1902, Mr and Mrs Bonnet arrived in Tourane (Đà Nẵng). They represented the British Foreign Bible Society (BFBS). For eight years, located in Tourane, Mr Bonnet did a great work in Chinese (*chữ nôm*) Bible distribution that prepared the ground for the arrival of the CMA missionaries later in 1911.[79] Bonnet was also praised publicly in the CMA's *The Alliance Weekly* in 1912, perhaps by A. B. Simpson, who wrote:

> The British and Foreign Bible Society, through their faithful agent, Mr. Bonnet, has labored in this field (Tourane, Annam) for seven or eight years, and has won for the Gospel of Jesus Christ a good reputation, and it was through this man we got this opening.[80]

In fact, besides Bonnet who was involved in the Bible distribution, there was a report of the Bible Society of France that appeared in "The Missionary Review of the World" in 1905:

> There is not a single important place in Cochin China, in the southern part of Annam and in the French Laos territory which has not many copies of the Holy Bible. More than 400 copies

---

78. Dayan requested a second trip to Tonkin in February 1903 to find a second Vietnamese language teacher (as the first had returned to Vietnam), but the Committee did not respond due to lack of funds. He waited for a response from the Board in New York. He was then frustrated that his proposal to enter Vietnam had been delayed and his plan to enter Vietnam's field from Saigon was not approved, instead the Committee and the Board wanted to enter Tonkin via Lung-Chow. For further details of the conflict, see Sawin, 25–29.

79. Lloyd G. Hughes, "A Momentous Crisis in the Quest of Annam," *The Alliance Witness* (26 August 1911): 337; Paul M. Hosler, "The Dawn of Protestant Missions in Annam," *The Alliance Witness*, (2 December 1911): 136–138. See also in Sawin, 42–46.

80. The Christian and Missionary Alliance, *The Alliance Weekly* (August 1912): 281. Cited by Sawin, 56–57.

of the Bible have been distributed among the Protestant colonists and soldiers, and more than 300 copies have gone into the hands of Roman Catholics who have asked for them. A large number of Vietnamese, Cambodians, Chinese and East Indian who have learned to read French have also eagerly received the Bible. This French society, which published the Scriptures in one language only, is finding by experience that an effective means of preaching the Gospel in all the world is by disseminating the Gospel everywhere.[81]

In Rev Phan Đình Liệu's "*Lịch sử Tin Lành truyền đến Việt Nam*" (The History of the Evangelical Mission to Vietnam), it is stated that the BFBS purchased Mr Phuc's property in Quảng Nam province in 1902 to establish a small center for distributing New Testaments and Gospel portions in Chinese under Mr Bonnet and three other Vietnamese (Am, Lo, and Yen).[82] The Society, in fact, became the largest agency in Vietnam to "propagate the Christian message by the printed page."[83] However, as for Bible publishing, the CMA missionaries in Indochina made their own efforts. Mr and Mrs W. C. Cadman were appointed to translate and print the Vietnamese Bible which used the standard Romanized script (or the *quốc ngữ*), instead of using the script of the BFBS's Chinese Bible. Such a decision was very wise and timely as stated in the article, "the message will bring (the Gospel) to many who cannot read the Chinese characters (neither the French)."[84] The decision of using the vernacular language *quốc ngữ* in Bible translation instead of Chinese or French (as the BFBS and the Bible Society of France had done) was a significant turn that followed the *quốc ngữ* trend promoted by Vietnamese nationalists and Vietnamese Catholics. Furthermore, it followed

---

81. The Christian and Missionary Alliance, "The Missionary Review of the World," *Alliance Magazine* (1905): 602. Cited by Sawin, 28–29.

82. Phan Đình Liệu, *Lịch sử Tin Lành truyền đến Việt Nam* [The history of the Evangelical mission to Vietnam], (unpublished manuscript, n.d.), 3–6. Cited by Lê Hoàng Phu, "Short History," 101.

83. Lê Hoàng Phu, "Short History," 101.

84. Jaffray, "Report of the Indo-China Mission, 1916," 184–185. See also in Sawin, *Christian and Missionary Alliance*, 150–155.

the vernacular Bible translation movement among East Asian Christian missionaries (e.g. Korean translation into the Hangul script from Manchuria).[85]

During 1910, at the Edinburgh Missionary Conference, for example, Pastor A. Boegner delivered a speech with an "optimistic view of the prospects of the future mission work in the French Colonies."[86] This attention perhaps stirred the mission work among the French Protestant churches that resulted in a number of missionaries arriving in Indochina.

In 1911 and 1912, letters from J. H. Freeman, a CMA missionary stationed in Lampoon, Siam (Thailand), were also addressed to Pastor A. Boegner of Société des Missions Évangéliques de Paris (SMEP), now known as Défap.[87] The familiar name that has been used in English is the Paris Evangelical Society of France. This name was used in various letters by the American Mission Board of the Presbyterian Church of USA (PC USA) and the Christian and Missionary Alliance (CMA) to the French Protestant Missions.[88] Nevertheless, this is, perhaps, the first account of the SMEP appearing as a missionary society to Indochina (Vietnam) which became the sending society for a number of French Protestant missionaries, including Ulysse Soulier, Paul Monet, and Georges Bois. Besides contacts with the French Catholic priests and the French Protestant pastors in Tonkin (the north of Vietnam) for the French-speaking churches, Mr Bonnet, working with the BFBS in Tourane (present day Đà Nẵng), was the key French Protestant person responsible

---

85. For further discussion of using *quốc ngữ* among the Vietnamese nationalists and Catholics, see Nguyen KimSon, "Catholic Church in Vietnam." For Korean Bible translation, see Samuel H. Moffett, *A History of Christianity in Asia*, 2 vols., vol. 2: 1500 to 1900 (Maryknoll, NY: Orbis Books, 1998), 531, 46 fn. 9.

86. See Lloyd G. Hughes, "Letter to A. Boegner on Sep 19, 1910," (CMA Headquarters, Wuchow, South China: Archives of Société des Missions Evangéliques des Paris [SMEP/Défap], 1910).

87. See J. H. Freeman, "Letters to A. Boegner on July 27, 1911 and March 12, 1912," (Lampoon, Siam: Archives of Société des Missions Evangéliques des Paris [SMEP/Défap]). The former name of Défap was Société des Missions Évangéliques de Paris (SMEP), from 1822 to 1971. Since 1971, it has been called Défap. See Jean-François Zorn, *Le Grand Siècle d'une Mission Protestante: La Mission de Paris de 1822 a 1914*, 2nd édition revue et augmentée ed. (Paris: Éditions Karthala, 2012), 22–24.

88. See Arthur J. Brown, "Lao Expansion No. 79," (Archives of Société des Missions Evangéliques des Paris [SMEP/Défap], 1912). In the letter dated 11/9/1912 to the Laos mission, Arthur J. Brown, Secretary of the Mission Board of the Presbyterian Church of USA (PC USA) addressed Rev. Daniel Couve, the Secretary of this Society, who was also a member of the Continuation Committee of the World Missionary Conference at Edinburg.

for the decision of choosing the city of Tourane to be the center of the CMA mission in Vietnam in 1911.[89]

Ulysse Soulier was among the first French Protestant missionaries to Indochina by the end of 1921, together with Pierre Samuel Vũ Tâm Thất and Paul Monet.[90] Soulier was ordained a pastor early in 1921. He had until then studied in France at the Preparatory School for Protestant Theology of Batignolles, and then at the Institute of Protestant Theology, where he apparently resided until leaving for Indochina. He was the key person of the SMEP to the French colonies of Indochina.[91] Most of the archival documents of Indochina found in Défap (SMEP) were marked as belonging to "U. Soulier."[92]

The archival documents reveal some important facts regarding the sometimes rough relationships among the French Protestant missions (SMEP), the French Church in Indochina (Église Protestante Francaise du Tonkin), and the CMA mission in the pioneering stage. Also, from the Défap/SMEP's archive, it appears that by 1922 there were some nationals who were the first converts of the French Protestant missionaries in Tonkin. These included Nguyễn Bang Tiến in Bắc Ninh, and Nguyễn Văn Tế in Hà Nội, both of whom later attended the CMA's Bible school in Tourane, Đà Nẵng in 1924. Besides these men, Pierre Samuel Vũ Tâm Thất and Louis Đường[93] were two

---

89. Here are five reasons why Tourane was strategic location for the CMA mission: (1) For a town in the tropics it is considered healthy; (2) Mr Bonnet desires to sell or rent his property to us. This would protect us from Roman Catholic interference; (3) By our beginning work in Tourane we would have the opportunity to become the heirs of the good-will of both officials and people which Mr Bonnet has no doubt deservedly secured during his eight years' residence in the place; (4) The Roman Catholic influence in this district is decidedly less than in other ports; and (5) It strikes about the centre of Annam. See in Paul M. Hosler and G. L. Hughes, "The South China Alliance Tidings," (August 1911): 3. Also, see Hughes, "Momentous Crisis," 337; Hosler, "Dawn of Protestant Missions," 136–138.

90. Bourdeaux, "Notes on an Unpublished Letter," 19.

91. See Ulysse Soulier, "L'appel de l'Indochine française" [The call of French Indochina], (Conference at Nantes in August 1920: Archives of Société des Missions Evangéliques des Paris [SMEP/Défap], 1920).

92. See Ulysse Soulier, "Copied Letters from 1907–1928," (Archives of Société des Missions Evangéliques des Paris [SMEP/Défap]). The Défap's library has not catologued these documents into archival documents, but they were boxed under *Indochina 1860-1924* and *Indochina 1925-1952*. Perhaps, these letters, pamphlets and documents, related to the field of Indochina, were collected by Soulier before he handed them over to the Défap/SMEP's archive.

93. Bourdeaux believes it was through Sergeant Louis Đường, a Protestant Vietnamese non-commissioned officer who was also an interpreter (he was of mixed race), that Soulier came to know another interpreter, one newly converted Pierre Samuel Vũ Tam Thất.

Vietnamese who, together with Ulysse Soulier and Paul Monet, were employed by the "exploratory commission to study the foundation of a French Protestant mission in Indochina," the commission that was founded on 29 April 1920 to support the missionary initiative.[94]

Vũ Tâm Thất in his two reports dated Hanoi 23 June 1922 and Hanoi 15 November 1922, indicated that he was a Vietnamese evangelist, but was affiliated with the Study Commission of the French Protestant Mission in Paris: "Evangéliste Annamite a Messieurs les Membres de la Commission d'Etudes en vue de la fondation d'une Mission Protestante Francaise en INDOCHINE à Paris" (Annamese Evangelist to the Honorable Members of the Study Commission for the founding of the French Protestant Mission in Indochina in Paris).[95] Perhaps, at the time this report was presented, Vũ Tâm Thất was in Hà Nội, though he might have been "demobilized in December 1919, and managed to stay in France and begin theological studies in Paris in order to become an evangelist."[96]

Among additional important influences of the French Protestant missions in Vietnam was the missionary work accomplished by Paul Monet and Georges Bois. Bois was also one of the most influential French Protestant missionaries in the early twentieth century in Tonkin (the North of Vietnam today). In 1952, Bois wrote his thesis on *Histoires des Missions Protestantes en Indochine,* summarizing the Protestant missions in Indochina from the late-nineteenth to the mid-twentieth centuries. Bois describes his mission work under Société des Missions Évangéliques de Paris (SMEP/Défap) together with Paul Monet, who had already been in Hanoi since 1923. Together, Monet and Bois planted a Vietnamese church in which they contextualized the worship and liturgy into Vietnamese culture – burning incense, using Psalms to worship in a Vietnamese way, and using Vietnamese music and melody rather than the Western hymns.[97] Unfortunately, their work had to stop because of some internal difficulties and criticism regarding their mission strategies.

---

94. Bourdeaux, "Notes on an Unpublished Letter," 16.

95. See Vu Tam That Samuel, "Rapport relatif à la Mission Américaine de Hanoi le 23 Juin, 1922 (Report on the American Mission in Hanoi in June 23, 1922)," (Archives of Société des Missions Evangéliques des Paris (SMEP/ Défap), 1922).

96. Bourdeaux, "Notes on an Unpublished Letter," 17.

97. See Đặng Ngọc Phúc, *Những người Tin Lành tại Việt Nam trong giai đoạn thăm dò*, 362–363.

Perhaps, the resistance was from the French Protestant believers in Vietnam who saw the practice as too Roman Catholic. Nevertheless, both Monet and Bois remained in Vietnam and carried on mission work among the nationals. If this account is true, perhaps further research into their contextualization efforts in Vietnam during this time is needed. Their efforts could be the second evidence of "contextualization" in Vietnam attempted by the Protestant missionary.[98] These strategies may encourage Vietnamese evangelicals today to contextualize the gospel message throughout the worship and liturgy of the church, as well as to make the Bible culturally relevant to the Vietnamese.

Attitudes toward Vietnamese Socio-Cultural and Religious Contexts

Most of the written or spoken accounts about the Vietnamese, their culture and religions by the CMA missionaries who visited Vietnam in the pioneering stage, were very superficial, offensive, and biased for today's readers. Here are some illustrations that indicate the bias against the nationals and their religious, cultural and political contexts. For instance, in one report in the *Missionary Alliance* about the New York Tabernacle October Convention in 1892, Simpson stated that, "It is an unhealthy country (Annam, Tonkin, Cochin-China and Cambodia) and entirely occupied by the Roman Catholic religion whose opposition will undoubtedly be found most persistent."[99] Again, in an *Annual Report* in October 1893, Simpson said, "This whole country is crowded with Roman Catholic priests and converts, and is the strongest mission of the Church of Rome in the heathen lands . . ."[100]

The CMA missionaries' attitude toward Vietnamese traditions, religious beliefs and other faiths in this period was often negative and sounded judgmental. Interfaith dialogue, even today, is an ongoing struggle, something regarded as a fad that should be outside of the evangelicals' radar. But the root of the Vietnamese evangelicals' isolation from other faiths today may be traced back to the ways that the native traditions, Vietnamese beliefs and

---

98. The articulation of the "three missionary principles" is the first account of an attempt at framing "contextualization" by any Protestant mission in Vietnam as seen in the above section, "French Protestant Missions in Resurgence," particularly pages 150–151.

99. Cited by Sawin, *Christian and Missionary Alliance*, 4.

100. Cited by Sawin, 5.

faiths were described in the writings of the early CMA missionaries. About religions in Vietnam, Robert A. Jaffray wrote:

> The religion of the people is chiefly Buddhism and Confucianism, with some additions to suit their tastes ... The Vietnamese people, it is said, are not an extremely religious race. However, Protestant Christianity has never been introduced among the Vietnamese; it speaks to the shame of the Church.[101]

Regarding the Roman Catholics in Vietnam, Jaffray seemed more critical of the Church than of local religions. The language sounds even harsher with labels such as a "system of making converts," "the awful shadows of Romanism," and "giants in the land." Jaffray published an article in 1899, from which the labels and quotations above and below are taken. Perhaps he had just taken an initial tour of the country, and did not yet have a full picture of who the Vietnamese people were. And yet, he wrote:

> Their (the Catholics in Vietnam) system of "making converts" is a wholesale one ...
>
> One is not surprised at such results, when such broad methods of missionary work are adopted. It is the old story of the awful shadows of Romanism which have cursed South America, Cuba, Puerto Rico, and the Philippines Islands. Opposition, if any, to Protestant missionary work, will come from these unscrupulous priests.
>
> We have come to Kadesh. Our report is: There be "giants in the land," there are many adversaries stronger than we. But bless God, though the natural prospects may be dark, yet silver linings shine on God's side of the cloud, and greater is He that is in you, than he that is in the world ... Oh, for the love of His appearing, heed the cry of these perishing souls.[102]

In the 1908 report, again Jaffray said:

> The native religions of these people are Buddhism, Confucianism, Spiritism and Roman Catholicism. The latter is of the same type

---

101. Robert A. Jaffray, "Việt Nam," *Christian Alliance* (July 1899): 65f. Cited by Sawin, 14.
102. Jaffray, "Vietnam," 65–67. Cited by Sawin, 14–16.

> of corrupt Romanism that is found in South America and other such countries . . . A slight knowledge of the facts of the case is sufficient to prove to the true Christian that the missions of the Roman Catholic Church cannot serve as a substitute for the pure Gospel of Jesus Christ. The fact that Romanism is there, is but an added reason why the True Light should shine amid darkness.[103]

In the report of 1909, Jaffray said:

> Romanism, as found in Annam, is in its most corrupt form. Far from being a substitute for the true Gospel, it is but an added reason for sending the pure Light to that benighted land.[104]

Whether the CMA missionaries in Vietnam were specifically influenced by Dr Simpson's views on other religions is not part of the current study, but these missionaries and the national leaders later struggled with issues of relating to other faiths and beliefs in Vietnam. It seems obvious that Dr Simpson saw other world religions as satanic counterfeits.[105]

Concerning the Vietnamese nationals, another CMA missionary also had an interesting observation. In his "First Impression of Annam" written in 1912, Frank A. Soderberg[106] described:

> For two years previous to the opening of Annam, the writer had prayed that the way might open for him to go. God graciously answered and it was my privilege to enter as one of the pioneer missionaries to this neglected land . . .
>
> There is an aggregate population of 22,000,000 – All these souls are without a ray of hope . . .

---

103. Jaffray, "The 'Lostness' of the People of Indo-China," *Alliance Magazine* (10 April 1908): 22f. Cited by Sawin, 31–34.

104. Jaffray, "A Plea for the Perishing," 49f. Cited by Sawin, 36–38.

105. See Gerald E. Mcgraw, "A. B. Simpson 1843–1919: From Home Missions to a World Missionary Movement," in *Mission Legacies: Biographical Studies of Leaders of the Modern Missionary Movement*, ed. Gerald H. Anderson, American Society of Missiology Series (Maryknoll, NY: Orbis Books, 1994), 41; Daryl Westmood Cartmel, "Mission Policy and Program of A. B. Simpson" (MA Thesis, Hartford Seminary Foundation, 1962), 61–62, 175–179.

106. In 1912, Soderberg was appointed to Vietnam and joined with Paul Hosler in Danang to begin language study. He later went to Hai Phong to study French in the home of Mr Bonnet. See "South China Minutes," (1 Feb 1912): 405; (16 Sep 1912): 412.

The moral condition of the people is very low – This is because of their heathen rites and practices. The vice that exists is simply astonishing! . . . Before I went to Annam it was said to me, "Why go to such immoral people? The Chinese are so much better!" But to me it was the more reason I should go, that the Gospel might manifest its power in the hearts and lives of this benighted race and thus emancipate them from the thralling bondage of Satan. Pray for the Annamese.[107]

The French Protestants, in contrast to the CMA missionaries, had a different attitude towards the local people, culture and religion. For instance, Mr Bonnet, who appeared to be the pioneering worker, "softened the ground" (in Tourane or Đà Nẵng and Quảng Nam province, Annam) through his Bible distribution. He had kept a good relationship with the local authorities and the people. In May 1911, R. A. Jaffray, who represented the executive committee of the South China Conference, along with Paul M. Hosler and Lloyd G. Hughes as pioneer missionaries, left for Tourane (in Annam).[108] By 17 June 1911, the Board met in New York to face a real dilemma – an open door and a lack of funds. The minutes of the meeting state that because of financial conditions the Board should "seriously consider if it is advisable to open Annam."[109] The decision to open a missionary base could not be made at the time and the matter was postponed for a later date and future action. Even though Hughes wanted so much to be part of the first missionary task force that would open Vietnam to the gospel, not just this "pioneering" trip alone, God called him to higher service on 25 August while he was vacationing in Hong Kong. Nevertheless, his friend, Mr Paul Hosler finally returned and stayed in Đà Nẵng as a houseguest of the Bonnets, and sought to learn the Vietnamese language during the few remaining months of 1911. "The long awaited desire of so many hearts had now become a reality. An Alliance missionary [Paul Hosler] had taken up residence in Vietnam."[110] In their

---

107. Frank A. Soderberg, "First Impressions of Annam," *The Alliance Witness* (21 December 1912): 185. See also in Sawin, *Christian and Missionary Alliance*, 57–59.

108. Hughes, "Momentous Crisis," 337; The Christian and Missionary Alliance, "Entering Annam," *The Alliance Witness* (7 October 1911): 9. See also in Sawin, 42–46.

109. The Christian and Missionary Alliance, *The Alliance Weekly* (14 October 1911): 25.

110. Sawin, *Christian and Missionary Alliance*, 51.

report posted in *Alliance Witness* in 1911, these CMA missionaries testified of the good work that had been done by Mr Bonnet (of the British and Foreign Bible Society, in Tourane or Đà Nẵng).

> We had been led to choose Tourane as our objective point by a series of providential leadings . . . Mr. Bonnet has been located at Tourane for eight years and has been the means of opening up this region to the Gospel . . . He has made many trips throughout Annam and has sold thousands of Scripture portions and Bibles in the Romanized and in the Chinese character. In this way, the soil has been prepared, the seed sown, and already the harvest has begun . . . we have a combination of circumstances which constitute in the truest sense an OPEN DOOR FOR THE GOSPEL. There is every encouragement to enter NOW and the responsibility and ability lies with the Church . . . the people are eager to know the Truth and will soon turn from idols to serve the true and living God.[111]

Chapter Conclusion

In this historical overview from the early Protestant missionary period to the birth of the CMA mission in Vietnam, some significant points relevant to the focus of this study have emerged. First, the earlier accounts of Protestant missions have usually been ignored. Leaving aside the impact of the Catholic missionaries that indirectly or directly prepared the Vietnamese people's hearts for Christian faith, the evangelical church needs to reconstruct its mission historiography in a more accurate and complete way to include the work of those forgotten French and the British Protestant missions whose presence was significant to the later development of Western missionary work. These include the French agencies and missionaries of the Reformed Church of France, the SMEP or Défap, the Society for the Evangelization of French Colonies, and the significant contributions of property and Bible distribution activities of the British Foreign Bible Society (BFBS). In other

---

111. Hughes, "Momentous Crisis," 337; Hosler, "Dawn of Protestant Missions," 136–138. See also in Sawin, 42–46.

words, Protestant/evangelical Christianity in Vietnam today is the missionary fruit of the French, the British, and the North American missions together. The first two prepared the ground for the arrival, growth, and development of the latter.

Second, some primary contextualization efforts which were done by the French and the American missionaries made little impact in the life of the Vietnamese people, however they are still noteworthy. The French missionaries, Adolphe de Richmond, Paul Monet and George Bois, in particular, knew that they needed to refrain from "making Protestants" and changing the Vietnamese people's "religious labels." They even attempted to contextualize the worship and liturgy for the Vietnamese by drawing on some meaningful aspects of the culture, but their contextualization efforts were shut down. It seems that Adolphe de Richemond's three missionary principles, published in "Foi et Vie," were not widely read, prematurely dismissed, and they certainly were not followed. Otherwise the results of Monet and Bois's contextualized attempts could have been more positively endorsed among the French Protestant believers instead of being harshly criticized. If a culturally sensitive attitude had been demonstrated and affirmed widely among the Protestant Christians at that time, perhaps the attention of the early CMA missionaries would have been drawn toward more positive ways to engage with Vietnamese culture. The CMA missionaries were in fact not in a better position, although they learned from the failure of the French in their missionary activity – for instance, distributing and using foreign language Chinese and French Bibles. By translating and printing the Bible in the vernacular Vietnamese (*quốc ngữ*), they took a step over the first barrier, the language, in communicating the gospel to the Vietnamese people. By using the ordinary language of Vietnamese people in translating and printing the Bible and Christian literature, the CMA missionaries opened the door more widely to reach the Vietnamese people. Such commitment to an indigenous project of translation is significant, similar to that done by William Carey in India which became the hallmark of all Protestant mission work. The CMA missionaries thus made their mark for sustained missionary activity in the field of Vietnam by allowing Jesus to speak directly to the Vietnamese.

Third and most importantly, the early Christian missionaries missed opportunities for contextualization as they used derogatory terms to describe a society and culture even before having had contact with them. Moreover, they were not ready to move beyond the manifestations of obvious religio-cultural forms and rituals to the actual Vietnamese spirituality which lay behind them. These Christian missionaries were mostly insensitive to the cultural context and did not significantly show that the gospel needs to relate to the Vietnamese culture. They did not look for ways in which the Christian faith could effectively and deeply penetrate the Vietnamese worldview that was already rooted deeply in the local beliefs in spirits, combined with Confucian, Daoist, and Buddhist traditions. So instead of engaging with the culture, their views towards Vietnamese traditions and beliefs were often antagonistic or simply dismissive. Christian faith, thus, was considered by the Vietnamese as a foreign faith that had little to do with the people.

This chapter has revealed the present paradigm of mission theology that has developed through the historical evolution of Christian missions in Vietnam, particularly through and by the French and American Protestant missions. The current paradigm of mission theology lacks cultural integration, meaning that the gospel has not been relevantly contextualized to the Vietnamese culture. Chapter 6 will propose a paradigm shift of Vietnamese evangelical mission theology, but not before taking a closer look in chapter 5 at how Christian faith is being challenged when engaging the Vietnamese culture.

CHAPTER 5

Christian Faith in Context

Vietnamese evangelicalism (or the *Tin Lành*) seems to be growing fast and flourishing, and yet the "Jesus-Western-face-God" introduced by the *Tin Lành* through the early Protestant and the CMA missionaries remains different from the Vietnamese concept of God, raising questions about the contextualization approach of the evangelical missionaries beginning with Dr Simpson's theology. The questions remain: Do the Vietnamese people need to escape their cultural concept of God to become evangelical Christians according to the ways of the missionary? Can a Vietnamese become a follower of Christ while maintaining their Vietnamese identity?

A Catholic Attempt at Addressing the "Three Teachings"

Upon the early Christian missionaries arriving in Vietnam in the sixteenth century (Alexander de Rhodes arrived at *Đàng trong* or Annam in 1624), they attempted to address the Confucianist-Daoist-Buddhist faith. Their apologetic response is revealed in these two documents: *Hội Đồng Tứ Giáo* (Conference of Four Religions," ca. 1800) and *Tam giáo chư vọng* (The errors of the Three Religions).[1] Although there is little evidence to prove that these

---

1. Detail about these two writings is beyond this study. For an excellent and comprehensive study, see Tran Quoc Anh, "Hội đồng tứ giáo (Conference of Four Religions): An Encounter of Christianity with Three Religions in Eighteenth-Century Vietnam" (STL Thesis, Jesuit School of Theology, 2006). Another name of this *conference* is called *Hội Đồng Tứ Giáo Danh Sư* (Conference of Distinguished Teachers of Four Religions). Tran Quoc Anh, "Tam giáo chư vọng (The errors of the Three Religions): A Textual and Analytical Study of a Christian Document on the Practices of the Three Religious Traditions in Eighteenth-Century Vietnam" (PhD diss., Georgetown University, 2011).

Roman Catholic missionaries had any direct interfaith dialogue with the Daoist, Confucianist and Buddhist indigenous faiths, such documents nevertheless are proof of an engaged Christian presence in the country. It is important to revisit these imaginative and apologetic conversations to learn how the early missionaries reacted when faced with those visible manifestations of rituals and practices deeply embedded in the Vietnamese culture by the Confucianist-Daoist-Buddhist values and beliefs. Nonetheless, the writings would be one of the early Christian contextualization efforts in the already "contextualized" context (between the local beliefs and Daoist-Confucianist-Buddhist faith from the outside) of early modern Vietnam.

In the context of eighteenth-century Vietnam, "*Hội Đồng Tứ Giáo*" (The "Conference of Four Religions": Confucianism, Buddhism, Daoism and Roman Catholicism) reveals the concerns and tensions regarding the reception and acceptance of Christianity as "a valid Vietnamese way of life."[2] However, the *Conference* bears a literary resemblance to earlier apologetic writings such as Matteo Ricci's *True Meaning*, Alexander de Rhodes's *Cathechismus,* and anonymous Vietnamese sources which inspired Adriano di St. Thecla's *Opusculum de sectis*.[3] The main arguments of this Conference were formulated as three rounds of debates on (1) the origin of the cosmos and human beings; (2) the proper conduct of human activity; and (3) the final destination of human fate.[4] Similarly to the style of dialogue in Ricci's *True Meaning of the Lord of Heaven,* the *Conference* is expressed as the Chinese-Western dialogue between a Christian priest, a Confucian scholar, a Daoist priest, and a Buddhist monk. Each of these representatives presented their views on the main issues according to their faith. For instance, the first debate (called *First Day*) discussed: the origin of humanity and the cosmos; the Confucian dialectic of *yin* and *yang* forces; the Daoist view of "from

---

2. See Tran Quoc Anh, "Hội đồng tứ giáo (Conference of Four Religions)," v.

3. Tran Quoc Anh, "Hội đồng tứ giáo (Conference of Four Religions)," 39–40. The *Conference* was written in the *Nôm* manuscript, but the *Quốc ngữ* version was first published in the 1880s. The English version was translated by Tran Quoc Anh in 2006 from the 1867 *Nôm manuscript* and was amended by the *Quốc ngữ* versions, both the first publication from the 1800s and the 13th printing in 1951. It is interesting to know that this *Conference* was written in many editions and reprinted in all three scripts of Vietnamese writing, the *Hán* (classical Chinese), the *Nôm*, and the *Quốc ngữ*. This was a quite popular work for almost a hundred years while it was in print (c. 1864–1959).

4. See Tran Quoc Anh, "Hội đồng tứ giáo (Conference of Four Religions)," 40–123.

emptiness to nothingness comes the great Đạo of nature"; the Buddhist view of "everything is made from the power of the Buddha"; and the Christian view of the biblical account of creation *ex nihilo*.[5]

Similarly to the Conference, *Tam giáo chư vọng* (The errors of the Three Religions, *ETR* hereafter) another important Christian document, was written to aid in understanding the Confucianist-Daoist-Buddhist teachings.[6] The *ETR* was also called *Dị đoan chi giáo* (Doctrine of superstitions) and may have been written by Hilario di Gesù.[7] It is difficult to trace the date and authorship of the *ETR*.[8] Nevertheless, the text is divided into three books to correspond respectively to the "errors" of Confucianism, Daoism, and Buddhism. Each book contains several articles and each article is a series of dialogues between a Christian scholar and a Confucian scholar in the style of Matteo Ricci's famous treatise *True Meaning*. Similarly to the *Conference*'s structure of dialogue, the *ETR* presents the dialogue between a "Western Scholar" (the author himself) and an "Eastern Scholar." Despite the apparent dialogical form, the *ETR* is not a true dialogue; it is, rather, the author's apologetic in the Western classic tradition of a Christian scholar's attempt to introduce, expound, and evaluate the teachings of Confucianist-Daoist-Buddhist doctrines without really displaying an understanding of them. For instance, nine of the eleven articles in Book Two (Articles 3–11) are devoted to exposing the

---

5. Tran Quoc Anh, 37, 48–61.

6. See Tran Quoc Anh, "Tam giáo chư vọng (The errors of the Three Religions)," 28–43. The manuscript of *The Errors of the Three Religions* (ETR) is a 10 x 15 cm undated notebook written in black ink and has been preserved in a good condition as Volume 1098 in the Archives of the Missions Étrangères de Paris (AMEP).

7. Tran Quoc Anh believes "the author was most likely Hilario di Gesù or one of his close associates, not excluding Adriano," written in various compositional stages from 1740s to 1750s. Hilario di Gesù (1697–1754) came to Tonkin in 1724, became bishop of Core (or Corycus) and co-adjudicator of East Tonkin in 1736 and took over the administration of the vicariate the following years. A prolific author, Hilario was also known to be a competent authority on religions in Tonkin, and published at least a dozen different works, including the *Dị đoan chi giáo* (Doctrine of superstitions), *Đại học chi đạo* (Path to great learning), and *Index historicus*.

8. This document was probably written during the same period as others, such as Matteo Ricci's *Tianzhu Shiyi* (1603), Alexandre de Rhodes's *Cathechismus* (1651), Adriano di Santa Thecla's *Opusculum de sectis* (1750), the anonymous *Phép giảng đạo thật* (1758), and *Hội đồng tứ giáo* (ca. 1800). For *Opusculum de sectis* (1750), see Adriano di Santa Thecla, *Opusculum de sectis apud Sinenses et Tunkinenses. A Small Treatise on the Sects among the Chinese and Tonkinese: A Study of Religion in China and North Vietnam in the Eighteenth Century*, trans. Olga Dror (Ithaca, NY: Cornell-SEAP, 2002).

"superstitious" acts, rituals, and beliefs associated with Daoism; and four of the twelve articles in Book Three (Articles 8–11) deal with Buddhist funeral practices and the treatment of the souls.[9] The evaluations are hardly objective, as they reflect on the visible ritual practices of the "Three Teachings" rather than on their doctrines. The real purpose of the *ETR* was, therefore, to demonstrate the superiority of the Christian faith in contrast to the existing spiritual and religious values and beliefs of Vietnam at that time.

The three-day *Conference* and the three-book *ETR* are imaginary conversations, pieces of apologetic material written to defend the legitimacy of Christianity while diminishing the intrinsic values of existing indigenous religions and doctrines. Such an argumentative position on certain events or practices does not come close to considering and unveiling fairly the actual meaning behind those manifestations. They also reveal that the Western missionaries' lack of understanding of the true meaning behind the practices inevitably led to a missed opportunity for contextualization which, in fact, existed in the core values or doctrinal philosophies of Confucianism, Daoism, Buddhism, and the local folk beliefs.

Protestant Missions in the Colonial Context

The French Protestant missions contributed to the early efforts of the Protestant missions in Vietnam, despite not making any significant contribution to either the theology or religious practices of Vietnamese evangelicalism. These missions included the Église Réformée de France (Reformed Church of France), Société des Missions Évangéliques de Paris (SMEP or Défap), and Société d'Évangélisation des Colonies Françaises (Society for the Evangelization of French Colonies).[10] The American Christian and Missionary Alliance (CMA) mission, on the other hand, has left their footprint with a

---

9. See Tran Quoc Anh, "Tam giáo chư vọng (The errors of the Three Religions)," 127–128. Also the text of these two Books and their articles appear in the *Quốc ngữ*, 648–705.

10. As seen in chapter 3, for instance, the Société d'Évangelisation des Colonies, one of the earliest missionary societies sent pastor Théophile Boisset to Hải Phòng in 1884 to minister to the French and European Protestants. And within the mission of the *Église Réformée de France*, the first Protestant church was started in Hải Phòng in 1894. Eventually, three other Protestant churches were founded: one in Hà Nội in 1902 which is now the church of the Evangelical Church of Vietnam (ECVN) in the North, another in Sài Gòn (Hồ Chí Minh City, after 30 April 1975), and one in Đà Lạt.

successful CMA church in Indochina (Vietnam), as well as implementing their CMA theology and practices that are reflected in various ways in the lives of Vietnamese evangelicals.[11] Except for occasional personal conflicts that one may become aware of when reading their archived communications,[12] the relationship between the two missions was generally mutually agreeable. Both missions were pioneering Protestant missions in Vietnam and therefore, they had similar interests and helped each other, rather than competing with each other. Both missions were young and therefore they lacked experience in dealing with the social, political, and religious complexity of early twentieth-century Vietnam. This lack of experience was reflected in their harsh reactions toward other Vietnamese belief systems and religions, including the Roman Catholic faith. Moreover, both missions were faced with challenges from the Catholics and the French Indochinese colonial authorities who were skeptical of their missionary motives. They attempted (especially the Americans) to keep a clearly "neutral" position toward the political agenda of the anti-colonial and national movements.

This section, therefore, discusses in detail some possibilities of successes and failures of these two missions, the French Protestant missions and the North American CMA.

Christian Mission and Colonization

The French Protestant mission in Vietnam was trapped between Christian mission and colonization. The French Protestant missionary movement in French Indochina often carried with it the stigma of European imperialism. Furthermore, the French missions were held in question and rejected by the anti-colonial movements and nationalists, both in French Indochina and in Paris.

---

11. The CMA missionaries, such as C. H. Reeves, arrived in Lạng Sơn province, the area of North Vietnam in 1897. Mr and Mrs Sylvan Dayan arrived in Hải Phòng in 1902; Robert A. Jaffray had already been in Hanoi since 1889. However, these missions were not successful in planting churches. It was only on the second visit to Tourane in 1911, the landmark year in the mission history of Vietnamese evangelicalism, that Mr Jaffray was successful in planting a church.

12. William C. Cadman, "Letters to U. Soulier" (Mission Évangélique de L'Indo-Chine Francaise-CMA (Hanoi, Tonkin): Archives of La Société des Missions Evangéliques des Paris (SMEP/ Défap), 5 Apr, 25 Apr, and 28 Apr 1923).

The first reason for a mostly unsuccessful mission of the French Protestants in Vietnam is that colonial missions propagated colonial imperialism while helping colonies to embrace the Lordship of Christ. The lack of ultimate success of the French Protestant mission in Indochina is that it was "new wine" (Protestantism) in an "old wineskin" (the old colonial-style mission of European Christendom). This style of evangelization preferred the "one size fixes all" motto, in which "we" (the missionaries) have a gospel (Christianity) for "them" (the nationals) that can change every social, political, and religious aspect of the culture. The accusations of post-colonial scholars and historians – who have criticized the role of Catholic missions for a long time as an extended arm of French imperialism and colonialism, or as "evidence of later French colonial ambitions in Vietnam" – can make colonial missions look even oppressive.[13] As Charles Patrick Keith observes, "Modern Vietnamese language historiography, especially on politically charged subjects, has long borne the weighty imprint of the legitimating narratives and priorities of the communist party-state."[14] But these accusations may have undermined the contributions of Catholic nationalists and revolutionists, who identified themselves with the marginalized and the oppressed, who experienced harsh persecution from various Vietnamese lords and kings, and their own people – the Vietnamese – who misunderstood them.

The French Protestant mission was in a similar position as this colonial mission process. Although it is not fair to just adopt the political perspective of Nguyễn Ái Quốc (better known as Hồ Chí Minh) to justify a theological-missional perspective in the case of the French Protestant mission in Indochina, it is quite reasonable to consider an intellectual piece of writing – Nguyễn Ái Quốc's letter to a French Protestant pastor – to shed some light on the causes of failure of the French mission in the whole picture of the social, geo-cultural, political, and religious complexity of the early twentieth century Vietnam.

---

13. Keith, *Catholic Vietnam*, 8. Such an argument is often seen in modern Vietnamese historiography, viewing the missionary presence in the Vietnamese kingdom as far back as the seventeenth century as evidence of later French colonial ambitions in Vietnam, for instance, in Nguyễn Văn Kiệm, *Sự du nhập của đạo Thiên Chúa Giáo vào Việt Nam từ thế kỷ XVII đến thế kỷ XIX* [The arrival of Roman Catholicism in Vietnam from the 17th century to the 19th century], (Hà Nội: Hội Khoa học Lịch sử Việt Nam, 2001).

14. See Keith, *Catholic Vietnam*, 8.

Nguyễn Ái Quốc criticized the matter of evangelization (mission) and colonization thus: "every civilizing mission – whether it is in the Antilles, Madagascar, Indochina, or Tahiti – is always towed by a so-called evangelizing mission."[15] Turning toward Vietnam (Indochina), Nguyễn Ái Quốc, in his letter sent to Ulysse Soulier in 1922, equated the French Protestant mission with the Catholic one in Vietnam.[16] The letter is one of many examples of how a Vietnamese nationalist viewed Christian mission – both the long existent Catholicism and the newer Protestantism – as being attached to other agendas, rather than purely as proclamation of the gospel of Christ.

Nguyễn Ái Quốc's reaction in the letter was perhaps coming from his encounter with Soulier's *L'appel de l'Indochine française* (The call of French Indochina),[17] together with his awareness of the anti-Protestantism in Paris that had spread from metropolitan France to the colonies even after the law of the Separation of Church and State in 1905.[18] Although Nguyễn Ái Quốc had experienced the Roman Catholics in Vietnam – a Christianity that was at once a source and motor of colonization, of the division of Vietnamese society (the Christian/non-Christian [bên đạo/ bên lương] distinction), and of an enforced occidentalization – his letter focused solely on his anti-colonial (political) propaganda rather than on a discussion of the Protestant mission.[19] Another example of Nguyễn Ái Quốc's remarks of the Vietnamese peasants under the French colonial regime is reflected in his writing later in 1924:

---

15. See Nguyen Ai Quoc, *Le procès de la colonisation francaise* (The process of French colonization).

16. See Nguyễn Ái Quốc, "Monsieur le Pasteur (to the Pastor)," (Paris: Archives of Société des Missions Evangéliques des Paris (SMEP/ Défap), 8 Sept. 1921); Hồ Chí Minh, "Unpublished Letter by Hồ Chí Minh." Thanks to Bourdeaux who initially discovered this letter at the SMEP/ Défap and discussed its content in the *Journal of Vietnamese Studies*. I also touched with my own hands and read this same letter for myself during my archival visit at the Défap in March 2015.

17. See Soulier, "L'appel de l'Indochine française (Call of French Indochina)."

18. Bourdeaux, "Notes on an Unpublished Letter," 14; Jean Baubérot and Valentine Zuber, *Une haine oubliée: L'anti-protestantisme avant le "pacte laïque" (1870–1905)* [A forgotten hatred: Anti-Protestantism before the "Secular Pact" (1870–1905)], (Paris: Albin Michel, 2000).

19. Bourdeaux, "Notes on an Unpublished Letter," 14. For "anticlericalism" see Philippe Delisle, *L'anticléricalisme dans les colonies françaises sous la Troisième République* [Anticlericalism in the French colonies under the Third Republic], (Paris: Les Indes Savantes, 2008). For "mission and colonization" see Jean-François Zorn, "Mission et colonisation: entre connivence et différence, point de vue protestant," in *Religions et colonisation*, eds. Dominique Borne and Benoît Falaize (Paris: Éditions de l'Atelier, 2009), 75–83.

> The Annamese [Vietnamese] in general are crushed by the blessings of French protection. The Annamese [Vietnamese] peasants especially are still more odiously crushed by this protection ... This is due to the fact that they are robbed on all sides and in all ways by the Administration, by modern feudalism, and by the Church ... One can see that behind a mask of democracy, French imperialism has transplanted in [Vietnam] the whole cursed medieval regime, including salt tax; and that the Annamese [Vietnamese] peasant is crucified on the bayonet of capitalist civilization and on the cross of prostituted Christianity.[20]

Nguyễn Ái Quốc thus urged the French Protestants that, "if you want to find a true Christian in Indochina [Vietnam], look for him in a good Indochinese [Vietnamese] man, but nowhere else."[21] The early missionaries to Vietnam seemed to be so intent on "making one more Christian" that they perhaps did not realize they were also "making one less Vietnamese." However, a genuine Vietnamese Christian is expected to be a good Vietnamese as well, as Nguyễn Ái Quốc said, "Being good Annamites does not stop them from being good Christians."[22]

Bourdeaux believed that Nguyễn Ái Quốc's letter was a response to a group of French Protestants, including Soulier, who hoped to undertake an exploratory mission in Indochina. But do Soulier and Paul Monet have different versions of the project known as *The Call*?[23] Whatever the case, Nguyễn Ái Quốc attacked the adjective "French" in the title of the pamphlet *The Call* because he believed that it was "a process that is doubtlessly laudable yet still quite contrary in nature, since evangelization was an accomplice to colonization."[24] Nguyễn Ái Quốc expressed it this way:

---

20. Hồ Chí Minh, *Hồ Chí Minh: Selected Works*, vol. 1 (Hanoi: Foreign Languages Publishing, 1960–1962), 62ff. Cited by Lê Hoàng Phu, "Short History," 6.
21. See Nguyễn Ái Quốc, "Monsieur le Pasteur (to the Pastor)."
22. See Nguyễn Ái Quốc, "Monsieur le Pasteur (to the Pastor)"; Hồ Chí Minh, "Unpublished Letter by Hồ Chí Minh," 3.
23. See Paul Monet as discussed in chapter 3.
24. Bourdeaux, "Notes on an Unpublished Letter," 25.

Like all things ideal, religion does not and should not have any borders, and those who take on the task of propagating it should be above any nationalism and any political interests. This is why, in my humble opinion, the word "Indochina" on its own, without an adjective, translates the idea of He [Christ] whom we all love, and the hope of those whom you would like to teach to love Him. But the adjective "French" placed before "Indochina" gives it an effect that is utterly contrary to that which you want and we want; for the work of Christ is, as you say, a work of liberation and emancipation, whereas colonialism, whatever the kind, is a work of oppression and subjugation. A controlled Indochina cannot be a truly Christian Indochina.[25]

Does Nguyễn Ái Quốc see "colonial mission" under the term "French" as resulting in an Indochina not free to be a truly indigenized (contextualized) Christian Indochina? Yes, it becomes obvious when one reads *The Call of "French" Indochina*. He thus sees that this project called *The Call* will continue to "control" rather than to "free" people.

Bourdeaux's pamphlet version of *The Call*, opens with an introduction signed by the "exploratory commission to study the foundation of a French Protestant mission in Indochina."[26] That same commission appeared in Vũ Tâm Thất's report, "Rapport relatif à la Mission Américaine de Hanoi le 23 Juin, 1922" (Report on the American Mission in Hanoi in 23 June 1922).[27] This was the commission that supported the missionary initiative which employed four men, two of whom were French (Ulysse Soulier, Paul Monet) and two Vietnamese (Louis Đường, Vũ Tâm Thất). Are these organizations – this commission, founded on 29 April 1920 and the Young Men's Christian Association (YMCA) that operated in Indochina – the same? If this is the case, then Nguyễn Ái Quốc was correct in raising the question of its missionary nature:

---

25. See Hồ Chí Minh, "Unpublished Letter by Hồ Chí Minh."
26. Bourdeaux, "Notes on an Unpublished Letter," 16.
27. See Vu Tam That Samuel, "Rapport relatif à la Mission Américaine de Hanoi le 23 Juin 1922 (Report on the American Mission in Hanoi in 23 June 1922)."

> It seems that the Y.M.C.A. in Indochina would only be open to former soldiers, to students, and to sons of Mandarins. Would it therefore be closed to the masses, even though they alone are most in need of consolation and of illumination?[28]

Nevertheless, the pamphlet *The Call*, which was the basis of Nguyễn Ái Quốc's polemic in his letter, raises several questions about how the colonial mission became embedded in the minds of the people of Indochina as a French colony.[29] This forty-eight-page pamphlet is comprised of two texts: one by Soulier (handwritten text) and the other was Paul Monet's outline of the situation in Indochina from his missionary point of view.[30] The pamphlet's cover gives this title: *The Missionary Project: France, Indochina: A Dragon, and Finally a Christian Cross are Superimposed*. Nguyễn Ái Quốc is responding to this document in order to present his critique of colonization.[31] Here are some provocative statements from this pamphlet that Nguyễn Ái Quốc asserted in his critical response:

> In the appeal by Captain Monet [Mr. le Capitain Monet], it was written that "lies and deceit are very laudable skills for the Annamite [Vietnamese]" . . . A little further on, it states that "such a trait of deceit or selfishness is merely a result of essential principles of 'Confucian philosophy' and of the Buddhist religion, etc." . . . Captain Monet says that "French Christians should understand that the Annamite people are living under <u>moral</u> oppression and are suffering from that oppression" . . . At the end of his appeal, Captain MONET says that the utmost

---

28. Hồ Chí Minh, "Unpublished Letter by Hồ Chí Minh," 2.

29. This 48-page pamphlet, of which roughly 2,000 copies were printed, was written between March and April 1921; for the price of one franc, it could be purchased in two places in Paris. See in Bourdeaux, "Notes on an Unpublished Letter," 16. While Soulier's *The Call* is a 47-page handwritten pamphlet which designates the following on the first page: Ulysse Soulier, Conférence, Nantes, Août, 1920, "L'appel de l'Indochine française."

30. See Bourdeaux, "Notes on an Unpublished Letter," 17. Soulier's *The Call* at the Défap details the inner development that led him to his religious vocation and then to his missionary call. He explains that since he had dealt with Annamite [Vietnamese] infantrymen when he was in charge of a barracks in Picardy during the war, he decided on Indochina.

31. Bourdeaux, "Notes on an Unpublished Letter," 16.

possible [efforts] must be made [to make] of the 3,000 students true Christians and good <u>Frenchmen</u>.[32]

Bourdeaux argued that Nguyễn Ái Quốc stressed "Captain" Monet – as Monet's writing revealed his personality – to help Soulier, a person of "kind-heartedness" to guard against Monet's distorted ideas about Indochina and its people.[33] While the original purpose of and motivation behind this pamphlet is unknown, the language speaks very clearly of a biased colonial missionary style. Let alone the various cultural-religious biases, the final idea that Monet presented alone can prove that he wanted to make one more Christian and one less Vietnamese. Nguyễn Ái Quốc questioned how can these 3,000 Vietnamese students fulfill their impossible roles of being both true Christians and good Frenchmen.[34] Are they not Vietnamese? Or do they need to be colonized or converted to be French before or at the same time, in order to be good Christians? A colonial mission of evangelization that propagates colonial imperialism thus cannot help the colonies to embrace the Lordship of Christ. And in the case of Indochina, this type of mission encountering the anti-colonial forces put an end to French Protestantism in Vietnam.

Another reason for the relative failure is that the French Protestant mission entered Indochina at an inopportune time in Vietnam's history – during the struggle for independence. The Vietnamese anti-colonialist and nationalistic movements had emerged earlier, but had not flourished during the first few decades of the twentieth century in Vietnam. The European powers, particularly the French, had colonized Asian lands protecting European trade and the enterprises operating there, exploring the availability of economic resources and exploiting them, and at the same time promoting European cultural, political and religious activities. This bitter experience left a big scar

---

32. It seemed Monet (and the YMCA in Indochina) targeted to "evangelize" for the goal of 3,000 Vietnamese students. This goal was seen impossible according to Nguyễn Ái Quốc's criticism, "It is materially impossible for a man or a society to fulfill two opposed missions at the same times; one of these is the most beautiful and the most noble: that of Evangelizing, of telling men to love their God and their neighbor; the other mission is to 'put into castles' a group of men and encourage them to renounce their own country, or at the very least make them love a country other than their own." See in Nguyễn Ái Quốc, "Monsieur le Pasteur (to the Pastor)"; Hồ Chí Minh, "Unpublished Letter by Hồ Chí Minh," 2–3.

33. Bourdeaux, "Notes on an Unpublished Letter," 18.

34. Hồ Chí Minh, "Unpublished Letter by Hồ Chí Minh," 3.

on the memories of the Asian people.[35] For instance, one of the first results of the French colonial conquest was to deprive the Vietnamese of the right to call their country by its proper name, requiring them instead to think of themselves as other than Vietnamese; they had to use the names of Tonkin, Annam, and Cochinchina.[36] For whatever reason, the change was very real and painful, despite memories of national unity conjured up by the name "Vietnam."[37] "Loss of linguistic autonomy was so internalized that even revolutionaries referred to themselves by the name given to them by their French masters – Annamites – a label that resonated with echoes of an earlier period of colonial rule under the T'ang dynasty."[38]

The self-realization of Vietnamese nationalism and anti-colonialism,[39] which emerged in the late nineteenth century, flourished in the early twentieth century when France added Laos and unified the area under a French governor general as French Indochina.[40] Anti-colonialism emerged as a central issue in Vietnam, giving birth to a variety of resistance movements during the nineteenth century.[41] However, "revolution and resistance" in Vietnam in the early twentieth century under the *Việt Minh*, became a force for independence as Vietnamese nationalism grew in the period which is described as "the Vietnamese struggle for independence."[42]

Several writings and histories of revolutions in this period show how Vietnam was desperate to re-establish identity through anti-colonial reactions and the ever-increasing growth of "radical" nationalism. In fact, the cause of "radicalism"[43] in Vietnamese history can be traced back to this period of

---

35. Patrick J. N. Tuck, *French Catholic Missionaries and the Politics of Imperialism in Vietnam, 1857-1914: A Documentary Survey* ([Liverpool]: Liverpool University Press, 1987), 26.

36. Hue-Tam Ho Tai, *Radicalism and the Origins*, 7.

37. See Cao Huy Thuan, "Christianisme et Colonialisme au Vietnam (1857–1914)" (Universite of D' Amiens; the Centre de Relations Internationales et de Science Politique 1969).

38. Hue-Tam Ho Tai, *Radicalism and the Origins*, 7.

39. Kenneth Perry, "Nationalism in Southeastern Asia," 8.

40. The name for Tonkin, Annam, Cochinchina, and Cambodia and Laos under French colonial administration.

41. Tarling, *Cambridge History of Southeast Asia, Volume Two*.

42. Schirokauer and Clark, *Modern East Asia*, 316.

43. "An essentially non-ideological current of reaction, both to colonial rule and to native accommodation to that rule, whose chief characteristics were iconoclasm and the marriage of the personal and the political. In this sense, radicalism is not a true 'ism' as conventionally understood, but more of a political mood." Hue-Tam Ho Tai, *Radicalism and the Origins*, 2.

nineteenth-century anti-colonialism and can be understood as a delayed reaction to colonial conquest. The first stage of French conquest was completed in the 1860s, creating the French colony of Cochinchina, and the second campaign ended in 1884, with the establishment of the protectorate of Annam in the South and the protectorate of Tonkin in the North of Vietnam.[44] This radicalism, though delayed, with its proponent's abiding concerns of freedom, security, needs of the individual, and the interests of the community, had been the foundation of anti-colonialism right from the beginning of French colonialism in the 1860s and throughout the first three decades of the twentieth century, ending with the triumph of communism led by Marxist-Leninist revolutionary Nguyễn Ái Quốc.[45] Such a triumph can be attributed to a peculiar conjunction of trends occurring in international world communism, in domestic problems and dynamics, and in the policies and practices of colonialism.[46] Moreover, the foundation for the success of the communist revolution in Vietnam was a national psyche rooted in Confucianism and Buddhism that rested upon village cohesion and a highly focused ethno-cultural identity centered on the figure of the king that was transferred to the country's revolutionary leader Hồ Chí Minh.[47]

During the second phase of Vietnam's colonial history, between the years of 1900 and 1945, several cultural and political movements took place. For thirty-one years, "from 1900 to 1931, anti-colonial activities manifested clear progress toward a more systematic organization into political parties that reflected the practice of modernized polities."[48] The French colonial authorities

---

44. See Patricia M. Pelley, *Postcolonial Vietnam: New Histories of the National Past* (Durham, NC: Duke University Press, 2002), 69; Hue-Tam Ho Tai, *Radicalism and the Origins*.

45. Hue-Tam Ho Tai, *Radicalism and the Origins*, 4.

46. See Hue-Tam Ho Tai; Brocheux and Hémery, *Indochina*.

47. See Brocheux and Hémery, *Indochina*, 281.

48. Trương Bửu Lâm, *Colonialism Experienced: Vietnamese Writings on Colonialism, 1900–1931* (Ann Arbor, MI: University of Michigan, 2000), 2. Clive J. Christie, *Southeast Asia in the Twentieth Century: A Reader* (London: Tauris, 1998), 80–81; David G. Marr, *Vietnamese Tradition on Trial, 1920–1945* (Berkeley, CA: University of California Press, 1981), 163–164. Good examples of this trend are the Đông Du (Going East) movement of Phan Bội Châu formed in 1905 that led to the political parties of the National Party of Vietnam (Việt Nam Quốc Dân Đảng, VNQDĐ) in 1927 and the Indochinese Communist Party (Đông Dương Cộng Sản Đảng, ĐDCSĐ) in 1930. Also at this time, political revolutions that began with the Yên Bái's rebellion, fomented by the Nationalist Party, shook the Vietnamese colony. Further were the strike-demonstrations and work stoppages of the industrial workers that took place every day,

dealt harshly with both revolutions, executing many of their leaders, and causing the survivors to go into exile or keep a low profile.[49] It was not until the beginning of the 1940s that the *Việt Minh* was able to merge the main political factions into one united front to fight against both Japanese fascism and French imperialism. On 2 September 1945, President Hồ Chí Minh gave a "Declaration of Independence" in Hanoi for the Democratic Republic of Vietnam (later renamed the Socialist Republic of Vietnam), which was a strong statement, in particular, against French imperialism.

> Nevertheless, for more than eighty years, the French imperialists, abusing the standard of Liberty, Equality, and Fraternity, have violated our Fatherland and oppressed our fellow-citizens. They have acted contrary to the ideals of humanity and justice. In the field of politics, they have deprived our people of every democratic liberty. They have enforced inhuman laws; they have set up three distinct political regimes in the North, the Center and the South of Vietnam in order to wreck our national unity and prevent our people from being united.[50]

It was the same *Việt Minh* that led the resistance against the French attempt at colonial re-conquest, which began in 1945.[51]

In the political turmoil created by colonial expansion (between the rise of anti-colonialist national forces, and the fight for independence intertwined with the legitimate desire of the Vietnamese to maintain their cultural identity), missionary efforts (perceived as a threat to it) were doomed to fail.

The Adjectives *American* and *français*

Unlike its French counterpart, the American CMA mission had a successful mission in Vietnam. The American CMA also had a news magazine *The Call*

---

coupled with armed uprisings of "worker-peasants" led by the local "Soviet" leadership of the Indochinese Communist Party.

49. Trương Bửu Lâm, *Colonialism Experienced*, 13.

50. See Hồ Chí Minh, *Hồ Chí Minh: Selected Works*, vol. 3. (Hanoi: Foreign Languages Publishing, 1960–1962), 17–21.

51. See Huỳnh Kim Khánh, *Vietnamese Communism, 1925–1945* (Ithaca, NY: Published under the auspices of the Institute of Southeast Asian Studies, Singapore, by Cornell University Press, 1982).

*of Indochina,*⁵² and yet neither adjective – "French" nor "American" – became important to them. In fact, as we have noted, it was due to the word *français* (French), that had become the object of Nguyễn Ái Quốc's criticism in the letter to Ulysse Soulier, that the French Protestants had to end both their mission and their French imperialist efforts in the mid-twentieth century. Why then could the American CMA mission remain in Vietnam longer, and not only that, but continue in partnership with the national church, the Evangelical Church of Vietnam (ECVN) for sixty-eight years (1927–1975)?

Eliminating any unnecessary adjective was a way of keeping the CMA away from any political involvement. Perhaps this was one of many wise decisions in the CMA's mission strategy. This politically neutral attitude was practiced during the later political conflicts in Vietnam by the Evangelical Church of Vietnam (ECVN) standing on this popular motto: *Tin Lành không tham gia chính trị* (The Evangelical Church of Vietnam does not get involved in politics).⁵³ The *Constitution* states clearly that,

> the Evangelical Church of Vietnam asserts that it is loyal to the Government and will not tolerate any propaganda against the government, within the Church. The Church resolutely refuses

---

52. *The Call*, the CMA News Magazine of Indochina Field, seems to have started in 1922 (many in CMA Box 4) and lasted until 1973. From 1922–1930 (March) it was called *The Call of French Indochina* (up to the Oct '29– Mar '30 no. 28). From 1930 (April)–1934, it was called *The Call of French Indochina and East Siam* (from April 1930 in the April–June no. 29, until the Oct '33–Sep '34 no. 39, 1934). From 1951–1953, it was called *The Call of Indochina* (5 Issues: the Spring and the Fall Issue in 1951, the Spring and the Fall Issue in 1952, and the 1953 Issue). From 1953–1965, the chronicles continued in Vietnam after Indochina became four autonomous fields of Vietnam, Cambodia, Tribes, and Laos (starting from 1 January 1953), *The Call of Indochina* was then called *The Call of Vietnam*. From 1966–1973, the CMA *Call of Vietnam* was called *Vietnam Today*. In fact, the last issue of *Vietnam Today* was the Summer Issue, no. 14, 1973, The CMA Archive: Box 14.

53. Lê Hoàng Phu believed that the ECVN "has developed steadily and has played a significant role in the country, not in the political arena but in the moral, religious, and social welfare realms." He gave an illustration of the ECVN's long-standing policy of "non-involvement in politics," stating that the ECVN's leaders declined the offer of Bao Dai (former emperor who returned to Vietnam) in the spring 1949, to form a nationalist government which composed of representatives of the "largest religious families" of the country included the Buddhists, the Roman Catholics, the Cao Dai, the Hoà Hảo, and the Tin Lanh (the ECVN). See Lê Hoàng Phu, "Short History," 6.

to have any part in anything connected with politics or anything else aside from its purpose as a church.[54]

Nevertheless, there was more than one reason that brought some success to the CMA mission throughout the colonial and post-colonial periods.

From the year of its entry into Vietnam, the CMA mission was already favored by several factors. The 1911 report about the "present outlook for missions" in Indochina showed the CMA enjoying certain favors.

> At the present time, there is a most remarkable opening for the preaching of the Gospel in Annam. Not for years has there been such favorable inducements to lead the Church to enter as now. The reason for this favorable condition of affairs is threefold, namely, (1) the political situation; (2) the disestablishment of the Catholic Church in France; (3) the colportage work of M. Bonnet.[55]

Regarding the first favorable condition (the political situation), the CMA mission understood the situation in Vietnam during these years as follows:

> The French have been desirous of restoring peace in Indochina and in Annam, particularly, the people have accepted the protectorate of France, and without a doubt their earthly lot is far better than in former years, when they were at war among themselves and the various tribes of Laos.[56]

Also, because of the colportage network of M. Bonnet, the CMA mission enjoyed a good relationship with "The Resident at Tourane [the governor who] has already assured us of his friendship and by courtesy and prudence we can strengthen our position with him and the Government."[57] This same

---

54. See Section VII – The Relationship of the Church and the Government, in Hội Thánh Tin Lành Việt Nam, *Constitution of the Evangelical Church of Vietnam (Điều Lệ của Hội Thánh Tin Lành Việt Nam)*, the 1956 amended text ed. (Saigon: Nhà in Tin-Lành, 1958), 18 (in English).

55. Hosler, "Dawn of Protestant Missions," 138.

56. Hosler, 136–138.

57. Hosler, 136–138.

political favor continued for the CMA mission during the period between 1954 and 1975.⁵⁸

The second favorable reason, "the disestablishment of the Catholic Church in France," was beneficial for all the Protestant missions in French territories.

> The disestablishment of the Church in France has put the Catholics at somewhat of a disadvantage in Annam. They had long enjoyed a strong position here because of their service to the Government. That their influence is diminishing is due partly, no doubt, to some of their questionable methods among the natives. After many years of persecution the position of the French Protestants is now regarded as being more consistent than that of the Catholics. Considering the attitude of the Church of Rome in the past, we gratefully praise God that such a hindrance to the preaching of the Gospel is being removed.⁵⁹

Moreover, the Roman Catholic Church's postwar self-realization and adjustment had helped the Catholics in Vietnam. Official documents issued by the Vatican, including Benedict XV's 1919 apostolic letter *Maximum Illud (On the propagation of the faith throughout the world)*, and Pius XI's 1926 encyclical *Rerum Ecclessiae*, marked a decisive reformation to mission policy and administration, as well as generating a transformation in the relationship between Rome, missions, and colonial regimes.⁶⁰

And the last reason, "the colportage work of M. Bonnet," who had softened the ground for the gospel, and the work of other French Protestants, who were assisting the early days of the CMA mission in Vietnam, represented crucial missional efforts that counted toward the steadily growing strength of the CMA mission.

---

58. The 1954 Geneva Accords signed in Geneva, Switzerland brought about the end of war in Indochina. In 1975, the northern Communist army of the Democratic Republic of Vietnam gained a final victory over the alliance of the United States and the Republic of Vietnam during the presidencies of US President Richard M. Nixon and the South Vietnamese President Nguyễn Văn Thiệu.

59. Hosler, "Dawn of Protestant Missions," 138.

60. Keith, *Catholic Vietnam*, 93–98. The full text of *Maximum Illud* is in Thomas J. M. Burke, S. J., 1957, *Catholic Missions: Four Great Missionary Encyclicals*, Incidental Paper of the Institute of Mission Studies, no.1, New York: Fordham University Press.

Thus, we can conclude that the CMA had some success in Vietnam. The French Protestant missions should not be considered as failures since they put forth missional efforts that helped prepare the soil for the formation of Vietnamese evangelicalism. Fortunately, the CMA mission indeed continued steadily in the field ever since it had started in the 1880s. From 1927 to 1975, the CMA mission remained strong and influential in the life of the young national church, the Evangelical Church of Indochina (ECIC), which later became the Evangelical Church of Vietnam (ECVN). And yet, the mission of the CMA had more success, not only because of their material support and personnel involved in the field, but also because of their CMA theology and practices.

"Foreign" Faith: An Issue of the Vietnamese Evangelicals

Although the Evangelical Church of Vietnam (ECVN) has shown itself an indigenous church through the "Three-Self Principle,"[61] the church is struggling to self-theologize as a relevant Vietnamese church. In order to articulate biblical faith in Vietnamese cultural terms, the gospel needs to relate locally and depart from the theological assumptions of Euro-American cultural discourse.[62] What follows are issues of christocentric theological views that become a fundamental doctrines of Vietnamese evangelicalism.

"The Fourfold Gospel"

The Fourfold Gospel – Christ our Savior, Christ our Sanctifier, Christ our Healer and Christ our Coming Lord – is the foundation of Simpson's theology and practice, and one of the distinctive characteristics of the CMA.[63] Vietnamese evangelicalism today is deeply rooted in this theology, including

---

61. Lê Hoàng Phu, "Short History," 3–4. A large number of local churches of the Evangelical Church of Vietnam were organized on this Three-Self principle in Vietnam before the 1950s.

62. Dyrness and Kärkkäinen, *Global Dictionary of Theology*, 192.

63. See Albert B. Simpson, *The Fourfold Gospel: Albert B. Simpson's Conception of the Complete Provision of Christ for Every Need of the Believer-Spirit, Soul and Body*, updated ed. (Camp Hill, PA: Christian Publications, 1984); John S. Sawin, "The Fourfold Gospel," in *The Birth of a Vision: Essays on the Ministry and Thought of Albert B. Simpson*, eds. F. David Hartzfeld and Charles Nienkirchen (Beaverlodge, Alberta: Buena Book Services, 1986).

the doctrine that humans are "sinful" and need a "redemptive" God.[64] There is no doubt of the success of the mission of the CMA in Vietnam as described above. A. B. Simpson's strong theology of mission and mission strategy led to the growth of the mission to become a denomination, the Christian and Missionary Alliance, as it is today. A review of the CMA archival documents related to Vietnam, revealed that, besides his role as the founder of the Alliance, Dr Simpson played another most important role as a strategic person and mission mobilizer. This is evident in several writings and in his preaching about the missionary urgency to reach the unoccupied world for the gospel, including Vietnam (seen in his initial concerns). And yet his role has largely been overlooked in the Vietnamese historiography as other more popular figures, including R. A. Jaffray, John Drange Olsen, William C. Cadman, and D. I. Jeffrey have been viewed as the pioneering workers in early Vietnamese evangelicalism.[65] Nevertheless, his famous document *The Fourfold Gospel* and some other writings have put forth a strong statement of his mission theology.[66]

Dr A. B. Simpson's theological views are strongly focused on Christology, the sanctification of the believer, pre-millennial eschatology, divine healing, and the baptism of the Holy Spirit.[67] Dr Simpson greatly emphasized "divine healing, premillennialism, and sanctification" and taught these fundamentalist doctrines in the CMA Bible schools.[68] In fact, Dr Simpson and the Missionary Training Institute "exerted a conservative and moderating influence on fundamentalism by channeling *fin-de-siècle* religious fervor into an inward experience, which was expressed outwardly in holy living and

---

64. See Simpson, *Fourfold Gospel*; John Drange Olsen, *Thần đạo học* [Theology], vol. 1 & 2 (Sài Gòn: Nhà in Tin-Lành, 1957).

65. Both Cadman and Jeffrey are important figures for further studies because of their roles and influences on the younger church, the ECVN (e.g. The *Thánh Kinh Báo* operation, the Bible school in Đà Nẵng then in Nha Trang, as Jeffrey revealed in his "Team Memories.")

66. Christian T. Collins Winn, ed. *From the Margins: A Celebration of the Theological Work of Donald W. Dayton* (Eugene, OR: Pickwick, 2007), 356–375. In re-interpreting Korean Christianity, Donald Dayton believes that "The Fourfold Gospel" is often associated with the work of A. B. Simpson, but actually this pattern is much wider and comes out of the heart of the Holiness movement itself. For further discussion on the origins of "The Fourfold Gospel," see Dayton's discussion on "The Four-Fold Gospel: Key to Trans-Pacific Continuities."

67. Mcgraw, "A. B. Simpson 1843–1919," 39–45.

68. See Gerald E. Mcgraw, "The Doctrine of Sanctification in the Published Writing of Albert Benjamin Simpson" (New York University, 1986); Mcgraw, "A. B. Simpson 1843–1919."

tireless evangelism."[69] These fundamentalist practices were also reflected in the mission policy and program later on, especially in the Vietnam mission field.[70] The early statement of purpose of the Alliance in 1887 declares that:

> The Christian Alliance was organized in the summer of 1887 at Old Orchard Convention for the purpose of uniting in Christian fellowship and testimony in a purely fraternal Alliance the large number of consecrated Christians in the various evangelical churches who believe in the Lord Jesus as Saviour, Sanctifier, Healer, and Coming Lord. It seemed to very many that there was a divine necessity for a special bond of fellowship among those who were being thus simultaneously called into closer intimacy with our coming Lord in order that we might give a more emphatic testimony to these great principles which might well be called at this time "Present truths," that we might encourage and strengthen each other's hearts by mutual fellowship and prayer, and that we might unite in various forms of aggressive work to give wider proclamation to these truths and prepare for the coming of our Lord. With this view the Alliance was formed and founded upon the special basis of the Fourfold Gospel as above expressed. In all other respects and with reference to all other doctrines its attitude is strictly evangelical.[71]

Christ Our Savior

Christ our Savior for Dr Simpson means that the only solution for the world that lacked an opportunity for salvation, is to be "saved and saved alone!" through Christ.[72] For Simpson the essential mission is to evangelize by proclaiming salvation in the crucified and resurrected Christ, the one whom

---

69. Virginia Lieson Brereton, "Protestant Fundamentalist Bible Schools, 1882–1940" (PhD diss., Columbia University, 1984), 186. See details of the context of these fundamentalist Bible schools in ch. 1 "The Context for a New Education," and ch. 2 "Beginnings."

70. See ch. 6 "A Missionary Church 1900–1919," and ch. 7 "Motives and Policies" in Cartmel, "Mission Policy and Program."

71. See *Christian Alliance Year Book* (1893) cited by Albert E. Thompson, *The Life of A. B. Simpson* (Brooklyn, NY: Christian Alliance Publishing, 1920), 128–130.

72. See "The Lord's Coming and Missions" in Albert B. Simpson, *The Challenge of Missions* (New York: Christian Alliance Publishing, 1926); Simpson, *Fourfold Gospel*, 25–26.

the gospel proclaims – not education or social or medical relief, because apart from Christ people remain eternally doomed.[73] Thus, there are several sermons and papers that were written and preached by Simpson, which are regarded as "The Missiology of A. B. Simpson," in which he urged the evangelization of the world in his generation.[74] Simpson shared his interests in the world's unoccupied fields in the early years of the Alliance, emphasizing that "it is a tremendous emergency . . . because of the insistence of the Master's command and commission about it."[75]

Vietnam was first mentioned in August 1882 as an unoccupied field.[76] Such an impact was later on reflected in Robert A. Jaffray's 1908 report to impress upon the North American Christians the importance of "the message of salvation" because of the "lostness" of the people of Indochina (Vietnam).[77] In fact, the merger of the Christian Alliance and International Missionary Alliance to become the Christian and Missionary Alliance (CMA) in April 1897 was not just to respond to the crises of "liberalism" and the "Pentecostal movement" at that time, but also for the sake of the work of missions in the world. As Simpson remarked, "It expressed the genius of our movement. We are an alliance of Christians for worldwide missionary work."[78]

Christ Our Sanctifier

Christ our Sanctifier is another one of Dr Simpson's important doctrinal concepts. Since the early days of his Louisville pastorate, Simpson found that a believer cannot survive if he lacks personal cleansing and anointing, and therefore the person must be empowered continually by the Holy Spirit.[79] Simpson emphasizes sanctification as a two-stage approach – a preparation

---

73. Mcgraw, "A. B. Simpson 1843–1919," 39.

74. See John S. Sawin, *Missionary Semons by A. B. Simpson* (unpublished manuscript, 1983).

75. See Sawin, *Missionary Semons by A. B. Simpson*.

76. See Albert B. Simpson, *The Word, the Work and the World* (August 1882). See also in Sawin, *Christian and Missionary Alliance*, 2.

77. Jaffray, *Alliance Magazine* (10 April 1908): 22f. Cited by Sawin, 30–34.

78. Aiden Wilson Tozer, *Wingspread* (Harrisburg, PA: Christian Publishing, 1943), 96; Robert L. Niklaus, John S. Sawin, and Samuel J. Stoesz, *All for Jesus: God at Work in the Christian and Missionary Alliance over One Hundred Years* (Camp Hill, PA: Christian Publications, 1986), 96–99.

79. Mcgraw, "Doctrine of Sanctification," 144–188; Simpson, *Fourfold Gospel*, 27–46.

for living and a preparation for dying which traditionalists considered as an unnecessary requirement.[80] But Simpson believes that "Christian holiness is ... Christ life, perfection in Christ, abiding in a perfect Christ." In fact, "Sanctification is the pathway to a deeper peace, even the 'peace of God which passeth all understanding' ... Sanctification brings the soul into harmony with God and the laws of its own being, and there must be peace, and there can be in no other way."[81] This is crucial for the Christian life because both the "focus on the cosmic work of Christ and the identification of the believer with Christ have important implications for the missionary task. The higher Christian life and missions directly complement each other, since Christ does not indwell or fill the believer merely to grant good feelings or experiences, but rather to enable the believer to live for Christ and his kingdom."[82]

In the Alliance's guiding principles, the role of the Holy Spirit is important as the Alliance emphasizes "the special agency and superintendency of the Holy Ghost in the work of missions, seeking only whole consecrated missionaries and holding the work under the constant direction of the Spirit of God."[83] Simpson believes that the role of the Holy Spirit is very important for believers, both in their individual spiritual journey with God, and in the work of missions to the world. Along with that, Simpson was open to the gifts and the manifestations of the Holy Spirit as revealed in his *Diary* quoted below. However, the Alliance experienced the withdrawal of some of its members to align themselves with the Pentecostal movement because of various reasons, including Simpson's position on the Pentecostal "evidence doctrine," tearing apart the fabric of Alliance unity. He strongly urged the Alliance not to lose its unity because it is a unity based on a "common experience" and "precious revelation" of Jesus as "Savior, Sanctifier, Healer and Coming Lord," and on a common commitment to the task of world evangelization. Therefore, he

---

80. Mcgraw, "A. B. Simpson 1843–1919," 44.

81. Albert B. Simpson, *Wholly Sanctified* (Harrisburg: Christian Publication, 1925; New York: Christian Alliance Publishing, 1890), 9–10.

82. Samuel J. Stoesz, "The Doctrine of Sanctification in the Thought of A. B. Simpson," in *The Birth of a Vision: Essays on the Ministry and Thought of Albert B. Simpson*, eds. F. David Hartzfeld and Charles Nienkirchen (Beaverlodge, Alberta: Buena Book Services, 1986), 119.

83. George P. Pardington, *Twenty-Five Wonderful Years* (New York: Christian Alliance Publishing, 1914), 104; Niklaus, Sawin, and Stoesz, *All for Jesus*, 84.

advised that, "the only way to meet error [is] to go all the way with truth."[84] The Alliance would remain united only as long as Alliance workers could see Christ in one another.[85] Although he made several public critiques of the "evidence doctrine," he was a "forerunner of Pentecostalism"[86] who himself was a private seeker of the Pentecostal baptism with tongues, as noted in one entry of his diary:

> Five years have passed since these memoirs were written (1907). No extraordinary manifestation of the Spirit in tongues or similar gifts have come. Many of my friends have received such manifestations, but mine has still been a life of fellowship and service. At all times my spirit has been opened to God for anything He might be pleased to reveal or bestow; but He has met me still with the old touch and spiritual sense and in distinct and marked answers to believing prayer in my practical life.[87]

Though he did not have the evidence of tongues – as many had in his time where the tongues movement took place in many states, before the Azusa Pentecostal movement in 1906 – he believed that the Holy Spirit empowers people to be those of Spirit-filled, holy living to reach the unoccupied world to "bring back the King."[88]

Christ Our Healer

Crist as our Healer is the third fundamental aspect of *The Fourfold Gospel*. Divine healing is a very important element in Simpson's ministry. This is because of his experience with Christ as Healer in Maine in 1881 where he himself was suddenly spared from anticipated death related to a diagnosed

---

84. Simpson, "Editorial," *The Alliance Weekly* (4 May 1907): 205; Simpson, "Editorial," *The Alliance Weekly* (12 June 1909): 180.

85. Albert B. Simpson, "Editorial," *The Alliance Weekly* (1 August 1908): 296.

86. See Charles Nienkirchen, "A. B. Simpson: Forerunner and Critic of the Pentecostal Movement," in *The Birth of a Vision: Essays on the Ministry and Thought of Albert B. Simpson*, eds. F. David Hartzfeld and Charles Nienkirchen (Beaverlodge, Alberta: Buena Book Services, 1986), 149.

87. See Simpson, diary entry for 6 October 1912, in John S. Sawin, "The Response and Attitude of Dr. A. B. Simpson and the Christian and Missionary Alliance to the Tongues Movement of 1906–1920," *Theological Research Exchange Network (TREN)* (1986): 28.

88. Albert B. Simpson, "Missionary Wings, Rev. 14:6," *The Alliance Weekly* (August 1891): 118.

heart condition.[89] That was a miracle for Simpson. Though he did not want to make divine healing the sole purpose of the gospel – but rather as one of "its constituent parts"[90] – he believed that faith comes when God confirms his word with healing signs, especially in the missionary tasks when communicating the gospel overseas.[91] So he said:

> Healing is the purchase of Christ's atonement and the gift of Christ's indwelling and resurrection life. Through the indwelling Christ, we are supernaturally quickened, sustained and enabled to rise above the power of disease, to overcome infirmity and to fulfill all of the work to which He calls us until our life work is completed and we rise to the higher life of immortal resurrection.[92]

Christ Our Coming Lord

Dr Simpson's eschatological view is pre-millennialist. As reviewed in *Conference for Prayer and Counsel* "The Testimony and Teaching of the Alliance" is that "The Alliance holds and teaches the personal and pre-millennial coming of the Lord Jesus."[93] Dr Simpson believes that the imminence of Christ's return is dependent on the effects of missionary endeavor, the motivation for missions coming from Matthew 24:14, that "Christ is ready and waiting to return as soon as the church has fulfilled its obligation."[94] Dr Simpson believes that "We know that our missionary work is not in vain, but in addition to the blessing of all, it is to bring Christ Himself back again. It puts in our hands the key to the bridal chamber and the lever that will hasten

---

89. Mcgraw, "A. B. Simpson 1843–1919," 40.

90. In the preface of *The Gospel of Healing*, Simpson noted: "It is most important that it should be ever held in its true place in relation to the other parts of the gospel. It is not the whole gospel, nor perhaps the chief part of it, but it is a part, and its due relationship to the whole, it will prove to be, like the gospel itself, 'the power of God to everyone that believeth.'" See Albert B. Simpson, *The Gospel of Healing*, 4th ed. (New York: Christian Alliance Publishing, 1890), 7–8.

91. Mcgraw, "A. B. Simpson 1843–1919," 40; Thomas and Draper, "A. B. Simpson and World Evangelization," 203, 206.

92. The Christian and Missionary Alliance, *The Word, the Work and the World* (July 1887): 2.

93. Sawin, "Fourfold Gospel," 21–24.

94. Thomas and Draper, "A. B. Simpson and World Evangelization," 204.

his return."⁹⁵ Therefore, in this fourth "fold" of *The Fourfold Gospel*, Christ as our coming Lord, Simpson believes that the church plays a significant role in "bringing back the King."⁹⁶ Through the two articles published in 1890 and 1892, "The Great Commission" and "Eloquent Figures for the Cause of Missions," he pleads for persons and resources to meet the urgent need for missions to achieve the evangelization of the world in his generation.

Although not going abroad himself as a missionary, Simpson inspired many people to go. In fact, he was called the father of a "sending" mission organization in that it "has demonstrated its viability in pioneering, sacrifice, evangelism, and church growth."⁹⁷ And though it may be an exaggeration, Walter Turnbull asserted that, "Simpson was the only missionary leader that associated the coming of the Lord with the completion of the missionary task."⁹⁸

The "Christological" *Fourfold Gospel*, which became the fundamental elements for the CMA mission and its young church in Vietnam, is manifested in their evangelism and conversion efforts which will be discussed next.

Evangelism and Conversion: Tension with the Culture

The CMA mission focused much of its efforts and resources toward evangelization. Dr Simpson's main concern for Vietnam was that "the great kingdom of Annam [Vietnam] should be occupied for Christ."⁹⁹ As a result, the CMA missionaries attempted (in 1897, 1889, and 1902) to "occupy Vietnam with the gospel as soon as possible."¹⁰⁰ This is very unlike the way of the early Jesuits in Vietnam, for example, Alexander de Rhodes' way – choosing the right people to pioneer the ministry – in planting the Vietnamese church. To enhance the speed of evangelization, the CMA missionaries in Tourane (Đà Nẵng) – the cradle of Vietnamese evangelicalism – encouraged their first converts, many of whom had a low level of education and low social

---

95. See "The Lord's Coming and Missions," in Simpson, *The Challenge of Missions*, 48.
96. Simpson, "Missionary Wings, Rev. 14:6," 118; Sawin, "Fourfold Gospel," 27.
97. Mcgraw, "A. B. Simpson 1843–1919," 45.
98. Walter Turnbull, *The Alliance Weekly* (November 1919): 98; Sawin, "Fourfold Gospel," 28.
99. The Christian and Missionary Alliance, *The Word, the Work and the World* (February 1887): 112, 28. Cited by Sawin, *Christian and Missionary Alliance*, 3.
100. See Phạm Xuân Tín, *Gospel First Came to Vietnam*.

status, to be active in the distribution of evangelistic tracts and personal witness through the facilities acquired from the British and Foreign Bible Society (BFBS).[101] Earlier, the main work of the BFBS – which was once one of the largest Christian agencies in Vietnam – was to "propagate the Christian message by the printed page."[102] Thus, during this early stage of Vietnamese evangelicalism, the CMA churches were greatly influenced by the enthusiastic evangelization agenda of the CMA that caused suspicious attention from both the existing church – the Roman Catholic Church in Vietnam – and the rulers and kings of Vietnam at the time.[103]

Ever since they arrived in Vietnam in the late nineteenth and the early twentieth centuries, the CMA missionaries had passed on to the local Vietnamese converts their enthusiasm for urgent evangelism and a doctrinal emphasis for the soul being saved, living a holy life to go heaven.[104] The young evangelical church – the Evangelical Church of Vietnam (ECVN) – did attempt to present an indigenous image by changing its name on two different occasions, in 1927 as *Hội Tin Lành Đông Pháp* (Evangelical Church of [French] Indochina) and then in 1950 as *Hội Thánh Tin Lành Việt Nam* (Evangelical Church of Vietnam) (ECVN).[105] Yet, changing its name to appear as an indigenous church has not helped the church to develop a Vietnamese ecclesiological dimension: a communal church life. Beside the name change, this evangelical church also attempted to make the gospel available to the Vietnamese people, through the Vietnamese Bible translation in 1926.

Most of the time "conversion" has been viewed as an individual decision or a "highly personal decision" rather than a communal conversion.[106] In contrast, the Vietnamese have a harmonized image of *Trời-Đất-Người*

---

101. Scholar Đào Duy Anh said, "Evangelicalism is good, but, only non-educated people can only believe." And an anonymous scholar asked a missionary, "Why don't you disciple a better educated people to evangelize with you?" quoted in Lê Hoàng Phu, "Short History," 387.

102. See Phan Đình Liệu, *Lịch sử Tin Lành truyền đến Việt Nam*. Cited by Lê Hoàng Phu, "Short History," 101.

103. See Charles Patrick Keith, "Protestantism and the Politics of Religion in French Colonial Vietnam," *French Colonial History* 13 (2012): 141-174.

104. For instance, Mrs Gordon H. Smith, *Victory in Vietnam* (Grand Rapids, MI.: Zondervan, 1965).

105. See Lê Văn Thái, *Bốn mươi sáu năm chức vụ (Hồi ký)*; Lê Hoàng Phu, "Short History"; Phạm Xuân Tín, *Lược sử giáo hội Tin Lành Việt Nam* [A short history of the Evangelical Church of Vietnam], (unpublished manuscript, 1991); Reimer, "Protestant Movement in Vietnam."

106. See Herendeen, "Conversion and Indigeneity."

(Heaven-Earth-Human) in their perception in which conversion or salvation is understood as being/living harmonized in the relationship with Heaven, Earth, and other human beings. In terms of reaching out to a community and turning that community or village (Vietnamese tend to live together in small groups called *thôn* or *làng* [village]) into a church place for the Vietnamese, the Vietnamese Catholic Church is in a better position. Therefore a major challenge for Vietnamese evangelicalism, is that, though the ECVN has practiced the Three-Self principles of Self-Support, Self-Government and Self-Propagation since the 1920s, it has not been able to develop its beliefs and practices in indigenous communal ways.

Fundamentalist Doctrines

The young evangelical church, the ECVN, has continued to hold onto the American fundamentalist doctrines of the CMA theologians, especially John Drange Olsen's *Thần đạo học* (Theology), as the theological foundation for church life ever since 1927. Violet B. James, who compared and contrasted the American CMA and Mennonites in Vietnam in her 1989 studies, said that, "the ECVN was modeled after the CMA Church in America. Ministers were trained by the missionaries from the Missionary Training Institute in New York with a similar curriculum. Thus the local Christians were not given the scope to develop their own pattern of worship and church life."[107] In fact, in 1972, Dr Lê Hoàng Phu suggested that "in addition to the three basic principles of the indigenous church policy universally accepted in Protestant mission circles (Three-Self), the Evangelical Church of Vietnam should also concentrate its efforts on 'self-nurture' and 'self-expression' which are vital to any indigenous movement and constitute a basis for a significant contribution of a national church to the worldwide Christian church and to the cultural heritage of its own country."[108]

John Drange Olsen, from Norway, studied at Nyack Missionary Training Institute under Dr Simpson before heading to Vietnam as an Alliance missionary. He translated part of the New Testament and Old Testament into Vietnamese as well as serving as one of the editors of the complete Vietnamese Bible (usually called the 1926 version). He also served as dean of the first

---

107. James, "American Protestant Missions," 354.
108. Lê Hoàng Phu, "Short History," 3–4.

evangelical Bible school in Đà Nẵng.[109] One of his greatest accomplishments is the two-volume systematic theological text, *Thần đạo học* (Theology), which he edited and which has had significant impact on the Vietnamese evangelical church life.

Olsen's *Thần đạo học* (Theology) consists of eleven books bound into two volumes with the following contents: (1) General Remarks on Theology; (2) the Scripture; (3) God; (4) Humanity; (5) Sin; (6) Christ; (7) the Holy Spirit; (8) Salvation; (9) Angels; (10) the Church; (11) the Second Coming/End of the World. This textbook was approved by the ECVN's annual committee meeting in 1950 in Đà Lạt, and received permission to be printed by the ECVN printing house in Đà Lạt.[110] Though this work is a systematic theological text, it lacks a systematic way of referencing the sources. In a few places Olsen mentions some theologians' names. For instance, Olsen quoted Dr R. A. Torrey when discussing "eternal death" in Book Five: "The Doctrine of Sin."[111] But, in Book Ten: "The Doctrine of the Church," Olsen forgoes referencing and attribution for a brief non-specific statement: "A theologian has written . . ." Moreover, when comparing Olsen's *Thần đạo học* (Theology) with Augustus Hopkins Strong's *Systematic Theology: A Compendium Designed for the Use of Theological Students*, written in 1907, both the outline and much of the content of the two works look similar.[112] Needless to say, Olsen's *Thần đạo học* (Theology) was deeply influenced by conservative Baptist theologians such as R. A. Torrey and especially A. H. Strong.[113]

Olsen's Book Ten: "The Doctrine of the Church" is also heavily influenced by Strong's Part Seven: "Ecclesiology, of the Doctrine of the Church" (vol.

---

109. Lê Hoàng Phu, 195–198.

110. See Olsen, *Thần đạo học*. The foreword was written by Rev Ông Văn Huyên, the chairman of the ECVN (South) at this time. For some reason, the textbook was hand-printed manually in the Bible school in Da Nang, likely due to the urgent need for it among the evangelical churches and the students of the Bible school.

111. Olsen, *Thần đạo học*, 309–370.

112. See Augustus Hopkins Strong, *Systematic Theology: A Compendium Designed for the Use of Theological Students* (Valley Forge, PA: Judson Press, 1907). Strong was a conservative Baptist theologian.

113. See Philip Khanh Van Trinh, "Toward a Doctrine of Sin in the Vietnamese Context: Elements in the Dialogue between the Vietnamese Indigenous Perceptions and Christian Teaching on Sin by Missionaries" (PhD diss., Graduate Theological Union 2004). Thank you to Dr Philip Khanh Van Trinh for discovering this parallel.

3).¹¹⁴ Though Olsen opens his discussion on this doctrine by relating how the word "Church" is understood in Vietnam and even in China, his ecclesiological perspective is informed by the general fundamentalist practices of the CMA blended with the conservative Baptist perspective of the Strong's *Systematic Theology*.¹¹⁵ Though he carefully chose the existing ecclesiological understanding of the church that had been popularized by the Catholics, for example, Nhà ở của Đức Chúa Trời (House of the Lord of Heaven), as used by Alexandre de Rhodes (as will be discussed in the next chapter), his ecclesiological perspective was of little help to the Vietnamese understanding of the church in the context of Vietnam.¹¹⁶

Thus, a critique of the Vietnamese evangelical perspective on ecclesiology is that Vietnamese evangelicalism in the nineteenth- and twentieth-century Vietnam was trapped in the context of the end of Western Christendom and the ongoing colonialism in Asia, in which the "Protestant approach to missions can be viewed in large measure as one of cargo."¹¹⁷ As a result, the church has assumed "God's truth to be timeless and culture-free" as did the Western missionaries.¹¹⁸ Darrell L. Whiteman argues that "non-Western Christians have learned a non-contextualized Christianity from their missionary teachers and have adopted it at a formal, behavioral level that still has not yet penetrated the deeper levels of their worldview."¹¹⁹ Vietnamese evangelicalism has relied heavily on the CMA theological works, for example, Olsen's *Thần đạo học* (Theology), rather than constructing its own ecclesiological perspective that is relevant to the context of Vietnam. As a result, Vietnamese evangelical ecclesiology has not reflected what makes the church "Church" from the Vietnamese perspective.

Reconstructing its ecclesiological perspective requires that Vietnamese evangelicalism must study and consider Vietnamese culture seriously to

---

114. Olsen, *Thần đạo học*, 765–838.

115. In "Book Six: Doctrine of Christ" of *Thần đạo học*, however, Olsen argued that Christ (Logos in Greek) is Đạo, not "Ngôi Lời" as seen in the Vietnamese Bible. This understanding of Đạo is stressed much in the Vietnamese-East Asian perspective ontologically. More discussion on this matter will be given in chapter 6.

116. Olsen, *Thần đạo học*, 763–768.

117. Shaw, "Beyond Contextualization," 209.

118. Shaw, 209.

119. Whiteman, "Contextualization," 6.

understand the outlook on life, beliefs, traditions, and rituals of the Vietnamese in order to frame its ecclesiology. For instance, Vietnamese evangelicals need to address the issue of ancestral veneration versus ancestor worship in a satisfactory manner since this issue has been a major hindrance to the acceptance of Vietnamese evangelicals by the Vietnamese.[120] Moreover, Vietnamese evangelicals need to examine the past contextualization efforts of the French Protestants in Vietnam during the late nineteenth century – burning incense, using psalms to worship in a Vietnamese way, and using Vietnamese music and melody rather than the Western hymns[121] – and the concepts of "self-nurture" and "self-expression" suggested by Rev Lê Hoàng Phu (1972).[122]

Chapter Conclusion

There is no doubt about the impact of the French and the American Protestant missions on the formation of Vietnamese evangelicalism. On one hand, it is laudable for Vietnamese evangelicals to show their appreciation for the hearts and minds of these early Protestant missionaries in Vietnam. However, on the other hand, they cannot continually rely on foreign missions and the Euro-American theological heritage to form its own theology and practices. "Indigenous agency" is one of the necessary measures to ensure Vietnamese church growth.[123] The twenty-first century Vietnamese church, in obedience to the Holy Spirit, needs to adapt by observing continually "the signs of the times," in order to construct a Vietnamese theological framework, so that the

---

120. Simon Chan, *Grassroots Asian Theology: Thinking the Faith from the Ground Up* (Downers Grove, IL: IVP Acadamic, 2014), 72. Chan believes a thorough understanding of the practice of ancestral veneration in Asian context can form "one of the most important backdrops for the contextualization of the gospel."

121. Bois, *Histoire des Missions*, 40–42; Đặng Ngọc Phúc, *Những người Tin Lành tại Việt Nam trong giai đoạn thăm dò*, 362–67. Paul Monet believes that in the Old Testament, the Jews used Psalms, which are their folk songs to worship God; thus, it is biblical for Vietnamese to use their folk songs [*ca dao* and *dân ca*] as ways to worship God. For further discussions on contextualization efforts done by Paul Monet and George Bois, see George Bois's thesis in 1952.

122. Bois, *Histoire des Missions*, 40–42.

123. Wilbert R. Shenk, ed. *Enlarging the Story: Perspectives on Writing World Christian History* (Maryknoll, NY: Orbis Books, 2002), xiv–xv. This edited book is a wonderful example of how to allow national voices (or "the unrecorded voices of Bible women, evangelists, catechists, translators, and counted faithful laypeople") who were, are, and will be initiating the story of World Christianity.

church can be "church" constantly relevant to its context.[124] While exploring the signs of the times, Vietnamese evangelicals must keep in mind that the process of making the Vietnamese church a "church" must be done in a way that brings people into being more like Christ, and yet not less Vietnamese. Thus, the future of Vietnamese contextual ecclesiology, while learning from its counterparts in East and Southeast Asia, depends on obedience to the prompting of the Holy Spirit, while participating in the mission of the triune God working in every aspect of Vietnamese culture.[125] Vietnamese evangelicals can be seen as facing two particular challenges, namely ecumenical engagement and addressing the religio-cultural realities.

First, ecumenically, Vietnamese evangelical churches should work together for the sake of Vietnamese Christianity, rather than for each church's own interests. Some collaborative initiatives, such as the Vietnamese Bible translation project, between the Catholic Church and the Evangelicals under the United Bible Society, have already been in place, from 1974 to 1993.[126] Evangelicals have also been in dialogue recently with the Vietnamese state.[127] Furthermore, in the past few years, some evangelical churches and theological educators have gathered for several mutual discussions, such as "Vietnamese Culture from an Evangelical Perspective."[128] Thus, it is very likely that there will be more dialogues in the near future among Vietnamese evangelicals, between the Evangelicals and the Catholics, and between the Christian Church and the Vietnamese State.

---

124. Peter C. Phan, ed. *The Asian Synod: Texts and Commentaries* (Maryknoll, NY: Orbis Books, 2002), 301–302; Joseph Dinh Duc Dao, "The Christian Formation of the Laity and Lay Missionary Efforts in Asia," in *Proclaiming Jesus Christ in Asia Today*, ed. Pontificium Consilium Pro Laicis (Rome: Libreria Editrice Vaticana-Vatican Press, 2010), 105–106.The full English text of *Ecclesia in Asia* can be found in Phan, *Asian Synod*, 286–340. Also in *Origins* 29, 23 (18 November 1999), 358–384. Federation of Asian Bishops' Conferences Plenary Assembly, *FABC at Forty Years: Responding to the Challenges of Asia: A New Evangelization*, vol. 2014, FABC Plenary Assemblies Series 12/8 (Xuan Loc; Hồ Chí Minh City: FABC, 2012).

125. For instance, Orrel N. Steinkamp, *The Holy Spirit in Vietnam* (Carol Stream, IL: Creation House, 1973).

126. See https://biblevietnam.org, accessed 11 December 2014.

127. http://btgcp.gov.vn/Plus.aspx/vi/News/38/0/248/0/1979/Hoi_thao_Dao_Tin_lanh_o_Viet_Nam_tu_nam_1976_den_nam_2011_%20Monday,%20June%2027,%202011, accessed 27 June 2011.

128. See http://hoithanh.com/Home/tin-tuc/4151-hoi-thao-than-hoc-lan-thu-2.html, accessed 11 December 2014.

Second, in participating in the mission of the triune God, Vietnamese evangelicals have an opportunity to be more serious in addressing the intertwined religio-cultural realities of Vietnam. While the future of the Catholic Church in Vietnam continues to be reshaped by the FABC's missiological approach which is best described as *missio inter gentes* (mission *among* the nations) rather than traditional *missio ad gentes* (mission *to* the nations),[129] and focused on various themes that have been set at the 2012 Vietnam FABC Plenary Assembly (the *Mega-Trends in Asia and Ecclesial Realities*),[130] the future of Vietnamese evangelicals is still unclear and perhaps complicated since they have not obligated themselves to share in one theological voice or one ecumenical body. However, Vietnamese evangelicals may benefit from the work of their counterparts in East and Southeast Asia, considering in particular the document "Critical Asian Principle" (CAP)[131] that was revised recently and is now called the "Guidelines for Doing Theologies in Asia."[132] The East and Southeast Asian context, for which this guideline has been developed, shares similarities with Vietnam. The guideline is to be used for constructing theological education and ultimately church theologies in the Asian context. Furthermore, the 2010 Cape Town Commitment (or *Lausanne III*), in which many Vietnamese evangelical church leaders participated, continues to remind the Vietnamese evangelicals to confess their faith as "For the Lord We Love," and the call to action as "For the Lord We Serve."[133]

---

129. For an excellent study of the mission theology of the FABC's official documents, see Jonathan Y. Tan, "Missio Inter Gentes: Towards a New Paradigm in the Mission Theology of the Federation of Asian Bishops' Conferences (FABC)," *Mission Studies* 21, no. 1 (2004).

130. Federation of Asian Bishops' Conferences Plenary Assembly, *FABC at Forty Years: Responding to the Challenges of Asia: A New Evangelization*, 7–13.

131. See Huang Po Ho, "Contextualization of Theological Education in South East Asia – Challenges and Responses: A Case Study of South East Asia Graduate School of Theology," *IV International WOCATI Congress and Jubilee of the ETE of WCC* (2008): 3–4. Mr. Huang provides the history of the phrase of "Critical Asian Principle" (CAP), which was introduced to and adopted as basic perspective for establishing and operating the doctoral studies program of the SEAGST in 1972. In 1975 at the ATESEA meetings in Taiwan, there was general consensus that the whole graduate school program of ATESEA is carried out in the light of the Critical Asian Principle. Huang quotes this from The Association for Theological Education in South East Asia and The South East Asia Graduate School of Theology, *Handbook* (version year 2005–2007), 84.

132. See Association for Theological Education in South East Asia, "Guidelines for Doing Theologies in Asia," *International Bulletin of Missionary Research* 32, no. 2 (2008).

133. See www.lausanne.org/content/ctc/ctcommitment, accessed 24 August 2012.

Also, Vietnamese evangelicals, the ECVN in particular, need to revisit the motto that *"Tin Lành không tham gia chính trị"* (the evangelical church does not get involved in politics) that had been popular during the political conflicts in Vietnam. Such understanding of politics has been applied to the church for certain situations and yet has paralyzed many Vietnamese evangelicals in responding to other needs of the people. For instance, how does an evangelical church respond to the people in Vietnam in terms of peace and reconciliation? How should a church respond peacefully to a particularly sensitive, potentially violent situation while still being faithful to the truth of the gospel of Christ?

"The task of the Christian church is to cooperate with God in shaping the society in light of the values of the coming kingdom of God, the kingdom of equality, justice, and peace."[134] The future of Vietnamese evangelicals should continue to be a "participatory ecclesiology"[135] at all levels as Miroslav Volf proposed, in following the prompting of the Holy Spirit in the process of making the church an inwardly transformed agent that leads to an outward expression in the context of Vietnam.[136]

---

134. Veli-Matti Kärkkäinen, *Christ and Reconciliation: A Constructive Christian Theology for the Pluralistic World*, vol. 1. (Grand Rapids, MI: Eerdmans, 2013), 377. Further helpful discussion on this particular is in "Reconciliation as the Church's Mission in the World," in Veli-Matti Kärkkäinen, *Christ and Reconciliation*, 364–380.

135. See Veli-Matti Kärkkäinen, *An Introduction to Ecclesiology: Ecumenical, Historical & Global Perspectives* (Downers Grove, IL: InterVarsity Press, 2002), 134–141.

136. Veli-Matti Kärkkäinen, "The Calling of the Whole People of God into Ministry: The Spirit, Church and Laity," *Studia Theologica* 54, no. 2 (2000): 154–155.

CHAPTER 6

A Paradigm Shift Proposal for Vietnamese Mission Theology

Before Christianity became a missionary movement from the West to the rest, had it not originated in Asia? Was the Bible, the very foundation of Christianity not written in its entirety by Asian writers? Was not the gospel first spread on this continent by the apostles, including the apostle Thomas, who according to tradition, is believed to have founded the Christian church in South India? If so, are not the characteristics of biblical Christianity very Asian in thinking, in culture and in life conditions?[1]

This chapter proposes a cultural integration for a renewed mission theology in Vietnam. The chapter offers a new perspective on how indigenous and Christian concepts and their practices can merge, creating a paradigm shift necessary for a renewed Vietnamese evangelical mission theology. The fact is that Christianity is still not at home in Vietnam, despite the "outward assimilation" of Christianity that had manifested itself as early as the East Syrian Christian visitors and settlers in Asia.[2] Asian Christianity, and more specifically Vietnamese evangelicalism, has several Western characteristics that have been blended within it. Perhaps the Western characteristics of Vietnamese Christianity began with the formation of Western imperialism because Christian missionary movements in Vietnam often coincided with Western colonial expansion. Vietnamese Christians have been considered

---

1. Saphir P. Athyal, *Church in Asia Today: Challenges and Opportunities* (Singapore: Asia Lausanne Committee for World Evangelization, 1996), 8–9.

2. Hans Küng described the encounters of Christianity and China in *seven* historical models, of which the "outward assimilation" is the first. For details of these models, see Küng and Ching, *Christianity and Chinese Religions*, 233–256.

as having betrayed their own culture and way of life to embrace a Western faith (Christianity). Even today this is the situation for Christianity in Asia where Christian faith is contrary to many contexts of Asian culture, the exceptional case being the Philippines. That the Asian churches have identified and wrestled with contextualization issues is evident, as seen from the many contextual theologies that have emerged in the context of Asia in the last fifty years.

Nevertheless, the challenges of assimilating (contextualizing) Christian faith into the syncretistic, already contextualized Asian spirituality remain the same today as in yesteryears. This study does not attempt to come up with another contextual theology for Asia at large. Yet, within the context of Eastern Asia, Vietnamese evangelicals could initiate the process of theologizing some of the most critical religio-cultural issues, namely the Vietnamese concepts of God and the family. These concepts need to be redeemed for a mission theology in the specific context of Vietnam. The processes of theologizing these concepts, therefore, would require a paradigm shift in mission theology so that the church in Vietnam can be "church" constantly relevant to its context.

Mission Theological Principles

Vietnamese evangelical mission theology must look at the cultural and theological issues as resources for organizing its principles. These principles would be drawn from what has already been done within the context of Vietnam and other similar cultures in East Asia.

Being Asian Evangelical

Generally, Asian theological trends tentatively focus in two directions: Asian contextual theologies and Asian evangelical theologies.

Asian Contextual Theologies

Within the twentieth century of post-colonialism and national independence, Asian theologies have emerged to accommodate various socio-political, and religio-cultural dimensions of the continent. Contextual Asian theologians have developed their theologies to respond to the needs, but more importantly, to wrestle with the challenges that Christianity has not been able to overcome for years, thus still lacking relevance to the Asian people.[3] Using the argument of God's incarnation and revelation in the Scripture coming through a specific cultural form (the Jewish and Hellenistic cultures to record his revelation), Asian theologies frequently focus on various Asian cultural forms to represent their specific contexts, for example, the pain-of-God theology (Japan), water-buffalo theology (Thailand), third-eye theology (China), Minjung theology (Korea), theology of change (Taiwan), and a score of other national theologies such as Indian theology, Burmese theology, and Sri Lankan theology.[4] Thus, because the focal point for theologizing is the context (socio-politically oriented, syncretistic, and normed by situational-social analysis), rather than by the primacy of Scripture, many Asian theologies have been branded as "contextual theologies," and not as authentic Asian evangelical theology.[5] Most prominently, in Bong Rin Ro's "Asian Theology," Asian theologies have been categorized into four groups: (1) syncretistic theology, (2) accommodation theology, (3) situational theology, and (4) biblical theology.[6]

Syncretistic theology: Bong Rin Ro believes that this trend tries to syncretize Christianity with a national religion (Hinduism, Buddhism, or Islam) in an attempt to contextualize theology into the national situation. According to Ro, this group includes some "liberal theologians" in India, such as Raymond

---

3. For instance, John C. England, *Asian Christian Theologies: A Research Guide to Authors, Movements*, Sources, 3 vols. (Delhi: ISPCK, 2002–2004).

4. The entry "Asian theology" listed these Asian theological trends in three categories before proposed the fourth one, "biblical theology." See Bong Rin Ro, "Asian Theology," in *Evangelical Dictionary of Theology*, ed. Walter A. Elwell (Grand Rapids, MI: Baker Academic, 2001), 106–108.

5. For instance, Christopher J. H. Wright holds that these "contextual theologies" believe that context does matter, that in the act of reading and interpreting the Bible, the questions of who you are, where you are, and whom you live among as a reader make a difference. See in Wright, *Mission of God*, 41–43. Others, such as Donald Leroy Stults, disagree with Asian "contextualized theology" by two criteria: (1) the parameters for contextualizing the gospel in Asia are not established by the Scripture; and (2) they cannot go beyond the non-negotiable *evangelical* doctrines or traditional formulations, including salvation by grace alone, the Great Commission, and the return of Christ. See specifically ch. 8 "The Parameters of Theological Contextualization," and ch. 9 "A Critique of Recent Contextualized Theology" in Donald Leroy Stults, *Developing An Asian Evangelical Theology* (Denver, CO: iAcademic Books, 2001), 133–188.

6. The discussion of these three categories and the biblical theology that Ro suggested is taken from Bong Rin Ro, "Contextualization: Asian Theology," in *The Bible and Theology in Asian Contexts: An Evangelical Perspective on Asian Theology*, eds. Bong Rin Ro and Ruth Eshenaur (Taipei, Taiwan: Asia Theological Association, 1984), 63–77; Ro, "Asian Theology," 106–108.

Panikkar (*Unknown Christ of Hinduism*) and M. M. Thomas (the cosmic Christ in a form of secular humanism).

Accommodation theology: Ro argues that this is another subtle attempt to contextualize theology in Asia, including attempts to accommodate other religious ideas that are observable, particularly in Buddhist countries. The Asian religious terminologies and concepts of Buddhism include *dharma*, the word selected by the Thailand Bible Society for the word Logos in John 1:1. Matteo Ricci chose the words *Tien Chu* as the name for God because that was the popular Chinese Buddhist concept of God and Chuan-Seng Song's *Third-Eye Theology* takes *satori* (enlightenment of the mind) of Japan's Zen Buddhism, to argue that the same Spirit is working in both Christianity and Buddhism. This approach therefore, promotes that the aim of Christian missions should be the interaction of Christian spirituality with Asian spirituality, that *dharma* and *sangha* be used to describe Christian "doctrine" and "body of Christ" (D. T. Niles's *Buddhism and the Claims of Christ*), and that the three basic characteristics of Buddhist existence – *anicca* (impermanence), *dukkha* (suffering), and *anatta* (no-self) – provide a comprehensive analysis of the human predicament that can become a basis for Christian theology.

Situational theology: Ro believes that this theology may not be in agreement with the biblical and historical doctrines of the Christian church, and yet it speaks to the concrete situation in Asia. This type of theology includes Kazoh Kitamori's pain-of-God theology in Japan, and the Minjung theology in Korea. This theology (*minjung* meaning of all the people) teaches that Jesus Christ is the liberator from social injustice, economic exploitation, political oppression, and racial discrimination.

Methodologically, the context sets the tone for most Asian contextual theologies that have emerged within the twentieth century, the period of post-colonial and national independence for several countries in Asia. If the argument that theology is birthed from the context is true, then Asian contextual theologies have manifested what they are in responding to the needy (as in the fourth criterion of the declaration *The Bible and Theology in Asia Today* which is discussed next). Such Asian contextual theologies are varied depending on their contexts. Some diverse and controversial (liberal theologies) theological trends, perhaps, indicate how varied the processes of contextualization could be. What is left over of the twentieth century Asian "contextual theologies" are the struggles of the post-colonial context, such as social injustice, economic exploitation, and political oppression, seemingly the same issues of today. It appears that the Asian churches must once again reinterpret what "church" means in each particular context of Asia for the twenty-first century and beyond.[7]

Fortunately, Asian Christianity has had the courage to initiate its national involvement and responsibility for its own post-colonial period context. For instance, the Catholic Church of Vietnam for the first time since the seventeenth century, has its own national leaders (Vietnamese bishops) to lead the church after a long period under foreign leadership.[8] Not only that, but the Asian theological processes are the result of tireless contextualization efforts done in Asia.[9] Although the processes of theologizing the gospel in Asia have been initiated by Asian theologians, the question of how to justify a theology as being evangelical has been a difficult issue to wrestle with. It is not enough just being "Asian" in terms of accommodating Asian cultures and religions or the social justice issues. It also needs to be done with a primary focus on the Scripture to be evangelical.

Evangelical, but How?

What makes an Asian theology *evangelical*? And what then are some guiding and organizing principles for contextualizing the gospel in Asia?

The word "evangelical" precisely means the "good news," *evangelion* in Greek. The term "evangelical" used today, however, has a variety of meanings and is almost confusing. Historian Molly Worthen recently commented, "Evangelicalism is a far more thoughtful and diverse world than most critics – and even most evangelicals themselves – usually realize."[10] Worthen has

---

7. These prominent issues in Asia and how theology ought to be done in responding these needs are beyond the scope of this study.

8. An excellent analysis of the Vietnamese Catholic Church done by Keith, *Catholic Vietnam*. Also, a brief study of the church as an example of contextualization in Nguyen KimSon, "Catholic Church in Vietnam."

9. For example, the Jesuits' inculturation in East Asia, and the Protestants' translation/adaptation efforts in India by William Carey, and in China by Hudson Taylor.

10. Molly Worthen, *Apostles of Reason: The Crisis of Authority in American Evangelicalism* (New York, NY: Oxford University Press, 2014), 2. Here, Worthen has specific "modern American evangelicals" in mind where their relationships fraught with secular reason and imagination are examined. See also Molly Catherine Worthen, "Unlike a Mighty Army: Anxiety and Authority in American Evangelicalism" (PhD diss., Yale University, 2011).

suggested that to understand "evangelicals" is to see them as Protestants that have historically been uniting themselves together around "three elemental concerns": (1) how to repair the fracture between spiritual and rational knowledge; (2) how to assure salvation and a true relationship with God; and (3) how to resolve the tension between the demands of personal belief and the constraints of a secularized public square."[11] More precisely, according to Worthen, it is "how to reconcile faith and reason; how to know Jesus; and how to act publicly on faith after the rupture of Christendom."[12]

A traditional view is that Christians who are "evangelical" are those who affirm "a few key doctrine and practical emphases," for instance, David Bebbington's four marks of "evangelical religion."[13] These evangelical hallmarks are: (1) conversionism, the belief that lives need to be changed; (2) activism, the expression of the gospel in effort; (3) biblicism, a particular regard for the Bible; and (4) crucicentrism, a stress on the sacrifice of Christ on the cross.[14] Later George M. Marsden added the fifth, "trans-denominationalism" to describe evangelicals' willingness to see other evangelicals as part of the

---

11. Worthen, *Apostles of Reason*, 4. See also Worthen, "Unlike a Mighty Army."

12. Worthen, *Apostles of Reason*, 6.

13. See http://www.wheaton.edu/ISAE/Defining-Evangelicalism/Defining-the-Term, accessed 28 February 2017. Besides, this site suggests to look at evangelicalism as "an organic group of movements and religious tradition." Within this context "evangelical" denotes a style as much as a set of beliefs, and an attitude which insiders "know" and "feel" when they encounter it. As a result, groups as disparate as black Baptists and Dutch Reformed Churches, Mennonites and Pentecostals, Catholic charismatics and Southern Baptists can all come under the evangelical umbrella – demonstrating just how diverse the movement really is. Also, according to this site, "a third sense of the term is as the self-ascribed label for a largely midwest-based coalition that arose during the Second World War. This group came into being as a reaction against the perceived anti-intellectual, separatist, belligerent nature of the fundamentalist movement in the 1920s and 1930s. Importantly, its core personalities (like Carl F. H. Henry, Harold John Ockenga and Billy Graham), institutions (for instance, Moody Bible Institute, Wheaton College, and Fuller Theological Seminary), and organizations (such as the National Association of Evangelicals and Youth for Christ) have played a pivotal role in giving the wider movement a sense of cohesion that extends beyond these 'card-carrying' evangelicals."

14. See particularly "Preaching the Gospel: The Nature of Evangelical Religion" in David Bebbington, *Evangelicalism in Modern Britain: A History from the 1730s to the 1980s* (London: Unwin Hyman, 1989), 7–18. A similar formulation worded differently is found in Alister E. McGrath, *A Passion for Truth: The Intellectual Coherence of Evangelicalism* (Downers Grove, IL: InterVarsity Press, 1996), 22.

same family despite denominational differences, and to share cooperative projects and evangelistic efforts.[15]

"*Evangelicalism* has perennially been disputed, and its sociological and theological boundaries will continue to be debated (emphasis in original)," as theologian Amos Yong observed.[16] He offers an "Asian American pent-evangelical" perspective within "the pentecostal and charismatic currents," and argues that "renewal theological instincts are no less Bible-based, Christ-centered, evangelistically and missionally motivated, and pietistically shaped than their evangelical forebears and cousins."[17] Thus, "a pent-evangelical category holds together meaningfully in the context of thinking about global evangelical theology" with Asian as well as Asian-American contributions.[18]

Bong Rin Ro's "Asian Theology" suggests the fourth type of theology "biblical theology" to argue for an Asian "evangelical" theology.[19] An evangelical Asian theology needs to be a "biblically oriented theology" which is not only relevant to the life situations in Asia, but also guards against the danger of syncretism and of the minimizing of fundamental scriptural teachings during the process of contextualization.[20] Ro takes his position on "biblical theology" from the four criteria of the twenty-page declaration of the Asian evangelical theologians, *The Bible and Theology in Asia Today*.[21] Four guiding principles for theology in different religious contexts of Asia are given: (1) the authority

---

15. George M. Marsden, *Evangelicalism and Modern America* (Grand Rapids, MI: Eerdmans, 1984), vii–xvi.

16. Amos Yong, *The Future of Evangelical Theology: Soundings from the Asian American Diaspora* (Downers Grove, IL: IVP Academic, 2014), 32, 36.

17. Yong, *Future of Evangelical Theology*, 36. See also Amos Yong, *The Spirit Poured Out on All Flesh: Pentecostalism and the Possibility of Global Theology* (Grand Rapids, MI: Baker Academic, 2005); Amos Yong, *In the Days of Caesar: Pentecostalism and Political Theology* (Grand Rapids, MI: Eerdmans, 2010).

18. Yong, *Future of Evangelical Theology*, 36.

19. Ro's three other types/areas of theology of "Asian Theology" have been mentioned earlier.

20. Ro, "Asian Theology," 108.

21. See ATA, "The Bible and Theology in Asia Today: Declaration of the Sixth Asia Theological Association Theological Consultation 1982," in *The Bible and Theology in Asian Contexts: An Evangelical Perspective on Asian Theology*, ed. Bong Rin Ro and Ruth Marie Eshenaur (Taichung, Taiwan, ROC: Asia Theological Association, 1982), 3–20; Ro, "Asian Theology," 108. At the Sixth Asia Theological Association Consultation in Seoul, Korea, 1982, some eighty evangelical theologians discussed Asian theology and jointly produced this: *The Bible and Theology in Asia Today*.

of the Bible is reaffirmed as the only infallible, inerrant Word of God; "The Bible, not theologians, is to speak in our theology"; (2) Jesus Christ, the only incarnate Son of God, is unique; (3) mission-centered theology aiming to communicate the gospel to the lost is the best protection against syncretism; and (4) love should be the essential part of an Asian theology; only as Christians identify with the needy do they contextualize the gospel.

Although Ro believes that there is no particular Asian theology with an "evangelical" label that is widely accepted by evangelical theologians, this evangelical joint-declaration gives some guiding principles for theologizing in the varied Asian contexts. While there is much agreement among evangelical theologians on the first two points as fundamental issues (the authority of the Bible and the uniqueness of Jesus Christ), the latter two points have become the most difficult issues in the contextualization efforts for Asian evangelicalism.

Hwa Yung suggests that Asian theologies must be "theologies of mission or missiological theologies," according to the following four concerns or criteria: (1) their ability to address the diverse socio-political Asian contexts in which the churches find themselves; (2) the empowerment they bring to the evangelistic and pastoral tasks of the churches; (3) the means by which they facilitate the inculturation (contextualization) of the gospel; and (4) their faithfulness to the Christian tradition.[22] But the question is, how far can a missiological theology go and still address the diverse socio-political Asian contexts (the first criterion)? And what are the means by which a missiological theology facilitates the contextualization of the gospel (the third criterion)? As already mentioned in chapter 1 ("Contextualization" section), Hwa Yung refuses "dualism" and argues firmly that "Asian evangelical theology" would help to construct an "authentic Asian Christian theology." What then is the alternative if Asian "multi-culturalism" were the replacement for "dualism"? What Asian terms can be used to frame "Asian evangelical theology" to make it less "bananas" and more "mangoes"?[23]

---

22. Hwa Yung, "Banana Or Mango?," 95–96; Hwa Yung, *Mangoes or Bananas?*, 57–58.

23. By *bananas*, Hwa Yung implied that Asian is yellow on the outside, but Western is white on the inside; and by *mangoes*, he meant the pure Asian tropical fruit to represent an authentic homegrown theological product.

A Paradigm Shift Proposal for Vietnamese Mission Theology   195

The following sections of this chapter discuss how a Vietnamese theology can be evangelical. Considering not only the non-negotiable and fundamental doctrines of the Bible's authority and the uniqueness of Jesus Christ, the study also attempts to provide parameters whereby Vietnamese evangelical theology can be both *Vietnamese* and *evangelical*. Thus, Vietnamese evangelicalism, in the processes of making its Christian faith relevant to the context of Vietnam, should maintain its evangelical faith within a Vietnamese perspective. But first, let us turn to the early Christian assimilation efforts in Vietnam.

Early Christian Assimilation Efforts

As discussed in the previous chapters 2, 3, and 4, prior to the efforts at contextualization by the early Catholic missionaries and the cultural adaptation of the French Protestants in Vietnam, there could have been some sort of assimilation of Christianity in early Vietnam, when Vietnam and China were not distinct geographical countries as they are today.[24] But, the question is, which historical encounters of Christian missionary movements in Vietnam are relevant to theological attention today? What happened before Christianity encountered (or "re-encountered") Vietnam and East Asia in a significant way? More specifically, what attempts at assimilation by the early Christians in Vietnam are significant for the current theologizing of Vietnamese evangelicalism?

Christians from the East Syrian Church, had a different approach in spreading Christian faith from that of later missionaries, whose purpose was conversion of the natives. The spread of the East Syrian Christianity in China is revealed on the famous stele of Xian, written in Syriac and Chinese (781 CE). These Christians, mostly merchants and monks, spread Christianity into India, Vietnam, Java, Tibet, Central Asia, and China (in 578 CE) in the sixth or seventh century. The Persian monk A-lo-pen, is believed to have arrived in Xian in 635 CE, according to the famous stele of Xian, excavated in

---

24. It was argued in ch. 2 that it is not necessary to make a geographical distinction between Vietnam and China since this boundary was not conceptualized at the time. For instance, Buddhist teachers invited at that time from the South (the southern indigenous people which originated in the northern region of Vietnam today) moved back and forth easily to the North (the northern Kingdom or China today) to share their Buddhist faith. See also Nguyễn Ngọc Thơ, "Văn Hoá Bách Việt Vùng Lĩnh Nam Trong Quan Hệ Với Văn Hoá Truyền Thống Ở Việt Nam."

1623.²⁵ As a result, the "outward assimilation" of Christianity was manifested historically through the existence of the East Syrian Christians in China as a group of migrants who sought to "survive" amid an alien culture and competing religions.²⁶

Although there is still no clear evidence that the East Syrian Church accomplished any significant work in Vietnam during their visits, the outward assimilation of this Christianity in the early centuries in the Southern kingdoms (the Vietnamese) might have taken place as it did in the North (China). While the case of the East Syrian Christians is assumptive, the rest of this chapter will deal with the late history in Vietnam, where there are records of active missionary efforts by the Roman Catholics for about five centuries (the Jesuit missionaries in Vietnam from the sixteenth century), and by Protestant missions (the French and the American missions) for one third of that period.

With the arrival of Roman Catholic missions in the sixteenth century in South and East Asia, Christianity re-encountered the Asian peoples of both South and East Asia. The Protestant mission which came later (a British Baptist missionary William Carey who first came to India in 1793) was another Christian missionary movement to this continent. Asian Christianity, however, was not solely a fruit of Western missionary movements, since there was an ongoing Christian witness from the first century in Asia. From the sixteenth to the twentieth centuries, Christianity was in a complicated position where it often carried with it the stigma of Western imperialism. It was very unfortunate that the Christian missionary movements in Asia went hand in hand with Western colonial expansion to the point that when colonialism was the enemy of the Asian people, Christianity was often their enemy by association.

From a social and economic perspective, Western missionaries had contributed to the civilizing process (or more accurately a Westernizing process) of these kingdoms. For instance, de Rhodes and his companions invented *quốc ngữ* writing that became the national script of the Vietnamese language

---

25. For Syrian Christians in China, see Tang, *East Syriac Christianity*; Tang and Winkler, *From the Oxus River*.

26. Küng and Ching, *Christianity and Chinese Religions*, 198. The East Syrian Christians also used Daoism as their basis for communicating the gospel. For instance, see Martin Palmer, *The Jesus Sutras: Rediscovering the Lost Scrolls of Taoist Christianity* (New York: Ballantine Books, 2001).

today. Not only so, but they also contributed to the development of the nations in many aspects of life, and of the Asian society at large in shaping values that cannot be measured, for example, the concept of the worth of individuals, and of social relationships. As Saphir P. Athyal commented, "Christian missions were instrumental in promoting rapid progress and providing models to follow. This is gratefully recognized even by the enemies of Christianity in Asia."[27] And, "Christianity finally completed the movement out of Western Europe to become a truly global faith – a process that began in the fifteenth century."[28]

Ironically, Christianity is still viewed as a Western religion in most places in Asia. While the Christian missionary efforts seem to meet some of the needs of the Asian people, Christian faith has been challenged to satisfy the minds and the hearts of the people. Perhaps, though the mission efforts were focused on how to spread the faith to the people, especially the poor and the needy, there was less effort by missionaries to promote understanding of Asian culture and a Vietnamese expression of Christian faith. The early Protestant missionaries in Vietnam constantly reacted negatively to Vietnamese culture and were insensitive to the values inherent in the culture.

Like other Asian people, the Vietnamese are also devout and religious people. The continent is the birthplace of all the major world religions: Hinduism, Buddhism, Islam, and Christianity. In addition, Confucianism and Daoism have greatly influenced the religio-cultural traditions of the East Asians, particularly the Vietnamese. However, Christian missionaries hardly understood the people's complex worldview which intertwined sacred and secular aspects. In other words, the syncretistic spirituality of the Asian people (the holistic worldview that integrated and synthesized the religious aspects with the secular life) was seldom appreciated by the missionaries.

As seen in the "Asian Syncretistic Context" (ch. 1), Asian spirituality is a complicated synthesis of animistic beliefs, Confucianism, Daoism and Buddhism, besides two other major religions – Hinduism and Islam. These religions are deeply rooted in the people's outlook on life and their daily practice. As Athyal observes, "Christianity, as it came from the West, seriously failed in understanding this holism, which is the core of Asian spirituality.

---

27. Athyal, *Church in Asia Today*, 13.

28. Scott W. Sunquist, *The Unexpected Christian Century: The Reversal and Transformation of Global Christianity, 1900–2000* (Grand Rapids, MI: Baker Academic, 2015), 176.

Nor did it present the gospel strictly in biblical terms of integrating the sacred and the secular for all of which Christ is the Lord."[29] And because of its having developed in the West, Christianity took on such Western cultural overtones and thought patterns that Asians found this faith to be alien and difficult to accept.

Although the efforts of the Jesuits and the Catholic missionary movements to accommodate (contextualize) Christian faith into the local Vietnamese culture (as in other places in Asia, such as China, Japan, and India) were remarkable, the processes of evangelizing the Vietnamese and the planting of local churches were modeled after their churches in the West. Whatever the strategy, it was not until the arrival of the Jesuits in the seventeenth century, that the church was able to be somewhat established in Vietnam.[30] Thus, the earliest form of Christianity in Vietnam was Roman Catholicism. Slowly it gained recognition and became one of the main religions in Vietnam. Yet, the Christian faith has not been a popular faith within Vietnamese spirituality.[31]

Whether or not the assimilation of early Christianity took place in Vietnam, the contextualization efforts done by the Catholic missionaries (as a the result of which, the national Vietnamese Catholic Church remained strong and well established during the post-colonial period) would serve as references for Vietnamese evangelicalism. The argument for this chapter lies chiefly on how the religio-cultural dimension of the Vietnamese context and of similar contexts of East Asia serve as a principle for Vietnamese evangelical mission theology.

Vietnamese Evangelical Mission Theology

This section advances three suggestions that should characterize a "Vietnamese evangelical mission theology" today. Principally, Vietnamese evangelicalism can be seen as very much in agreement with the "four evangelical marks"[32] as well as with the first two criteria of the 1982 evangelical joint-declaration

---

29. Athyal, *Church in Asia Today*12.
30. See Nguyen KimSon, "Mission History of Vietnamese Evangelicalism."
31. As seen in the Roman Catholic mission in Vietnam (ch. 4).
32. See particularly "Preaching the Gospel" in Bebbington, 7–18. These four evangelical hallmarks, however, were broad categories by which to trace the "evangelical religion" in "modern Britain," predominantly the Protestant Reformation in the modern Europe.

as mentioned above.³³ This means that the faith and practice of Vietnamese evangelicalism is firmly anchored in the beliefs that lives need to be changed ("conversionism"); the gospel is expressed or lived out in daily life ("activism"); there is a particular regard for the Bible ("biblicism"); and there is stress on the sacrifice of Christ on the cross ("crucicentrism").³⁴ In terms of the 1982 Asian evangelical joint-declaration, Vietnamese evangelicalism holds onto the first two criteria: (1) The authority of the Bible as the only "infallible, inerrant Word of God,"³⁵ and that the foundation of theology and practice is Scripture and not the dictates of theologians; and (2) the uniqueness of Jesus Christ, the only incarnate Son of God, who is their Lord and Savior.

In practice, Vietnamese evangelicalism has been struggling with the last two criteria of the joint-declaration – (3) that mission-centered theology, which aims to communicate the gospel to the lost, is the best protection against syncretism; and (4) that love should be the essential part of an Asian theology; only as Christians identify themselves with the needy do they contextualize the gospel. How should a mission-centered theology be constructed that will communicate the gospel to the Vietnamese and yet be protected against syncretism? The "needy" are seen there, and "love" is the essential part in their identity, and yet, Vietnamese evangelicals still wrestle

---

33. ATA, "Bible and Theology in Asia Today," 3–20; Ro, "Asian Theology," 108.

34. Among these marks, *biblicism* is the most prominent characteristic of the Vietnamese evangelicalism. See, for example, Nguyen Le Quynh-Hoa, "Tin Lanh: The Bible and the Construction of an Evangelical Vietnamese Christian Identity (1975–2007)" (PhD diss., Claremont Graduate University, 2013).

35. Here, this concept needs to be examined historically from the Western Enlightenment perspective. Molly Worthen argued that, "history – rather than theology or politics – is the most useful tool for pinning down today's evangelicals." According to Worthen, one can easily trace the evangelical roots all the way back to the European Pietists' zeal for private Bible study and personal holiness following on the heels of the Protestant Reformation. Worthen added, "Evangelical catchphrases like 'Bible-believing' and 'born again' are modern translations of the Reformers' slogan *sola scriptura* and Pietists' emphasis on internal spiritual transformation." See, Worthen, *Apostles of Reason*, 4. In England, the Pietist movement ("Methodist") began after 1738 by the brothers John (1703–1791) and Charles (1708–1788) Wesley who began a crusade of popular preaching in the Church of England. In Germany, Lutheran Pietism, led by Philipp J. Spener (1635–1705) and Emanuel Swedenborg (1688–1772), followed a pattern similar to Methodism. Swedenborg's movement in Sweden began as an effort to reconcile science and revelation; after Swedenborg's death, it became increasingly emotional and mystical. Spener, in Germany, stressed Bible study, hymn singing, and powerful preaching. The Moravian movement sprang from his background. Under the sponsorship of Count Nicholaus von Zinzendorf (1700–1760), it spread to the frontiers of Europe and to the English colonies in America (see http://history-world.org/age_of_enlightenment.htm, accessed 28 Feb 2017).

with how to contextualize the gospel in the midst of the syncretistic spirituality of Vietnam.

Therefore, three suggested characteristics for a Vietnamese evangelical mission theology will be briefly sketched below:

Continuity with Christian Tradition

First, historically and biblically, Vietnamese evangelical mission theology must be faithful in continuity with the larger Christian tradition. Such theology must both "embrace rightly oriented belief and confession and rightly oriented action and affection, and resist any bifurcation of head and heart, mind and soul, spirit and body."[36] That means Vietnamese evangelical theology, while shaped by the Christian faith received from the missionary, but expressed locally and authentically, must have substantial continuity with the history of the church, a continuation of the history of Jesus Christ. In other words, a Vietnamese theology and its Christianity are in "historical continuity with the story of Jesus Christ's life, death, resurrection, ascension, sending of the Spirit and parousia."[37]

Theologically speaking, the Vietnamese evangelical mission theology must be a mission-centered theology, modeled after the missionary activity of the triune God (*missio Dei*). As God the Father has sent Jesus the Son through the empowering of the Spirit, the church is sent into the world. In that *missio Dei*, the church is prompted to carry on its *mission* until the return of Christ, fulfilling the Great Commission (Matt 28:19–20). In the latest Lausanne document, *The Cape Town Commitment* (2010), evangelicals reaffirmed the unchanging realities of the world that human beings are lost, and therefore, the church's mission goes on with the good news of the gospel.[38] The church's mission in Vietnam, thus, is to take the whole gospel of the kingdom to the unreached world, regardless of social-political-cultural-religious contexts.

---

36. Amos Yong, "Whither Asian American Evangelical Theology?," *Evangelical Review of Theology* 32, no. 1 (2008): 36-37.

37. Chan, *Grassroots Asian Theology*, 12.

38. See http://www.lausanne.org/en/documents/ctcommitment.html, accessed 6 December 2013. Since all human beings are lost when they are separated from Christ, they are still in need of the gospel that can reach them wherever they are. Though there is no specific statement in *The Cape Town Commitment* as to how evangelicals see the world in terms of the number of people groups, their understanding that the world is *lost* has been the same throughout the 20th century and continues into the beginning of the 21st century.

In other words, Vietnamese evangelical mission theology is not only about "proclaiming and living out a holistic soteriology in terms of being explicit about the personal, confessional, embodied, social, environmental, spiritual, and eschatological dimensions of the saving work of Christ by the Spirit, but also rejecting any attempt to reduce the redemptive work of the Trinitarian God to any one of these aspects."[39]

The gospel is the unique and ultra-important message of "the biblical good news of the saving work of God through Jesus Christ" to the Vietnamese. The good news of the gospel is defined as a restoration of the relationship between human beings and God through Christ. The gospel message, therefore, needs to be proclaimed in the power of God's Spirit, who "illumines the minds of God's people so that the Bible continues to speak God's truth in fresh ways to people in every culture."[40]

God's Action

Second, the Vietnamese evangelical mission theology must be willing to see God's action in the religio-cultural context of Vietnam-East Asia. A Vietnamese evangelical mission theology in the twenty-first century cannot proceed by ignoring the Vietnamese spirituality of today.[41] This is a complex, integrated matrix of local beliefs in God(s), spirits, the Confucianist-Daoist-Buddhist faiths, a syncretistic hybrid assimilation of both Asian and Western

---

39. Yong, "Whither Asian American," 37.

40. See http://www.lausanne.org/en/documents/ctcommitment.html, accessed 8 December 2013.

41. Some Asian theologians are willing to learn and dialogue with Daoist, Confucian, Buddhist, and other Asian religious traditions to enable more confident dialogue that leads to witness. See, for instance, Bruce J. Nicholls, ed. *The Unique Christ in Our Pluralist World* (Grand Rapids, MI: Baker Books House, 1994); Ken Gnanakan, *Proclaiming Christ in a Pluralistic Context* (Bangalore: Theological Book Trust, 2002); Amos Yong, *Pneumatology and the Christian-Buddhist Dialogue: Does the Spirit Blow through the Middle Way?*, Studies in Systematic Theology (Leiden, Netherlands), v. 11. (Leiden: Brill, 2012); Heup Yong Kim, *Wang Yang-ming and Karl Barth: A Confucian-Christian Dialogue* (Lanham, MD: University Press of America, 1996); Heup Yong Kim, *Christ and the Tao* (Hong Kong: Christian Conference of Asia, 2003); Heup Yong Kim, "Life, Ecology, and Theo-tao: Towards a Life Theology of Theanthropocosmic Tao," *Madang: International Journal of Contextual Theology in East Asia* 11 (2009); Heup Yong Kim, "An Asian Journey Seeking Christian Wholeness: Owning Up to Our Own Metaphors (Theotao)," in *Asian and Oceanic Christianities in Conversation: Exploring Theological Identities at Home and in Diaspora*, ed. Heup Yong Kim, Fumitaka Matsuoka, and Anri Morimoto, Studies in World Christianity and Interreligious Relations 47, The Church and Theology in Context Series (Amsterdam, New York: Editions Rodopi B. V., 2011); Hub-yong Kim, *A Theology of Dao*, Ecology and Justice Series (Maryknoll, NY: Orbis, 2017).

philosophical and social-religious aspects. As Bruce J. Nicholls suggests, "Let us not be so fearful of syncretism that we fail to attempt the task of contextualization in the cross-cultural communication of the gospel."[42]

Theology ought to be done while observing God's intent and God's desire for the Vietnamese, while having the Bible continue to speak God's truth in fresh ways to the Vietnamese. Such theology is grounded not only by the view of God's speech in the Scripture (What God said), but also by the view of "God's act of speech" (the world of the scriptural text) which can be heard in classics of Vietnamese-East Asian philosophy and religions as well as from the reality of those who are marginalized and voiceless in the world of religions.[43] Here, theologian Paul S. Chung uses the term "irregular theology" to argue that the "irregular post-foundational and hermeneutical" reflection of "God's act of speech" helps us to see that "extrabiblical" words of God and "intratextuality" are not in contradiction, but are rather complementary.[44]

Asian contextual theologians have long sought to provide "astute social analyses of the pervasive poverty" as theologian Amos Yong observes, but they "fail to offer religious and spiritual answers that concretely engage the masses of Asia."[45] Similarly, the tendency of liberation theology, coming from the church in Latin America, which is inspired by the socio-political conditions as the source for theologizing, has alarmed most evangelicals.[46] Thus, "a theological hermeneutic based on the good news of the incarnation remains plausible in the modern world since it can and does meet the spiritual

---

42. Bruce J. Nicholls, "A Living Theology for Asian Churches: Some Reflections on the Contextualization-Syncretism Debate," in *The Bible and Theology in Asian Contexts: An Evangelical Perspective on Asian Theology*, ed. Bong Rin Ro and Ruth Marie Eshenaur (Taichung, Taiwan, ROC: Asia Theological Association, 1984), 131–132.

43. Christian faith and East Asian religions and cultures can learn from and complement each other in mutuality and partnership. See, for instance, a model proposed that is argued as the "most appropriate for Christian mission" from a Vietnamese Roman Catholic experiment in an article by Peter C. Phan, "An Asian Christian? Or a Christian Asian? Or an Asian-Christian? A Roman Catholic Experiment on Christian Identity," in *Asian and Oceanic Christianities in Conversation: Exploring Theological Identities at Home and in Diaspora*, ed. Heup Yong Kim, Fumitaka Matsuoka, and Anri Morimoto, Studies in World Christianity and Interreligious Relations 47. Church and Theology in Context Series (Amsterdam; New York, NY: Editions Rodopi B. V., 2011).

44. Chung, *Constructing Irregular Theology*, 3.

45. Yong, "Whither Asian American," 29.

46. Gilliland, *Word among Us*, 2.

needs of people whose lives are deeply religious to begin with."⁴⁷ That means Vietnamese theological hermeneutical processes (that are based on the good news of the incarnation) are not guided by "evangelical" principles only, but also by being thoroughly Vietnamese. They pay attention to the spiritual needs of the Vietnamese whose lives are deeply religious. This is where such theology should begin, not relying only on social reform (e.g. the Dalits theology in India) or only on evangelistic proclamation (e.g. seen mostly in the early CMA missionaries and the ECVN).⁴⁸

Here, the Asian concept(s) of God, learned from the wisdom of the Vietnamese-East Asian philosophy and religions, provide a voice to help construct the Vietnamese-East Asian theology.⁴⁹ Although it may sound "irregular" to Western theologians, it offers a helpful nuance for theology from the Asian perspective. Such an argument has recently emerged to provide a "both-and" approach to core doctrines of Christianity. For instance, in the work of theologian Jung Young Lee, the Trinity can be seen as a "becoming" or as the principle of change itself from the Daoist perspective. As the *Đạo*, the "supreme ultimate" is characterized by the harmony of opposites, the *yin* and *yang*, then "what is intrinsic to the *yin-yang* relationship is not its entity or being, but its change."⁵⁰

Therefore, to have the Vietnamese mission theology in which the Bible continues to speak God's truth in "fresh ways" to the Vietnamese, it has to begin with Vietnamese ways or forms. That theology will work when it is able

---

47. Yong, "Whither Asian American," 29.

48. Simon Chan, "The Problem of Transcendence and Immanence in Asian Contextual Theology," *Trinity Theological Journal* 8 (1999): 17. Observing the work of Vishal Mangalwadi (in India) and Wang Ming Dao (in China), Simon Chan states that, "those who are so concerned about making Christ immanent in Asia have ended up making the church powerless and irrelevant." Also, a similar observation was made earlier; see in Bruce J. Nicholls, "Salvation and Humanisation in the Theology of Evangelism," in *Voice of the Church in Asia: Report of Proceedings Asia Theological Association Consultation* (Singapore: Asia Theological Association, 1975), 154–163.

49. This could be "the beginnings of a self-theologizing i.e. authentically true to the Asian context and i.e. built on the very pluralism of the continent"; see Allen Yeh, "Asian Perspectives on Twenty-First-Century Pluralism," in *The Gospel and Pluralism Today: Reassessing Lesslie Newbigin in the 21st Century*, ed. Scott W. Sunquist and Amos Yong (Downers Grove, IL: IVP Academic, 2015), 215–232.

50. Jung Young Lee, *The Trinity in Asian Perspective* (Nashville, TN: Abingdon Press, 1996), 27.

to "prophetically critique the accommodations of previous formulations of evangelical theology to any kind of ideological captivity."[51]

Forms of Thinking

Third, the Vietnamese evangelical mission theology must be organized by Vietnamese "forms" of thinking. Here, two specific forms of the Vietnamese perspective will be discussed: (1) the Vietnamese concept of God, and (2) the extended family narrative. Both are argued from the assimilation-resistance characteristics of Vietnamese spirituality. While the concept of God is seen through the Vietnamese spirituality (as already discussed in ch. 2), it seems disconnected from the other two loci of theology, the Trinity (the relationship among God, Jesus Christ and the Holy Spirit) and the church (including the place of ancestors in the Christian community).

Specifically, a robust mission theology for Vietnamese evangelicalism needs to resonate with the argument of "God-in-our-midst" (ch. 1), seeing that an understanding of God has been both assimilated and resisted throughout the history of the Vietnamese. Such a dual force demonstrates how Vietnamese spirituality was both able to resist the religio-cultural influences from the outside and yet assimilate moderately (not absorbing completely all of one single religious doctrine) the essentials of the outside influences that are of specific interest to the Vietnamese people (such as in the Cao Dai).[52]

The core Vietnamese spirituality is the *Đạo* (the way) in which the process of syncretism has created an integrated unique form of spirituality specific to the Vietnamese people. Honoring certain realities from daily encounters with nature, respecting the living saints or heroes when they were alive, or venerating them as spirits or deities after death, and venerating Heaven (*Thiên, Ông Trời*) as seen in the Sacrifice to Heaven, are just some of the manifestations of Vietnamese spirituality. And thus, to follow the *Đạo* is to harmonize and observe fully all these realities regarded as truths.

Then, the Vietnamese family perspective can become a framework for developing an understanding of the triune God relationship and the issue

---

51. Yong, "Whither Asian American," 36.

52. The Cao Dai in Vietnam is among some "newer Asian religions" developed in Asia which have been 'inspired' or 'shaped' by their encounter with Christianity in the 20th century. See Sunquist, *Unexpected Christian Century*, 164–167.

of ancestor veneration. Within the context of the Confucian teaching on family relationship, especially on the role of the eldest son, Jesus is viewed as "the eldest son and ancestor," or "the ancestor-mediator."[53] In the context of Africa, Bujo Bénézet argues that the title "Proto-Ancestor" is reserved for Jesus Christ, because "The term 'ancestor' can only be applied to Jesus in an analogical sense, or eminent way, since to treat him otherwise would be to make of him only one founding ancestor among many . . . This signifies that Jesus did not only realize the authentic ideal of the God-fearing African ancestors, but also infinitely transcended that ideal and brought it to new completion."[54] This study, however, argues that when the Trinity is viewed according to the Vietnamese concept of God, whose being is connected within the "family relationship" of Father-Son, the ancestor veneration issue is treated as an "extended family" where the church is a community for both the living and deceased, a "communion" that is large enough to welcome not only the living, but the ancestors who are not "spirits," but are remembered and venerated by the living. Simon Chan argues that a more adequate way of organizing an Asian theology is to center it in the doctrine of the triune God as the divine family. He believes that it reflects faithfully the fundamental way in which the first two persons of the triune God are revealed, namely, as Father and Son. Moreover, "in much of Asia a person's foremost identity is defined in relation to his or her family, and not just the immediate family but also the extended family, which may include an entire clan, and the linear family, which includes deceased ancestors."[55]

With these "three suggestions" in mind, the next two sections offer some approaches on how the Vietnamese evangelical mission theology should begin, namely with "God-in-our-midst," a Vietnamese concept of God and a Vietnamese extended family perspective for both the Trinitarian relationship – God the Father, God the Son, and God the Holy Spirit – and the Vietnamese Christian community of both the living and the deceased ancestors. Both

---

53. See, for instance, "Jesus the Christ with Asian Face," and "Jesus as the Eldest Son and Ancestor" in Phan, *Christianity with an Asian Face*, 98–145. A similar argument views Jesus as "the ancestor-mediator" (priest) in Chan, *Grassroots Asian Theology: Thinking the Faith from the Ground Up*, 91–127.

54. Bénézet Bujo, *African Theology in Its Social Context*, trans. John O'Donohue, Faith and Cultures Series (Eugene, OR: Wipf & Stock, 2006), 77–87.

55. Chan, *Grassroots Asian Theology*, 42–43, 66–67.

concepts need to be redeemed through Christ, because "all cultures, like the humans that form them, are fallen and therefore in need of redemption."[56] This is not the only way to construct a Vietnamese theology within the Asian theological trend, but it underscores the meaning of Vietnamese-ness when developing a Vietnamese evangelical mission theology.[57] Also, it provides a hope that this study could answer those questions raised earlier in chapter 4: (1) Do the Vietnamese need to escape their cultural concept of God to become Christians according to the ways of the missionary? and (2) Can a Vietnamese become a follower of Christ and still maintain their Vietnamese identity?

God in Our Midst: A Vietnamese Concept of God

This section, specifically views the concept of God from the Vietnamese evangelical perspective to redeem it for the Vietnamese Christian understanding of God. This is done from the Vietnamese religio-cultural perspective, rather than from a systematic theology of the doctrine of God.

The Đạo

The Vietnamese concept of God is the most critical point to be redeemed in this new paradigm shift, namely the identity and nature of the Đạo. David J. Bosch argued that the old theological paradigm is a monolithic approach and such a paradigm has to shift to a "critical hermeneutic" in which the biblical text is recognized as contextual in its very nature.[58] Thus, God has interacted with human beings through time and space and in multiple contexts so as to communicate God's intent and God's desire to be in relationship with human beings, wherever they are found.

The old Christian paradigm introduced a strange, alien understanding of God to the Vietnamese. Although such a theology of God, despite being historically, culturally, and linguistically conditioned and shaped, was from

---

56. Sunquist, *Understanding Christian Mission*, 250–252.

57. For example, German theologian Hans Küng urged Chinese theologians a few decades ago to take the Asian concept of God seriously. See, "Focal Points of Chinese Theology: Understanding of God, Christ, and Spirit" in Küng and Ching, *Christianity and Chinese Religions*, 261–268. See also Xinzhong Yao, "Confucian Christ: A Chinese Image of Christianity," in *Identity and Marginality: Rethinking Christianity in North East Asia*, ed. Werner Ustorf and Toshiko Murayama (Frankfurt am Main: P. Lang, 2000).

58. Bosch, *Transforming Mission*, 421–425.

the early missionary period of Vietnam, it had not connected to the God that was known in the hearts and minds of the Vietnamese.[59] This "foreign" God, as introduced by the missionaries, was one of the biggest barriers (besides the forbidding of ancestral practices) to acceptance of the Christian faith among the Vietnamese. It is important to construct a theology of God that not only carries on the historic tradition (the nature of "translatability" of Christians who have lived and witnessed the gospel in different times and places throughout the centuries), but which is also understood by the Vietnamese culturally and linguistically.

It is critically important to search for the Vietnamese-East Asian concept of God (the *Đạo*) while trying to make sense of the Christian concept of God. Long before the arrival of Christian missionaries, the Vietnamese have acknowledged the notion of God, whether in forms of the *Đạo* (Way) as in Daoism, or of the *Trời* (*T'ien*/Heaven) as in Confucianism or even *Shang-ti* (Lord-on-High). Such forms of the *Đạo* (Way) and obeying the Will of the Way of the Vietnamese-East Asians do not diminish the visibility of seeing or knowing God. Certainly, such divine forms do not equate pagan unknown gods with the Christian God. But, these divine phenomena and understandings of "God" may indicate that the people in East Asia are open to God's intent to be known.[60] Perhaps, it also indicates that the people are ready to come into the full knowledge of God incarnate, Jesus the Christ. This is God, the Word who incarnated himself into the world (John 1:10) and became flesh and lived among humanity. Jesus Christ, living among humanity, in

---

59. For instance, Phan Khôi (a Vietnamese scholar who was part of the Vietnamese Bible translation from 1920–1925) argued that God could be known to humanity (God's image), not an abstract perception (power). See, Phan Khôi, "Giới Thiệu và Phê Bình Thánh Kinh Báo" [Introduction and critque of Bible magazine], *Phụ Nữ Tân Văn* 74 (10/16/1930) (http://www.thuvientinlanh.org/phan-khoi-gioi-thieu-va-phe-binh-thanh-kinh-bao/, accessed 9 December 2016). In one place in the first issue of *Thánh Kinh Báo* published on January 1931: "*Thế gian không phải tự nhiên mà có. Nhưng phải nhờ có một quyền phép lớn lắm mà đã dựng nên trời đất, và quyền phép lớn ấy tức là Đức Chúa Trời*" (This world is not created from nowhere. The earth and heaven were created by a massive power, and such *power* is God). Mr Phan argued that equating God with such massive *power* is not biblically accurate, and is not God's intention to be known by humanity.

60. For instance, Chinese scholars have recently attempted to make ancient understanding of the divine nuanced to the Chinese Christian God. See Chan Kei Thong and Charlene L. Fu, *Finding God in Ancient China: How the Ancient Chinese Worshiped the God of the Bible* (Grand Rapids, MI: Zondervan, 2009).

local culture, is God's revelation of who God is so that human beings can once again be reconciled with the Creator God.

The concept of *Đạo* must be redeemed for Vietnamese mission theology.[61] Although the approach of the early Christian missionary Alexander de Rhodes, to coin a new expression *đức Chúa trời đất* ("the honorable Lord of heaven and earth") for the term *God* is remarkable, this approach is questionable because it does not recognize the identity and nature of the *Đạo* philosophically.[62] Nevertheless, de Rhodes invoked one of the fundamental principles of Vietnamese philosophy, *Trời-Đất-Người* (Heaven-Earth-Human) which must always be viewed in strict unity with one another.[63] When branding this new term, *đức* is an honorific title; *Chúa* means "Lord" and was used as the title of the heads of the states; *trời* means "heaven" or "firmament"; and *đất* means "earth."[64] But, is the *Chúa* (Lord) of heaven-earth-humanity (*trời-đất-con người*) not the *Đạo* among the Vietnamese intelligentsia?

The concept of *Đạo* (Way) and the notion *đạo* (way) are two different concepts, but are related to each other. In the writings of *Lao-tzu*, the *Đạo* is indeterminate as seen in the famous line of *Lao-tzu*'s text, "The Way (*Tao*) that can be spoken of, is not the constant [true] Way (*Tao*)."[65] The nameless *Đạo* or unidentified *Way* (indeterminate) is the first principle from which all things proceed to become determinate. Although this understanding of the *Đạo*'s nature appears to be a philosophical attempt to conceptualize an earlier, religious belief, the *Đạo* is not the subject of human worship. Here, like in the Confucian classics, "Lord-on-high" (a supreme diety) and

---

61. The discussion on the *Đạo* has been given much detail in ch. 1, section 1.

62. The argument is rather on the nature and identity of the *Đạo*, although the Daoist ethics of simplicity, humility and non-resistance had drawn much attention by the Chinese Christians recently. For instance, there was Lin Yutang, the Chinese humanist who rejected the Christianity of his childhood to become a Daoist for 40 years, only to return to the faith of his parents in his old age. See, Jianming He, "Dialogue between Christianity and Taoism: The Case of Lin Yutang," in *Christianity and Chinese Culture*, eds. Miikka Ruokanen, Baoluo Huang, and Paulos Zhanzhu Huang (Grand Rapids, MI: Eerdmans, 2010); Hieromonk Damascene, *Christ the Eternal Tao*, 3rd ed. (Platina, CA: Valaam Books, 2002); Zhiming Yuan, *Lao Tzu and the Bible: A Meeting Transcending Time and Space*, trans. Chen Shangyu (Bloomington, IN: AuthorHouse, 2010).

63. Here is a very deep Vietnamese triune concept which would echo the Buddhist trinity: the Buddha-dharma-sangha.

64. In *Cathechismus*, de Rhodes explained that "heaven" is not divine but created. See Phan, *In Our Own Tongues*, 164.

65. Quoted in Küng and Ching, *Christianity and Chinese Religions*, 132.

"Heaven" have been given a progenitor's or creator's role as that which gives birth to all things. The *Đạo* as the natural "Way" as well as the human way, is the "Way" of all "ways."[66] As the (indeterminate) *Đạo* is the origin of the (indeterminate) universe, the beginning of all (determinate) beings is that everything (determinate) is governed by the *Đạo* (the law of the universe); then does not the nature of the *Đạo* sound like the Creator God and *YHWH* (in the Old Testament), or the Word (*logos*) and the Way (*hodos*) (in the New Testament)?[67] This word *Đạo* has been used in Chinese translations of John's Prologue – "In the beginning was the *Đạo*" – and the essence thereof is echoed in the line 'I am the Way, the Truth and the Life.'[68] In contrast, the Vietnamese translations of the Bible used the words *ngôi lời* (Word) and *Đường đi* (Way) respectively which are ambiguous and make little sense for the Vietnamese understanding of the *Đạo* (the Way) philosophically. Thus, to make the translation more understandable to the Vietnamese, the word *Đạo* should be applied to these verses in the Vietnamese Bible: "*Ban đầu đã có 'Đạo'*" (In the beginning was the Word) (John 1:1), and "*Ta là 'Đạo,' chân lý, và sự sống*" (I am the Way, the truth and the life) (John 14:6).[69]

Surprisingly, Olsen's *Theological Work* (in Vietnamese, as seen in ch. 4) on Christology (Book Six) also argued Christ is "*Đạo*." In section 4 "The Incarnation of Christ," Olsen recognized Christ is the *Đạo* both in humanity and divinity. For instance, Olsen translated John 1:1 "*Đạo* is God" and argued that *Đạo* (Logos Christ) is not only being with God, but this *Đạo* is

---

66. *Đạo* has taken over *Heaven* (*Trời*) in *Lao-tzu*, whereas they appeared interchangeable in *Chuang-tzu*.

67. For instance, the 1823 French version of Dao De Jing shows this similarity, quoted in Robert Ernest Hume, *The World's Living Religions: With Special Reference to Their Sacred Scriptures and in Comparison with Christianity: An Historical Sketch* (1924. Reprint, New York: Scribner & Clark, 1959), 138–143.

68. Küng and Ching, *Christianity and Chinese Religions*, 132; Chung, "Mystery of God," 254; Chung, *Constructing Irregular Theology*, 69. Another way of understanding Đạo and how it corresponds with the Greek word "logos" is that it can be translated "The Expression" to describe Christ as the expression of the Truth. See the comparison of Đạo and logos in "Chapter 9: All Truth Is God's Truth" in Thong and Fu, *Finding God in Ancient China*.

69. Exceptionally, two other Vietnamese Bible versions: Rev Phạm Xuân Tín Version (BDPX) and Nhuận Chánh Version (NC), use *Đạo* for Christ in their translations. Such efforts of translating "Logos/ Word" into the essence of the Vietnamese spirituality, which is the *Đạo*, are similar to the Chinese Bible translation efforts, since thus the approach is not new because the Church has done this for ages.

God ("*Theo câu này, 'Đạo' [Logos Christ] không những là ở cùng Đức Chúa Trời, nhưng chính 'Đạo' ấy là Đức Chúa Trời*").[70]

When discussing the authority of Christ in salvation, Olsen argued that Christ fulfills salvation because (1) "Christ *là 'Đạo'* (Logos) *của Đức Chúa Trời*" (Christ is Đạo [Logos] of God), and (2) "*Christ là con người*" (Christ is humanity).[71]

Instead of acknowledging the *Đạo* (the Way), the early missionaries (de Rhodes) decided to develop a new expression, *đức Chúa trời đất*. They had some clues about the explicit recognition of the presence of God among the Vietnamese belief and practice through the *đạo* (way), but not of the *Đạo* (Way). As seen in de Rhodes' own words:

> Having heard of the Law which they call *đạo* in scholarly language and *đàng* in popular tongue, which means *way*, . . .
>
> I decided to announce it to them under the name of the Lord of heaven and earth, finding no proper word in their language to refer to God . . .
>
> I decided to employ the name used by the apostle Saint Paul when he preached to the Athenians who had set up an altar to an unknown God, . . .[72]

Of course, the words *đạo, đàng, Phật,* or *Bụt* (the way, or Buddha) as de Rhodes learned (from Confucianism in particular) were common terms to describe the notion of the *đạo* (way) which is identified and determinate. But the *Đạo* (Way) which is indeterminate should have been chosen instead of the *đức Chúa trời đất* (Lord of heaven and earth).[73] The *Đạo* always has been understood by the Vietnamese. They have encountered different concepts of God and yet could "assimilate" the "One" that is specific for them.

Principally, the new expression *đức Chúa trời đất* replaces the common misconception among the Vietnamese that the material heaven (*trời*)

---

70. See chapter 4: "Christ the Incarnate God" (Book Six: Christology) in Olsen, *Thần đạo học*. Here, Olsen is ontologically in line with the Vietnamese perspective on the *Đạo*, as well as the Chinese Christian Bible translations of Logos (the Word) is *Đạo* (Way).

71. See chapter 8: "Salvation" (Book Six: Christology) in Olsen, *Thần đạo học*.

72. *Histoire du Royaume*, 129–130, cited by Phan, *In Our Own Tongues*, 163.

73. See de Rhodes' *Đức Chúa Trời* (or *blời*) *đất* in Đỗ Quang Chính and Nguyễn Văn Hậu, *Hoà mình vào xã hội Việt Nam* [Inculturating into the Vietnamesese culture and soceity], (Hà Nội: Nxb Tôn giáo, 2008), 95–102.

is divine. It does not replace the *Đạo* in the Vietnamese concept of God. Although the connotation of *đức Chúa trời đất* has been well accepted among the Vietnamese Christians – using the short form *Đức Chúa Trời* in the Bible and in ritual practices – it still has not satisfied, but has confused the understanding of the *Đạo* by the Vietnamese (though the Cao Dai resonated with the Vietnamese way of understanding the *Đạo*) when referring to the One True God.[74] There is no term or expression in the Vietnamese language that is adequate for the name of God, for the *Đạo* is the nameless and unidentified "One." The concept of the *Đạo* (the Way) therefore needs to be reserved as the most reverent and honorable One, in the same manner as YHWH of the Israelites. Such understanding of God, the concept of the *Đạo*, indeed needs to be redeemed for Vietnamese evangelicalism, because the Vietnamese experience and reason of the *Đạo*'s identity and nature is philosophically, biblically, and theologically profound, and yet not less concrete in perception.

The Supreme One

The concept of the "Supreme One," like the *Đạo* above, needs to be redeemed for Vietnamese mission theology. Here, the *Đạo* is expressed in various forms throughout Premodern and Early Modern Vietnam.[75] These forms or names express the identity and nature of the *Đạo* and prove the fact that Vietnamese spirituality has been an integrated form of spirituality, both able to resist the religio-cultural influences from the outside and to assimilate the essentials that are specific to the needs of the Vietnamese throughout history. Each form depends on how the Vietnamese embraced (assimilated) and/or resisted it in history according to the people's spirituality at the time.[76]

---

74. When the *đất* (earth) was dismissed in the term used by both the Vietnamese Catholics and Evangelicals, is unknown. But, the Vietnamese Catholicism and Evangelicalism are indebted to de Rhodes in their use of this Vietnamese expression of God, "*Đức Chúa Trời*" today, for example, in the oldest version of the Evangelical Bible version, the 1926 (known as *Bản truyền thống*).

75. The Premodern Vietnam period during which period the *Việt* people, struggled against Northern domination (up to the tenth century, 939 CE), and finally established an independent nation under five different dynasties: Ngô, Đinh, Lê, Lý and Trần from the tenth to fourteenth centuries. The second period or Early Modern Vietnam, included the fifteenth to nineteenth centuries, during which there was the expansion of the southward influence, encroaching upon existing populations of the Cham and Khmer ethnic groups under the Nguyễn dynasty.

76. For instance, Tạ Chí Đại Trường, *Thần, Người và Đất Việt*.

The encounter with Confucianism brought changes to the meaning of the term *trời* (heaven) in Vietnamese animistic spirituality. The word *trời* (heaven) now carries double meanings; one describes the sky, or perhaps the place of God's presence; another understanding is *Thiên* (or *Ông Trời*, Mr Heaven literally).[77] The latter has usually been personified as *Thiên* or *Ông Trời* (Mr Heaven), referring to the Vietnamese animistic belief that consists essentially of the "cult of heaven," the spirits, and the ancestors.[78] Religiously, at the head of the hierarchy of spirits, the Vietnamese place *Thiên* or *Ông Trời* above all deities, immortals, spirits, and genies. From the Daoist perspective, the Vietnamese see *Thiên* or *Ông Trời* (the *Đạo*) as the relational, transcendent, benevolent, and just God, creator of the universe, source of life, and supreme judge. This is why there is no cult of heaven at the popular level; the rendering of cult to this God (Heaven) was reserved for the emperor who once a year (since the nineteenth century once every three years) offered a solemn sacrifice, known as *Tế Nam Giao*, in the name of the entire people.[79]

The concept of *Thiên* (Heaven), as seen mostly in Premodern and Early Modern Vietnam, does not replace the understanding of the *Đạo* (Way).[80] In

---

77. See, for example, the traditional Vietnamese concept of *Trời* in Trương Văn Thiên Tư, "Mệnh Trời: Toward a Vietnamese Theology of Mission" (PhD diss., Graduate Theological Union, 2009), 143–160.

78. This is why Rhodes hesitated to use *Ông Trời* for *God*, because he was afraid that it might suggest that the material heaven (*trời*) is divine, which he believed to be a common misconception among the Chinese and the Vietnamese.

79. As seen in Phạm Đình Hổ's *Vũ trung tuỳ bút*, Bento Thien's *History of the Country of Annam* which is discussed in section "Belief in Heaven and Other Folk Belief" (ch. 2). See also Cadière, *Croyances et pratiques religieuses des Viêtnamiens*, I:85–129. Picturing Jesus as "the eldest son" offering worship to God the Father, Jesus can "be compared with the Vietnamese emperor in his role of high priest during the *Tế Nam Giao*." Peter C. Phan argues that, "If we leave aside the sacrifices to earth, spirits, and imperial ancestors during the Te Nam Giao and focus on the sacrifice to heaven, we can see in the role of the emperor that of Christ as the *Thiên Tử* (Son of God) and the high priest or 'minister of the sanctuary and of the true tent' (Heb 8:2) offering the perfect and eternal sacrifice to God, as magnificently expounded by the letter to the Hebrews. In the name of all of us, whom 'he is not ashamed to call . . . brothers and sisters' (Heb 2:11), Jesus, the eldest brother, offers his perfect sacrifice of filial obedience (Heb 1:5; 12:1–11) to God his Father," Phan, *Christianity with an Asian Face*, 136–138.

80. The concept of Heaven in Confucianism was advocated and sincerely studied by the Jesuits in China, for example, Matthew Ricci as he believed ancient China could already have known the true God (both *Shang-ti* and *T'ien*) believing and worshiping him, but overlooking the concept of *Dao* in Lao-tzu's *Dao De Jing*, as seen in Johannes P. Bettray, *Die Akkommodationsmethode des P. Matteo Ricci S.I. in China*. (Romae: Apud aedes Universitatis Gregorianae, 1955), 236, 81; Nicolas Trigault and Matteo Ricci, *De Christiana expeditione apud*

fact, these two are interchangeable in the Vietnamese literature.[81] As seen in the "Rationalizing the Essentials" in chapter 2, Nguyễn Bỉnh Khiêm's stele inscription of the Three Teachings Temple shows that, "What Heaven imparts to man is called human nature; To follow our nature is called the Way; It is rooted in the Mind and lodged in the Teachings; The forms through which it has been bequeathed to us are full of dignity, eternal and ageless as Heaven."[82] Nguyễn Bỉnh Khiêm argued that the nature of the Đạo (Way) or Thiên (Heaven) is syncretized in the Three Teachings and Vietnamese animistic beliefs as the common threads: "Aren't all of them the teachings that follow human nature in order to cultivate the Way (Đạo)?" In the same vein, Trần Trọng Kim who regarded Confucianism as the national essence of Vietnam, also believed that the essence of Confucianism started from the Way (Đạo), "If humans adopt the middle course, behave according to the Way of Heaven (Thiên Đạo or Đạo của Trời), and nurture their feelings, they will acquire benevolence (nhân)."[83]

The concept of Thiên (Heaven) was associated with the cult of Ngọc Hoàng Thượng Đế (Great Lord – Jade Emperor) and was popular in Vietnam in the sixteenth century, as well as with the Cao Dai (Caodaism) in the twentieth century.[84] In the context of the sixteenth century, Heaven (Thiên) in Nguyễn Bỉnh Khiêm's writing, viewed as the Supreme One (Thượng đế), became very

---

Sinas suscepta ab societate Jesu (Augsburg1615), 116. quoted in Lưu Hồng Khanh, Lão Tử Đạo Đức Kinh [Lao-tzu's Dao De Jing], (Hồ Chí Minh City: Nxb Trẻ, 2005).

81. Unlike Vietnam, through the long history of China, the meanings of Shang-ti (上帝; Lord-on-High), T'ien (天; Heaven), the two terms for God, underwent significant changes. The Jesuits finally settled for T'ien-chu (天主; Lord of Heaven), Lord of whatever Heaven may represent to the Chinese for Shang-ti and T'ien, while continuing occasionally to refer to the Lord of Heaven as Lord-on-High or simply, Heaven. Further discussions, see in Ching, Confucianism and Christianity; Legge, Notions of the Chinese; Tsu-Kung Chuang, "Shangdi: God from the Chinese Perspective," in The Global God: Multicultural Evangelical Views of God, ed. Aída Besançon Spencer and William David Spencer (Grand Rapids, MI: Baker Books, 1998); Thong and Fu, Finding God in Ancient China.

82. See in Nguyễn Nam, "Being Confucian in Sixteenth Century Vietnam: Reading Stele Inscriptions from the Mac Dynasty," in Confucianism in Vietnam (Hồ Chí Minh City: Vietnam National University and Hồ Chí Minh City Publishing, 2002), 143; Nguyen Nam, "Writing as Response," 298–300; Dutton, Werner, and Whitmore, Sources of Vietnamese Tradition, 115.

83. Trần Trọng Kim, Nho giáo, i, ix–x, xii–xiii, xv–xvii, xix–xx, xxii–xxvi, 389–172, trans. Luu Doan Huynh, Jayne Werner, and John Whitemore, quoted in Dutton, Werner, and Whitmore, Sources of Vietnamese Tradition, 414–424.

84. For the cult of Ngọc Hoàng Thượng Đế, see Đinh Khắc Thuân, "Contribution à l'histoire de la Mac (1527–1592) du Viet Nam," 275–284.

popular in Vietnamese spirituality.[85] With this perception of *Thiên* (heaven, the Supreme One), it was believed that "goodness" can be rewarded and evil will be judged by Heaven, according to the Buddhist principle of "karmic" retribution and cause-and-effect.[86] Therefore, worshiping *Thiên* (Heaven) became a more common ritual in the Vietnamese religious belief system, for instance, in the Cao Dai in twentieth century Vietnam.

The meanings and connotations of the *Đạo* (Way) and *Thiên* (Heaven) as the "Supreme One," have been carried on by the Cao Dai into the modern period of Vietnam.[87] Here, Caodaism, a brand-new religion at the time, emerged out of the need to fill the gap between the Vietnamese belief in popular spirits and the faiths coming from the outside, including the Three Teachings, the European Christian faith (e.g. the new expression *đức Chúa trời đất*), and other religious precepts of the world. More importantly, this Vietnamese faith was an attempt to unify all Vietnamese spirituality to resist the foreign faiths (as seen in the discussion of the Cao Dai in chapter 2). Perhaps, such resisting by assimilating the essentials of other faiths, which has already been the second nature of the Vietnamese, is again proven in the Cao Dại (Caodaism).[88]

As the Vietnamese compared themselves with other peoples in the world, Cao Dai recognized that *Đấng Cao Cả* (the Supreme God) was with them and for them, especially in the midst of their suffering under the oppression of the colonial regime. The first group of the Cao Dai's disciples (of whom many were Vietnamese intellectuals) acknowledged that the One True God or the Supreme Being, the Creator that the Vietnamese have known throughout the history is indeed the Only One. The Cao Dai then believed that the Vietnamese are the chosen people of the Supreme God or Jehovah God to

---

85. The Vietnamese evangelicals have used this term *Thượng đế* (the Supreme One) interchangeably with *Đức Chúa Trời* (God).

86. Nguyen Nam, "Writing as Response," 308.

87. As seen in the "Unifying Form of Spirituality" in chapter 2.

88. Although the Cao Dai offers a unifying form of spirituality uniquely specific to the context of colonial Vietnam as well as the global context, these offers, however, are beyond the scope of this study which mainly argues about how the concept of God (as the *Đạo*, the *Thiên* which is indeed the Supreme One) has been preserved and carried on in this particular Vietnamese religion. In other words, the argument is based on the Cao Dai's religio-cultural aspects ontologically, rather than in socio-political aspects practically which are more controversial in postcolonial Vietnam.

reveal the third and final attempt in a "mysterious way" or "method" to save human beings from their transgressions.[89]

The Third Period of Salvation, moreover, is for all human beings who should follow this Way/Great Path (*Đạo*). The Vietnamese who believe in *Đức Cao Đài* are to carry on the mission of Jesus (who is proclaimed by the gospel, but, according to them, has not been heard from, or has been distorted by the French colonial presence and Vietnamese Catholics), to bring *Đức Cao Đài*'s salvation to the world. This understanding, perhaps, had a more political tone when Caodaism entered into the process of de-colonialization. But, the acknowledgement of "God-in-our-midst" has been the concept running through the Vietnamese for generations. It is, therefore, important for the new Vietnamese mission theology not just to recognize the concept, but to make it a significant contribution to Vietnamese spirituality. Such understanding has been manifested in the belief and practices that there is the Only One True God, the One who has been in the midst of the Vietnamese for generations.

Theologically, that the One True God came (incarnated) into the midst of the Vietnamese, means that the *Đạo, Thiên, Đức Cao Đài* or *Đấng Cao Cả* is the One and Only One, and yet in the form of a human being, the God-man Jesus Christ has revealed the fullness of the One and the fulfillment of the "God-in-our-midst" concept. Methodologically, the Vietnamese then, can understand the nature of God's incarnation better in their perception of family, the relationship between God-Jesus Christ, and the Spirit in the concept of divine family.

God with Us: A Vietnamese Hermeneutic

We turn now to provide a hermeneutical interpretation of the meaning of Jesus and the Christian church from a Vietnamese perspective. This section argues that Jesus the Immanuel is "God with us" by the power of the Spirit in a continual and relational way. From the Vietnamese perspective of the

---

89. According to the Cao Dai (a parallel might be Mormonism in the US – having a special calling for a particular nation), the First Period of Salvation was chronologically associated with Moses, Buddha Dipankara, and Chinese deities Fu Hsi and T'ai Shan Dao Guan. The Second Period of Salvation was represented by Buddha Shakyamuni, Confucius, Lao Tzu, Jesus Christ, and Mohamed. See http://caodai.com.vn/en/news-detail/brief-outline-of-history-and-philosophy-of-caodaism.html, accessed 10 June 2016.

extended family specifically, the relationships between God-Jesus as Father-Son, and the church as a community of believers are explored.

Jesus Christ: The Incarnate God

Jesus Christ, the Immanuel is God with us. Jesus Christ in the power of the Spirit is in our midst relationally and continually. The concept of the triune God viewed from the family perspective is profoundly practical in Vietnam. The concept of family would be best to bridge the gap between the One True God (which has been understood as given above) and Jesus Christ the Lord and the Holy Spirit as relational beings, with reciprocal relationships.

Jesus Is the Way (Đạo)

It is difficult for the Vietnamese to understand that Jesus is God (the Way) in relationship with God the Father.[90] When the Vietnamese hear Jesus's statement, "I am the Way, the Truth, and the Life," it sounds like blasphemy as it did to the Jewish people at the time of Jesus, because the Vietnamese cannot understand how Jesus is related to and connected with the concept of *God*. Religiously speaking, the Vietnamese have strictly revered God as *Đạo*, *Thiên* (*Trời*), *Thượng đế*, and *Đấng cao cả* in a respectful way. The Vietnamese commonly address *God* as *Ông Trời*, the prefix *Ông-* is reserved for the most powerful and ultimate One who is reverently worshipped. In Daoism, the Supreme *Đạo* is not even spoken of.[91] In Confucianism, *Thiên* respectively is exclusively venerated by the king (as seen in Heaven veneration) on behalf of the entire kingdom. As seen in the Cao Dai, Jesus is placed at the third level of their worship, the "way of the saints." In the Cao Dai, Jesus does not offer a great number of teachings. Rather, Jesus is simply treated as Jehovah God's obedient child, and the filial obligations are understood by the Confucian

---

90. Jesus's titles, teachings and actions that show who he is from the synoptic biblical perspective are beyond the scope of this study. Nevertheless, the gospels of Matthew, Mark, Luke, and especially John have presented who Jesus is. For instance, "Jesus according to the Synoptists" and "Jesus according to John" in Darrell L. Bock, *Jesus According to Scripture: Restoring the Portrait from the Gospels* (Grand Rapids, MI: Baker Academic, 2002). Also, the recent work of Darrell L. Bock with Benjamin I. Simpson shows that the Gospels argue that full array of Jesus's acts explains that Jesus the promised Messiah is also the divine Lord. He is the Son of Man who combines humanity and divine prerogatives in unique ways. See Darrell L. Bock and Benjamin I. Simpson, *Jesus the God-Man: The Unity and Diversity of the Gospel Portrayals* (Grand Rapids, MI: Baker Academic, 2016), 65–121.

91. For *Đạo*, see "the one that can be named is not the real Dao" first line in the *Dao De Jing*. Chinese translations use *Dao* for λόγος (logos or the "Word" as in John 1:1).

model (*Đức Chúa Jésus Christ làm con hiếu hạnh*). Furthermore, Jesus speaks to the Cao Dai disciples to follow the *Đạo* (Way). Jesus is also treated as a junior "brother" in this Vietnamese-East Asian pantheon according to the teaching of the elderly sages, and was placed three levels below Confucius, Lao Tzu, and the Buddha. Thus, the disconnection between Jesus Christ the Son and God the Father is a big gap in the mind of the Vietnamese.

Philosophically speaking, the Father God and Jesus the Son are related to each other in a way that God is the source of all things which is the *Đạo*, the beginning of all, and the Way of all ways. As seen in Daoist tradition, *Đạo* is "transcendentally immanent and immanently transcendental. The immanence of *Đạo* refers to the way of the universe which is the driving force in [the] flux of all life and nature. It is called the Mother of the world in terms of giving life to all living sentient creatures."[92] If the *Đạo* is understood better as the concept of God in Vietnamese, then, theologically speaking, the Vietnamese only know this *Đạo* (God) through Jesus Christ who has revealed the Father's love to humanity. This view of God from the Daoist perspective is relevant to the Christian understanding of the meaning of Jesus Christ.

To explain this further, for the Vietnamese, Christ is seen as both high priest and ancestor; he is our "greatest ancestor" in the household of faith. Salvation is the restoration to a right position in the family of God, where people are called the "holy brothers."[93] It is, however, the understanding of the Vietnamese concept of God (the *Đạo*) which would help to bridge the gap in the mind of the Vietnamese that Jesus is not another god, but the Incarnate God who came down to be with the Vietnamese as with any other people in the world. Thus, "the Word became flesh and lived among us" (John 1:14 NRSV) is a critical statement for the Vietnamese. The incarnation is also the

---

92. Chung, "Mystery of God," 247.

93. Chan, *Grassroots Asian Theology*, 91–127, 18–97. These suggestions would be controversial, particularly the practice of ancestral worship. But they introduce an authentic "flavor" into global ecumenical Christianity, and challenge the issue of how theology ought to be done in an Asian context. See Nguyen KimSon, "Grassroots Asian Theology: Thinking the Faith from the Ground Up," *International Bulletin of Missionary Research* 39, no. 1 (2015).

"massive act of translation" as Andrew Walls believed.[94] In sum, the Word is God now come in the flesh.[95]

Jesus reveals God because he was with God and is God.[96] Jesus Christ was the Đạo (Way) in the beginning and Jesus Christ is the Đạo (Way) for all human beings who acknowledge and follow this Only Way. As John Drange Olsen argued that the pre-incarnate Christ has two positions: (1) as the Đạo (Logos) of God, Christ is the Creator who was involved in the creation from the beginning (Gen 1:1). God through Christ, the second person in the triune God, directly finished the creation with God (John 1:3; Col 1:16; Heb 11:3); and (2) Christ is the Sustainer of the creation. From the beginning, God through Christ, has protected and taken care of the whole universe (Col 1:17; Heb 1:3).[97]

Thus, Jesus is the Way to God the Father (John 14: 1–14) because "No one has ever seen God. It is God the only Son, who is close to the Father's heart, who has made him known" (John 1:18 NRSV). He is also the enlightened light, the revealer of who God is and what God is doing, through his Church (John 1:9; Ps 119:105).

The Trinitarian Faith

The Trinitarian relationship is better understood from the Vietnamese perspective as the father-son relationship within a hierarchical structure of society. The Vietnamese family is a hierarchical structure. The ordered relationships between family members are mutually related and subordinated. That means that a community built upon a hierarchical social structure would automatically embrace and reflect the family model and dynamic in which elders are respected and members within the community, as within the family, adopt a hierarchically ordered position in relationships. As Korean theologian Jung

---

94. Walls, *Cross-Cultural Process*, 29. See also chapter 3: "The Translation Principle in Christian History," in Walls, *Missionary Movement in Christian History: Studies in the Transmission of Faith*, 26–42; Sanneh, *Translating the Message*.

95. See Bock, *Jesus According to Scripture*, 410–416.

96. Bock, 421. Also, John has another answer to the identity of the Word/Wisdom/Torah of God. He has become incarnate in the person of Jesus Christ. He, not the Law of Moses, is the key to the meaning of life. Neither was the first of God's creation, but is part of God himself, eternal and uncreated, as seen in John W. Pryor, *John: Evangelist of the Covenant People: The Narrative and Themes of the Fourth Gospel* (Downers Grove, IL: InterVarsity Press, 1992), 8.

97. See chapter 3: "Christ Pre-incarnation" (Book Six: Christology) in Olsen, *Thần đạo học*.

Young Lee argues, one who is in the social classes of a hierarchy as reflecting a pattern would understand the "functional hierarchy in the Trinity."[98] Each member of the Trinity is hierarchically ordered, but not equal in function. However, Vietnamese evangelicalism has taken the Trinitarian faith from the Western perspective (for instance, the work of Olsen as seen in chapter 4), which stressed the equality of the three persons of the Godhead. Modern theology from the West, even among Western evangelicals, has struggled with the concept of a hierarchical relationship. For instance, a prominent evangelical theologian Karl Barth sees that both "divine superiority" and "divine subordination" reveal their respective "modes of being."[99] That means the apparent subordination is based on the hypostatic distinction of Father and Son, not an essential distinction, therefore it does not imply subordination at all.[100]

The triune God's relationship therefore, should be viewed from both the perspective of a relational and reciprocal relationship of Father-Son, as seen in the relational mode of being, rather than the perspective of an equal "mode of being" which is stressed much by the egalitarians in the West.[101] When this relational perception is comprehended, the Vietnamese would understand that Jesus is the Logos or the Đạo (Way) and would see no contradiction with the concept of God that the Vietnamese understand. Again, since the Vietnamese, like many Asians, value the concept of family, this narrative nuances the continuity and relationship between the One True God called the Father God and the Son Jesus Christ, and the Spirit, as well as the place of ancestors in the church as a community, which will be discussed in the next section.

When viewed from a hierarchical relationship perspective, the Father and the Son are seen as two distinct "modes," and yet are mutually relational and reciprocal beings. This means that the Father's generation of the Son and

---

98. Lee, *Trinity in Asian Perspective*, 204–205.

99. For Karl Barth, the glory of the Trinity is seen in the Father's sending his Son who, in his obedience to the Father, reveals what the inner Trinitarian relationship is like. See in Karl Barth, *Church Dogmatics*, vol. 4.1 (Edinburgh: T&T Clark, 1957), 203–204, 9–10.

100. Chan, *Grassroots Asian Theology*, 47–68. Chan favors the triune family as analogy for the relationship of the persons within the Trinity.

101. For instance, Elaine Storkey, "Evangelical Theology and Gender," in *The Cambridge Companion to Evangelical Theology*, ed. Timothy Larsen and Daniel J. Treier (Cambridge, MA: Cambridge University Press, 2007), 161–176.

aspiration of the Spirit imply personal distinction and order, yet the relationship can also be described as mutually dependent.[102] The mutual and reciprocal relationship is biblical as the Scripture reveals Jesus's statement about his relationship with the Father. Jesus the Son depended on the Father, and yet the Father reveals his redemptive purpose for the world through Jesus in the power of the Spirit. This means that although Jesus declared, "The Father and I are one" (John 10:30 NRSV), a relationship of equality, Jesus acknowledged his dependency on the Father when he said "The word that you hear is not mine, but is from the Father who sent me" (John 14:24b NRSV).

In the end, it is necessary to read and interpret Scripture through the lens of philosophical thoughts (Daoist and Confucianist), and still the omnipotence of God is not conditioned by a historical period or ideology, but by history as a whole. "The Mysteries of the Most Holy Trinity and of the Incarnate God were anciently known to the Chinese nation."[103] This statement appears in the translation of *Dao De Jing* (*Tao Te Ching*) presented to the British Royal Society in 1788.[104] A triune God can be seen, as it were, darkly through Chinese and Vietnamese traditions.

From this ordered and hierarchical relationship between the Father God and Jesus the Son, the Vietnamese can see the continuity of God with us (Immanuel) in the world. The meaning can be gleaned in John's prologue "In the beginning was the Word, and the Word was with God, and the Word was God" (John 1:1 NRSV), and Jesus's declaration "I am the way, and the truth, and the life. No one comes to the Father except through me" (John 14:6 NRSV); therefore, Father and Son are connected. Jesus the Son was in the beginning with God but was incarnated into the world to show the way to the Father God (the Đạo). In other words, the Incarnate God through Jesus is profoundly understood by the Vietnamese when associating God with the Đạo and Jesus with the Đạo (Way).

---

102. Chan, *Grassroots Asian Theology*, 67–68. The traditional Catholic and Orthodox doctrine of the monarchy of the Father understands that the Father is the one "without origin" and the "sole principle" by whom the Son is generated and from whom the Spirit proceeds, as seen in Vladimir Lossky, *Orthodox Theology: An Introduction*, trans. Ian and Ihita Kesarcodi-Watson (Crestwood, NY: St Vladimir's Seminary Press, 1989), 47–48.

103. Quoted in Chung, *Constructing Irregular Theology*, 49.

104. This was accomplished by Jesuit missionaries in China. See James Legge, *The Sacred Books of China: The Texts of Taoism*, reprint ed., vol. 1, Series pt. 1 (New York: Dover Publications, 1962), xiii.

But we have only spoken about Father and Son in the Trinity. What about the Holy Spirit? Theologically speaking, the family narrative in Scripture helps to clarify the "interrelatedness" of the triune God's relationship of God, Jesus Christ and the Holy Spirit. While the doctrine of the Trinity is central to the Christian faith, in the context of Vietnam (as in many other cultures in Asia), there are different implications as seen in the Cao Dai in terms of Jesus's relationship to God the Father. From this family perspective, the Holy Spirit is the bond of unity of the Father and the Son. Principally, the Spirit is the bond of love and unity between the Father and the Son, and the church (believers).[105] But, how about the relationship of the Holy Spirit to the context of spirits which is very much a part of everyday life in Vietnam (ch. 2)?[106] Understanding the relationship of the Holy Spirit to the world is equally as important as the work of the Spirit in the Trinity and through the church.[107] As The Cape Town Commitment *A Confession of Faith*, in re-emphasizing the importance of the Holy Spirit to the mission of the church, says:

> We love the Holy Spirit within the unity of the Trinity, along with God the Father and God the Son. He is the missionary Spirit sent by the missionary Father and the missionary Son, breathing life and power into God's missionary Church. We love and pray for

---

105. See Chan, *Grassroots Asian Theology*, 129–156.

106. Here the work of the Holy Spirit plays a critical role, as argued by Gary Tyra that "the Holy Spirit will speak to us through our imaginative dialogue with the biblical text and cultural context," and therefore, contextualization should "involve a conversation with three entities not two: the biblical text, the cultural context and the Spirit of mission!" in Gary Tyra, *The Holy Spirit in Mission: Prophetic Speech and Action in Christian Witness* (Downers Grove, IL: IVP Academic, 2011), 139.

107. The work of the Holy Spirit in the context of spirits of Vietnam is beyond the scope of this study. As the study attempts to provide theological articulation for syncretism and incarnational justification of God in Christ (the Đạo), the study wishes to also penetrate the role of the Holy Spirit from a Vietnamese Christian perspective. Such direction would help to construct a Vietnamese evangelical pneumatology for the context of tremendous awareness of spirit(s) in Vietnam and East Asia as seen in chapter 3's "Popular Animist Beliefs." Nevertheless, some theological trends that have developed recently in Christian theology promote that Pneumatology is the foundational principle to see the universal presence of the Spirit or to discern the Spirit(s) which would be greatly beneficial for a Vietnamese evangelical pneumatology. See, for instance, Amos Yong, *Beyond the Impasse: Toward a Pneumatological Theology of Religions* (Grand Rapids, MI: Baker Academic, 2003); Yong, *Spirit Poured Out*; Amos Yong, *Renewing Christian Theology: Systematics for a Global Christianity* (Waco, TX: Baylor University Press, 2014); Kirsteen Kim, *The Holy Spirit in the World: A Global Conversation* (Maryknoll, NY: Orbis Books, 2007); Koo Dong Yun, *The Holy Spirit and Ch'i (Qi): A Chiological Approach to Pneumatology*, Princeton Theological Monograph Series 180. (Eugene, OR: Pickwick, 2012).

the presence of the Holy Spirit because without the witness of the Spirit to Christ, our own witness is futile. Without the convicting work of the Spirit, our preaching is in vain. Without the gifts, guidance and power of the Spirit, our mission is mere human effort. And without the fruit of the Spirit, our unattractive lives cannot reflect the beauty of the gospel.[108]

Again, the Spirit is the bond of love and unity between the Father and the Son, but also of the church. This perspective echoes the Christian traditions when referring to the Holy Spirit as the Spirit of communion (fellowship) (2 Cor 13:14).[109] The Holy Spirit is the "condition and medium" of the fellowship between the Father and the Son and "only on this basis may the imparting of the Spirit to believers be seen as their incorporation into the fellowship of the Son with the Father."[110] The Spirit is the bond of love and unity between the church and its head, Christ and access is by "one Spirit to the Father" (Eph 2:18). "Through the Spirit's indwelling the church, the church is united to Christ as his body and ultimately to the Father, the source of all things . . . Thus only in and through the church does creation find its true meaning and fulfilment."[111] The church as the Spirit-indwelled community to manifest 'God with us' is further explored below.

The Church: The Center of God's Purpose

The church as a Vietnamese Christian community lives out the presence of God, a place which manifests "God with us" (Immanuel) or, more specifically, to show that God is in our midst. That means as Jesus Christ is the head of the church, the purpose of God in the world is manifested through a community of all Christians, both the living and the deceased.

---

108. https://www.lausanne.org/content/ctc/ctcommitment#p1-1, accessed 8 February 2017. See also "Our God Is a Missionary God," in John R. W. Stott, *The Contemporary Christian: Applying God's Word to Today's World* (Downers Grove, IL: InterVarsity Press, 1992), 321–326 (as cited by Wright, *Mission of God*, 24, fn. 2).

109. For instance, Joseph Ratzinger, "The Holy Spirit as Communio: Concerning the Relationship of Pneumatology and Spirituality in Augustine," *Communio* 25, no. 2 (Summer 1998).

110. For instance, Wolfhart Pannenberg, *Systematic Theology*, vol. 1 (Grand Rapids, MI: Eerdmans, 1991), 316.

111. Chan, *Grassroots Asian Theology*, 156.

The House of God's Presence

The church is firstly seen as the place of God's presence. Early in the history of the Catholic mission in Vietnam, under the Jesuits, the churches that were founded by de Rhodes were first understood as "quasi-religious communities of catechists" in both Tonkin, Annam, and Cochinchina (North, Central, and South Vietnam today).[112] When things became more stable these quasi-religious organizations were called *Nhà Đức Chúa Trời* (House of the Lord of Heaven), whose members lived in the presbytery with the parish priests.[113] The Vietnamese evangelicals also called the church *Nhà Chúa* (House of the Lord). This is less common among the evangelicals today where the church is normally called *Nhà thờ* (House of worship). But, whether the "House of the Lord" or "House of worship," the meaning of the church is understood as the place of God's presence (the dwelling place of God as seen in the Jewish tradition in the Old Testament). In the New Testament, the "household of God" or the "house of God" appears to imply managing one's own household which leads to managing God's house or church, as seen in 1 Timothy 3:5, Ephesians 2:19, Hebrews 10:21, and 1 Peter 4:17. The early Christian understanding of church (*Nhà Chúa*) was *oikos ekklesias* (Latin: *domus ecclesiae*) or *oikos kyriakou* (the Lord's House).[114] From these early Christian uses of the metaphor of "oikos" (house) by the New Testament writers, and still present in the Orthodox theological paradigm of *oikonomia* ("economy," e.g. divine economy or ecclesial economy)[115] which is an important biblical and early Christian *ecclesial* understanding, then, this metaphor "oikos" expresses well the understanding of *nhà* and *nhà Chúa* by the Vietnamese.

Besides the Venerating Heaven ritual that was reserved for the emperor (who once a year performed the sacrifice as an act of worshiping Heaven), the Vietnamese have a tradition of worshiping in communal houses or temples

---

112. Phan, *Mission and Catechesis*, 38–68, 101.

113. Phan, 102. See also Đỗ Quang Chính, *Lịch sử chữ Quốc Ngữ 1620–1659*, 329–378.

114. For instance, see Eusebius, *Historia Ecclesiastica* (Turnhout: Brepols Publishers, 2010), VII.30.19, VIII.1; Eusebius, *History of the Church*, trans. Rufinus of Aquileia and Philip R. Amidon, *The Fathers of the Church: A New Translation*, vol. 133 (Washington, DC: Catholic University of America Press, 2016). See also "oikos tou theou" in Hippolytus, *The Apostolic Tradition of Hippolytus (with Introduction and Notes)*, trans. Burton Scott Easton (Cambridge: Cambridge University Press, 1934).

115. See, for instance, Vladimir Lossky, John H. Erickson, and Thomas E. Bird, *In the Image and Likeness of God* (Crestwook, NY: St Vladimir's Seminary Press, 1985).

(*đình, chùa*). These temples honor those who have founded or protected the village and the nation (ch. 2).[116] On a regular basis, Vietnamese "home" worship is more popular than worship at the "communal houses" or "temples" which is done on certain occasions only (for instance, the Lunar New Year, or a death anniversary). In fact, in Vietnam as well as in the rest of Asia, "the primary locus of religious life is the home" where it finds its most conspicuous expression in ancestor veneration.[117] Nevertheless, these temples are usually associated with the religious and ritual practices of their spirit beliefs, for instance, worshiping the village guardian deities (*thành hoàng*).[118] It reveals that the Vietnamese have in mind that the communal houses or temples are the place where the people as a community gather to worship.

Theologically, there is no contradiction when viewing the nature of "the House of the Lord" from that Vietnamese perspective. Thus, the meaning of the "house" and the "church" from the Christian perspective are similar to the Vietnamese perspective, for instance, "for my house shall be called a house of prayer for all peoples" (Isa 56:7 NRSV). That "house" of the Lord is designated as the place for worshiping God, and it is also the place of prayer where the community gathers to be in God's presence. The Lord Jesus said to the people who changed the purpose of the house that, "It is written, 'My house shall be called a house of prayer'; but you are making it a den of robbers" (Matt 21:13 NRSV). Therefore, the church as the "house of the Lord," is where the Vietnamese community of God's people are in God's presence. And this community is going forth to manifest God's purpose in the world as a relational community, not as independent individuals. Vietnamese life is communal. Christian life is also communal.

---

116. A communal house (*đình*) or temple (*chùa*) is place where the spirits received people's worship, whereas shrine (*đền, miễu*) is where the spirits resided.

117. Chan, *Grassroots Asian Theology*, 162.

118. *Thành hoàng* is a folk belief which worships the highest spirit (*thần*) who protected a village. It was more popular in the North (*Đàng ngoài cũ*) of Vietnam compared to the South (*Đàng trong cũ*). In the North, *Thành hoàng* was functioning as a combination of a *đền* (or shrine) and a *đình* (or temple), whereas in the South, *đình thần* (spirited temple) combining all the spirits (from separate shrines) to worship in one place. See particularly "*Hệ thống thần địa phương mới: thành hoàng làng*" [New local spirits system: Village's *thành hoàng*] in Tạ Chí Đại Trường, *Thần, Người và Đất Việt*, 162–183.

A Relational Community

The church secondly is a relational community of the living, where its members are considered as brothers and sisters. But this community includes the deceased ancestors, as seen from the Vietnamese perspective (the extended family). As an extended family, the church also reaches to the people have gone before us. They are the ancestors, the respected people of the Bible (the saints). This does not mean the living worship the dead or their spirits, rather they venerate or honor them in a way that upholds their lives and teachings as still of significant value for our present time. They are part of our community. A Vietnamese relational community as an extended family, therefore, comprises both the living and the deceased.[119] As an extended family, the church is not only for the living, but also the place where the ancestors are venerated. For the community of the living, more discussion is given in the next section. But, one should note at this point that the ancestor issue is very troublesome for many Vietnamese evangelicals. The *Constitution of the Evangelical Church of Vietnam* (1956) states that "He [a church member] must not take part in ancestor worship, spirit worship, and various superstitions."[120] This needs greater clarification, and further study by Vietnamese evangelicals.[121]

---

119. This has also called "a communion of saints," as seen in Chan, *Grassroots Asian Theology*.

120. See Part 1 – Qualifications for Church Membership of Section VII – Church Membership in Hội Thánh Tin Lành Việt Nam, *Constitution of the Evangelical Church of Vietnam (Điều Lệ của Hội Thánh Tin Lành Việt Nam)*, 6–7 (in English); 8–9 (in Vietnamese). This *Constitution*, based on the *Constitution of the Evangelical Church of Indochina* in 1928, was recognized by The Annual General Assembly of the Evangelical Church of Vietnam met in the My-Tho church (South Vietnam) on at the 5 July 1928. The 1928 *Constitution* stated *clearly* that a member of the ECVN "must put away his idols and give up his ancestral worship," and "cease from any employment unworthy of the Gospel" such as "selling wine, tobacco, or things pertaining to idolatry," namely "incense, lamps, paper money," quoted in Lê Hoàng Phu, "Short History," 182. Dr Lê commented that this particular statement in the 1928's *Constitution* was to deal with the sensitive problem which has confronted the Christian Churches in East Asia, both Catholic and Protestant. But, he noted that "the cult of ancestors [was] being considered by the [American] missionaries as another form of idolatry."

121. The world of spirits is very much a part of everyday life in Vietnam as likewise in Asia. Therefore, how the doctrine of the Spirit (pneumatology) is related to the church in the Vietnamese spirit beliefs context is very important and suggested for further study. An example can be seen in "The Holy Spirit and Spirituality" in Chan, *Grassroots Asian Theology*, 129–156; Simon Chan, "Asian Christian Spirituality in Primal Religious Contexts," in *Walking with God: Christian Spirituality in the Asian Context*, ed. Charles Ringma (Manila, Philippines: OMF Literature; Asian Theological Seminary, 2014), 32-52.

Culturally, the Vietnamese venerate their ancestors as seen in chapter 2.[122] Vietnamese spirituality is much more complicated when one thinks about what this veneration means.[123] Is it worship? These two words are as confusing in Vietnamese as they are in English. Both are action verbs in Vietnamese: "worship" is expressed by *thờ* while "venerate" is *kính*. As seen in the *Tales of Twenty-Seven Spirits* ("Popular Animist Beliefs" section in ch. 2), when one worships (*thờ*) someone (such as heroes, saints) it means that they are worthy to be venerated (*kính*). If they are heroes (because of doing good things for the community or nation) while they are living, they would also be good spirits/saints protecting the people continually even after death. Death does not mean the end of life, but a transitional mode of being into spirit.[124] From an animistic spirit belief perspective, those *Twenty-Seven* heroes are "good spirits" who continually are not only being venerated, but also being worshiped. In this sense, Vietnamese can combine these two verbs into one action verb, "venerably worship" (*thờ kính*). Those heroes or saints, therefore,

---

122. Léopold Cadière also described that, "This presence of the ancestors in the midst of the family is not a purely passive state. They act. Ordinarily their influence is exercised for the well-being of the living members of the family. When the latter fulfill their obligations of filial piety punctually, then the ancestors, furnished on ritual days with all that they need, [being happy and tranquil], make their presence felt by distributing all sorts of good things to their descendants. But if they have chosen a defective place for burial, or if they forget to make requisite offerings or if they are cheap, the ancestors will take revenge, or more precisely, they will punish the guilty. Then a geomancer or sorcerer must be consulted, and following their advice, the bones must be relocated, an expiatory sacrifice made in honor of such displeased ancestors." See Cadière, *Croyances et pratiques religieuses des Viêtnamiens*, I:39.

123. For instance, Léopold Cadière analyzed Vietnamese philosophical popularity that was associated with the spiritual world, including the cosmology (heaven, earth, and the pantheon of occult beings), and the ancestors and their relationship with descendants, see Léopold Cadière, *Croyances et pratiques religieuses des Viêtnamiens*, 3 vols., vol. 3 (Paris: Ecole Française d'Extrême-Orient, 1957). See also Nguyen Joseph Huy Lai, *La tradition religieuse spirituelle et sociale au Vietnam: sa Confrontation avec le Christianisme*, Beauchesne religions 11 (Paris: Beauchesne, 1981), 53–126.

124. Vietnamese animistic spirit belief makes no clear distinction between *soul* (*hồn*) and *spirit* (*linh*) as in the Western worldview, see, for instance, in Reginald Eugene Reimer, "The Religious Dimension of the Vietnamese Cult of the Ancestors," *Missiology: An International Review* 3, no. 2 (1975): 155–168. Reimer argues that one can understand Vietnamese cults of the ancestors by understanding Vietnamese beliefs concerning the *soul*. For the Vietnamese "entire man" perspective that is "body and soul," see Cadière, *Croyances et pratiques religieuses des Viêtnamiens*, vol. 3.

as good spirits, are venerably worshiped, and then in return, bestow upon the worshiper wealth and health, as well as protect them from evil spirits.¹²⁵

When someone is venerated (*kính*) it does not necessarily mean being worshiped (*thờ*). In this sense, the word "venerate" is understood as an action of paying respect, *tôn kính or hiếu kính* (meaning "honor" in English) which are nouns (for instance, he pays or shows his/her veneration/honor to someone).¹²⁶ Of course, the difference between being "venerably worshiped" and "venerated" (or honored) is a very thin line. One can worship the one he or she is respectfully venerating (or honoring). Here is where many Vietnamese evangelicals (and the CMA missionaries to Vietnam) have misunderstood the subtle complexity of the Vietnamese ancestor veneration and simply required forsaking the ancestors" when they became Christians. For instance, the CMA missionary Paul M. Hosler said, "Ancestral-worship is another form of religion and to this the worship of all gods and genii is subordinate. The morals and customs of the people are founded upon it and all social and domestic life is governed thereby. Truly, 'The dead rule the living.'"¹²⁷

If ancestors are not subjected to Christian worship, which is forbidden according to the first commandment: "you shall have no other gods before me" (Exod 20:3 NRSV), then, how shall the ancestors be treated according to the third commandment: "Honor your father and your mother" (Exod 20:12 NRSV)? Perhaps, the word "honor" (and venerate) here could be referring to the living parents. How then can the minds and hearts of the Vietnamese fulfill their devotion and love for the deceased? Here, the Vietnamese perception of the extended family is inclusive of both the living, their ancestors, and the members or relatives in their clans who already have passed away. Each time a Vietnamese extended family (or a clan) gathers together at important events, such as a death anniversary (*đám giỗ, đám kỵ*), ancestors are prayed for (*khấn*) and remembered (*tưởng nhớ*). Of course, Vietnamese Christians are not supposed to pray to the dead, and worship the dead as "other gods" (according to the first commandment). But, the Vietnamese regard ancestor

---

125. Whether these *good* spirits came to protect people from *evil* spirits or not, and the religious rituals that are accompanied with this spirit belief and practices, is beyond the scope of this study.

126. As seen in Emperor Kang-Xi's argument in Thong and Fu, *Finding God in Ancient China*.

127. Hosler, "Dawn of Protestant Missions," 137.

veneration as a pious regard for those who came before.[128] They do not believe their ancestors have a "God like status" requiring worship (as Christians worship God). The question remains, then, how should the Vietnamese Christians venerate or honor ancestors in a way that is biblically (as in the third commandment) and culturally appropriate?

What then are the alternatives to the ancestor practices for Vietnamese evangelicals? Some critical suggestions have been made by some Asian and African theologians as seen above, for instance, Phan's "Jesus as the Eldest Son and Ancestor," Chan's "the Ancestor-Mediator (Priest)," and Bujo's "Proto-Ancestor" which could help to further the thinking about the meaning of Christ (christological proposal) for the issue of ancestor veneration among the Vietnamese evangelicals.[129] Also, some practical ways as seen elsewhere in Asia could be a point of reference. For instance, in Taiwan, a common practice of the Taiwan Presbyterian Church members is to display the Ten Commandments, Bible verses, and a picture of Christ on the central wall of their house. At the same time, these Christians are present with their non-Christian relatives at ancestral sacrifice gatherings for maintaining fellowship with the relatives and to show them that they have not forsaken the ancestors and the clan.[130] In China, Christians have an annual memorial meeting on a special "Ancestor's Day" or a "Memorial Day" when "services are held in the church or at the cemetery in commemoration of the departed parents. Such a day is also observed by individual Christian families."[131]

---

128. For instance, to argue for the view of Christ as the eldest son within the context of Vietnamese ancestor worship and to respond to the "objection" that there is no ancestor worship among the Jews, Peter C. Phan says that, "Vietnamese ancestor veneration sometimes contains, especially at the popular level, magical practices assimilated from Taoism [Daoism]. But shorn from these superstitious practices, ancestor veneration as a religious manifestation of deep gratitude and filial piety to one's forbears and of a living communion with them does not seem to be foreign to the Jews." See "Jesus as Eldest Son and Model of Filial Piety," in Phan, *Christianity with an Asian Face*.

129. For the Vietnamese Roman Catholic perspective, see chapter 4 "*Vấn đề cúng bái tổ tiên*" [Ancestor worship issue] in Đỗ Quang Chính and Nguyễn Văn Hậu, *Hoà mình vào xã hội Việt Nam* [Inculturating into the Vietnamesese culture and society], 184–242.

130. See David Liao, "Christian Alternatives to Ancestor Worship in Taiwan," in *Christian Alternatives to Ancestor Practices*, ed. Bong Rin Ro (Taichung, Taiwan, ROC: Asia Theological Association, 1985), 214.

131. See *China Christian Yearbook* (Shanghai: Christian Literature Society, 1917), 296, cited by Liao, "Christian Alternatives," 215–216. We note that many Western (Christian) nations also have a "Memorial Day."

It can be argued that Vietnamese evangelicals need to make sense of their faith in practical ways rather than ignoring them and finding more excuses to repress the ancestor veneration issue. Ontologically, the Vietnamese cannot understand why Vietnamese evangelicals celebrate the death of Jesus (as in the Lord's Supper) in their regular worship, but do not do so with their own ancestors. Even when argued that the Lord's Supper is just a memorial (in "remembrance of Jesus"), the sacrament should be an act of worship, not just merely remembering his death. Biblically speaking, Jesus Christ is the Way (God), and Jesus Christ is God with us, then such celebration is considered as an act of worship of the One True God, or at least, a part of Christian worship for centuries in the Christian church.[132] The Apostle Paul also argued, "But in fact Christ has been raised from the dead, the first fruits of those who have died" (1 Cor 15:20 NRSV). Then would the Lord's Supper be seen as an act of veneration of Jesus in Christian worship?

Ancestor veneration is also a theological issue since theology is birthed from a specific cultural context. This is one of the main contextualization issues that is suggested for further study so that ancestor veneration might become a culturally, theologically, and biblically appropriate practice for Vietnamese evangelicals. As seen from Korean and Chinese Christian perspectives, Vietnamese evangelicals should not abandon completely ancestor worship since it is a beautiful tradition that God has given us and it does point to God's commandments. Rather this tradition must be reclaimed to reflect a Vietnamese Christian perspective. As one Korean theologian has said, "ancestor veneration calls Christians to an enlarged theological vision of salvation, as a holistic, community salvation, encompassing the deceased and the not yet born in the communion of saints."[133] Korean theologian Jung Young Lee also suggests that "we should provide a Christian liturgy, instead of a Confucian one, in terms of which Christians can make ancestor worship in a Christian

---

132. The meaning of the Lord's Supper with its various practices is one of important themes in systematic theology, for instance, see "The Lord's Supper and Christian Worship" in Wolfhart Pannenberg, *Systematic Theology*, trans. Geoffrey W. Bromiley, vol. 3, T & T Clark Academic Paperbacks (Grand Rapids, MI: Eerdmans, 1993), 283–336.

133. Heup Yong Kim, "Ancestor Veneration and Christianity in Asia," in *The Cambridge Dictionary of Christianity*, ed. Daniel Patte (Cambridge, MA: Cambridge University Press, 2010), 32.

family worship together with ancestral souls."[134] Since this issue is so complex for Vietnamese evangelicals, it should be examined and studied carefully from various angles: from the Vietnamese culture (Vietnamese syncretistic spirituality), other East Asian cultures, and biblical interpretation (idolatry in the Bible, or the first commandment given in Exod 20:3–4). Here, a "joint declaration on ancestor practices" could be helpful to define an "evangelical" approach to ancestor practices for Vietnamese evangelicals.[135] In sum, ancestor veneration which is honoring the ancestors "must be distinguished from ancestor cult or worship with specific rituals for caring for the dead" that being practiced popularly in East Asia.[136]

Moreover, a relational community also means that in obedience to God (modeling after the *missio Dei*) and being prompted by the Spirit, the living are able to relate to others who need to be in this community to experience the presence of God, which is the focus of the next section.

A Missional Community

The church thirdly is not a static institution, but always, and at the same time, a movement. The church is a missional community which means that the church is the center of God's cosmic purpose for the world. Within the Eastern Orthodox tradition, the church and its mission center around communion of being, or ecclesial communion. This means that being a member of the church, one becomes an "image of God," and exists as God himself exists, that is, taking on God's "way of being."[137] In this sense, the church is "church" when it is in communion with the triune God, and with one another among

---

134. See "Ancestor Worship: From a Theological Perspective," in Jung Young Lee, ed. *Ancestor Worship and Christianity in Korea*, vol. 8, Studies in Asian Though and Religion (Lewiston, NY: E. Mellen Press, 1988), 83–91. See also, Jung Young Lee, *The Theology of Change: A Christian Concept of God in an Eastern Perspective* (Maryknoll, NY: Orbis Books, 1979).

135. See "A Working Document Towards a Christian Approach to Ancestor Practices" (by 98 evangelical theologians, pastors, and missionaries from nine countries in Asia met in Taipei, ROC, December 26–31, 1983) in Bong Rin Ro, ed. *Christian Alternatives to Ancestor Practices* (Taichung, Taiwan: Asia Theological Association, 1985), 3–10.

136. Scott W. Sunquist, "Ancestor Veneration and Christianity: Overview," in *The Cambridge Dictionary of Christianity*, ed. Daniel Patte (Cambridge, MA: Cambridge University Press, 2010), 30.

137. John Zizioulas, *Being as Communion: Studies in Personhood and the Church* (Crestwood, NY: St Vladimir's Seminary Press, 1985), 134, 45–49.

the church members through the eucharist (the Lord's Supper). It means that wherever the local eucharistic gathering is, there is the church of God.[138]

The adjectival form of the word mission, "missional," coined in the 1990s, is used widely today to recover the missional nature of every local church, and it gives us a clearer picture that mission is not from the church, but "from the heart of God, to each context, and it is carried out in suffering in this world for God's eternal glory."[139] And since "mission begins with God himself, not merely because He is the God of mission, but because his very character is mission," the task of mission for the Vietnamese Christian community is to participate in the mission of the triune God (*missio Dei*) as "the prophetic voice" that launches the church from the place (house) of worship and fellowship into "the frontiers of God's sovereign rule."[140]

The mission of the church is from the essence of the nature of the triune God since it is from the mission of the Son and the mission of the Holy Spirit that it draws her origin, in accordance with the decree of God the Father.[141] The triune God is God the Father who created and redeemed his creation. God the Son, whom the Father sent, was begotten to redeem the whole creation. And God the Holy Spirit, who proceeded through the Son (*filioque*), helps to carry on "inwardly His saving work and prompt the church to spread out."[142]

The church therefore is the community of Christ's disciples (catechists) in the "House of the Lord, " meaning not the buildings, but the living people. This community belongs to anyone who has received the Lordship of Christ. One then is justified by God's grace through faith in God's Son, the Lord Jesus, the One and Only Way (*Đạo*), no other way. This community of the living is therefore, "to give prophetic witness to the gospel of Jesus Christ, to engage together in worship of God, and to serve others," because each individual

---

138. Zizioulas, *Being as Communion*, 148–149. Zizioulas argues that, *communion* is not just an ontological category of God, but also of the church, because we bear the image of the triune God who likewise is "one in many," and conversely, "many in one."

139. Sunquist, *Understanding Christian Mission*, xii, 8–9.

140. Gnanakan, *Kingdom Concerns*, 67; Sunquist, *Understanding Christian Mission*, xiii, 136.

141. See *Ad Gentes*, "Decree *Ad Gentes* on the Mission Activity of the Church," ed. Pope Paul VI (1964).

142. See *Ad Gentes* #2 and #4.

in the church has different "gifts and abilities that are at work as gifts of the Spirit (*charisms*) in serving Christ's church and its tasks" as in Paul's list in 1 Corinthians 12.[143] This missional community therefore "looks to the Holy Spirit" because it can "accomplish [its] mission only in obedience to the prompting of the Holy Spirit."[144] Moreover, this community must manifest the essential attributes of the church, to be "holy and catholic."[145] This church (as a missional community) is "holy" because "it is sanctified by Jesus Christ its Lord."[146] This church is "catholic" because it presents variety in an actual congregation, and especially in its life of worship.[147] This means that the missional community is the house of God welcoming all those who are thirsty for the "living water" (John 4:10–15), having such thirst which the Spirit himself has created and which Jesus the Savior alone can fully satisfy.[148]

Chapter Conclusion

This chapter has proposed a cultural integration for a Vietnamese evangelical mission theology in terms of redeeming the Vietnamese concept of God, and the Vietnamese extended family perspective for both the Trinitarian relationship – the Father, the Son and the Holy Spirit – and the Vietnamese Christian community of both the living and the ancestors. This is a new perspective on how Vietnamese and Christian concepts and practices can be merged,

---

143. This statement is in both the Joint Roman Catholic–Evangelical Lutheran Commission's report "Das geitsliche Amt in der Kirche" (1981) and the Lima Report (1982), quoted in Pannenberg, *Systematic Theology*, 373.

144. Phan, *Asian Synod*, 301–302; Joseph Dinh Duc Dao, "Christian Formation of the Laity," 105–106. The full English text of *Ecclesia in Asia* can be found in Phan, *Asian Synod*, 286–340. Also in *Origins* 29, 23 (18 November 1999), 358–384.

145. As seen in the Apostles Creed.

146. Pannenberg, *Systematic Theology*, 406. The argument is as for individual life, so for the fellowship of the church, the baptismal cleansing from sin is a theme for life, accompanying the church throughout its history for a constantly renewed turning aside from the sin of the world and for a deepening of fellowship with Jesus Christ.

147. See Pannenberg, 406–415. Pannenberg warns against any particular church that claims only its own order and tradition is catholic to exclusion of all other churches. Thus, he believes, although catholicity is the most comprehensive aspect of the unity of the church, it can also be the striking feature that causes "constant threats," that is, manifestations of the phenomena of schism, heresy, and apostasy.

148. Phan, *Asian Synod*, 301–302; Joseph Dinh Duc Dao, "Christian Formation of the Laity," 105–106. The full English text of *Ecclesia in Asia* can be found in Phan, *Asian Synod*, 286–340. Also in *Origins* 29, 23 (18 November 1999), 358–384.

creating the paradigm shift required for a renewed Vietnamese evangelical mission theology. This new missiology should exhibit three characteristics as summarized below.

First, historically and biblically, Vietnamese evangelical mission theology must be faithful in continuity with the larger Christian tradition. At the same time, this mission theology must be a mission-centered theology, modeled after the missionary activity of the triune God (*missio Dei*). Second, this mission theology must be willing to see God's action in the religio-cultural context of Vietnam and East Asia. This means that theology ought to be done while observing God's intent and God's desire for the Vietnamese, and while having the Bible continue to speak God's truth in fresh ways to the Vietnamese. And third, Vietnamese evangelical mission theology must be organized by Vietnamese forms of thinking. Two specific forms of Vietnamese perspective have been discussed: (1) the Vietnamese concept of God, and (2) the extended family narrative.

With these three characteristics, a preliminary approach has been proposed for a Vietnamese evangelical mission theology. First, viewing "God in our midst" is a starting point to bridge the gap in the minds of the Vietnamese regarding the concept of the *Đạo* or *Thiên* (*Ông Trời*). Second, from a Vietnamese perspective on an extended family, "God with us" is interpreted as the continual and relational way for the framework of Trinitarian faith and of the church of Jesus Christ. From this perspective, Jesus Christ, the Incarnate Son, is interpreted as the continuity of God the Father in a relational way, namely Father-Son. The fullness of the Creator God or the indeterminate *Đạo* (Way) has been revealed (incarnated) to humanity and identified so that Jesus is the Word (*Đạo*) and the Way (*Đạo*). Jesus Christ as the head of the church has called all human beings who believe in him to be reconciled with God the Father. The union, as seen in the marriage metaphor, between the church as the bride and Christ as bridegroom, shows the bridegroom looking for the bride in Revelation 19:7–9; 21:1–22:21 (this narrative is also mentioned in Mark 2:19–20; John 3:29). This inclusive community of saints of the past, present and future is called to manifest the glory and the presence of the Father on earth. Moreover, this missional community carries on the mission of God to the world to proclaim the redemptive message to the end of the earth in the power of the Holy Spirit (Acts 1:8) till the return of Christ.

In the final analysis, the Vietnamese concept of God and the extended family perspective need to be redeemed for a Vietnamese mission theology to be relevant in the specific context of Vietnam. The processes of theologizing these concepts will promote a paradigm shift in mission theology so that the church in Vietnam can be "church" constantly relevant to its context; an essentially Vietnamese church.

CONCLUSION

Theological Missiological Reflections

This book has identified a gap between the Vietnamese syncretistic spirituality and the Christian faith introduced by the Protestant Christian missionary movements in Vietnam. Within the larger context of East Asia, the study has navigated the religio-cultural dimensions of Vietnamese spirituality that have posed a challenge for the Christian faith's assimilation into the complex syncretistic framework of the Vietnamese belief system from the beginning, identifying failed attempts at contextualization. The Vietnamese evangelicals practice, for the most part, a Western evangelicalism which disrupts the Vietnamese cultural and spiritual patterns. They still find it difficult to "nurture" or to "express" themselves theologically in the Vietnamese cultural context in which they exist. Thus, what this study has brought forth is a way to move from practice to theory (a reverse methodology) for constructing a Vietnamese evangelical mission theology in a way that would help the leadership of the church to move forward.

Within the larger East Asian syncretistic context, the Vietnamese have shown, throughout their long history their ability to syncretize and to integrate their animist beliefs with the outside religio-cultural influences, whether the process was simply osmotic or the result of centuries of foreign rule. As a result, the Vietnamese spirituality is a complex, integrated matrix of local beliefs in God(s), spirits, Confucianist-Daoist-Buddhist concepts, and Christian faith, forming a syncretistic hybrid of both Oriental and Western philosophical and socio-religious aspects. This study has identified that within this long process of assimilation, the dialectic interplay of dual forces – resistance and assimilation – has shaped how the Vietnamese were able to both resist the religio-cultural influences from the outside and to assimilate moderately the essentials of the outside influences that were of specific interest to them. As seen in this research, the failure of the Christian missionaries to identify this resisting and assimilating interplay, by rationalizing the essentials and unifying them with local popular animistic beliefs toward a single religious doctrine to be discarded, became the reason why Christian contextualization efforts failed. However, at the same time, it seems promising that contextualization efforts in Vietnam are possible once the dual-force nature is recognized. We see what needs to be resisted and what are the crucial religio-cultural elements or concepts that need to be or can be assimilated. This identification and acknowledgement would serve as the lens through which the contextualization processes would review the essential elements or concepts of Vietnamese spirituality which can be redeemed for evangelical Christian beliefs and practices.

Among these essential elements that a new approach in missionary efforts in the twenty-first century must revisit and capitalize upon, is the concept of the Đạo (the Way) which is at the core of the Vietnamese-East Asian worldview. This study has showed that the Vietnamese understanding of the divine nature of the Đạo indicates that the Vietnamese would be, by analogy, open to God's intent to be known, or simply to experience God in our midst. The Đạo is the essence of Vietnamese spirituality. Centuries before encountering the Western Christian God introduced by missionaries, the Đạo has been the central metaphysical concept understood by the Vietnamese. The early Christian missionaries, however, upon their arrival in Vietnam, encountered the immediately visible forms of traditional practices and common ritual ceremonies practiced over many centuries, as completely foreign to them and to their own faith. Missionaries failed to understand the meaning behind these religio-cultural traditions, not recognizing the essence underlying these manifestations. Hence, they were not able to find ways to contextualize the gospel to the Vietnamese. The opportunity for contextualization existed all the time, but was not seen. God's incarnation through Jesus the Christ (the Đạo) is the "massive" translation of the gospel into human history. This translatable nature is now becoming more visible to the modern Christian scholars of East Asian Christianity. We can see that contextualization studies can reveal the connection between the perception of the Incarnate God and the Đạo in the Vietnamese perspective of God. Ontologically, the argument that Christ is the Đạo makes concrete sense to the Vietnamese view of God. Theologically, it is providential that God's intent to be known by the Vietnamese is the God who came down in flesh to reveal the Đạo of God. In sum, Christ is the Đạo.

Contextualization efforts, then, remain an ongoing and necessary task for Vietnamese evangelicalism to make known God's intention to the Vietnamese. The current study has identified the unique Vietnamese cultural and spiritual premises that indicate the reason why Christian contextualization efforts failed, and, at the same time, has strongly suggested that any attempt at Christian contextualization in Vietnam cannot overlook the "dual force" and the nature of the Đạo of Vietnamese spirituality.

From this study of Vietnamese evangelicals in the context and the ongoing contextualization efforts in Asia, it has been argued that it is necessary to present the Christian faith in such a way that allows the Vietnamese to follow Christ and yet remain within their Vietnamese culture. This present study, therefore, offers some relevant contributions to Vietnamese contextualization efforts by proposing a paradigm shift in Vietnamese mission theology that honors being both evangelical and Vietnamese. A robust Vietnamese mission theology has some outstanding characteristics that are considered necessary for Vietnamese evangelicals to make Christian faith both evangelical and Vietnamese at the same time.

The first argument for the new approach in contextualization efforts promotes continuity with the Christian tradition at large. A Vietnamese mission theology must be faithful to continue the redemptive work of the Trinitarian God, the saving work of God through Jesus Christ (the Đạo) by the Holy Spirit that has been passed down through the Church of Christ since Pentecost. Such theology then enables the church to proclaim the good news of the gospel as a reconciliation and restoration of the relationship between humankind and God through Christ, the Đạo. And in the power of the Holy Spirit, Christ the Đạo enlightens the minds and hearts of the Vietnamese so that the Bible continues to speak God's truth in fresh ways to them. Vietnamese mission theology must be Christian.

The second part of the argument of integration is rationalizing from the Vietnamese forms of thinking. As seen earlier, the French and American Protestant missionaries in early twentieth-century Vietnam seemed to be intent on making the native Vietnamese more Christian, overlooking, perhaps, that in the process, they were also making each one less Vietnamese. But, a genuine Vietnamese evangelical is expected to be a good Vietnamese first who continually upholds and respects the traditional values that are an intrinsic part of Vietnamese identity and spiritual makeup. That means at both the fundamental and ontological level, a Vietnamese mission theology must begin with the Vietnamese concept of the divine, the *Đạo* which is Jesus Christ, the Incarnate God. Theoretically, this organizing principle for a Vietnamese mission theology would be the right direction to follow. Philosophically and theologically, acknowledging that the *Đạo* is Christ, the Incarnate God, is the key to unlock the problem of believing in a God who is alien and strange to the Vietnamese. "Immanuel, God with us," carries the Vietnamese connotation of the *Đạo*. Christ the *Đạo* is with the Vietnamese. The *Đạo* was with God and is God who came down to earth in flesh for humankind (John 1), including the Vietnamese.

This current study also invites several further studies of the dimensions of the family of the triune God and the contextual ecclesiology from the Vietnamese perspective. Two specific suggestions are given below.

First, this present research has focused on the religio-cultural dimensions of Vietnamese spirituality, identified local popular animistic beliefs, some religions from the outside, including Christianity, as well as some indigenous religions of which the most notable one is the Cao Dai. Thus, the study can be the foundation for interested Vietnamese evangelicals to conduct a comprehensive study of these religions and faiths in Vietnam from the historical, social, and political dimensions of these religions.

Second, a Vietnamese systematic theology must construct the doctrine of the Trinity, namely the doctrines of God and Christology, that are relevant to the Vietnamese. For instance, John Olsen's *Thần đạo học* (Theology) attempted to portray a Vietnamese Christology that identified Jesus Christ as the *Đạo*. But more than just changing terminology, the concept of the *Đạo* needs to be perceived as it is in the Vietnamese and East Asian perspective. The way of understanding the *Đạo* as navigated in this study can be a framework for Vietnamese evangelical theological study in a thematic and systematic way for Vietnamese evangelicals to work on the religio-cultural heritage and the relevance of their faith in the Vietnamese context.

As a concluding remark, Christian faith is expected to be both relevant and indigenous in Vietnamese form, style, language, and meaning, not only at one point in time, but being so constantly in the present and the future. Such Christian faith must reflect God the Đạo at the fundamental and ontological level at all times. That faith then will meet the deepest needs of the Vietnamese and will penetrate their worldview of the One True and Only God, the Đạo who is the source of all things. The vision of a fully evangelical Vietnamese contextual community was the initial thought and driving force behind the present study. A strong hope, that the church of Christ in Vietnam, which is built on Christ and against which the gates of hell shall not prevail (Matt 16:18 ESV), will continually be the catalyst for spiritual awakening for the Vietnamese till the day of Christ's second coming.

APPENDIX

Inculturation vs Contextualization

The term "inculturation" has been preferred by some authors, predominantly used by Roman Catholic missiologists – see, for example, "inculturation" entry in Virginia Fabella and R. S. Sugirtharajah, eds., *Dictionary of Third World Theologies* (Maryknoll, NY: Orbis Books, 2000), 104–106, and several articles in Stephen B. Bevans, *Mission and Culture: The Louis J. Luzbetak Lectures*, American Society of Missiology Series 48 (Maryknoll, NY: Orbis Books, 2012). The term denotes:

1. the nature of mission as a process which combines "the theological principle of incarnation with the social-science concept of acculturation (adapting oneself to a culture)" in Robert J. Schreiter, *Constructing Local Theologies* (Maryknoll, NY: Orbis Books, 1985), 5;
2. mission as inculturation because "the church since its interception has always seen the scope of its mission as universal and all embracing. It entails crossing all human boundaries and meeting peoples of all cultures and religious traditions," in Francis Anekwe Oborji, *Concepts of Mission: The Evolution of Contemporary Missiology* (Maryknoll, NY: Orbis Books, 2006), 17–21;
3. inculturation as a model for the *insertion* of faith *into* culture, in Aylward Shorter, *Toward a Theology of Inculturation* (Maryknoll, NY: Orbis Books, 1989), 10–11;
4. *contextualization* as more superficial than *inculturation* and as allied to the idea of adaptation, in Gerald A. Arbuckle, *Earthing the Gospel: An Inculturation Handbook for Pastoral Workers* (Maryknoll, NY: Orbis Books, 1990), 21;

5. inculturation as "the whole process which leads to a synthesis between Christianity and national cultures," in Xiaochao Wang, *Christianity and Imperial Culture: Chinese Christian Apologetics in the Seventeenth Century and Their Latin Patristic Equivalent*, Studies in Christian Mission Series 20 (Leiden: Brill, 1998), 223;
6. as a variant of mission as contextualization, mission shifting from mission as accommodation to mission as inculturation for the question "Could a 'fourth self' be added to the classical 'three selfs' – self-theologizing?" in David Jacobus Bosch, *Transforming Mission: Paradigm Shifts in Theology of Mission*, American Society of Missiology Series 16 (Maryknoll, NY: Orbis Books, 1991), 447–457; Norman E. Thomas, *Classic Texts in Mission and World Christianity* (Maryknoll, NY: Orbis Books, 1995), 206–222.

The term "contextualization," however, is preferred in this book as the best way of describing the process of theologizing, because contextualization indicates "a shift of emphasis from the center to what had been considered the periphery and from the missionary to local church." The task of theologizing now becomes "more dialogical and less a matter of one-way applications." Stanley H. Skreslet, *Comprehending Mission: The Questions, Methods, Themes, Problems, and Prospects of Missiology*, American Society of Missiology Series 49 (Maryknoll, NY: Orbis Books, 2012), 88. Thus, *contextualization* has been widely supported by the Theological Education Fund in 1972, the Asian Bishops in 1979 (*FABC Newsletter*, April 1979) and can replace the older terminology, including *adaptation, indigenization, acculturation*, and *inculturation*. See Bosch, *Transforming Mission: Paradigm Shifts in Theology of Mission*, 420–432; Thomas, *Classic Texts in Mission*, 169–184; Stephen B. Bevans, *Models of Contextual Theology*, Faith and Cultures Series (Maryknoll, NY: Orbis Books, 1992), 26–27. For further discussion on "contextualization," see ch. 2: "Contextualization in Christian Mission Theology."

Bibliography

Aagaard, Johannes. "Some Main Trends in Modern Protestant Missiology." *Studia Theologica* 19, no. 1–2 (1965): 238–259.

———. "Trends in Missiological Thinking during the Sixties." *International Review of Mission* 62, no. 245 (1973): 8–25.

Ad Gentes. "Decree *Ad Gentes* on the Mission Activity of the Church." Edited by Pope Paul VI, 1964.

Adriano di Santa Thecla. *Opusculum de sectis apud Sinenses et Tunkinenses. A Small Treatise on the Sects among the Chinese and Tonkinese: A Study of Religion in China and North Vietnam in the Eighteenth Century.* Translated by Olga Dror. Ithaca, NY: Cornell-SEAP, 2002.

Anderson, David L. *The Columbia History of the Vietnam War.* New York: Columbia University Press, 2011.

Arbuckle, Gerald A. *Earthing the Gospel: An Inculturation Handbook for Pastoral Workers.* Maryknoll, NY: Orbis Books, 1990.

Ashford, Bruce Riley. *Theology and Practice of Mission: God, the Church, and the Nations.* Nashville, TN: B & H Academic, 2011.

Asselin, Pierre. *Hanoi's Road to the Vietnam War, 1954–1965: Series from Indochina to Vietnam 7.* Berkeley: University of California Press, 2013.

Association for Theological Education in South East Asia. "Guidelines for Doing Theologies in Asia." *International Bulletin of Missionary Research* 32, no. 2 (2008): 77–80.

Asia Theological Association. "The Bible and Theology in Asia Today: Declaration of the Sixth Asia Theological Association Theological Consultation, 1982." In *The Bible and Theology in Asian Contexts: An Evangelical Perspective on Asian Theology*, edited by Bong Rin Ro and Ruth Marie Eshenaur, 3–20. Taichung, Taiwan, ROC: Asia Theological Association, 1982.

Athyal, Saphir P. *Church in Asia Today: Challenges and Opportunities.* Singapore: Asia Lausanne Committee for World Evangelization, 1996.

Barth, Karl. *Church Dogmatics.* Vol. 4. Edinburgh: T & T Clark, 1957.

Baubérot, Jean, and Valentine Zuber. *Une haine oubliée: L'anti-protestantisme avant le "pacte laïque" (1870–1905)* [A forgotten hatred: Anti-Protestantism before the "Secular Pact" (1870–1905)]. Paris: Albin Michel, 2000.

Beaver, Pierce R. "The Legacy of Rufus Anderson." *Occasional Bulletin of Missions Research* 3, no. 3 (1977): 94–97.

Bebbington, David. *Evangelicalism in Modern Britain: A History from the 1730s to the 1980s*. London: Unwin Hyman, 1989.

Bettray, Johannes P. *Die Akkommodationsmethode des P. Matteo Ricci S. I. in China*. Romae: Apud aedes Universitatis Gregorianae, 1955.

Bevans, Stephen B. *Mission and Culture: The Louis J. Luzbetak Lectures*. The American Society of Missiology Series 48. Maryknoll, NY: Orbis Books, 2012.

———. *Models of Contextual Theology*. Maryknoll, NY: Orbis Books, 2002.

———. *Models of Contextual Theology*. Faith and Cultures Series. Maryknoll, NY: Orbis Books, 1992.

Bevans, Stephen B., and Roger Schroeder. *Constants in Context: A Theology of Mission for Today*. Maryknoll, NY: Orbis Books, 2004.

Bock, Darrell L. *Jesus According to Scripture: Restoring the Portrait from the Gospels*. Grand Rapids, MI: Baker Academic, 2002.

Bock, Darrell L., and Benjamin I. Simpson. *Jesus the God-Man: The Unity and Diversity of the Gospel Portrayals*. Grand Rapids, MI: Baker Academic, 2016.

Bois, Georges. "Eglises et Missions Protestantes d'Indocine (de 1949 à 1951)." *Journal des Missions Évangéliques* 5, no. 23 (1952): 122–131.

———. *Histoire des Missions en Indochine et les Protestants Francais*. Villeneuve-les-Avignon: Manuscrits, 1952.

———. "Les Resultats de L'Enquete Missionnaire en Indochine" [The results of missionary inquiry in Indochina). Archives of Société des Missions Evangéliques des Paris (SMEP/ Défap), 1924.

Bokenkamp, Stephen R., and Peter S. Nickerson. *Early Daoist Scriptures*. Taoist Classics. Berkeley: University of California Press, 1999.

Bonk, Jonathan J. "The Defender of the Good News: Questioning Lamin Sanneh." *Christianity Today*, October 2003.

Bosch, David Jacobus. *Transforming Mission: Paradigm Shifts in Theology of Mission*. American Society of Missiology Series 16. Maryknoll, NY: Orbis Books, 1991.

Bourdeaux, Pascal. "Notes on an Unpublished Letter by Hồ Chí Minh to a French Pastor (8 September 1921) or the Art of Dissenting Evangelization." *Journal of Vietnamese Studies* 7, no. 2 (2012): 8–28.

Brereton, Virginia Lieson. "Protestant Fundamentalist Bible Schools, 1882–1940." PhD diss., Columbia University, 1984.

Brocheux, Pierre, and Daniel Hémery. *Indochina: An Ambiguous Colonization, 1858–1954.* Translated by Ly Lan Dill-Klein, with Eric Jennings, Nora Taylor and Noémi Tousignant. Berkeley, CA: University of California Press, 2009.

Brown, Arthur J. "Lao Expansion No. 79." Archives of Société des Missions Evangéliques des Paris (SMEP/ Défap), 1912.

Bujo, Bénézet. *African Theology in Its Social Context.* Translated by John O'Donohue. Faith and Cultures Series. Eugene, OR: Wipf & Stock, 2006.

Cadière, Léopold. *Croyances et pratiques religieuses des Viêtnamiens.* Vol. 3. Paris: Ecole Française d'Extrême-Orient, 1957.

———. *Croyances et pratiques religieuses des Viêtnamiens.* Vol. 1. Hanoi: Impremerie d'Etrême Orient, 1944.

———. *Croyances et pratiques religieuses des Viêtnamiens.* Vol. 2. Saigon, Paris: Ecole Française d'Extrême-Orient, 1955.

Cadman, William C. "Letters to U. Soulier." *Mission Évangélique de L'Indo-Chine Francaise-CMA (Hanoi, Tonkin): Archives of La Société des Missions Evangéliques des Paris (SMEP/ Défap), Apr 5, Apr 25, and Apr 28, 1923.*

Cao Huy Thuan. "Christianisme et Colonialisme au Vietnam (1857–1914)." Diss., Universite of D' Amiens; the Centre de Relations Internationales et de Science Politique, 1969.

Cartmel, Daryl Westmood. "Mission Policy and Program of A. B. Simpson." MA Thesis, Hartford Seminary Foundation, 1962.

Chan, Simon. "Asian Christian Spirituality in Primal Religious Contexts." In *Walking with God: Christian Spirituality in the Asian Context*, edited by Charles Ringma, 32–52. Manila, Philippines: OMF Literature, Asian Theological Seminary, 2014.

———. *Grassroots Asian Theology: Thinking the Faith from the Ground Up.* Downers Grove, IL: IVP Acadamic, 2014.

———. "The Problem of Transcendence and Immanence in Asian Contextual Theology." *Trinity Theological Journal* 8 (1999): 5–18.

Chan, Wing-tsit. "The Natural Way of Lao Tzu." In *A Source Book in Chinese Philosophy*, edited by Wing-tsit Chan, 136–176. Princeton, NJ: Princeton University Press, 1963.

———, ed. *A Source Book in Chinese Philosophy.* Princeton, NJ: Princeton University Press, 1963.

———. "Spiritual Dimensions: The Doctrine of the Mean." In *A Source Book in Chinese Philosophy*, edited by Wing-tsit Chan, 95–114. Princeton, NJ: Princeton University Press, 1963.

Chang, Carsun. *The Development of Neo-Confucian Thought.* London: Vision Press, 1958.

Chapman, Jessica M. *Cauldron of Resistance: Ngo Dinh Diem, the United States, and 1950s Southern Vietnam.* Ithaca, NY: Cornell University Press, 2013.

Chen, I-Hsin. "Connecting Protestantism to Ruism: Religion, Dialogism and Intertextuality in James Legge's Translation of the Lunyu." PhD diss., University of Manchester, 2014.

Ching, Julia. *Confucianism and Christianity: A Comparative Study*. Tokyo: Kodansha International, 1977.

———. *To Acquire Wisdom: The Way of Wang Yang-ming*. Studies in Oriental Culture 11; Oriental Monograph Series 16. New York: Columbia University Press, 1976.

Christie, Clive J. *Southeast Asia in the Twentieth Century: A Reader*. London: Tauris, 1998.

Chuang-tzu. *Wandering on the Way: Early Taoist Tales and Parables of Chuang Tzu*. Translated by Victor H. Mair. Honolulu: University of Hawaii Press, 1998.

Chuang, Tsu-Kung. "Shangdi: God from the Chinese Perspective." In *The Global God: Multicultural Evangelical Views of God*, edited by Aída Besançon Spencer and William David Spencer, 189–206. Grand Rapids, MI: Baker Books, 1998.

Chung, Paul S. *Constructing Irregular Theology: Bamboo and Minjung in East Asian Perspective*. Studies in Systematic Theology 1. Leiden: Brill, 2009.

———. "The Mystery of God and Tao in Jewish-Christian-Taoist Context." In *Asian Contextual Theology for the Third Millenium: Theology of Minjung in Fourth-Eye Formation*, edited by Paul S. Chung, Kyoung-Jae Kim and Veli-Matti Kärkkäinen, 243–266. Eugene, OR: Wipf & Stock, 2007.

Clark, Allen D. *A History of the Church in Korea*. Seoul: Christian Literature Society of Korea, 1971.

Coe, Shoki. "Contextualizing Theology." In *Third World Theologies*, edited by Gerald H. Anderson and Thomas F. Stransky, 19–24. New York: Paulist Press, 1976.

Collins Winn, Christian T., ed. *From the Margins: A Celebration of the Theological Work of Donald W. Dayton*. Eugene, OR: Pickwick, 2007.

Confucius. *Analects*. Translated by David Hinton. Berkeley: Counterpoint, 2014.

———. *The Analects of Confucius*. Translated by Arthur Waley. London: Allen & Unwin, 1956.

———. *The Analects of Confucius: A Philosophical Translation*. Translated by Roger T. Ames and Henry Rosemont. Classics of Ancient China. New York: Ballantine Books, 1999.

Conn, Harvie M., Manuel Ortiz, and Susan S. Baker, eds. *The Urban Face of Mission: Ministering the Gospel in a Diverse and Changing World*. Phillipsburg, NJ: P&R, 2002.

Cook, Matthew, and Rob Haskell, eds. *Local Theology for the Global Church: Principles for an Evangelical Approach to Contextualization*. Pasadena: World Evangelical Alliance Theological Commission, 2010.

Corrie, John, Samuel Escobar, and Wilbert R. Shenk, eds. *Dictionary of Mission Theology: Evangelical Foundations*. Downers Grove, IL: InterVarsity Press, 2007.

Costa, Ruy O. *One Faith, Many Cultures: Inculturation, Indigenization, and Contextualization*. Maryknoll, NY: Orbis Books, 1988.

Dai Nam thuc luc. [The Veritable Records of Dai Nam]. Translated by Nguyễn Ngọc Tỉnh. vol. 10. Hà Nội: Nxb Khoa Học Xã Hội, 2004.

Damascene, Hieromonk. *Christ the Eternal Tao*. 3rd ed. Platina, CA: Valaam Books, 2002.

Đặng, Ngọc Phúc. *Những người Tin Lành tại Việt Nam trong giai đoạn thăm dò* [Protestant Christians in Vietnam in the exploratory period]. San Diego, CA: unpublished book, 2011.

Đặng, Thế Đại. "Tính đặc sắc Nam bộ và truyền thống văn hóa Việt Nam qua một dòng tôn giáo." [Southern characteristics and Vietnamese traditional cultures through a religious practice]. *Tạp Chí Nghiên Cứu Tôn Giáo* 58, no. 4 (April 2008), 43–52.

Đào Duy Anh. *Việt Nam văn hóa sử cương* [An outline of Vietnamese culture]. Hà Nội: Nxb Văn học, 2010.

Delisle, Philippe. *L'anticléricalisme dans les colonies françaises sous la Troisième République* [Anticlericalism in the French Colonies under the third republic]. Paris: Les Indes Savantes, 2008.

Đinh Khắc Thuân. "Contribution à l'histoire de la Mac (1527–1592) du Viet Nam" [Contribution to the history of the Mac (1527–1592) of Vietnam]. Doctoral dissertation, Ecole des hautes études en sciences sociales, 2000.

———. *Văn Bia Thời Mạc* [Stele inscriptions of the Mac period]. Hà Nội: Nxb Khoa học Xã hội, 1996.

Ditchfield, Simon. "The Jesuits: In the Making of a World Religion." *History Today* 57, no. 7 (2007): 52–59.

Đỗ Hữu Nghiêm. *Lịch sử giáo hội Tin Lành Việt cận đại* [History of the contemporary Evangelical Church of Vietnam]. Unpublished manuscript, 2010.

———. "Phương pháp truyền giáo của Tin Lành giáo tại Việt Nam" [Mission methodology of Protestant religion in Vietnam]. MA Thesis, s.n., 1968.

Đỗ, Quang Chính. *Lịch sử chữ Quốc Ngữ 1620–1659* [History of Quoc Ngu writing, 1620–1659]. Hà Nội: Nxb Tôn giáo, 2008.

Đỗ, Quang Chính, and Văn Hậu Nguyễn. *Hoà mình vào xã hội Việt Nam* [Inculturating into the Vietnamesese culture and soceity]. Hà Nội: Nxb Tôn giáo, 2008.

Đỗ, Quang Hưng. "Đạo Tin Lành ở Việt Nam: Một cái nhìn tổng quát" [Protestantism in Vietnam: An overview]. Ban Tôn giáo Chính phủ (Government Committee for Religious Affairs). Accessed 27 August

2019, http://btgcp.gov.vn/Plus.aspx/vi/News/38/0/240/0/1395/Dao_Tin_lanh_o_Viet_Nam_mot_cai_nhin_tong_quat.

Đoàn Triệu Long. "Đạo Tin Lành buổi đầu vào Việt Nam" [Beginning of evangelicalism in Vietnam]. *Nghiên Cứu Tôn Giáo* 1 (2012): 43–49.

Dutton, George E., Jayne S. Werner, and John K. Whitmore. *Sources of Vietnamese Tradition*. New York: Columbia University Press, 2012.

Dyrness, William A., and Veli-Matti Kärkkäinen, eds. *Global Dictionary of Theology: A Resource for the Worldwide Church*. Downers Grove, IL: IVP Academic, 2008.

Encrevé, A. *Les Protestants en France de 1800 À Nos Jours* (Protestants in France from 1800 to today). Paris: Stock, 1985.

England, John C. *Asian Christian Theologies: A Research Guide to Authors, Movements, Sources*. 3 vols. Delhi: ISPCK, 2002–2004.

Eusebius. *Historia Ecclesiastica*. Turnhout: Brepols Publishers, 2010.

———. *History of the Church*. Translated by Rufinus of Aquileia and Philip R. Amidon. The Fathers of the Church: A New Translation 133. Washington, DC: Catholic University of America Press, 2016.

Fabella, Virginia, and R. S. Sugirtharajah, eds. *Dictionary of Third World Theologies*. Maryknoll, NY: Orbis Books, 2000.

Federation of Asian Bishops' Conferences Plenary Assembly. *FABC at Forty Years: Responding to the Challenges of Asia: A New Evangelization*. Vol. 2014. FABC Plenary Assemblies Series 12/8. Xuan Loc & Hồ Chí Minh City: FABC, 2012.

Flemming, Dean E. *Contextualization in the New Testament: Patterns for Theology and Mission*. Downers Grove, IL: InterVarsity Press, 2005.

Flett, John G. *The Witness of God: The Trinity, Missio Dei, Karl Barth, and the Nature of Christian Community*. Grand Rapids, MI: Eerdmans, 2010.

Freeman, J. H. "Letters to A. Boegner on July 27, 1911 and March 12, 1912." Lampoon, Siam: Archives of Société des Missions Evangéliques des Paris (SMEP/ Défap).

Funk, A. E. "The Need of Annam: Annual Report May 1908." In *The Christian and Missionary Alliance in Indo-China (1925–1930)*, John S. Sawin. Unpublished manuscript.

Gilliland, Dean S. "Contextual Theology as Incarnational Mission." In *The Word among Us: Contextualizing Theology for Mission Today*, edited by Dean S. Gilliland, 10–11. Dallas, TX: Word, 1989.

———. "Contextualization." In *Evangelical Dictionary of World Missions*, edited by A. Scott Moreau, Harold A. Netland, Charles Edward Van Engen and David Burnett, 225–228. Grand Rapids, MI: Baker Books, 2000.

———, ed. *The Word among Us: Contextualizing Theology for Mission Today*. Dallas, TX: Word, 1989.

Gnanakan, Ken. *Kingdom Concerns: A Biblical Exploration towards a Theology of Mission*. Bangalore, India: Theological Book Trust, 1989.

———. *Proclaiming Christ in a Pluralistic Context*. Bangalore: Theological Book Trust, 2002.

———. "Some Insight into Indian Christian Theology." In *Global Theology in Evangelical Perspective: Exploring the Contextual Nature of Theology and Mission*, edited by Jeffrey P. Greenman and Gene L. Green, 116–132. Downers Grove, IL: IVP Academic, 2012.

Gorospe, Adonis Abelard O. "Spirituality and Christianity." In *The Gospel in Culture: Contextualization Issues through Asian Eyes*, edited by Melba Padilla Maggay. Manila: OMF Literature and Institute for Studies in Asian Church and Culture, 2013.

Hammer, Olav, and Mikael Rothstein. *Handbook of the Theosophical Current: Brill Handbooks on Contemporary Religion*. Leiden, Boston: Brill, 2013.

He, Jianming. "Dialogue between Christianity and Taoism: The Case of Lin Yutang." In *Christianity and Chinese Culture*, edited by Miikka Ruokanen, Baoluo Huang and Paulos Zhanzhu Huang. Grand Rapids, MI: Eerdmans, 2010.

Herendeen, Dale Sims. *Conversion and Indigeneity in the Evangelical Church of Viet Nam*. Pasadena, CA: Fuller Theological Seminary, 1975.

Hesselgrave, David J., and Edward Rommen. *Contextualization: Meanings, Methods, and Models*. Grand Rapids, MI: Baker, 1989.

Hesselgrave, David J., and Ed Stetzer, eds. *Missionshift: Global Mission Issues in the Third Millennium*. Nashville, TN: B&H Academic, 2010.

Hiebert, Paul G. *Anthropological Insights for Missionaries*. Grand Rapids, MI: Baker Book House, 1985.

———. "Critical Contextualization." *International Bulletin of Missionary Research* 11, no. 3 (July 1987): 104–112.

———. *The Gospel in Human Contexts: Anthropological Explorations for Contemporary Missions*. Grand Rapids, MI: Baker Academic, 2009.

———. "The Gospel in Human Contexts: Changing Perceptions of Contextualization." In *Missionshift: Global Mission Issues in the Third Millennium*, edited by David J. Hesselgrave and Ed Stetzer, 84–99. Nashville, TN: B&H Academic, 2010.

———. "Syncretism and Social Paradigm." In *Contextualization and Syncretism: Navigating Cultural Currents*, edited by Gailyn Van Rheenen. Pasadena, CA: William Carey Library, 2006.

Hippolytus. *The Apostolic Tradition of Hippolytus (with Introduction and Notes)*. Translated by Burton Scott Easton. Cambridge: Cambridge University Press, 1934.

Hồ, Chí Minh. "Unpublished Letter by Hồ Chí Minh to a French Pastor (8 September 1921)." Translated by Kareem James Abu-Zeid, *Journal of Vietnamese Studies* 7, no. 2 (2012): 1–7.

———. *Hồ Chí Minh: Selected Works*. Vol. 3. Hanoi: Foreign Languages Publishing House, 1961.

———. *Hồ Chí Minh: Selected Works*. Vol. 1. Hanoi: Foreign Languages Publishing House, 1960.

Hội Thánh Tin Lành Việt Nam. *Constitution of the Evangelical Church of Vietnam* [Điều Lệ của Hội Thánh Tin Lành Việt Nam]. The 1956's amended text ed. Saigon: Nhà in Tin-Lành, 1958.

Hoskins, Janet Alison. *The Divine Eye and the Diaspora: Vietnamese Syncretism Becomes Transpacific Caodaism*. Honolulu, HI: University of Hawaii Press, 2015.

———. "An Unjealous God? Christian Elements in a Vietnamese Syncretistic Religion." *Current Anthropology* 55, no. S10 (2014): S302–S311.

Hosler, Paul M. "The Dawn of Protestant Missions in Annam." *The Alliance Witness* (2 December 1911).

Hosler, Paul M., and G. L. Hughes. "The South China Alliance Tidings." (August 1911): 3.

Huang, Po Ho. "Contextualization of Theological Education in South East Asia – Challenges and Responses: A Case Study of South East Asia Graduate School of Theology." *IV International WOCATI Congress and Jubilee of the ETE of WCC* (2008).

Hue-Tam Ho Tai. *Radicalism and the Origins of the Vietnamese Revolution*. Cambridge, MA: Harvard University Press, 1992.

Huệ Khải. *The Emergence of Caodaism in Cochinchina*. Hồ Chí Minh City: Cơ quan Phổ thông Giáo lý Đại Đạo; Nxb Tôn giáo, 2008.

———. *Lược Sử Đạo Cao Đài: Khai Minh Đại Đạo 1926* [A concise Cao Dai history: The 1926 inauguration]. Hà Nội: Nxb Tôn giáo, 2015.

Hughes, Lloyd G. "Anam the Neglected." *The Alliance Witness* (January & February 1904).

———. "Letter to A. Boegner on Sep. 19, 1910." CMA Headquarters, Wuchow, South China: Archives of Société des Missions Evangéliques des Paris (SMEP/Défap), 1910.

———. "A Momentous Crisis in the Quest of Annam." *The Alliance Witness* (26 August 1911).

———. "A Personal Letter." *The Christian and Missionary Alliance* (7 July 1906).

Hugo, Victor. *Conversations with Eternity: The Forgotten Masterpiece of Victor Hugo*. Translated by John Chambers. 1st ed. Boca Raton, FL: New Paradigm Books, 1998.

———. *Victor Hugo's Conversations with the Spirit World: A Literary Genius's Hidden Life*. Translated by John Chambers. Rev. and expanded 2nd ed. Rochester, VT: Destiny Books, 2008.

Hume, Robert Ernest. *The World's Living Religions: With Special Reference to Their Sacred Scriptures and in Comparison with Christianity: An Historical Sketch*. New York: Scribner's Sons, 1959.

Huỳnh, Kim Khánh. *Vietnamese Communism, 1925–1945*. Ithaca, NY: Cornell University Press, 1982 (published under the auspices of the Institute of Southeast Asian Studies, Singapore).

Hwa, Yung. *Mangoes or Bananas?: The Quest for an Authentic Asian Christian Theology*. Oxford: Regnum, 1997.

———. "Theology and Mission in the Asian Church." DMiss diss., Asbury Theological Seminary, 1995.

Irvin, Dale T., and Scott W. Sunquist. *History of the World Christian Movement. vol. II: Modern Christianity from 1954–1800*. Maryknoll, NY: Orbis Books, 2012.

Irwin, Edwin Franklin. *With Christ in Indo-China: The Story of Alliance Missions in French Indo-China and Eastern Siam*. Harrisburg, PA: Christian Publication, 1937.

Jaffray, Robert A. "Vietnam." *Christian Alliance* (July 1899).

———. "The 'Lostness' of the People of Indo-China." *Alliance Magazine* (10 April 1908): 22f.

———. "The Annual Report for 1905." *Alliance Magazine* (1906).

———. "The Indo-China Mission for 1916." *The Alliance Weekly* (23 June 1917).

———. "A Plea for the Perishing of South China and Annam." *The Christian and Missionary Alliance* 33, no. 4 (23 October 1909).

———. "Report of the Indo-China Mission, 1916." *The Alliance Witness* (23 June 1917).

———. "To Dr. Simpson (10 February)." *Christian Alliance* (May 1899).

James, Violet B. "American Protestant Missions and the Vietnam War." PhD diss., University of Aberdeen, 1989.

Jebens, Holger. *Cargo, Cult, and Culture Critique*. Honolulu, HI: University of Hawaii Press, 2004.

Ji, Jingyi. *Encounters between Chinese Culture and Christianity: A Hermeneutical Perspective* (includes summary in Dutch on pp. 221–226). Münster: Lit Verlag, 2007.

Joseph Dinh Duc Dao. "The Christian Formation of the Laity and Lay Missionary Efforts in Asia." In *Proclaiming Jesus Christ in Asia Today*, edited by Pontificium Consilium Pro Laicis, 85–109. Rome: Libreria Editrice Vaticana-Vatican Press, 2010.

Kärkkäinen, Veli-Matti. "The Calling of the Whole People of God into Ministry: The Spirit, Church and Laity." *Studia Theologica* 54, no. 2 (2000): 144–162.

———. *Christ and Reconciliation: A Constructive Christian Theology for the Pluralistic World*. Vol. 1. Grand Rapids, MI: Eerdmans, 2013.

———. *An Introduction to Ecclesiology: Ecumenical, Historical & Global Perspectives*. Downers Grove, IL: InterVarsity Press, 2002.

Keith, Charles Patrick. *Catholic Vietnam: A Church from Empire to Nation*. Berkeley, CA: University of California Press, 2012.

———. "Catholic Vietnam: Church, Colonialism and Revolution, 1887–1945." PhD diss., Yale University, 2008.

———. "Protestantism and the Politics of Religion in French Colonial Vietnam." *French Colonial History* 13 (2012): 141–174.

Kim, Heup Yong (Hub-yong). "Ancestor Veneration and Christianity in Asia." In *The Cambridge Dictionary of Christianity*, edited by Daniel Patte, 32. Cambridge, MA: Cambridge University Press, 2010.

———. "An Asian Journey Seeking Christian Wholeness: Owning Up to Our Own Metaphors (Theotao)." In *Asian and Oceanic Christianities in Conversation: Exploring Theological Identities at Home and in Diaspora*, edited by Heup Yong Kim, Fumitaka Matsuoka and Anri Morimoto, 25–38. Studies in World Christianity and Interreligious Relations 47. Amsterdam; New York: Editions Rodopi, 2011.

———. *Christ & the Tao*. Hong Kong: Christian Conference of Asia, 2003.

———. "Life, Ecology, and Theo-tao: Towards a Life Theology of Theanthropocosmic Tao." *Madang: International Journal of Contextual Theology in East Asia* 11 (2009): 75–94.

———. *A Theology of Dao*. Ecology and Justice Series. Maryknoll, NY: Orbis Books, 2017.

———. *Wang Yang-ming and Karl Barth: A Confucian-Christian Dialogue*. Lanham, MD: University Press of America, 1996.

Kim, Kirsteen. *The Holy Spirit in the World: A Global Conversation*. Maryknoll, NY: Orbis Books, 2007.

Kohn, Livia. *Introducing Daoism*. State College, PA: Journal of Buddhist Ethics Online Books, 2008. http://worldreligionsbooks.com/eBooks/daoism/.

Koontz, Gayle Gerber, and Andy Alexis-Baker, eds. *Theology of Mission: A Believers Church Perspective*. Downers Grove, IL: InterVarsity Press, 2014.

Koyama, Kosuke. *No Handle on the Cross: An Asian Meditation on the Crucified Mind*. Maryknoll, NY: Orbis Books, 1977.

Kraft, Charles H., ed. *Appropriate Christianity*. Pasadena, CA: William Carey Library, 2005.

———. "The Development of Contextualization Theory in Euroamerican Missiology." In *Appropriate Christianity*, edited by Charles H. Kraft, 15–34. Pasadena, CA: William Carey Library, 2005.

———. "Is Christianity a Religion or a Faith?" In *Appropriate Christianity*, edited by Charles H. Kraft, 83–98. Pasadena, CA: William Carey Library, 2005.
———. "Why Appropriate?" In *Appropriate Christianity*, edited by Charles H. Kraft, 3–14. Pasadena, CA: William Carey Library, 2005.
Küng, Hans, and Julia Ching. *Christianity and Chinese Religions*. New York: Doubleday, 1989.
Kwan, Simon S. M. "From Indigenization to Contextualization: A Change in Discursive Pratice Rather than a Shift in Paradigm." *Studies in World Christianity* 11, no. 2 (2005): 236–250.
Landon, Kenneth Perry. "Nationalism in Southeastern Asia." *The Far Eastern Quarterly (pre-1986)* 2, no. 2 (1943): 139–152.
Lao Tse. *Tao Te Ching, or, the Tao and Its Characteristics*. Translated by James Legge. Auckland, NZ: Floating Press, 2008.
———. *The Wisdom of Laotse*. Translated by Lin Yutang. New York: Modern Library, 1948.
Latourette, Kenneth Scott. *A History of Christianity*. 1st ed. New York: Harper& Row, 1953.
Lê, Hoàng Phu. "A Short History of the Evangelical Church of Viet Nam (1911–1965)." PhD diss., New York University, 1972.
Lê, Văn Thái. *Bốn mươi sáu năm chức vụ (Hồi ký)* [Forty-six years in ministry: Memoir]. Sài Gòn: Nhà In Tin-Lành, 1970.
Le, Vince. "The Pentecostal Movement in Vietnam." In *Global Renewal Christianity: Spirit-Empowered Movement Past, Present, and Future, Vol. 1: Asia and Oceania*, edited by Vinson Synan and Amos Yong, 181–195. Lake Mary, FL: Charisma House, 2016.
Lee, Jung Young, ed. *Ancestor Worship and Christianity in Korea*. Studies in Asian Though and Religion 8. Lewiston, NY: E. Mellen, 1988.
———. *The Theology of Change: A Christian Concept of God in an Eastern Perspective*. Maryknoll, NY: Orbis Books, 1979.
———. *The Trinity in Asian Perspective*. Nashville, TN: Abingdon, 1996.
Legge, James. *The Notions of the Chinese Concerning God and Spirits: With an Examination of the Defense of an Essay, on the Proper Rendering of the Words* Elohim *and* Theos *into the Chinese Language*. Edited by William J. Boone. Hong kong, 1852. https://archive.org/details/notionsofchinese00legg/page/n4.
———. *The Sacred Books of China: The Texts of Taoism*. Vol. 1. Series part 1. New York: Dover Publications, 1962.
Liao, David. "Christian Alternatives to Ancestor Worship in Taiwan." In *Christian Alternatives to Ancestor Practices*, edited by Bong Rin Ro, 209–218. Taichung, Taiwan, ROC: Asia Theological Association, 1985.
Littlejohn, Ronnie L. *Daoism: An Introduction*. London: I. B. Tauris, 2009.

Lossky, Vladimir. *Orthodox Theology: An Introduction.* Translated by Ian and Ihita Kesarcodi-Watson. Crestwood, NY: St Vladimir's Seminary Press, 1989.

Lossky, Vladimir, John H. Erickson, and Thomas E. Bird. *In the Image and Likeness of God.* Crestwook, NY: St Vladimir's Seminary Press, 1985.

Lundström, Klas. "Gospel and Culture in the World Council of Churches and the Lausanne Movement with Particular Focus on the Period 1973–1996." Doctoral diss., Svenska Institutet för Missionsforskning, 2006.

Lutheran World Federation. "Together in God's Mission: An LWF Contribution to the Understanding of Mission." Geneva: Lutheran World Federation, 1988.

Lưu Hồng Khanh. *Lão Tử Đạo Đức Kinh.* Hồ Chí Minh City: Nxb Trẻ, 2005.

Luzbetak, Louis J. *The Church and Cultures: New Perspectives in Missiological Anthropology.* American Society of Missiology Series 12. Maryknoll, NY: Orbis Books, 1988.

Lý Tế Xuyên. *Departed Spirits of the Viet Realm* [Việt Điện U Linh Tập]. Translated by Brian E. Ostrowski and Brian A. Zottoli. Southeast Asia Program. Ithaca, NY: Cornell University, 1999.

MacIlvaine, Rodman W. "What Is the Missional Church Movement?" *Bibliotheca sacra* 167, no. 665 (2010): 89–106.

Marr, David G. *Vietnamese Tradition on Trial, 1920–1945.* Berkeley, CA: University of California Press, 1981.

Marsden, George M. *Evangelicalism and Modern America.* Grand Rapids, MI: Eerdmans, 1984.

Martin, Luke S. *An Evaluation of a Generation of Mennonite Mission, Service and Peacemaking in Vietnam 1954–1976: Vietnam Study Project.* Akron, PA: Mennonite Central Committee, 1977.

McGrath, Alister E. *A Passion for Truth: The Intellectual Coherence of Evangelicalism.* Downers Grove, IL: InterVarsity Press, 1996.

Mcgraw, Gerald E. "A. B. Simpson 1843–1919: From Home Missions to a World Missionary Movement." In *Mission Legacies: Biographical Studies of Leaders of the Modern Missionary Movement,* edited by Gerald H. Anderson, 37–47. American Society of Missiology Series 19. Maryknoll, NY: Orbis Books, 1994.

———. "The Doctrine of Sanctification in the Published Writing of Albert Benjamin Simpson." PhD diss., New York University, 1986.

Mejudhon, Ubolwan. "The Way of Meekness: Being Christian and Thai in the Thai Way." DMiss diss., Asbury Theological Seminary, 1998.

Minamiki, George. *The Chinese Rites Controversy from Its Beginning to Modern Times.* Chicago, IL: Loyola University Press, 1985.

Miyamoto, Ken Christoph. *God's Mission in Asia: A Comparative and Contextual Study of This-Worldly Holiness and the Theology of Missio Dei in M. M. Thomas and C. S. Song.* American Society of Missiology Monograph Series 1. Eugene, OR: Pickwick, 2007.

Moffett, Samuel H. *A History of Christianity in Asia, Vol. 2, 1500 to 1900*. Maryknoll, NY: Orbis Books, 1998.

Moreau, A. Scott. *Contextualization in World Missions: Mapping and Assessing Evangelical Models*. Grand Rapids, MI: Kregel Academic, 2012.

———. "Syncretism." In *Evangelical Dictionary of World Missions*, edited by A. Scott Moreau, Harold A. Netland, Charles Edward Van Engen and David Burnett, 924–925. Grand Rapids, MI: Baker, 2000.

Munro, Donald J. *The Concept of Man in Early China*. Michigan Classics in Chinese Studies 6. Ann Arbor, MI: Center for Chinese Studies, University of Michigan, 2001.

Neill, Stephen C. *Creative Tension*. London: Edinburgh House Press, 1959.

———. *A History of Christian Missions*. Pelican History of the Church 6. Harmondsworth: Penguin Books, 1966.

Newbigin, Lesslie. *The Gospel in a Pluralist Society*. Grand Rapids, MI: Eerdmans, 1989.

———. *Trinitarian Faith and Today's Mission*. Richmond, VA: John Knox, 1964.

Ng, Peter Tze Ming. *Chinese Christianity: An Interplay between Global and Local Perspectives*. Religion in Chinese Societies 4. Edited by Kenneth Dean, Richard Madsen and David Palmer. Leiden: Brill, 2012.

Ngô, Sĩ Liên. *Đại Việt sử ký toàn thư* [Complete book of the historical records of great Viet]. Hà Nội: Viện Khoa học Xã hội Việt Nam, 1993.

Nguyen, Ai Quoc. *Le procès de la colonisation francaise* [The process of French colonization]. Paris: Imprimerie et Librairie du Travail, Première Série, Mœurs Coloniales, 1926.

Nguyễn, Ái Quốc. "Monsieur le Pasteur" [To the pastor]. Paris: Archives of Société des Missions Evangéliques des Paris (SMEP/ Défap), 8 September 1921.

Nguyễn, Cao Thanh. "Đạo Tin Lành ở Việt Nam từ 1975 đến nay, tư liệu và một số đánh giá ban đầu" [The evangelicalism in Vietnam from 1975 to the present, sources and initial comments]. *Ban Tôn giáo Chính phủ*. Accessed 29 November 2014, http://btgcp.gov.vn/Plus.aspx/vi/News/38/0/240/0/2737/Dao_Tin_lanh_o_Viet_Nam_tu_1975_den_nay_tu_lieu_va_mot_so_danh_gia_ban_dau.

Nguyễn, Đăng Trúc. *Đạo làm người (La Culture et le Sens De'l Humanite de L'homme),* [in Vietnamese and French]. Reichstrett, France: Định Hướng Tùng Thư, 2012.

Nguyễn, Du. *The Tale of Kieu: A Bilingual Edition of Truyen Kieu*. Translated by Huỳnh Sanh Thông. New Haven, CT: Yale University Press, 1983.

Nguyễn, Dữ. *Truyền kỳ mạn lục* [Collection of strange tales]. Translated by Trúc Khê and Ngô Văn Triện. Hồ Chí Minh City: Nxb Trẻ & Nxb Hồng Bàng, 1768.

Nguyen, Joseph Huy Lai. *La tradition religieuse spirituelle et sociale au Vietnam: sa Confrontation avec le Christianisme*. Beauchesne religions 11. Paris: Beauchesne, 1981.

Nguyen, KimSon. "The Catholic Church in Vietnam: An Example of Contextualization." *Asia Journal of Theology* 29, no. 1 (2015): 74–87.

———. "Grassroots Asian Theology: Thinking the Faith from the Ground Up." *International Bulletin of Missionary Research* 39, no. 1 (2015): 46.

———. "Mission History of Vietnamese Evangelicalism in the Pioneering Stage: A Vietnamese Perspective." *Journal of Asian Mission* 16, no. 2 (October 2015): 51–67.

Nguyen, Le Quynh-Hoa. "Tin Lanh: The Bible and the Construction of an Evangelical Vietnamese Christian Identity (1975–2007)." PhD diss., Claremont Graduate University, 2013.

Nguyen, Nam. "Writing as Response and as Translation: 'Jiandeng Xinhua' and the Evolution of the Chuanqi Genre in East Asia, Particularly in Vietnam." PhD diss., Harvard University, 2005.

———. "Being Confucian in Sixteenth-Century Vietnam: Reading Stele Inscriptions from the Mac Dynasty." In *Confucianism in Vietnam*, 139–157. Hồ Chí Minh City: Vietnam National University and Hồ Chí Minh City Publishing House, 2002.

Nguyễn, Ngọc Thơ. "Văn Hoá Bách Việt Vùng Lĩnh Nam Trong Quan Hệ Với Văn Hoá Truyền Thống Ở Việt Nam" [Bach Viet Culture of the Linh Nam in the Relation with Traditional Culture in Vietnam]. Luận Án Tiến Sĩ Văn Hoá Học, Doctoral diss., Ho Chi Minh City University of Social Sciences and Humanities, 2011.

Nguyễn, Tài Thư. "'Tam Giáo Đồng Nguyên': Hiện Tượng Tư Tưởng Chung của Các Nước Đông Á" [Unified source of the Three Teachings: A common ideological phenomenon of East Asian countries]. *Tạp Chí Hán Nôm (Journal of Han-Nom Studies)* 3, no. 40 (1999): 11–17.

Nguyễn, Thế Nghi. *Tân biên truyền kỳ mạn lục: Tác phẩm Nôm thế kỷ XVI* [New version of Truyen Ky Man Luc: A Nom work of the sixteenth century]. Translated by Hoàng thị Hồng Cẩm. Hà Nội: Nxb Văn hoá Dân tộc, 2000.

Nguyen, Tu Cuong. *Zen in Medieval Vietnam: A Study and Translation of the Thien Uyen Tap Anh*. Honolulu: University of Hawai'i Press, 1997.

Nguyễn, Văn Kiệm. *Sự du nhập của đạo Thiên Chúa Giáo vào Việt Nam từ thế kỷ XVII đến thế kỷ XIX* [The arrival of Roman Catholicism in Vietnam from the 17th century to the 19th century]. Hà Nội: Hội Khoa học Lịch sử Việt Nam, 2001.

Nha Trang, Công Huyền Tôn Nữ. *Vietnamese Folklore: An Introductory and Annotated Bibliography*. Berkeley, CA: Center for South and Southeast Asia Studies, University of California, 1970.

Nicholls, Bruce J. "A Living Theology for Asian Churches: Some Reflections on the Contextualization-Syncretism Debate." In *The Bible and Theology in Asian Contexts: An Evangelical Perspective on Asian Theology*, edited by Bong Rin Ro and Ruth Marie Eshenaur, 119–138. Taichung, Taiwan, ROC: Asia Theological Association, 1984.

———. "Salvation and Humanisation in the Theology of Evangelism." In *Voice of the Church in Asia: Report of Proceedings Asia Theological Association Consultation*, 154–163. Singapore: Asia Theological Association, 1975.

———, ed. *The Unique Christ in Our Pluralist World*. Grand Rapids, MI: Baker Books House, 1994.

Nienkirchen, Charles. "A. B. Simpson: Forerunner and Critic of the Pentecostal Movement." In *The Birth of a Vision: Essays on the Ministry and Thought of Albert B. Simpson*, edited by F. David Hartzfeld and Charles Nienkirchen, 125–164. Beaverlodge, Alberta: Buena Book Services, 1986.

Niklaus, Robert L., John S. Sawin, and Samuel J. Stoesz. *All for Jesus: God at Work in the Christian and Missionary Alliance over One Hundred Years*. Camp Hill, PA: Christian Publications, 1986.

Oborji, Francis Anekwe. *Concepts of Mission: The Evolution of Contemporary Missiology*. Maryknoll, NY: Orbis Books, 2006.

Olsen, John Drange. *Thần đạo học* [Theology], vol. *1 & 2*. Sài Gòn: Nhà in Tin-Lành, 1957.

Ott, Craig, Stephen J. Strauss, and Timothy C. Tennent. *Encountering Theology of Mission: Biblical Foundations, Historical Developments, and Contemporary Issues*. Encountering Mission. Grand Rapids, MI: Baker Academic, 2010.

Palmer, Martin. *The Jesus Sutras: Rediscovering the Lost Scrolls of Taoist Christianity*. New York: Ballantine Books, 2001.

Pannenberg, Wolfhart. *Systematic Theology, vol. 1*. Grand Rapids, MI: Eerdmans, 1991.

———. *Systematic Theology*. Translated by Geoffrey W. Bromiley, vol. 3. T&T Clark Academic Paperbacks. Grand Rapids, MI: Eerdmans, 1993.

Pannier, Jacques. "Les Protestantes Francais in Extrême-Orient au XVII Siècle." *Bulletin de la Société de l'Histoire du Protestantisme Français (1903-)* 53, no. 6 (1904): 481–492.

Pardington, George P. *Twenty-Five Wonderful Years*. New York: Christian Alliance, 1914.

Pelley, Patricia M. *Postcolonial Vietnam: New Histories of the National Past*. Durham, NC: Duke University Press, 2002.

Phạm, Bích Hợp. *Người Nam Bộ và Tôn Giáo Bản Địa: Bửu Sơn Kỳ Hương, Cao Đài, Hòa Hảo* [The southern people and local religions]. Hà Nội: Nxb Tôn Giáo, 2007.

Phạm, Đình Hổ. *Vũ trung tuỳ bút* [Following the brush amid the rains]. Translated by Đông Châu Nguyễn Hữu Tiến. Hồ Chí Minh City: Nxb Văn Nghệ, 1998.

———. *Vũ trung tuỳ bút* [Following the brush amid the rains]. Translated by Tran Thi Kim Anh. Hà Nội: Nxb Khoa học Xã hội, 2003.

Phạm, Xuân Tín. *The Gospel First Came to Vietnam*. Mennonite Biblical Seminary and Mennonite World Conference, 1970.

———. *Lược sử giáo hội Tin Lành Việt Nam* [A short history of the Evangelical Church of Vietnam]. Unpublished manuscript, 1991.

Phan, Đình Liệu. *Lịch sử Tin Lành truyền đến Việt Nam* [The history of the Evangelical mission to Vietnam]. Unpublished manuscript, n.d.

Phan, Khôi. "Giới Thiệu và Phê Bình Thánh Kinh Báo" [Introduction and critque of Bible magazine]. Phụ Nữ Tân Văn 74 (16 Oct 1930).

Phan, Peter C. "An Asian Christian? Or a Christian Asian? Or an Asian-Christian? A Roman Catholic Experiment on Christian Identity." In *Asian and Oceanic Christianities in Conversation: Exploring Theological Identities at Home and in Diaspora*, edited by Heup Yong Kim, Fumitaka Matsuoka and Anri Morimoto. Studies in World Christianity and Interreligious Relations 47. The Church and Theology in Context Series, 57–74. Amsterdam; New York, NY: Editions Rodopi B. V., 2011.

———, ed. *The Asian Synod: Texts and Commentaries*. Maryknoll, NY: Orbis Books, 2002.

———. *Christianity with an Asian Face: Asian American Theology in the Making*. Maryknoll, NY: Orbis Books, 2003.

———. *In Our Own Tongues: Perspectives from Asia on Mission and Inculturation*. Maryknoll, NY: Orbis Books, 2003.

———. *Mission and Catechesis: Alexandre de Rhodes and Inculturation in Seventeenth-Century Vietnam*. Faith and Cultures Series. Maryknoll, NY: Orbis Books, 1998.

Phan, Phát Huồn. *History of the Catholic Church in Việt Nam, vol. 1: 1533–1960*. Long Beach, CA: Cứu Thế Tùng Thư, 2000.

Pocock, Michael, Gailyn Van Rheenen, and Douglas Mcconnell. *The Changing Face of World Missions: Engaging Contemporary Issues and Trends*. Grand Rapids, MI: Baker Academic, 2005.

Priest, Robert J. "Researching Contextualization in Churches Influenced by Missionaries." In *Communities of Faith in Africa and the African Diaspora: In Honor of Dr. Tite Tiénou with Additional Essays on World Christianity*, edited by Casely B. Essamuah and David K. Ngaruiya, 299–318. Eugene, OR: Pickwick Publications, 2013.

Pryor, John W. *John: Evangelist of the Covenant People: The Narrative and Themes of the Fourth Gospel*. Downers Grove, IL: InterVarsity Press, 1992.

Ramachandra, Vinoth. *Faiths in Conflict?: Christian Integrity in a Multicultural World*. Downers Grove, IL: InterVarsity Press, 1999.

Ramsay, Jacob. *Mandarins and Martyrs: The Church and the Nguyen Dynasty in Early Nineteenth-Century Vietnam*. Stanford, CA: Stanford University Press, 2008.

Ratzinger, Joseph. "The Holy Spirit as Communio: Concerning the Relationship of Pneumatology and Spirituality in Augustine." *Communio* 25, no. 2 (Summer 1998): 324–339.

Reimer, Reginald Eugene. "The Protestant Movement in Vietnam: Church Growth in Peace and War among the Ethnic Vietnamese." MA Thesis, Fuller Theological Seminary, 1972.

———. "The Religious Dimension of the Vietnamese Cult of the Ancestors." *Missiology: An International Review* 3, no. 2 (1975): 155–168.

———. *Vietnam's Christians: A Century of Growth in Adversity*. Pasadena, CA: William Carey Library, 2011.

Richemond, A. *L'évengile en Indo-Chine*. n.d.

Ro, Bong Rin. "Asian Theology." In *Evangelical Dictionary of Theology*, edited by Walter A. Elwell, 106–108. Grand Rapids, MI: Baker Academic, 2001.

———, ed. *Christian Alternatives to Ancestor Practices*. Taichung, Taiwan: Asia Theological Association, 1985.

———. "Contextualization: Asian Theology." In *The Bible and Theology in Asian Contexts: An Evangelical Perspective on Asian Theology*, edited by Bong Rin Ro and Ruth Eshenaur, 63–77. Taipei, Taiwan: Asia Theological Association, 1984.

Rogers, Glenn. *A Basic Introduction to Missions and Missiology*. Bedford, TX: Mission and Ministry Resources, 2003.

Rule, Paul A. *K'ung-Tzu or Confucius?: The Jesuit Interpretation of Confucianism*. East Asia Series (Sydney, NSW). Sydney; Boston: Allen & Unwin, 1986.

Russell, William P. *Contextualization: Origins, Meaning and Implications*. Rome: Pontifica, 1995.

Sanneh, Lamin O. *Translating the Message: The Missionary Impact on Culture*. American Society of Missiology Series 42. 2nd ed. Maryknoll, NY: Orbis Books, 2009.

Sawin, John S. *The Christian and Missionary Alliance in Indo-China (1882–1924)*. Unpublished manuscript.

———. "The Fourfold Gospel." In *The Birth of a Vision: Essays on the Ministry and Thought of Albert B. Simpson*, edited by F. David Hartzfeld and Charles Nienkirchen, 1–28. Beaverlodge, Alberta: Buena Book Services, 1986.

———. *Missionary Semons by A. B. Simpson*. Unpublished manuscript, 1983.

———. "The Response and Attitude of Dr. A. B. Simpson and the Christian and Missionary Alliance to the Tongues Movement of 1906–1920." Theological Research Exchange Network (TREN) (1986).

Scherer, James A. *Gospel, Church, and Kingdom: Comparative Studies in World Mission Theology*. Minneapolis, MN: Augsburg, 1987.

Schirokauer, Conrad, and Donald N. Clark. *Modern East Asia: A Brief*. Belmont, CA: Thomson/Wadsworth, 2004.

Schloesing, E. *Les Missions Protestantes en Indochine*. n.d.

Schreiter, Robert J. *Constructing Local Theologies*. Maryknoll, NY: Orbis Books, 1985.

———. "Contextual Theology." In *Christianity: The Complete Guide*, edited by John Bowden, 281–282. London: Continuum, 2005.

———. "Defining Syncretism: An Interim Report." *International Bulletin of Missionary Research* 17, no. 2 (1993): 50–53.

Shaw, Daniel R. "Beyond Contextualization: Toward a Twenty-First-Century Model for Enabling Mission." *International Bulletin of Missionary Research* 34, no. 4 (October 2010): 8.

Shaw, Daniel R., and Charles Edward Van Engen. *Communicating God's Word in a Complex World: God's Truth or Hocus Pocus?* Lanham, MD: Rowman & Littlefield, 2003.

Shenk, Wilbert R. *Changing Frontiers of Mission*. Maryknoll, NY: Orbis Books, 1999.

———, ed. *Enlarging the Story: Perspectives on Writing World Christian History*. Maryknoll, NY: Orbis Books, 2002.

———. "John Howard Yoder's Mission Theology: Context and Contribution." In *Theology of Mission: A Believers Church Perspective*, edited by Gayle Gerber Koontz and Andy Alexis-Baker, 13–33. Downers Grove, IL: InterVarsity Press, 2014.

Shorter, Aylward. *Toward a Theology of Inculturation*. Maryknoll, NY: Orbis Books, 1989.

Simpson, Albert B. *The Word, the Work and the World* (August 1882).

———. *Annual Report* (1896).

———. *Annual Report* (October 1895).

———. "Aggressive Christianity." *The Christian and Missionary Alliance Weekly* 23 (23 September 1899).

———. *The Challenge of Missions*. New York: Christian Alliance, 1926.

———. "Distinctive Teaching." *The Word, the Work and the World*, no. 9 (July 1887): 1–5.

———. "Editorial." *The Alliance Weekly* (4 May 1907).

———. "Editorial." *The Alliance Weekly* (12 June 1909).

———. "Editorial." *The Alliance Weekly* (1 August 1908).

———. "The Evangelization of Annam." *The Christian Alliance* (15 January 1897).
———. *The Fourfold Gospel: Albert B. Simpson's Conception of the Complete Provision of Christ for Every Need of the Believer-Spirit, Soul and Body.* Updated and edited. Camp Hill, PA: Christian Publications, 1984.
———. *The Gospel of Healing.* 4th ed. New York: Christian Alliance, 1890.
———. "Missionary Wings, Rev. 14:6." *The Alliance Weekly* (August 1891).
———. *Wholly Sanctified.* Harrisburg: Christian Publication, 1925.
Skreslet, Stanley H. *Comprehending Mission: The Questions, Methods, Themes, Problems, and Prospects of Missiology.* American Society of Missiology Series 49. Maryknoll, NY: Orbis Books, 2012.
Smith, Gordon H., Mrs. *Victory in Vietnam.* Grand Rapids, MI: Zondervan, 1965.
Smith, Ralph B. "An Introduction to Caodaism 1: Origins and Early History." *Bulletin of the School of Oriental and African Studies*, University of London 33, no. 2 (1970): 335–349.
———. "An Introduction to Caodaism 2: Beliefs and Organization." *Bulletin of the School of Oriental and African Studies*, University of London 33, no. 3 (1970): 573–589.
Soderberg, Frank A. "First Impressions of Annam." *The Alliance Witness* (21 December 1912).
Soulier, Ulysse. "Copied Letters from 1907–1928." *Archives of Société des Missions Evangéliques des Paris (SMEP/ Défap).*
———. "L'appel de l'Indochine française" [The call of French Indochina] 47. *Conference at Nantes in August 1920*, Archives of Société des Missions Evangéliques des Paris (SMEP/ Défap), 1920.
Star, Jonathan. *Tao Te Ching: The New Translation from Tao Te Ching.* New York: Jeremy P. Tarcher/Penguin, 2008.
Steinkamp, Orrel N. *The Holy Spirit in Vietnam.* Carol Stream, IL: Creation House, 1973.
Stoesz, Samuel J. "The Doctrine of Sanctification in the Thought of A. B. Simpson." In *The Birth of a Vision: Essays on the Ministry and Thought of Albert B. Simpson*, edited by F. David Hartzfeld and Charles Nienkirchen, 107–123. Beaverlodge, Alberta: Buena Book Services, 1986.
Storkey, Elaine. "Evangelical Theology and Gender." In *The Cambridge Companion to Evangelical Theology*, edited by Timothy Larsen and Daniel J. Treier, 161–176. Cambridge, MA: Cambridge University Press, 2007.
Stott, John R. W. *The Contemporary Christian: Applying God's Word to Today's World.* Downers Grove, IL: InterVarsity Press, 1992.
Strong, Augustus Hopkins. *Systematic Theology: A Compendium Designed for the Use of Theological Students.* 3 vols. Valley Forge, PA: Judson Press, 1907.
Stults, Donald Leroy. *Developing an Asian Evangelical Theology.* Denver, CO: iAcademic Books, 2001.

Sun, Anna Xiao Dong. *Confucianism as a World Religion: Contested Histories and Contemporary Realities*. Princeton, NJ: Princeton University Press, 2013.

Sunquist, Scott W. "Ancestor Veneration and Christianity: Overview." In *The Cambridge Dictionary of Christianity*, edited by Daniel Patte, 29–30. Cambridge, MA: Cambridge University Press, 2010.

———. *Understanding Christian Mission: Participation in Suffering and Glory*. Grand Rapids, MI: Baker Academic, 2013.

———. *The Unexpected Christian Century: The Reversal and Transformation of Global Christianity*, 1900–2000. Grand Rapids, MI: Baker Academic, 2015.

Sunquist, Scott W., and Amos Yong. *The Gospel and Pluralism Today: Reassessing Lesslie Newbigin in the 21st Century*. Downers Grove, IL: IVP Academic, 2015.

Tạ, Chí Đại Trường. *Thần, Người và Đất Việt* [Spirits, people and the lands of the Viet]. Hà Nội: Nxb Nhã Nam & Nxb Tri Thức, 2014.

Tan, Jonathan Y. "Encounter between Confucianism and Christianity." In *The Oxford Handbook of Christianity in Asia*, edited by Felix Wilfred, 428–443. New York: Oxford University Press, 2014.

———. "Missio Inter Gentes: Towards a New Paradigm in the Mission Theology of the Federation of Asian Bishops' Conferences (FABC)." *Mission Studies* 21, no. 1 (2004): 65–95.

Tang, Li. *East Syriac Christianity in Mongol-Yuan China*. Wiesbaden: Harrassowitz, 2011.

Tang, Li, and Dietmar W. Winkler. *From the Oxus River to the Chinese Shores: Studies on East Syriac Christianity in China and Central Asia*. Orientalia-patristicaoecumenica, v. 5. Zürich; Berlin: Lit Verlag, 2013.

Tang, Yi Jie. *Confucianism, Buddhism, Daoism, Christianity, and Chinese Culture*, vol. 3. Cultural Heritage and Contemporary Life Series 3, Asia. Peking; Washington, DC: University of Peking; Council for Research in Values and Philosophy, 1991.

Tarling, Nicholas. *The Cambridge History of Southeast Asia, Volume Two: The Nineteenth and Twentieth Centuries*. Vol. 2. New York, NY: Cambridge University Press, 1992.

Taylor, Keith Weller. *The Birth of Vietnam*. Berkeley, CA: University of California Press, 1983.

———. *A History of the Vietnamese*. New York, NY: Cambridge University Press, 2013.

The Association for Theological Education in South East Asia and The South East Asia Graduate School of Theology. *Handbook*, 2005–2007.

The Christian and Missionary Alliance. *Alliance Magazine* (31 January 1903).

———. *The Alliance Weekly* (14 October 1911).

———. *The Alliance Weekly* (August 1912).

———. "Annual Report for 1910." (1911).

———. *Christian Alliance* (15 January 1892).
———. *Christian Alliance* (June 1893).
———. *Christian Alliance* (January 1894).
———. *Christian Alliance* (June 1894).
———. *Christian Alliance* (August 1894).
———. *Christian Alliance* (January 1896).
———. *Christian Alliance* (January 1903).
———. *Christian Alliance* (August 1895).
———. "Entering Annam." *The Alliance Witness* (7 October 1911).
———. "The Missionary Review of the World." *Alliance Magazine* (1905).
———. *The Word, the Work and the World* (February 1887).
———. *The Word, the Work and the World* (July 1887).
Thomas, M. M. "Christ-Centred Syncretism." *Religion and Society* 26 (March 1979): 26–35.
———. *Man and the Universe of Faiths*. Madras: Published for the Christian Institute for the Study of Religion and Society, Bangalore, by the Christian Literature Society, 1975.
Thomas, Norman E. *Classic Texts in Mission and World Christianity*. Maryknoll, NY: Orbis Books, 1995.
Thomas, T. V., and Ken Draper. "A. B. Simpson and World Evangelization." In *The Birth of a Vision: Essays on the Ministry and Thought of Albert B. Simpson*, edited by F. David Hartzfeld and Charles Nienkirchen, 195–218. Beaverlodge, Alberta: Buena Book Services, 1986.
Thompson, Albert Edward. *The Life of A. B. Simpson*. Brooklyn, NY: Christian Alliance, 1920.
Thong, Chan Kei, and Charlene L. Fu. *Finding God in Ancient China: How the Ancient Chinese Worshiped the God of the Bible*. (Previously published as *Faith of Our Fathers*.) Shanghai: China Publishing Group Orient Publishing Center, 2006. (Originally published in simplified Chinese.) Grand Rapids, MI: Zondervan, 2009.
Tiénou, Tite. "Contextualization of Theology for Theological Education." In *Evangelical Theological Education Today* 2. Agenda for Renewal, edited by Paul Bowers. Nairobi, Kenya: Evangel Publishing House, 1982.
Toà, Thánh Tây Ninh (Tay Ninh Holy See). *Tân Luật* [The new code]. The Cao-Dai Temple of New South Wales' E-book v. 2011 ed. Thủ Đức, Việt Nam: Nhà in Trung Tâm Giáo Hoá Thiếu Nhi Thủ Đức, 1972.
———. *Thánh Ngôn Hiệp Tuyển* [Official spirit messages]. The Cao-Dai Temple of New South Wales' E-book v. 2011 ed. Thủ Đức, Việt Nam: Nhà in Trung Tâm Giáo Hoá Thiếu Nhi Thủ Đức, 1972.
Tổng, Cục Thống Kê. "The 2009 Vietnam Population and Housing Census: Completed Results." Hanoi, Vietnam, 2009.

Tozer, Aiden Wilson. *Wingspread*. Harrisburg, PA: Christian Publishing, 1943.

Trần, Ngọc Thêm. *Cơ sở văn hóa Việt Nam* [Vietnamese culture]. Nxb Giáo Dục, 1999.

Tran, Q Anh. "Inculturation, Mission, and Dialogue in Vietnam: The Conference of Representatives of Four Religions." In *Beyond Conversion and Syncretism: Indigenous Encounters with Missionary Christianity, 1800–2000*, edited by David Lindenfeld and Miles Richardson, 167–194. New York: Berghahn Books, 2012.

Tran Quoc Anh. "Hội đồng tứ giáo [Conference of four religions]: An Encounter of Christianity with Three Religions in Eighteenth-Century Vietnam." STL Thesis, Jesuit School of Theology, 2006.

———. "Tam giáo chư vọng [The errors of the Three Religions]: A Textual and Analytical Study of a Christian Document on the Practices of the Three Religious Traditions in Eighteenth-Century Vietnam." PhD diss., Georgetown University, 2011.

Trần, Quốc Vượng. "Về danh hiệu 'Hùng Vương.'" In *Hùng Vương dựng nước (King Hung established the nation)*, edited by Uỷ ban Khoa học Xã hội, 353–355. Hà Nội: Khoa học Xã hội, 1973.

———, ed. *Việt sử lược* [Short history of Dai Viet], 1960. Reprint, Huế: Nxb Thuận Hoá, 2005.

Trần, Thế Pháp. *Lĩnh nam chích quái liệt truyện* [Arrayed tales of collected oddities from south of the passes]. Translated by Lê Hữu Mục. Saigon: Khai Trí, 1960.

Trần, Trọng Kim. *Nho giáo* [Confucianism]. Sàigòn: Nxb Tân Việt, n.d.

Trigault, Nicolas, and Matteo Ricci. *De Christiana expeditione apud Sinas suscepta ab societate Jesu*. Augsburg 1615.

Trinh, Philip Khanh Van. "Toward a Doctrine of Sin in the Vietnamese Context: Elements in the Dialogue between the Vietnamese Indigenous Perceptions and Christian Teaching on Sin by Missionaries." PhD diss., Graduate Theological Union 2004.

Trompf, G. W. *Cargo Cults and Millenarian Movements: Transoceanic Comparisons of New Religious Movements*. Religion and Society 29. Berlin: Mouton de Gruyter, 1990.

Trương, Bửu Lâm. *Colonialism Experienced: Vietnamese Writings on Colonialism, 1900–1931*. Ann Arbor, MI: University of Michigan, 2000.

———. *A Story of Viet Nam*. Honolulu, HI: 2012. Kindle edition.

Truong, Van Thien Tu. "Mệnh Trời: Toward a Vietnamese Theology of Mission." PhD diss., Graduate Theological Union, 2009.

Tu, Weiming. *Centrality and Commonality: An Essay on Chung-Yung*. Monograph no. 3 of the Society for Asian and Comparative Philosophy. Honolulu, HI: University Press of Hawaii, 1976.

———. *Neo-Confucian Thought in Action: Wang Yang-ming's Youth (1472–1509)*. Berkeley: University of California Press, 1976.
Tuck, Patrick J. N. *French Catholic Missionaries and the Politics of Imperialism in Vietnam, 1857–1914: A Documentary Survey*. Liverpool: Liverpool University Press, 1987.
Turnbull, Walter. *The Alliance Weekly* (November 1919).
Tyra, Gary. *The Holy Spirit in Mission: Prophetic Speech and Action in Christian Witness*. Downers Grove, IL: IVP Academic, 2011.
Van Engen, Charles Edward. "Critical Theologizing: Knowing God in Multiple Global/Local Contexts." In *Evangelical, Ecumenical, and Anabaptist Missiologies in Conversation: Essays in Honor of Wilbert R. Shenk*, edited by Wilbert R. Shenk, James R. Krabill, Walter Sawatsky and Charles Edward Van Engen. Maryknoll, NY: Orbis Books, 2006.
———. "Five Perspectives of Contextually Appropriate Missional Theology." In *Appropriate Christianity*, edited by Charles H. Kraft and Dean S. Gilliland, 183–202. Pasadena, CA: William Carey Library, 2005.
———. "Mission Described and Defined." In *Missionshift: Global Mission Issues in the Third Millennium*, edited by David J. Hesselgrave and Ed Stetzer, 7–29. Nashville, TN: B & H Academic, 2010.
———. *Mission on the Way: Issues in Mission Theology*. Grand Rapids, MI: Baker Books, 1996.
———. "Toward a Contextually Appropriate Methodology in Mission Theology." In *Appropriate Christianity*, edited by Charles H. Kraft and Dean S. Gilliland, 203–226. Pasadena, CA: William Carey Library, 2005.
Van Rheenen, Gailyn. "Modern and Postmodern Syncretism in Theology and Mission." In *The Holy Spirit and Mission Dynamics*, edited by C. Douglas McConnell, 164–207. Pasadena, CA: William Carey Library, 1997.
———. "Syncretism and Contextualization: The Church on a Journey Defining Itself." In *Contextualization and Syncretism: Navigating Cultural Currents*, edited by Gailyn Van Rheenen. Pasadena, CA: William Carey Library, 2006.
Verkuyl, Johannes. *Contemporary Missiology: An Introduction*. Grand Rapids, MI: Eerdmans, 1978.
Vicedom, Georg F. *The Mission of God: An Introduction to a Theology of Mission*. St Louis, MO: Concordia, 1965.
Vu, Tam That Samuel. "Rapport relatif à la Mission Américaine de Hanoi le 23 Juin, 1922" [Report on the American Mission in Hanoi in June 23, 1922]. Archives of Société des Missions Evangéliques des Paris (SMEP/ Défap), 1922.
Vũ, Tuấn Sán, and Đinh Khắc Thuân. "Bài văn bia tạo tượng Tam Giáo, chùa Cao Dương của Trình Quốc Công" [The stele inscription on the statues of the Three Teachings at Cao Duong Pagoda by Trinh Quoc Cong]. *Tạp Chí Hán Nôm [Journal of Han-Nom Studies]* 1, no. 8 (1990).

Vu, Van Vinh. "Development of Confucianism in the Tran Dynasty and the Struggle of Confucian Scholars against Buddhism at the End of the XIV Century." Vietnam Social Science 2 (1999): 55–60.

Waldenfels, Hans. "Contextual Theology." In *Dictionary of Mission: Theology, History, Perspectives*, edited by Karl Müller, Theo Sundermeier, Stephen B. Bevans and Richard H. Bliese. Maryknoll, NY: Orbis Books, 1997.

Walls, Andrew F. *The Cross-Cultural Process in Christian History: Studies in the Transmission and Appropriation of Faith*. Maryknoll, NY: Orbis Books, 2002.

———. "In Quest of the Father of Mission Studies." *International Bulletin of Missionary Research* 23, no. 3 (1999): 98.

———. *The Missionary Movement in Christian History: Studies In the Transmission of Faith*. Maryknoll, NY: Orbis Books, 1996.

Wang, Xiaochao. *Christianity and Imperial Culture: Chinese Christian Apologetics in the Seventeenth Century and Their Latin Patristic Equivalent*. Studies in Christian Mission Series 20. Leiden: Brill, 1998.

WCC/TEF. "Ministry in Context: The Third Mandate Programme of the Theological Education Fund (1970–1977)." Edited by the TEF-staff. Bromley, Kent: Theological Education Fund, 1972.

Whiteman, Darrell L. "Contextualization: The Theory, the Gap, the Challenge." *International Bulletin of Missionary Research* 21, no. 1 (1997): 1–7.

———. "Models of Contextualization." In *Encyclopedia of Mission and Missionaries*, edited by Jonathan J. Bonk, 90–96. New York, NY: Routledge, 2007.

Whitmore, John K. "Social Organization and Confucian Thought in Vietnam." *Journal of Southeast Asian Studies* 2, no. 15 (1984, 1984): 296–306.

Woodside, Alexander. *Vietnam and the Chinese Model: A Comparative Study of Nguyen and Ching Civil Government in the First Half of the Nineteenth Century*. Cambridge, MA: Harvard University Press, 1971.

Worthen, Molly. *Apostles of Reason: The Crisis of Authority in American Evangelicalism*. New York, NY: Oxford University Press, 2014.

Worthen, Molly Catherine. "Unlike a Mighty Army: Anxiety and Authority in American Evangelicalism." PhD diss., Yale University, 2011.

Wright, Christopher J. H. "The Christian and Other Religions: The Biblical Evidence." *Themelios* 9, no. 2 (January 1984).

———. *The Mission of God: Unlocking the Bible's Grand Narrative*. Downers Grove, IL: IVP Academic, 2006.

Wu, Jackson. "The Honor of God in the Shame of Christ for Salvation: A Theological Contextualization from Chinese Culture." PhD diss., Southeastern Baptist Theological Seminary, 2012.

Yao, Xinzhong. "Confucian Christ: A Chinese Image of Christianity." In *Identity and Marginality: Rethinking Christianity in North East Asia*, edited by Werner Ustorf and Toshiko Murayama, 250. Frankfurt am Main: P. Lang, 2000.

———. *An Introduction to Confucianism*. New York, NY: Cambridge University Press, 2000.

Yeh, Allen. "Asian Perspectives on Twenty-First-Century Pluralism." In *The Gospel and Pluralism Today: Reassessing Lesslie Newbigin in the 21st Century*, edited by Scott W. Sunquist and Amos Yong, 215–232. Downers Grove, IL: IVP Academic, 2015.

Yoder, John Howard. "Anabaptist Vision and Mennonite Reality." In *Consultation on Anabaptist Mennonite Theology*, edited by A. J. Klassen, 1–46. Fresno, CA: Council of Mennonite Seminaries, 1970.

———. *The Priestly Kingdom: Social Ethics as Gospel*. Notre Dame, IN: University of Notre Dame Press, 1984.

Yong, Amos. *Beyond the Impasse: Toward a Pneumatological Theology of Religions*. Grand Rapids, MI: Baker Academic, 2003.

———. "Discerning the Spirit(s): A Pentecostal-Charismatic Contribution to Christian Theology of Religions." PhD diss., Boston University, 1999.

———. *The Future of Evangelical Theology: Soundings from the Asian American Diaspora*. Downers Grove, IL: IVP Academic, 2014.

———. *In the Days of Caesar: Pentecostalism and Political Theology*. Grand Rapids, MI: Eerdmans, 2010.

———. *Pneumatology and the Christian-Buddhist Dialogue: Does the Spirit Blow through the Middle Way?* Studies in Systematic Theology Vol. 11. Leiden: Brill, 2012.

———. *Renewing Christian Theology: Systematics for a Global Christianity*. Waco, TX: Baylor University Press, 2014.

———. *The Spirit Poured Out on All Flesh: Pentecostalism and the Possibility of Global Theology*. Grand Rapids, MI: Baker Academic, 2005.

———. "Whither Asian American Evangelical Theology?" *Evangelical Review of Theology* 32, no. 1 (2008): 22–37.

Yuan, Zhiming. *Lao Tzu and the Bible: A Meeting Transcending Time and Space*. Translated by Chen Shangyu. Bloomington, IN: AuthorHouse, 2010.

Yun, Koo Dong. *The Holy Spirit and Ch'i (Qi): A Chiological Approach to Pneumatology*. Princeton Theological Monograph Series 180. Eugene, OR: Pickwick, 2012.

Zizioulas, John. *Being as Communion: Studies in Personhood and the Church*. Crestwood, NY: St Vladimir's Seminary Press, 1985.

Zorn, Jean-François. "Mission et colonisation: entre connivence et différence, point de vue protestant" [Mission and colonization: Between complicity and difference, protestant point of view]. In *Religions et colonisation*, edited by Dominique Borne and Benoît Falaize, 75–83. Paris: Éditions de l'Atelier, 2009.

Zorn, Jean-François. *Le Grand Siècle d'une Mission Protestante: La Mission de Paris de 1822 a 1914*. 2nd édition revue et augmentée ed. Paris: Éditions Karthala, 2012.

Index of Names

A
A-lo-pen (Persian monk) 23, 195
Allen, Roland 12
Anderson, Rufus 12, 13, 68
Ashford, Bruce Riley 53
Athyal, Saphir P. 197

B
Baker, Susan S. 53
Barth, Karl 56, 60, 73, 219
Bebbington, David 192
Benedict XV 169
Bénézet, Bujo 205
Bento Thien 102
Bevan, Stephen B. 45
Boegner, A. 143
Bois, Georges 128, 130, 143, 145
Boisset, Théophile 126, 139
Bong, Rin Ro 189, 193
Bonnet, M. 168
Bosch, David 70, 73, 75–77, 206
Brunner, Emil 72

C
Cadman, William C. 137, 142
Carey, William 58, 74
Chaigneaux, Jean Baptiste 128, 130
Chan, Simon 203, 205
Ching, Julia 25
Chu Hsi 38, 40
Chuang-tzu 25, 27–29
Chung, Paul S. 202
Clement of Alexandria 80

Coe, Shoki 66
Confucius 32, 33, 35, 37

D
Đào, Duy Anh 107, 178
Dayan, Sylvan 138, 140, 141, 157
de Rhodes, Alexander 3, 44, 106, 118, 122, 153, 154, 208
de Richemond, Adolphe 129, 139, 151
Đỗ, Hữu Nghiêm 129
Đỗ, Quang Chính 102, 210
Đường, Louis 144, 161

F
Flemming, Dean 53, 62
Freeman, J. H. 143

G
Gilliland, Dean S. 52, 59
Gnanakan, Ken 64

H
Harnack, Adolf von 56
Hartenstein, Karl 18, 72, 73
Herendeen, Dale Sims 16
Hesselgrave, David J. 44, 45
Hiebert, Paul 47, 60, 67, 71
Hồ, Chí Minh 165, 166
Hoekendijk, Johannes Christian 68
Hoskins, Janet Alison 114
Hosler, Paul 137, 149, 227
Hughes, Lloyd 137, 149
Hugo, Victor 110

Hwa Yung 49

I
Irwin, E. F. 16, 128

J
Jaffray, Robert A. 136, 137, 140, 147, 149, 173
James, Violet 2, 14, 16, 179
John Paul II, Pope 46

K
Kardec, Allan 110
Keith, Charles Patrick 158
Kitamori, Kazoh 190
Koyama, Kosuke 67
Kraft, Charles H. 44, 53, 82
Kreamer, Henrick 56
Küng, Hans 206

L
Lamont, Clarence H. 136
Lao-tzu 25–29
Lê, Hoàng Phu 13, 16, 127, 130, 179, 182
Lê, Thánh Tông, king 101
Lê, Văn Thái 127
Lee, Jung Young 203, 219, 229
Legge, James 37
Lelacheur, David 134
Loyola, Ignatius 74
Luzbertak, Louis J. 53
Lý, Tế Xuyên 88

M
Marsden, George M. 192
Martin, Luke S. 14
Martyr, Justin 80
Mateo Ricci 32
McGavran, Donald 69
Mencius 35
Mereadier, G. M. 139
Monet, Paul 143–145, 160, 161
Moreau, A. Scott 46, 58, 60

Mou, Bo 91
Musasiwa, Roy 47

N
Neil, Stephen 75, 76
Nevius, John L. 12, 13
Ngô, Văn Chiêu 109
Nguyễn, Ái Quốc 4, 158–163, 165, 167
Nguyễn, Bang Tiến 144
Nguyễn, Bỉnh Khiêm 97–100, 213
Nguyễn, Dữ 103
Nguyễn, Văn Tế 144
Nicholls, Bruce J. 202

O
Olsen, John Drange 11, 179, 218, 238
Origen 63, 80, 83

P
Panikkar, Raymond 190
Pannier, Jacques 131
Phan, Peter C. 228
Pierre Samuel Vũ Tâm Thất 144
Pius XI 169

R
Rahner, Karl 61
Ramachandra, Vinoth 63, 71
Reeves, Clarence H. 136, 138, 157
Reimer, Reginald E. 16
Ricci, Matteo 3, 36, 154
Rommen, Edward 44
Roy, Raja Ram Mohan 64

S
Sanneh, Lamin 50, 79
Schreiter, Robert 55, 60–62
Shaw, Daniel R. 77
Shenk, Wilbert R. 70
Simpson, Albert B. 11, 131, 133, 135, 139, 141, 146, 153, 170–177, 179
Soderberg, Frank A. 137, 148
Soulier, Ulysse 143–145, 159, 161, 167

St Thecla, Adriano di 154
Stetzer, Ed 59
Strong, Augustus Hopkins 11, 180
Stults, Donald Leroy 189

T

Tang, Yi-Jie 28
Taylor, Hudson 58
Thất, Pierre Samuel Vũ Tâm 144
Thomas, M. M. 63, 64, 190
Tiénou, Tite 55
Torrey, R. A. 180
Tran, Quoc Anh 155
Trần, Trọng Kim 98, 100, 213
Turnbull, Walter 177

V

Van Engen, Charles E. 47, 54, 71
Van Rheenen, Gailyn 57, 60
Venn, Henry 12
Verkuyl, Johannes 74
Vũ, Tâm Thất 145, 161

W

Walls, Andrew F. 50, 58, 70, 80, 218
Whiteman, Darrell L. 81, 181
Worthen, Molly 191
Wright, Christopher J. H. 56, 68, 189
Wu, Emperor 39
Wu, Jackson 50

X

Xavier, Francis 3

Y

Yao Xinzhong 38
Yoder, John Howard 62, 69
Yong, Amos 193
Yung, Hwa 82, 194

Index of Subjects

A
accommodation 36, 57, 63, 70, 71
activism 199
Ad Gentes 231
agency, indigenous 182
alchemy, cult of 29
American Mission Board of PC USA 143
Analects of Confucius 34, 35
anatta (no-self) 190
ancestor worship 225
Ancestor's Day, celebration of 228
anicca (impermanence) 190
Animism 22
anthropology, missiological 81
anti-colonialism 124, 165
Asia Theological Association, principles for theologizing 194
Assemblies of God 15
assimilation 17, 18, 57, 63, 90, 198, 235
  cultural 65, 80
attitude, of CMA missionaries 146

B
Bàn thờ Ông Thiên (Mr Heaven's altar) 16
baptism, with tongues 175
belief in spirits, Vietnamese 87
belief system, syncretistic 95
beliefs
  animistic 28, 86, 212, 213, 235, 238
  indigenous 22, 52

beliefs and practices 57
  local 48, 51
  Vietnamese 9
benevolence, in Confucianism 99
Bible
  Chinese 151
  Vietnamese 142, 151, 178, 179, 181
Bible translation
  vernacular 143
  Vietnamese 6, 183
biblical theology, Vietnamese 50
biblicism 199
Book of Changes 29, 34
Book of Mencius 34, 35
Book of Odes 34
Bourdeaux 163
British and Foreign Bible Society (BFBS) 127, 131, 138, 141, 178
Buddhism 22, 24, 38, 39, 90, 92, 93, 101, 154
  Chinese 22
  Mahayana 22
  Theravada 63
  Vietnamese 92
  Zen 22
  Zen (Japanese) 190
Bửu Sơn Kỳ Hương 107

C
Cao Dai 107, 109, 238. *See also* Caodaism
Caodaism 18, 86, 114, 213, 214
  contextualization 109

273

contextualization effort 110
conversion 109
Đạo Trời 108
Đức Cao Đài 107, 108, 110, 111, 115, 215
   Spirit messages (Thánh Ngôn Hiệp Tuyển) 108
   syncretistic religion 116
   Vietnamese 31
Catholic Church of Vietnam 9, 124, 191
Catholicism, Vietnamese 123, 124
China Christian Council 13
Christendom 192
   Western 181
Christian and Missionary Alliance (CMA) 1, 16, 127, 131, 132, 138, 143, 144, 150, 156, 166–170, 173, 177
Christianity
   as a translated religion 82
   Asian 49, 187, 196
   assimilation of 23
   East Asian context 24
   East Syrian 23, 195
   Vietnamese context 5
Christians
   East Asian 23
   East Syrians 23
   Hellenistic 81
chữ nôm 86
Chuang-tzu 101
church(es)
   as a missional community 230
   as a Vietnamese community 222
   House of the Lord 223
   House of Worship 223
   non-registered 11, 14
   place of God's presence 223
   relational community 225
   Christian and Missionary Alliance (CMA) 10
Cochinchina 165
colonialism 123, 181, 196

French 106
   rise of 48
colonization 157, 159
communication 43, 44, 48, 50, 52
   good interpretation 53
   with superiority 47
communism 165
concept
   "three-self" 1, 2, 12, 13, 66
   Church Growth 69
concept of God
   Vietnamese 204, 232, 233
   Vietnamese-East Asian 207
Confucian Classics 33, 35
Confucianism 3, 24, 28, 31, 32, 36, 39, 40, 90, 92, 93, 107, 154, 212, 213, 216
   as filial piety (hiếu thảo) 105
   classical 31
   four concepts 38
   Han 31
   integration with Daoism and Buddhism 96
   Jesuit understanding 32
   Vietnamese 96
Confucians 33
   Han dynasty 39
   Vietnamese 40, 95, 96
Confucius, worship of 39
Công Giáo. *See* Vietnamese Catholic Church
context, East Asian 43, 235
contextualization 3, 6, 17, 18, 21, 22, 41, 43–46, 49, 54, 55, 57–59, 61, 69, 70, 72, 78, 82, 146, 151, 188, 190, 23–237, 267
   as communication 47
   as interpretation 50, 54
   Christian 21, 43
   critical 51, 71
   cultural 50
   definition 44, 53
   East Asian 65
   evangelical statement 52

evangelical view 47
exegetical 50
failed 236
first account 129
historical evolution 44
local theologies 66
local theologizing 67
minimal 56, 67
process of 65
processes 59
uncritical 56
Vietnamese 5, 64, 237
conversion 63, 65, 76, 178, 195
efforts 18
individual 64
resistance to 114
conversionism 199
converts, Vietnamese 178
cosmology 226
East Asian 114
Critical Asian Principle 184
crucicentrism 199
cultural adaptation 59, 67
culture
Vietnamese 3, 5, 7, 9, 16–18, 31, 44, 90, 93, 237
Vietnamese 105

D
Dao De Jing 24
Daoism 24–28, 31, 39, 40, 90, 92, 93, 154, 156, 197
philosophical 25
religious 28, 30
Daoist Immortals 111
Declaration of Independence, Vietnamese 166
decolonization 107
Democratic Republic of Vietnam 166
destiny 104
dharma 190
dialogue, interfaith 146, 154
doctrine, "Huang-Lao" 39
Doctrine of the Mean 36

dualism 194
Platonic 49
dualism perspective 49
dukkha (suffering) 190

E
East Syrian(s) 121, 187
East Syrian Church 195
ecclesiology 70, 238
Vietnamese 183
Vietnamese evangelical 181
education, theological 184
educators, theological 183
Église Réformée de France (Reformed Church of France) 126, 156
enlightenment, Buddhist 110
ethnic groups
Cham 9, 16, 87, 107, 123
Khmer 9, 16, 87, 107, 123
ethnocentrism 81
eucharist 231
Evangelical Church of Indochina (ECIC) 16, 138
Evangelical Church of Vietnam (ECVN) 1–3, 5, 11, 14–16, 18, 121, 125–127, 138, 167, 170, 178, 179, 185
evangelicalism
Vietnamese 3, 6, 9–11, 18, 19, 121, 123, 125, 129, 153, 156, 170, 171, 177–179, 181, 182, 187, 195, 198, 199, 211, 219, 237
Western 235
evangelicals 46
Vietnamese 3, 5, 6, 10, 11, 185, 235, 238
evangelists, foreign 66
evangelization 158–160, 163, 177
Protestant 131
Evangelization of French Colonies 131
evil spirits 30
ex nihilo 155
exegesis
of the culture 51

of the Scripture 51
exorcisms 30, 31

F
Faith and Order 1927 74
family
 extended 232, 233
 extended, narrative 204
fascism, Japanese 166
fasting 28
filioque 231
First Principle 40
Five Classics of Confucianism 91
Five Elements 29
folk beliefs, Vietnamese 90
folk narratives, oral 103
folk religion, Chinese 22
folk songs, in worship 182
fortune-telling 31
foundations, epistemological 48
Fourfold Gospel 10, 170, 171, 175, 177
French Indochina 106, 114, 124, 138, 157, 164
funeral practices, Buddhist 156

G
Gnosticism 80
God, as a missionary 75
God-in-our-midst, Vietnamese concept 204, 205, 215
God's intention 50, 65, 72, 78
gospel
 authentic 65
 contextualization 5
 distortion of 53, 81
Gospel Tabernacle, New York City 136
Guidelines for Doing Theologies in Asia 184

H
Hanoi Christian Fellowship 15
Heaven 26, 35, 100, 101, 103, 110, 209, 212–214
 in Confucianism 32, 33
 in Daoism 27
 Sacrifice to Heaven (Giao Lễ or Nam Giao) 101
 worship of 214
hermeneutic
 critical 70
 missional 68
 Vietnamese 215
hermeneutical bridge 51
hermeneutical processes, Vietnamese 203
Hinduism 22
 reformation 64
historiography
 Vietnamese 171
 Vietnamese evangelical 125
 Vietnamese mission 131
history
 shaped by God 64
 Vietnamese 17
Hoà Hảo (Peace and Harmony) 107
Hội Đồng Tứ Giáo (Conference of Four Religions 153
Hội Thánh Tin Lành Việt Nam 178, 225. *See also* Evangelical Church of Vietnam
Hội thánh Tư gia (Vietnamese House Churches) 14
Hội Tin Lành Đông Pháp (Evangelical Church of [French] Indochina, ECIC) 178
Holy Spirit 221
 power of 79
 role 174
 work of 60
House of the Lord 224
humanity, principles of 37
humanization 67, 69
hygiene, cult of 29

I
identity, Vietnamese 238
ideologies, Communist 109
Immortal Bodhisattva-Mahasatva 111

imperialism 124
　colonial 158, 163
　cultural 81
　French 107, 166
　Western 187, 196
incarnation 43, 62, 65, 70, 77, 78, 82, 189, 217
incense 31
inculturation 3, 61, 66, 267
　Catholic 114
indigenization 12, 43, 66
indigenous 3, 5, 22, 60, 82, 178
Indochina 4, 6, 161, 168
International Congress on World Evangelization 69
International Missionary Council (IMC) 73, 74
interpretation 43, 44
　comprehensive 53
　East Asian 54

J

Japan 22, 24
Jerusalem Council 54, 55
Jesuit priests 10, 23, 123
Jesuits 10, 36, 37, 44, 58, 106, 122, 123, 177, 198, 213, 223
Jesus Christ
　as ancestor 217
　as ancestor-mediator 205
　as Creator 218
　as high priest 217
　as Sustainer 218
　his position 114
　Vietnamese perspective 216
justice 66, 68

K

Kardecism 109, 110
karma 105
Kinh. *See* Vietnamese
knowing God 71
knowledge, mystical 28
Kyrios 81

L

language, vernacular 142
Lao-tzu 101
L'appel de l'Indochine française (Call of French Indochina) 159
Life and Work 1925 74
Lĩnh nam chích quái liệt truyện (LNCQLT) 7, 87
literature, nôm 103
LNCQLT. *See* Lĩnh nam chích quái liệt truyện
Lord's Supper 229
Lunar New Year 30

M

Mạc dynasty (1528–1592) 95, 123
Mandate of Heaven 101
Manichaean 29
masters, Neo-Confucian 39
Maximum Illud 169
Mennonites 127
　American 14
　in Vietnam 179
metaphysics, Buddhist 40
missio Christi 75, 76
missio Dei 18, 19, 68, 69, 72, 74–76, 200, 230
missio ecclesia 75
missio ecclesiarum 74
mission 73
　ecclesiocentric 75
　French Christian 4
　French Protestant 157, 158, 163
　of the triune God 75–77
　Protestant 5
　theocentric 75
mission theology
　"three-self" 68
　Vietnamese 5, 6, 19, 187, 188, 198, 200, 201, 204, 206, 232, 235, 237
missionaries 118
　Catholic 154, 198
　Christian 236

CMA 136, 137, 142, 146, 148–151, 153, 177, 178
East Asian 143
French Protestant 143, 144, 149
Protestant 5, 129, 153, 197
Western 156, 196
missions
American Protestant 121
British Protestant 150
Catholic 158
Christian 16, 18
CMA 12
colonial 158
French 129
French Protestant 121, 127, 139, 150, 170
in trinitarian dimensions 77
Jesuits 21
Protestant 5, 150, 156
Roman Catholic 121, 122
model
accommodation 45
adaptation 45
Christendom 70
Confucianism 114
countercultural 53
inferential 77
inferential. *See* relevance theory of communication
translation 45
modernization, French 106
moral values 104
Moravian movement 199
movement
"three-self" 12
Pentecostal 173, 174
music, Vietnamese 145, 182

N
narratives, folk 87
nationalism, Vietnamese 164
Neo-Confucianism 24, 31, 35, 39, 40
East Asian 40
neo-orthodoxy 73

New York Tabernacle October Convention, 1892 146
Nguyễn dynasty 9, 87, 123, 124, 128
Nhà ở của Đức Chúa Trời (House of the Lord of Heaven) 181
non-contextualization 48
Northern Kingdom 92

O
oikos ekklesias. See House of the Lord
Ông Táo (the kitchen god) 31
Ông Trời (Mr Heaven/God) 16, 212
orthodoxy, Confucian 94

P
paper talismans, burning of 31
paradigm shift 5, 19, 63, 70, 187, 188, 206, 237
Pentecost 79, 80
Pentecostalism 175
people, Vietnamese 4, 7–9, 16, 63, 88, 100
phenomenon, house church 15
philosophy
Confucian 29, 104, 162
Daoist 24–26, 29
Vietnamese 208
Vietnamese-East Asian 202, 203
pluralism
East Asian 23
religious 81
post-colonialism 64, 188
pre-millennialist 176
pre-registered churches. *See* non-registered churches
priest, Daoist 31
Protestant missions, French 125
Protestantism, conciliar 68

Q
quốc ngữ 86, 87, 102, 106, 107, 124, 143, 196

R
radicalism 165
re-contextualization 71
refugee crisis 116
registered churches 11, 14
reincarnation 104
relationship, Trinitarian 5, 19
relevance theory of communication 77
religions, Vietnamese-East Asian 203
Rerum Ecclessiae 169
resistance 17
　in Vietnamese culture 85
resistance and assimilation 85, 106, 116, 118, 235
Roman Catholic Church, in Vietnam 178
Roman Catholicism 139

S
sacrifice, ancestral 228
sangha 190
Scripture, authority of 60
secularism 66
self-expression 2
self-nurture 2
self-revelation 56, 57, 63
self-theologizing 2
Separation of Church and State, 1905 159
Shang-ti (Lord-on-High) 33, 35, 36, 207, 212, 213
Shen 36
Shintoism 22, 24
social development 68
Socialist Republic of Vietnam 166
Société des Missions Évangéliques de Paris (SMEP/Défap) 126, 143, 145, 156
Société d'Évangélisation des Colonies Françaises (Society for the Evangelization of French Colonies) 126, 128, 139, 156
Society of Jesus 74

South China Executive Committee 140
Southern kingdom 92
spirit messages 108
Spiritism, French 110
spirits, communication with 31
Spiritualism, European 109
spirituality
　Asian 188, 190, 197
　East Asian-Vietnamese 17
　Vietnamese 85, 86, 201, 204, 235, 238
syncretism 17, 21, 22, 41, 43, 55, 56, 58, 60, 64, 68, 193, 199, 202, 235
　Christ-centred 63
　definition 56–58
　discussion of 62
　East Asian 55, 63
　evangelical fears 55
　fear of 61
　in Confucianism 32, 38, 39
　Vietnamese 18, 55, 63, 85
syncretistic spirituality 17, 90
　East Asian 21, 197
　Vietnamese xv, 5, 17, 64, 200, 230, 235

T
T'ai-chi 36
Taiwan Presbyterian Church 228
Tam giáo chư vọng (The errors of the Three Religions) 153, 155, 156
Tambaram (Madras) International Missionary Council (IMC) 75
Tao-tsang (Taoist canon) 29
Tây Sơn regime 123
Temple of Literature (Văn Miếu) 94
Tết (Lunar New Year) 102
Thần đạo học 11, 179, 180, 181, 238
theologians
　Asian 64
　contextual Asian 188, 202
　Western 49

theologies
  Asian 184
  contextual 68, 188, 190
  local 55
theologizing 68, 70, 188
  local 47
theology
  accommodation 190
  Asian 194
  Asian evangelical 189
  biblical 193
  Black (Africa) 68
  Burmese 189
  contextual 17, 46
  covenant 71
  Dalit (India) 68
  evangelical 18
  Indian 189
  irregular 202
  liberation 68, 202
  Minjung (Korea) 68, 189, 190
  mission-centered 200
  missional 18, 49, 56, 61–63, 67, 69, 73, 171
  of change (Taiwan) 189
  pain-of-God (Japan) 189, 190
  situational 190
  social justice, Asian 191
  Sri Lankan 189
  syncretistic 189
  third-eye (China) 189
  Vietnamese-East Asian 203
  water-buffalo (Thailand) 189
theorists, Protestant mission 12
Third Period of Salvation 215
three-life principles of breath 30
three missionary principles 129, 146
Three Religions 9, 112
Three Teachings 91, 95, 103, 105, 111, 153, 156, 213, 214
Three Teachings Temple (Tam Giáo Tự) 95, 97
three-self concept 13

Three-Self Patriotic Movement (TSPM) 13
Three-Self Principle 170
Thượng đế 100, 214
T'ien 33–36, 212, 213
T'ien-chu 36, 213
T'ien-dao 37
T'ien-ming 35
Tin Lành 125, 153. *See* evangelicalism: Vietnamese
Tourane 138, 141
trans-denominationalism 192
transformation 71, 96, 169
  cultural 123, 124
  political 123, 124
  religious 124
  social 123, 124
translatability 43, 58
  definition 79
  nature of 79
  of Christianity 65, 78
  of the gospel 83
  process of 80, 82
translatable faith 65, 79
translation, indigenous 151
Trinitarian faith, Western perspective 219
Trinitarian relationship, Vietnamese perspective 218
Trinity, doctrine of 221, 238
triune God 72, 75, 219
  family perspective 216
  mission of the 19
Trời-Đất-Người (Heaven-Earth-Human) 179, 208
Truyện Kiều (The Tale of Kiều) 103, 104
Truyền kỳ mạn lục (Collection of Strange Tales) 103

U
United Bible Society 183

V

values, traditional 238
Vatican 169
Vatican's influence 114
venerably worship (thờ kính) 226
Venerating Heaven ritual 223
veneration
    ancestor 3, 16, 17, 86, 89, 90, 111, 182, 205, 224, 226–230
    of Heaven 216
    of Jesus 229
veneration vs. worship 226
Việt điện u linh tập (VĐULT) 16, 87, 88, 89, 93
Việt Minh 164, 166
Việt people 23, 86, 88, 93.
    See Vietnamese
Vietnam War 127, 139
Vietnamese Catholic Church 122, 124, 179
Vietnamese Civil War 128
Vietnamese House Churches 14

W

Way of Heaven 36, 107
World Council of Churches (WCC) 66, 69, 74
World Missionary Conference, 1910 74
World Student Christian Fellowship (WSCF) 69
worldview 58
    Vietnamese-East Asian 236
worship
    ancestor 182, 229
    of village guardian deities 224
    Vietnamese 224

Y

YHWH 79, 209, 211
yin-yang 29, 35, 203
Young Men's Christian Association (YMCA) 161

Langham Literature, with its publishing work, is a ministry of Langham Partnership.

Langham Partnership is a global fellowship working in pursuit of the vision God entrusted to its founder John Stott –

> **to facilitate the growth of the church in maturity and Christ-likeness through raising the standards of biblical preaching and teaching.**

Our vision is to see churches in the majority world equipped for mission and growing to maturity in Christ through the ministry of pastors and leaders who believe, teach and live by the Word of God.

Our mission is to strengthen the ministry of the Word of God through:
- nurturing national movements for biblical preaching
- fostering the creation and distribution of evangelical literature
- enhancing evangelical theological education

especially in countries where churches are under-resourced.

Our ministry

Langham Preaching partners with national leaders to nurture indigenous biblical preaching movements for pastors and lay preachers all around the world. With the support of a team of trainers from many countries, a multi-level programme of seminars provides practical training, and is followed by a programme for training local facilitators. Local preachers' groups and national and regional networks ensure continuity and ongoing development, seeking to build vigorous movements committed to Bible exposition.

Langham Literature provides majority world preachers, scholars and seminary libraries with evangelical books and electronic resources through publishing and distribution, grants and discounts. The programme also fosters the creation of indigenous evangelical books in many languages, through writer's grants, strengthening local evangelical publishing houses, and investment in major regional literature projects, such as one volume Bible commentaries like the *Africa Bible Commentary* and the *South Asia Bible Commentary*.

Langham Scholars provides financial support for evangelical doctoral students from the majority world so that, when they return home, they may train pastors and other Christian leaders with sound, biblical and theological teaching. This programme equips those who equip others. Langham Scholars also works in partnership with majority world seminaries in strengthening evangelical theological education. A growing number of Langham Scholars study in high quality doctoral programmes in the majority world itself. As well as teaching the next generation of pastors, graduated Langham Scholars exercise significant influence through their writing and leadership.

To learn more about Langham Partnership and the work we do visit **langham.org**

Protestant Christianity in Vietnam is unique: arriving late, it was dominated by one denomination for most of the century – the Christian and Missionary Alliance. In addition, Protestant Christianity came in the last decades of French colonialism, and it came in a very North American Protestant form. KimSon Nguyen has done all Vietnamese, not just Vietnamese Christians, a great service in explaining how the history of early Protestantism shows the struggles that took place as Christianity sought for a home in Vietnamese soil. Much of this history is difficult to read. However, this fascinating study goes further in suggesting ways forward as Christianity develops more and more as a Vietnamese religion, encompassing all of life and culture. I believe that Vietnamese readers will respond with recognition and appreciation; non-Vietnamese readers will respond as if being enlightened about how Vietnamese culture lives and develops. It is a great story – it is a Vietnamese story.

Scott W. Sunquist, PhD
Professor of Missiology,
President, Gordon-Conwell Theological Seminary,
South Hamilton, Massachusetts, USA

Radically evangelical, thoroughly contextual, deeply missional, and theologically and biblically syncretistic! How? Prior generations of evangelical scholars would never have been described in this way, but KimSon Nguyen represents the vanguard of mission theologians in the twenty-first century. Read this book to be challenged for the sake of the mission of God in a pluralistic and post-colonial global world.

Amos Yong, PhD
Professor of Theology and Mission,
Dean, School of Theology and the School of Intercultural Studies,
Fuller Theological Seminary, Pasadena, California, USA

In this richly researched book, Dr KimSon Nguyen relentlessly seeks to identify the unintended lopsidedness of Western evangelicalism planted in the East Asian context of Vietnam and offers tour-de-force proposals for an integrated mission theology that calls for serious reflection and correction. Its analysis of the religio-cultural dimensions of Vietnamese spirituality with its dual forces of "resisting and assimilating" is to be wrestled by all who care about mission in our global village in the twenty-first century.

Rev Linh H. Doan, PhD
President, Union University of California
Senior Pastor, Thanh Le Church, Anaheim, California, USA

www.ingramcontent.com/pod-product-compliance
Lightning Source LLC
Chambersburg PA
CBHW051536230426
43669CB00015B/2622